TREATING
THE
DIFFICULT
DIVORCE

TREATING THE DIFFICULT DIVORCE

A Practical Guide for Psychotherapists

Jay L. Lebow

AMERICAN PSYCHOLOGICAL ASSOCIATION
Washington, DC

Published by
American Psychological Association
750 First Street, NE
Washington, DC 20002
www.apa.org

APA Order Department
P.O. Box 92984
Washington, DC 20090-2984
Phone: (800) 374-2721; Direct: (202) 336-5510
Fax: (202) 336-5502; TDD/TTY: (202) 336-6123
Online: http://www.apa.org/pubs/books
E-mail: order@apa.org

In the U.K., Europe, Africa, and the Middle East, copies may be ordered from
Eurospan Group
c/o Turpin Distribution
Pegasus Drive
Stratton Business Park
Biggleswade, Bedfordshire
SG18 8TQ United Kingdom
Phone: +44 (0) 1767 604972
Fax: +44 (0) 1767 601640
Online: https://www.eurospanbookstore.com/apa
E-mail: eurospan@turpin-distribution.com

Typeset in Goudy by Circle Graphics, Inc., Columbia, MD

Printer: Sheridan Books, Chelsea, MI
Cover Designer: Nicci Falcone, Gaithersburg, MD

Library of Congress Cataloging-in-Publication Data
Names: Lebow, Jay, author.
Title: Treating the difficult divorce : a practical guide for
   psychotherapists / by Jay L. Lebow.
Description: First Edition. | Washington, DC : American Psychological
   Association, [2019] | Includes bibliographical references and index.
Identifiers: LCCN 2018022292 (print) | LCCN 2018041327 (ebook) | ISBN
   9781433830204 (eBook) | ISBN 1433830205 (eBook) | ISBN 9781433829895
   (hardcover) | ISBN 1433829894 (hardcover)
Subjects: LCSH: Family psychotherapy. | Divorce. | Divorced people.
Classification: LCC RC488.5 (ebook) | LCC RC488.5 .L425 2019 (print) | DDC
   616.89/156--dc23
LC record available at https://lccn.loc.gov/2018022292

British Library Cataloguing-in-Publication Data
A CIP record is available from the British Library.

Printed in the United States of America

http://dx.doi.org/10.1037/0000116-000

10 9 8 7 6 5 4 3 2 1

CONTENTS

Preface .... *vii*

Introduction 3

Chapter 1.   Working in the Territory of Difficult Divorce 13

Chapter 2.   Divorce Today 35

Chapter 3.   Considerations in Psychotherapy With Clients
Contemplating Divorce 57

Chapter 4.   Intervention With Divorce 75

Chapter 5.   Structuring Treatment in Difficult Divorce 95

Chapter 6.   Specific Treatment Strategies in Difficult Divorce 129

Chapter 7.   Interacting With the Legal System and
Other Professionals 165

Chapter 8.   Special Challenges and Problems
in Difficult Divorce 189

Chapter 9.   The Therapist's Interface With Difficult Divorce 225

Chapter 10.   Adaptations for Less Difficult Divorces 237

Chapter 11.   Case Examples: Working With Difficult Divorce 261

References 281

Index 309

About the Author 325

PREFACE

I have been working with difficult divorces in therapy for 40 years. I came to working with difficult divorce somewhat by happenstance, without the careful preparation that I recommend in this book. I was a director of clinical services, and one of the families seen in our clinic was embroiled in a dispute about custody and visitation centered on whether a parent should have access to the children. The other parent was highly politically connected and represented by one of the most aggressive family attorneys in the country. Amid threats of lawsuits, I, bravely and naively (with my only background in this area being therapy with high-conflict families and having done several child custody evaluations), took over the treatment of the case. All the work surrounding the case was highly acrimonious. A private investigator followed me for a few days, with a primary goal of being intimidating. Ultimately, there were mandated appearances in court in relation to this case, a trying cross-examination, and the very unusual outcome in court of the attorneys for one side being fined and sanctioned for their behavior. Somehow, the therapy did help the family make progress in moving out of the most dysfunctional range to more ordinary negative feelings, although being a therapist in this case was very stressful.

One might think that this experience would have driven me away from any future contact with such cases. Most therapy is simpler, involves more connection, and is more personally satisfying. However, this experience, and others like it soon after (albeit ones somewhat less dramatic), opened a new vista for me. These were families in great pain, as much so as any I had seen. Narratives were incredibly powerful; clearly, each parent and child believed wholeheartedly in the radical (and often dysfunctional) positions they were verbalizing. The patterns of systemic problem maintenance I had learned about in postgraduate training in family systems were dramatically evident. Most often, one person's bad behavior begat another person's worse behavior and so on, and those efforts that did appear on someone's part to act better were ignored. And, so often, the family members described being caught up in a Kafkaesque legal system in which they were relentlessly misconstrued and under attack, with appearances in court at random intervals where sometimes something happened and sometimes nothing occurred. Most of all, there were the children in these families, almost all of whom were deeply wounded and often troubled. It struck me that the conflict in these families represented a major public health problem; toxic effects were ever-present for almost everyone involved.

Thus, I wanted to see whether there were ways that therapists might better help these families and the individuals in them. What soon became clear was that many of the typical ways of approaching families and individuals in therapy were not well suited to these families. Therapists even became ensnared in the pathogenic process as they offered support that likely would have helped in some other context but served to enable their clients in their difficult behaviors. Over time, I developed ways of working with these families and individuals better suited to the task.

Many years later, I also went through a divorce. This provided a much different perspective about such conflicts. Although my own divorce was mostly cooperative and would qualify as a "good divorce," the vortex of feelings during that process was powerful. Going through divorce also forces one to place oneself in the powerful evolving dialogue about the place of divorce in our society. My personal experience prompted a great deal of further thinking and learning from the writing and research of others about divorce. This, in turn, led to additional questions about the families and individuals experiencing difficult divorce who are the focus of this book. What is different about these families from most families that manage their way through such challenging times? Even more important, are there ways to help reduce the enormous damage to all involved?

In my research for this book, I discovered how few books are written about therapy with divorcing individuals, couples, and families (even though 40% to 50% of couples in the Western world divorce; Cherlin, 2009) compared with the many books written about couple therapy and other problems that affect far fewer people. This book is designed to fill that void. A quick search on Amazon also reveals that there are several books about high-conflict divorce or divorce involving child custody and visitation issues for lay audiences and that many of those books actually serve to prompt greater conflict (e.g., with titles such as *How to Come Out Ahead in Your Custody Dispute*). I intend this book as an antidote to such writing and the forces that help move these families toward greater difficulties. Wise therapists can play a vital role in helping people move slowly and deliberately toward better solutions and mitigating the damage once such a systemic process is underway.

My thanks to Susan Reynolds, Elizabeth Budd, Elizabeth Brace, and Ida Audeh at the American Psychological Association, who patiently helped nurture this book into its present form.

TREATING
THE
DIFFICULT
DIVORCE

INTRODUCTION

Much has been written about the negative effects of divorce (Wallerstein & Lewis, 2004), and surely for most adults and children, this life transition is a challenging time. Yet most people do negotiate this painful experience: The great majority of adults and children move through it without falling into intractable conflict or other forms of disaster and eventually recover their balance (Hetherington & Kelly, 2002). Yet for some, the interpersonal processes and individual effects are much more disruptive and disabling.

This book focuses primarily on this latter group of families and the individuals within them, for whom divorce is more arduous. Most of these families are characterized by high conflict—most often between the divorcing couple but also frequently between parents and children. Some of these families feature major cutoffs (Bowen, 1978) in which any positive contact that might be expected, such as between a parent and children or between two parents about coparenting, stops. Many experience the collapse of the structure for

http://dx.doi.org/10.1037/0000116-001
Treating the Difficult Divorce: A Practical Guide for Psychotherapists, by J. L. Lebow

and presence of effective parenting. Still other families experience the emergence or exacerbation of problems in individuals (either parents or children) over the time of the divorce, complicating the complex interpersonal tasks involved in divorce. For many families, the judicial process around these issues is integral.

Even without extensive court involvement, risk for family members is high, and therapists readily can fall into patterns that enable problems as much as help. Further, psychotherapies are conducted with the ever-present possibility that the therapy itself might become relevant within the legal process. Clients are inevitably under great stress and may be functioning poorly, often experiencing a state described by Mavis Hetherington as "not me," that is, in which they feel like someone other than their typical selves (Hetherington, 1999). As a by-product, family members also often feel as if they no longer know each other, sometimes accompanied by a deep sense of betrayal. Such systemic patterns as symmetrically escalating conflict, cycles of demand and withdraw, and even complete withdrawal of family members from others are commonplace. Furthermore, families, friends, the legal system, and even helping professionals all often serve as agents that may intensify difficulties.

Difficult divorces, especially those with high levels of conflict, reverberate through the family and the legal system. Such difficult divorces are now frequently encountered, in the United States and across the world. Although estimates suggest that difficult divorces make up only 10% to 15% of divorcing families (Drozd, Saini, & Olesen, 2016; Galatzer-Levy, Kraus, & Galatzer-Levy, 2009), this remains a great number of families who are subject to destructive effects, which play out over many years and often affect multiple generations. Additionally, the utilization of mental health service by these families, both mandated by the court and of their own volition, is far greater than for other families. These are families and individuals whom attorneys and judges frequently refer to therapists, given the obvious problems present, and who also often self-refer. They present to therapists in a variety of ways, be it by requesting therapy for a child alone, an adult seeking therapy for himself or herself, or two former partners looking for help with coparenting or seeking therapy for the whole family. Given their special characteristics and their frequent interface with the legal system, there is a great need for a special approach to therapy with these families and their individual members.

This book is intended to fill what is a major gap in the literature about relational problems. Although there are many exemplary books and methods for treating couples to help them improve and even save their marriages (Christensen, Doss, & Jacobson, 2014; Epstein & Baucom, 2002; Gottman, 1999; L. S. Greenberg & Goldman, 2008; Johnson, 2015), few have focused on helping those going through the process of divorce and even fewer on helping those going through the most challenging divorces (Johnston, Roseby, & Kuehnle, 2009). There have been far more books about how to help the court evaluate decisions concerned with conflicts over child custody (i.e., how to help the court help these families; Ackerman, 2001; Galatzer-Levy et al., 2009; Gould & Stahl, 2000) than texts focused on how to help those mired in such conflicts directly. Clearly, there is a need for special knowledge and methods tailored to these specific circumstances.

Difficult divorces present a special problem for mental health treatment. This is particularly the case when conflict is high or there are unresolved issues about custody and division of time with children that migrate into the judicial system. Many of the best-established ways of helping families and individuals need to be significantly augmented and altered in the context of families struggling with this change in family structure and what it means. When families are simultaneously involved with the court and attorneys at a moment of such a crescendo of emotions, there are special challenges.

WHAT IS DIFFICULT DIVORCE?

Part of the problem in approaching this topic is that "difficult" divorce is heterogeneous in terms of the specific behaviors manifested by the participants. What is "difficult" divorce, and how does one differentiate it from the more normative variant? Professionals who encounter divorcing people regularly have no trouble recognizing that some families and the individuals in them cross some boundary of difference. Yet specifying what exactly is different about them is harder than it might initially seem.

First, "easy" divorces are rare. Few life events are as stirring, and even those who divorce well typically experience considerable distress during the process (Amato, 2010). If you encounter most people going through divorce on a bad day, the levels of upset, symptoms, conflict, and problematic sequences are considerable. Thus, in normative divorce, it is possible to find lower grade and transient examples of some of the problematic patterns in difficult divorce. Yet for some, the depth, duration, and effects of the plunge run deeper and longer than for others. A process is launched that picks up momentum like a snowball moving downhill, typically sparking systemic circular processes of action and reaction potentiating problems. Although as we shall see, some of the characteristics of those who cross this boundary are easy to label (e.g., those with personality disorders are overrepresented among those in difficult divorces), a precise formula for which divorces will be difficult and to what extent is elusive. Sometimes, two very unbalanced partners can disengage successfully (perhaps distracted by new involvements), whereas two of what otherwise looked to be well-functioning partners can become mired in an escalating dispute. How one copes with divorce is complex and governed by many factors.

Second, difficult divorce encompasses a complex array of behaviors, thoughts, and feelings. Although there are almost always common underlying pathways of deep hurt and anger, coupled with systemic processes that potentiate difficulties, the specific behavioral problems that occur vary considerably across difficult divorces (see Chapter 1). Most common (and in focus throughout much of this book) is high conflict between the divorcing couple that interferes with necessary processes that are part of the life course for a divorcing couple, such as getting divorced and coparenting. Yet there are many other variations in difficult divorce, including parent–child conflicts, parents more quietly being unable to arrive at arrangements for custody and time with children, divorcing couples being unable to arrive at postdivorce financial arrangements, child–parent cutoffs (often described as *alienation*), parent–parent cutoffs, conflicts that involve extended family, conflicts that involve new partners, and a variety of other lower conflict patterns that undermine joint decision-making and problem-solving. For many of those in difficult divorce, although not all, the processing of such issues extends into extensive involvement within the legal system, which, in turn, typically increases acrimony.

Let's add here that difficult divorce can occur in brief marriages or long-standing ones, in what had been happy marriages for a time and those that were never happy, across every cultural context; across gay and straight marriages, and in those with children and those without children. Some of those in what I am here referring to as *difficult divorce* never even marry, as when there are contested issues about child custody between unmarried people.[1] Additionally, although the label *difficult divorce* is useful in demarcating a special territory that calls for a special approach to treatment, here we are really talking about a continuum rather than one uniform grouping. There are those for whom divorce is normative, characterized by strong feelings and transient problematic states. Further along the continuum are those who are additionally challenged, with more pronounced drifts in and out of more problematic behaviors, patterns, and effects. At the far pole of the continuum are those for whom the divorce process is an unmitigated disaster. At this extreme lie domestic terrorism, constant conflict, endless triangulation of children, and severe damage to almost all involved.

Notably, society and its legal system devote more time to the psychological effects of divorce when children are involved. Children provide a highly valued focus for ongoing conflict and typically bind parents together

---

[1]These cases do not technically qualify as legal divorces, but they feature most of the same sorts of issues and conflicts.

in contact to some extent even after divorce is finalized. Their welfare is also a focus about which the state has a vested interest (beyond the individual welfare of divorcing adults). Those without children can and most often do go their separate ways; most with children do not do this (although some do, leaving what truly is then a single parent). Because of this, most referrals in difficult divorce involve conflicts about children, but this does not mean that other conflicts are less treacherous. Given the frequency of referral surrounding problems involving children, much of this book accentuates that context, but the role for psychotherapy is no less important for those without children.

It also is important to emphasize that divorce is a process. This has two further ramifications for considering what is meant by difficult divorce. First, the confusion and conflict that may come with the emergence of a decision to divorce on the part of one or both partners do not yet mean that families have crossed the boundary into difficult divorce. As the proverbial dust settles, most families move into more or less functional patterns that endure (although notably, narratives about events that transpired at the time of the decision to divorce or separate often become a key ingredient in how long-standing problems develop). Second, although this book primarily focuses on the time during which families are divorcing, there are many families for whom the problems linger many years after the divorce. Some families even have few problems while divorce is occurring, only to be have major issues emerge around divorce-related subjects, such as coparenting teenagers years later or determining who will pay for the children's college down the road. These sorts of issues are also subsumed here under difficult divorce.

AN INTEGRATIVE APPROACH TO THERAPY
WITH DIFFICULT DIVORCE

This book focuses on an approach to intervention with these families that I have developed and written about over the past 20 years. This approach has been summarized in a number of articles in peer-reviewed journals and book chapters, as well as in professional presentations over the past decade (Lebow, 2002, 2005, 2008, 2015b; Lebow, Chambers, Christensen, & Johnson, 2012; Lebow & Rekart, 2007). This is the first book describing this approach and one of the few books for professionals focused on the treatment of these cases. The approach is intended for the reader to consider in two overlapping ways. First, it is a comprehensive systemic approach to treating difficult divorce, intended as a therapy that one therapist or a team of therapists can use as a template for how to intervene with divorcing family systems. In this sense, it is analogous to other integrative family systems–based therapies for approaching specific problems and developmental crises that draw on multiple treatment formats (e.g., individual, subsystem, and whole family sessions) to enact change. Comparable examples are multisystemic therapy for adolescent conduct disorder (Henggeler, Schoenwald, Borduin, Rowland, & Cunningham, 2009), multidimensional family therapy for adolescent delinquency (Liddle, 2016), and Maudsley therapy for eating disorders (Eisler, Le Grange, & Lock, 2016).

However, in an equally important way, the model and the content of this book is intended to speak to therapists who are not treating the entire family system but instead are engaged with a subsystem within these families, such as a parent and child, two former partners, or even a single adult or child. This is actually the typical way therapists become engaged with those in difficult divorce, often resulting from a very specific referral for treatment of a specific person or a family subsystem. For those treating only one part of the family system, this book is also intended as a guide to treating particular members of systems in which difficult divorce is occurring. These two threads in this book work in tandem. A central thesis of this book is that all therapies with members of these families need to retain the same core elements: a systemic focus, knowledge about the processes in difficult divorce, implementation of effective strategies of change, comprehensive case formulation, setting appropriate and limited treatment goals, adapting to the interactions with the judicial system, and coordination with other therapists and professionals. Thus, this book describes a method for working with these families as a therapist who has access either to the entire family system or to a part of the system but wants to maximize his or her impact. The approach described in this volume is based in a pragmatic integrative view about how to work with these families and the individuals that comprise them. Typically, in each case, there are a multitude of concepts from different theoretical orientations that can be readily applied and an endless variety of ways to intervene. There are enough problems in these families to fill multiple individual adult therapies, child therapies, parent–child therapies, and family therapies. Yet the therapeutic task must be to pragmatically help these families and individuals with the available resources and to parsimoniously enable individual clients and the family system to ameliorate the difficulties experienced as much as possible while maximizing the cost-effectiveness of treatment. This calls for the generation of a formulation of what is occurring and a prudent plan for setting goals and offering help.

Theoretically, the approach described in this book is grounded in the traditions of integrative therapy and systems theory. From the integrative tradition, it draws on the notion of understanding and working with clients on multiple levels (e.g., behavioral, cognitive, emotion-focused, psychodynamic, systemic), considering systemic and individual processes, mixing therapy formats (family, subsystem, and individual sessions), and arriving at a way of working with a specific family that has the best possible fit with that specific family. From systems theory, it draws on the notion of examining systemic processes, working with multiple subsystems (e.g., the dissolving marital dyad, the evolving nuclear family and family of origin, and the legal system), and keeping central the focus on a successful transition to a new family structure as a core task (and challenge) for these families. This book centers on how to conduct a parsimonious, integrative therapy that mitigates the difficulties in these families and their individual members. The treatment approach also combines generic elements of intervention that have proven helpful in psychotherapy, with specific ways of adapting those common factors and shared strategies of intervention to the context of high conflict and highly traumatic life changes (Lebow, 2014), with more specific adaptations to this special context. This treatment model is related to and overlaps with many core principles of integrative systemic therapy (Pinsof et al., 2018), although it varies in some key ways from that model.

This book is written primarily for therapists and student therapists (whether they see themselves as systems, family, couple, individual adult, or individual child therapists) who work with or want to work with these cases. It likely will also have relevance for those working with divorce cases in other roles, such as judges, attorneys, parenting coordinators, mediators, and physicians involved in psychopharmacology with these clients. Given that difficult divorce is a worldwide problem, it also is intended for an international audience, although the exposition about interactions with the judicial system is based in typical procedures in the United States.

This book presents both a guide to broadly understanding and working with difficult divorce and a specific therapeutic toolkit for doing so. The key take-home point intended for the reader lies in the core tenets of this approach. The treatment model accentuates situating treatment in an understanding of the relevant discourse about divorce in our society today and in the extensive research about divorce. It centers on bringing a patient, caring, yet assertive frame to therapy; working from a case formulation about what is occurring and what needs to change; and then eliciting common factors and drawing from an extensive therapeutic toolkit in the work with these families and individuals. Always, realistic goal-setting and progress-tracking are emphasized.

The optimal therapeutic toolkit suggested is viewed as ranging widely across theoretical orientations, but the breadth of that range is seen as less important than holding to these core principles for working with these cases. A foundation of this approach is that there are many paths to change (and that all of them are arduous with these cases). Therapists are served by having many options available to them to work through the blocks that appear in

therapy with these clients. Nonetheless, those therapists with strong preferences and skills in some of the intervention strategies described are invited
to draw on the content of this book while remaining primarily anchored
in those strategies. It is hoped that in clinical practice with these families,
therapists may find relevant some of the methods presented here that lie
outside of their typical purview. Similarly, students might best use various
strategies presented to the extent they have mastered their basic content,
beginning with a more limited set of strategies and adding to those over time
(Lebow, 2014). The essence of this approach lies less in having the "right"
intervention (this is not a method that adopts such an idea, given that there
are many pathways to change) or even a breadth of intervention strategies,
but in holding a broader way of approaching these families and individuals.

OUTLINE FOR THIS BOOK

This book begins with a description of the aspects of difficult divorce
in Chapter 1. Chapter 2 widens the lens, examining divorce more broadly,
reviewing the most important research about divorce and considering it in
the context of the shifting attitudes about divorce in Western society. It is
essential to understanding and working with divorcing families and individuals
that therapy, and the information presented within it, be solidly grounded in
the basic research about divorce. It is also essential to place this work in the
context of the shifting meanings of divorce in the Western world. Whereas
divorce was once a rarely crossed threshold, experienced by most as shameful,
it has become a normative event in family life today, touching nearly 50% of
families (Amato & Irving, 2006). In this transitional era, ideas about divorce
in families clash, leaving family members with very different narratives about
this life experience, ranging from tragic or traumatic to necessary to moving toward growth. The ambivalence of the society about divorce makes
processing issues surrounding it complex. Chapter 3 segues from considerations about divorce in society to considerations about the topic of divorce
in psychotherapy. It highlights problems in how the topic of the possibility
of divorce is typically approached in the context of individual and couple
therapy, leading to an examination of pathways to divorce therapy and the
appropriate place for it.

Most of this book, and especially Chapters 4, 5, and 6, centers on presenting an integrative approach to treating difficult divorce. Chapter 4 begins
with a summary of the various structures for intervention in difficult divorce
(e.g., mediation, parenting programs). It then considers the differences in
therapy with normative and difficult divorce, highlighting why special treatments are needed in difficult divorce. The chapter concludes with a discussion

of the importance of holding a systemic perspective in difficult divorce and a summary of the treatment model. Chapter 5 focuses on various aspects of structuring therapy in the model, including the therapeutic contract, alliance formation, initial assessment, goal setting, and planning. Aspects of the therapeutic contract are elaborated and set out more explicitly than in many other therapies, given the legal interface that often presents in these cases. Therapy emphasizes establishing and maintaining a multipartial alliance with each family member. Assessment focuses on a multilevel understanding of the various processes occurring within and between family members and the stage of change of each person in relation to these issues. Case formulation and goal-setting target the problems and processes to be addressed in the treatment. A therapeutic plan is developed for each case based on the goals for that case and the strengths and problems in the family.

Chapter 6 describes intervention strategies and formats for therapy used in the model. Intervention is always adapted to the particular family or individual(s) and includes a range of strategies, including psychoeducational, behavioral, cognitive, emotion-focused, psychodynamic, and systemic methods. Various session formats (individual, parent–child, parent–parent, family) are used, selected in relation to what is most likely to be responsive to the reason for referral and acceptable and helpful in a specific case. Therapy ideally ends when the family stabilizes, but termination also frequently occurs due to extratherapeutic factors, necessitating an approach that anticipates such possible endings (Lebow, 1995).

The next chapters look at a range of specific issues that arise in therapy with difficult divorce. Chapter 7 discusses the interface with the legal system. Legal and ethical considerations are especially important when doing this work, as is an understanding of the specifics of the jurisdiction in which one practices. Chapter 8 examines several specific kinds of problems and issues that occur and how treatment is adapted in the presence of specific problems. Chapter 9 focuses on the therapist's self-care in this work and how to mitigate burnout.

Central to this book is a focus on those who fall at the high end of the continuum in difficulty in divorce. Many of the tenets of the approach have been developed with this very special population in mind. However, the model in this book is also applicable, with modification, to working with more normative divorce. Therefore, a version of the approach for less difficult divorce is offered in Chapter 10. The book concludes with Chapter 11, which describes two extended case examples of treating difficult divorce.

All the case examples in this book are composites based on cases in clinical practice, but they have been merged and fully deidentified in ways such that names, identifying information, and specifics have been changed so that there would be no resemblance to actual individuals. Throughout this book, the words *marital* and *couple* are used interchangeably. These problems also extend across all ethnic and religious groups and lesbian, gay, bisexual, transgender, or queer (LGBTQ) and heteronormative couples. Like many other difficulties, this is not one that discriminates. However, the law does matter in most of these cases, and that law may be quite different for married versus never-married couples. It goes without saying that in locations where LGBTQ couples cannot marry, further complexities ensue. Both married and unmarried couples present with the difficult endings described here.

Finally, a word about research and practice in this book. I have written extensively about the interface of research and practice, emphasizing how research must inform practice (Lebow, 2006; Lebow & Jenkins, 2018; Sexton et al., 2011). Practice in working with divorce likewise must incorporate the insights from research on divorce (summarized in Chapter 2) and the research on the impact of strategies of intervention in the context of other problems. This book is anchored in such understandings. However, divorce therapy has seldom, if ever, been studied for its impact. There are constraints to such research. In the realm of research on psychotherapy, there has always been more funding for treatment of specific *Diagnostic and Statistical Manual of Mental Disorders* (American Psychiatric Association, 2013) diagnoses than for relational problems such as minimizing the negative effects of divorce. Further, the frequent coexistence of matters in court make research on these treatments unlikely. Therefore, substantial parts of this book are written from the perspective of a clinician who has worked with these problems over many years and my observation of how other skillful clinicians work with these problems. These considerations are always informed by relevant available research, especially about intervention strategies that have been found effective in related problems, as well as basic research knowledge about both divorce broadly and difficult divorce more specifically. However, the suggestions for clinical practice presented here inevitably must extend beyond the narrow band of methods that have been demonstrated to have an impact in controlled research specifically assessing intervention in difficult divorce. I do try to distinguish as much as possible throughout this book between what is the voice of the experienced clinician and the reporting of well-established research findings.

1

WORKING IN THE TERRITORY OF DIFFICULT DIVORCE

The practice of psychotherapy is replete with complex decision-making. Choices about goals of treatment vary across the individuals seen and kind of therapy, and there are many effective alternate strategies for accomplishing specific goals (Lebow, 2014; Pinsof, Breunlin, Russell, & Lebow, 2011). Yet there are no decisions in therapy as complex and open to multiple diverse perspectives as decisions to divorce and how best to work with families approaching and going through this transition.

For example, consider this family:

> Angela and Roberto entered therapy during a marital crisis. Although Angela had complained for several years about their lack of connection and frequent fighting, Roberto had been unwilling to change and reluctant to engage in marital therapy. However, when Angela retained a lawyer and filed for divorce, Roberto desperately wanted to take whatever measure might save their marriage. The children, in part in relation

http://dx.doi.org/10.1037/0000116-002
Treating the Difficult Divorce: A Practical Guide for Psychotherapists, by J. L. Lebow

to their father's reaction, responded with significant distress. Roberto and Angela then initiated therapy as a couple. Roberto's goal was to restore the marriage, but Angela remained steadfast that, although she was willing to come in for therapy with Roberto, she had decided that she wanted to separate and divorce.

What should the role of the therapist be in such a therapy? Is the therapist's primary task to rescue the marriage? Is it to at least provide them an opportunity to discuss staying married? Or would it be to have them part as amicably as possible with a minimum of conflict? And what about the children? Would the best service be to involve the children to help detriangulate them from the parental conflict and help them through this transition? In the service of various possible treatment goals, would it be better to see them as a family, the couple, or triage all of them to different individual therapists?

Here is a second common situation:

> George and Gabrielle had a contentious, difficult marriage. When Gabrielle discovered that George was having an affair, she immediately filed for divorce. Their children, Todd (age 16) and Karen (age 13), had always been closer to their mother. When the marriage exploded, neither child wanted to spend time with George. Even though George and Gabrielle continued to live in the same house during the period just after Gabrielle filed, Todd and Karen spent almost no time with their father. Gabrielle held that it was up to the children how they incorporated their father into their lives. Considerable conflict between George and Gabrielle and between George and the children ensued. In the proceedings of the divorce, George and Gabrielle struggled about how to divide time with the children, and an attorney was appointed to support the needs of the children.

In a family situation like that of George and Gabrielle's, in which acrimony is overwhelming and feelings are deeply anchored, what might therapy accomplish? With feelings so raw, does it even make sense to have family members meet together in sessions? What might the therapist's role be in repairing the relationship between George and the children? What should be the role of children in therapy? How might a therapist best contend with the complex matters that occur in court regarding child custody?

THERAPISTS IN A STRANGE LAND

Psychotherapists mostly are skillful and have considerable success. Meta-analyses indicate they have a substantial positive effect in three of four cases (Lambert & Ogles, 2016; Smith & Glass, 1979). They are particularly effective in treating difficulties such as anxiety, depression, and couple distress, especially when clients are highly motivated to change and when there are clear, well-established pathways to promote change (Barlow, Bullis, Comer, & Ametaj, 2013; Lebow, Chambers, Christensen, & Johnson, 2012; Nathan & Gorman, 2015). Most therapists are also enthusiastic about seeing clients. They are highly committed to their work and derive satisfaction from the therapy process (Orlinsky & Rønnestad, 2005). Further, if they are in a private or group practice, they typically are gratified when there is a new referral and are very open to engaging with new clients.

Families engaging in difficult divorce, especially the high-conflict variation of divorce, present a much different territory for therapists. Even very skilled experienced therapists often feel well out of their comfort zone when they encounter such cases. Emotional reactivity in these families is extremely high. Clients are often in the phase of life described by Mavis Hetherington as "not me" (Hetherington, 1999)—that is, a time of enormous transition when they do not feel like their normal selves. This is a time in which family members are often capable of difficult behaviors, in which they may or may not notice that they are engaged. Further, as clients, they often come to treatment because of the intervention of a third party, perhaps the court or concerned family members who think they need help and may only be motivated for others to change. The legal system with its rules, and the possibility of deposition and testimony about what is occurring the family, may be directly involved and remains a constant consideration for therapists who may not want those experiences to be part of their professional lives. Finally, there a few guides to working with these families. Yet, although there are hundreds of self-help books about how to survive or thrive in a divorce (Baker, Bone, & Ludmer, 2014; Emery, 2004; Hetherington & Kelly, 2002; H. Miller & Shepherd, 2016), there have been few expositions on how therapists might help these families. One can be a terrific emotionally focused couple therapist or cognitive behavioral family therapist and have little training and experience in working with these systems.

Thus, therapists often tend to avoid these cases. A place where I once worked listed summaries of intakes so that therapists might select those clients whom they were most interested in treating. The difficult divorces of this kind clearly were the least often selected, sometimes remaining on the list for days before they were processed in some other way. The reasons for therapists' reluctant involvement in these cases are readily understandable. The thought of encountering aggressive lawyers and being called for deposition may be experienced as threatening. The anger, cutoffs, and strong emotions often seen in these clients may promote strong countertransference, or simply a desire to have less stressful workdays. How much nicer to engage with clients who have a specific problem, such as anxiety and depression, and who will work diligently toward treatment goals, appreciate the therapist, and have a greater probability of treatment success.

Further, if therapists are unfamiliar with this territory, their understanding may fail them. What may be highly effective in other contexts may be ineffective or even iatrogenic here. For example, if a therapist was seeing Gabrielle, the standard common factor of providing support, if presented without care and careful qualification, might readily turn into encouragement of her destructive stance toward George's parenting.

This is a land full of minefields, yet they can be known and negotiated. This book aims to help therapists and therapists in training develop their abilities to work with divorcing and postdivorce families, particularly those who are having particular difficulty with this life transition. The foundations of this work lie in the following:

1. *Developing a good working knowledge of the issues that arise in divorce and postdivorce life.* Here, there is a large empirical and clinical literature that can serve as a foundation for treatment.
2. *Drawing from an integrative, transtheoretical, and pragmatic body of knowledge that can be flexibly applied in working with these families or with specific family members.* Family, couple, and individual sessions are all possible formats for therapy, and one therapy may draw on multiple formats.
3. *Setting appropriate, achievable goals.* Part of the complexity of these cases is that there might be so many goals that overlapping interminable therapies might be thought necessary. Proximate goals for therapy may range from managing the present, to dealing with the ghosts of the past marital family life, to exploring multiple family-of-origin experiences, to considering a bevy of overlapping other factors. Goals must be chosen carefully and collaboratively in these families.
4. *Mastering interactions with the legal system and other people involved in trying to ameliorate problems.* The legal system can be an ally or a constraint; often the difference depends on the therapist's skill in working with the legal system.

CHARACTERISTICS OF DIFFICULT DIVORCE

There are few easy divorces; in fact, "easy divorce" is usually an oxymoron. Almost invariably, when a couple decides to divorce, most of the people involved are highly energized and upset. During the first few months of separation and divorce, many people meet criteria for a significant mental health diagnosis, most often in the domains of anxiety, depression, or posttraumatic stress disorder (see Chapter 2). Parenting also suffers, especially monitoring, and children are typically upset. Yet we must also separate "normative" divorce from the "difficult" divorce. In normative divorce, there is conflict, but only so much; there are strong feelings, but there is almost always some ability to regulate those feelings. And in normative divorce, after a period (for most, about 2 years), strong feelings die down, and life moves on.

In contrast, in difficult divorce something is off-kilter in a major way. Difficult divorces vary, so they cannot be stereotyped, but they often include several notable features. This section describes several of these characteristics. Only a few families have them all, but most difficult divorces feature many of them. Several apply only to divorcing partners with children, given that parents face the special challenge of needing to create and maintain some ongoing arrangement having to do with children over time, extending the complexity and long-term impact of possible problems, and elongating the time over which to develop issues.

1. Feelings are not just intense, they are often fully dysregulated.

Jose and Maria continued to live together while they were getting divorced. Several times a week, they would argue about who should be with their children at a specific time. Each disagreement would quickly degenerate into shouting, name-calling, and threats. In these arguments, both Jose and Maria felt and acted out of control in their emotions, as primal biological "fight" neurotransmitters in each dominated in the interaction.

Either because of personality characteristics or the immediate strains of the moment, many of those in difficult divorce have no ability to regulate painful feelings. These may be manifested as outbursts or as withdrawal; either way, the ability to manage how one feels is at times fully lost. A by-product of this is that various conflicts are not contained in subsystems (e.g., the partner subsystem) but become well known to all around, including children, regardless of the content or impact of those feeling states on those present. Contributing to this is that in difficult divorce, the loss of ability to mentalize and empathize with one another is almost universal and profound. For many, a solution to the deep sense of hurt is to lose all empathy for others in the family, most especially their former partners, as they are overwhelmed by their own feelings.

2. Family structures enter a period of uncertainty.

When Mia discovered that Kevin was having an affair, she confronted him. Kevin told her he was in love with the other woman, and thus Mia initiated divorce proceedings. Although Kevin and Mia agreed that divorce was the best option, they disagreed about when the children should be with each of them. Mia adamantly argued for the children spending 12 out of 14 days with her, whereas Kevin looked for a 50–50 split in time. Because they were unable to resolve this difference, they continued to live with one another despite the volatility of their situation. Two years, several lawyers, and one child custody evaluation later, they have yet to arrive at where they each would live and what the new structure would be for the allocation of time for the children with each parent.

Here, the old family structure is lost, and thus, so too are the necessary core building blocks of family structure that provide the foundation of family life (clear boundaries, consistent appropriate but flexible alliances, and a fair set distribution of power) described by Salvatore Minuchin (1974), and thus the process of developing a new family organization to replace the old one is arrested. The earlier family organization (e.g., a two-parent family) with clear roles is no longer functional, but a new one (e.g., each parent and the children as separate entities with a clear notion of the extent of coparenting) of a postdivorce family cannot emerge because the family is locked in intractable conflict about that structure. Additionally, often, no parental coalition of any kind about any issue is in place, providing fertile ground for other structural difficulties.

3. Children and others become triangulated into parental conflict.

Sharon is 13 and her bat mitzvah in the Jewish faith falls during her parents' separation as they are moving toward divorce. Sharon and Louise, her mother, have a meeting with the rabbi during which they choose how various family members will be involved in the bat mitzvah service. All the people selected to participate in the bat mitzvah are from the mother's side of the family or her mother's friends. When Harold, Sharon's father, hears about this and complains about him and his family not being involved, Louise replies that children should make such decisions about their bat mitzvah and that Sharon does not want him or his family involved. In this way, who will participate in what way in Sharon's bat mitzvah becomes a matter before the court.

Helping children remain free from parental conflict is among the most difficult tasks in divorce. As family therapists Salvatore Minuchin (1974) and Murray Bowen (1978) highlighted long ago, when there is conflict, and most especially a lack of any parental coalition, one of the simplest solutions is to bring third parties into the conflict in a process labeled *triangulation*. Such alliances may have far more power than would one party vis-à-vis the other in matters such as interparental conflict or may offset other differences in power between parents. Children in this way can represent a potential powerful ally against the other parent. What develops often aptly deserves the title *perverse triangle* that Jay Haley (1963) once applied to such alliances, given the damaging effects for all concerned. Few life events are as powerful as having your children join against you. Those with wisdom manage to avoid the temptation of such alliances, which inevitably will be destructive for the children involved. After all, children benefit from the best possible relationship with both parents except in the most exceptional circumstances. Further, this is a dangerous tactic because once children experience such power in triangulation, the triangle may shift over time. More than a few children begin siding with one parent only to shift to siding with the other later after they realize how they have been triangulated.

There is both an overt version of such triangulation and a covert one. In the *overt* version, parents' bids for sympathy and support are clearly stated. In the extreme, comments that are strongly alienating of the relationship with the other parent are frequent and directly promote triangulation ("Mom just doesn't care about us"). In the subtler, *covert*, version of this phenomenon, present in the example of Sharon and her family, triangulation is engaged by following and supporting a dysfunctional thought or behavior by a child. In this subtler circumstance, parents often say and think (as in Sharon's family) that they aren't undermining or engaging in a coalition but rather just supporting the wishes of their child. No truly parental balanced wisdom is offered (e.g., in a more normative divorce, a parent may ask the other, "What are we going to do about Sharon wanting this?" and engage a discussion or may more simply make a more direct parental structuring intervention with Sharon, telling her that some members of her father's family need to be involved). Both the overt and covert forms of triangulation are highly destructive. Notable here is that parents who only engage in the covert method often pride themselves in self-statements about their level of fairness because they do not engage in overt, highly critical statements about the other parent.

4. Closely related to the triangulation of children is a lack of appropriate boundaries between the parental conflict and children.

Tom became outraged when he learned Marie had been having an affair with someone she worked with and separated from Marie. When he explained the separation to the children, he went into great detail about Marie's involvement and, to be sure they believed him, showed them pictures of Marie and her lover taken by a private detective he had hired.

In the presence of strong feelings of hurt and anger, normal expectations for boundaries are often violated. Few would see Tom's behavior as appropriate, no matter the cultural context. In difficult divorce, the violations are not subtle, nor do they fall into the zone where wise people might have different ideas about what is appropriate.

When parents agree about some realistic set of expectations (these may vary) and work within those expectations, the transition through divorce occurs with less difficulty. It's important here to highlight that in getting to such a shared vision, even the best of parents may initially disagree about expectations around boundaries. Is it best to keep children fully insulated from the drama and conflicts that occur? For example, if there is a major conflict about money, should the children be told? Should children know who initiated a divorce? The answer to such questions can be debated. On one side, there is the idea of protecting the children from destructive conflict. On the other side, children seeing parents being upset and being forced to do their own detective work to figure out what is going on is also less than ideal. And there are the merits of being honest with one's children. A common example of too little sharing occurs when parents agree to, or one parent argues for, the merits of setting an unrealistic set of expectations about shielding children and others from knowledge about separation and divorce well after the transition has begun. In those circumstances, it is almost certain that children will be upset about the boundary for information between the coparents and the children having been too rigid.

Ultimately, many issues about boundary and information are not amenable to there being one correct answer; these are aspects of life much governed by personal values, cultural context, and the specifics of one family's situation. Having said that, in this variant of the difficult divorce, there is rarely any doubt that something dysfunctional is occurring. Boundaries for information sharing that are best not crossed are crossed—and typically often and provocatively. The result is increasing the emotional charge for children, further enabling the possibilities for triangulation and interparental and parent–child conflict.

5. Developmental tasks are not completed in a timely manner.

Margo and Steve initiated their divorce 2 years ago. At the time of their separation, their son Matt's school had identified that he had severe learning disabilities and needed neuropsychological testing. Margo strongly favored the testing and quickly identified someone to do it. Steve doubted the importance of the testing. Two years later, the testing had yet to begin.

Life tasks continue while people are divorcing. Children may face academic challenges, need braces, require treatment for more serious diseases, or need help with an emerging drug problem. Adults may go through job changes, establish new residences, or deal with their own health issues. In difficult divorce, many such tasks are postponed or remain out of focus. The result is often the accrual of further difficulties, which, in turn, raises the overall level of stress.

6. Coparenting atrophies or never develops.

Wilma and Ben had a traditional division of labor during their marriage with Ben working long hours and Wilma taking care of almost all the parenting tasks. Around the time of their separation, Nick, age 17, was arrested for shoplifting. Wilma was inclined to take him for therapy and set no consequence, believing that his acting out was a response to his parents' impending divorce and that he primarily needed to have his feelings understood. Ben wanted to set a significant consequence of Nick losing his car privileges for 6 months. They could not arrive at a mutually acceptable plan and thus wound up with two plans. Ben set up a major consequence of his not being allowed to go out evenings when in his home, while Wilma had him begin to see an individual therapist, and disowned the consequence Ben had set.

When parents part, some degree of coparenting is expected (or at least parallel parenting in which major issues do not stir up too much conflict). For some, coparenting extends to even the smallest decisions. For others, it may be restricted to particularly significant decision-making, leaving each parent to parent in his or her own way otherwise. Both are functional models. With either model, however, there is a need for some coordination and clarity about decision-making.

Many divorcing families lose or may never have had such coparenting processes. Wilma and Ben demonstrate an especially problematic situation because they never have actually coparented, with the less involved parent (often, as Ben is, the father in a heterosexual couple) never having developed much of a repertoire of parenting skills or participated actively in parental decision-making. Given that divorce almost inevitably means some time alone with each parent being assigned to the children, usually for at least 2 days at a time, such constellations can be rife with opportunities for problems to emerge. In such instances, parents need to develop coparenting rather than restore it, even as they are dealing with the complex tasks of separating their lives. Additionally, in such families, children and one parent may have to fully develop a relationship from a rudimentary connection, rather than more simply figure out how to extend and adapt that relationship in the absence of the other parent. In other difficult divorces, coparenting may have been adequate or even a strength before the divorce process began but may have totally atrophied in the wake of the hurt feelings in the divorce, leaving little basis for coordination between parents.

7. Communication breaks down.

When Susan and Monica split up, both were deeply hurt. Conversations about any subject easily led to upset and sometimes conflict. As a result, Monica decided to cut off all contact with Susan, not only not speaking to her but also not reading or responding to her e-mails and texts. This made for major gaps in the flow of information, such as when the children were sick, and negated any opportunities for even the simplest acts of coparenting.

A minimal level of communication between parting partners is needed in divorcing and postdivorce families if there are children or other mutual interests that need attention. Absent such communication, problems inevitably ensue. What is enough communication will vary with the specific family. For example, a family in which a child has a major medical or mental health issue needs to have more communication between parents (and for that matter, between each child and parent) than one in which children have less pervasive issues.

As with the other ongoing concerns in these families, the communication problem that emerges is not subtle. It may involve not only parental communication but sometimes communication between one parent and a child or the children.

One variation on this theme is the complete cutoff in communication in which at least one party decides he or she will not communicate with another party. Another is where communication between dyads (parent–parent or parent–child) is accompanied by high levels of acrimony. A third variation is the divorce equivalent of the demand–withdraw cycle seen in couple relationships (Eldridge & Christensen, 2002). Here, one former partner radically restricts communication while the other sends an onslaught of inquiries, reminders, and other bids for engagement (albeit often negative engagement). Inevitably, the withdrawer feels justified in withdrawing, given the degree of the onslaught, and the pursuer feels justified in the need for vigorous pursuit because he or she lacks crucial information.

8. Legal actions are particularly acrimonious.

Bud and Janine have many differences about their divorce that they are unable to resolve. Janine has several million dollars in a trust from her family. Bud believes that this should matter in the allocation of assets and in terms of child support, but Janine disagrees. Janine has been actively concerned about Bud's drug use, an allegation that Bud denies, despite Janine's having reports from friends about his going out to clubs and using drugs. In their divorce, which has been going on for about a year, several emergency petitions have been filed in court by their attorneys. As is common in such petitions, concerns in these petitions are presented in a dramatic and contemptuous way. When a hearing is held about Bud's time with the children, Janine's lawyer is especially provocative and attacking, challenging him with the findings about what he does in the evening compiled by a private investigator.

Interaction with the legal system is an important factor in many of these cases (see Chapter 7). Sometimes lawyers pursue aggressive ways of achieving what they see as the best possible outcome for their clients. Other times lawyers seek more balanced solutions, only to discover their clients find these unsatisfactory. Some litigants may even seek new attorneys who are prepared to be more aggressive.

Some aspects of the legal system are structured as a win–lose contest, and despite the best efforts of family court judges to reduce acrimony, presentations are often dramatic and exaggerated. Sometimes the intent of attorneys in the judicial system is to present the most convincing case—for example, by creating doubt about children's safety with a parent, either because there is real danger or to raise doubts. Other times the intent of attorneys lies in a war of attrition, testing whether the other parent will stay with his or her position when the cost to self-esteem and reputation may be high.

John Gottman has pointed out the difficult role that contempt has in marriage and how it is inextricably linked to marital demise (Gottman & Gottman, 2015). Stripped of any positive sentiment override, contemptuous communication through the voice of attorneys or documents filed in court sets and promotes a runway to a process of mutual derogation. It is rare in difficult divorce that anyone can maintain the attribution that only the attorney is the scoundrel here. Attorneys are often blamed, but almost always in the context of placing primary blame on one's former partner, whether or not the partner was the source of the particular attack. Ironically, the lawyers may meet with one another for coffee after the hearing in court, but the divorcing partners (and, for that matter, the children and others in the family, if they are called in to participate in the criticism of the partner in focus) do not.

9. Families engage in kin-wars.

Arjun and Prisha were married for 15 years. While they were together, they had many conflicts over how much time they and their children would spend with each of their families of origin. One annual conflict was over which family they would visit for the Christmas holiday. When they separated, conflict between each and the other's family of origin magnified. Arjun and his family blamed Prisha for her decision to initiate the divorce. Various family members on each side were witnesses in the divorce proceedings, testifying to the alleged bad behavior of the other spouse. When son Aadir graduated high school, a heated argument broke out between the respective families over who would have the opportunity to take him out to dinner and congratulate him first.

Janet Johnston labeled a certain kind of involvement of extended family in these systems as *kin-wars* (Johnston & Campbell, 1986), a perfect term to describe these conflicts. Kin-wars represent the dominance of primitive tribal behavior over reason. In each tribe, a strong sense of mutual support emerges in which there is little appropriate feedback about difficult behavior, whereas the behaviors and personalities of those on the other side in the conflict are blamed for all problems. Such patterns have a powerful effect. Family loyalty becomes more important than the general welfare. Further, such forces readily establish coalitions that hold shared beliefs and further restrict movement toward the general best interest. Occasionally, in a variation on these themes, one or more members of one kin network join with the partner to whom they do not have a blood relationship in this cycle of blame.

10. New partners are prematurely brought into relationships with children.

> Mike was shocked when Sarah told him she was filing for divorce. He quickly (many might say on the rebound) formed a new relationship with Jill. Given the strength of his positive feelings for Jill, he believed it would best for his children to join him in his new happiness 1 month into the relationship, and he began to include Jill in the time he spent with the children. This resulted in a great uproar among the children, who began to express reluctance to spend time with their father if it meant also being with Jill.

New partners, in divorcing and postdivorce families, emerge as issues in both normative and difficult divorce. For most adults, the successful resolution of a divorce eventually leads to a new relationship, and with that the process of building connections between new partners and children, as well as to other people in the parent's life (including to some extent their former partner; Papernow, 2013). Yet the question remains what the process for segueing into the remarried family life will be and how fast that process will occur. Divorce typically makes for two developmental transitions: The first is from married life to divorce, and the second is from divorced life to a new married life.

Often, in difficult divorce, as in Mike's case, the need to allow time for everyone to digest the first change is ignored, with negative consequences. The loving feeling of being in a new relationship can lead to a sense that others will share the enthusiasm and to a lack of empathy for how others may experience this change. This problem is amplified when the leaving partner exits when he or she is already in a relationship with a new partner, a configuration that often has negative short- and long-term consequences for relational life (with the involvement of the first partner while married becoming the focus of attention). A related scenario that emerges in some difficult divorce occurs when a pregnancy in the new relationship very quickly follows the end of the marriage or occurs during the divorce process.

11. New partners are experienced negatively.

Chris and Sally had little conflict in their divorce and were great coparents. After divorcing, they continued to participate in many events together with their children, ranging from school events to Thanksgiving dinner. However, conflict emerged when Sally entered a significant relationship with Barry a year later. The children found Barry too rough and mean in interactions and complained to their mother. Dinners together quickly ended, with their son, Mick, bringing many complaints to Sally about Barry.

Another variation in difficult divorces centers on the behavior of new partners. When new partners are experienced negatively by children or the former spouse, a sequence can set off or revive new systemic problems. Although such problems can occur any time in the life of the divorced family, the problems are typically most acute when the entry of the new partner is closely linked in time to separation and divorce. Common sources of difficulty include when

- the new partner acts in difficult ways, such as having psycho-pathology or behaviors that challenge norms in the older nuclear family;
- there is a premature entry of the new partner into the structuring aspects of parenting without sufficient time to establish an attachment;
- there is a sense of competitive parenting in which a parent experiences the stepparent as a threat;
- someone thinks that the new relationship was instrumental in the demise of the marriage;
- the new partner's presence makes for greater distance between the former couple; or
- new involvements spark the reprocessing of old wounds.

Remarkably, there are some divorces in which a high level of cooperation between parents and children can occur until these new partners enter, which then segue into a difficult phase that directly or indirectly centers on the new parent's role and behavior. Chris and Sally provide a prime example of when the entry of a new partner challenges a developing plan for ongoing connection among the original family members and the behavior of the new partner conflicts with previously normative ways of interacting or may be intrinsically harmful.

12. There is a specter of intrafamilial violence.

Doug was very hurt when Sonia told him she was filing for divorce. She asked him to leave the marital home, but he would not agree. For weeks thereafter, they lived together with their children, moving in and out of conflict. One evening, after having several drinks, Doug lost control during an argument and started to pummel Sonia. Their small children tried to intervene, but Sonia wound up with significant bruising on her face and body. She then filed an order of protection, and Doug was ordered to leave the marital home.

Intrafamilial violence is not the most frequent problem in difficult divorce, but it is a problem with enormous salience. The statistics here are sobering. In the transition to divorce, the rates of partner aggression and physical confrontations between parents and children drastically increases. Fifty percent of couples in custody disputes report some level of intimate partner violence (Rossi, Holtzworth-Munroe, & Rudd, 2016). In the judicial system, the number of orders of protection granted point to the extent of this problem. According to recent U.S. government statistics, separated families (i.e., those in the process of divorce) had the highest rates of intimate partner violence compared with married or divorced families (see https://www.bjs.gov/content/pub/press/ipv9310pr.cfm). Rates of homicide are also highest in families during this transition compared with any other time in life. Statistics indicate that both men and women become violent, but men do the preponderance of physical damage. To be sure, most families, even in difficult divorce, do not become violent, but violence and threats of violence are a major problem in many families, as are related behaviors such as stalking or persistent emotional abuse. Thus, therapists must always inquire about violence and threats to safety and make safety a priority.

13. A parent has a personality disorder.

Molly and Sam had a tumultuous relationship. Throughout their marriage, they argued a great deal about a wide variety of subjects. During those fights and at other times as well, Molly would become emotionally dysregulated. Although Sam was clearly equally responsible for the arguing, Molly's dysregulation, in which she would scream, throw things, and punch and kick, made long-term repair impossible. When they separated, Molly continued this pattern, without any of the positive connection they had previously. In this context, resolution of any issue became impossible. Molly would blame Sam for all her difficulties, and Steve would return the favor by pointing to what he termed Molly's "borderline personality disorder" (accurately describing her condition but also speaking in a highly provocative way that only served to worsen the interaction).

Therapists widely recognize that personality disorders make working with any problem more difficult (Hooley & Germain, 2008). There is strong evidence that psychotherapy outcomes for those with personality disorders tend to be worse than with other clients (Ogrodniczuk, Uliaszek, Lebow, & Piper, 2014), and therefore a number of special treatments for those with these difficulties have emerged (Linehan, 2015). In conflicts around divorce, the presence of a personality disorder is a difference that makes a difference, moving problems from difficult to seemingly impossible to resolve.

14. A parent has other severe psychopathology.

Mel had a long history of bipolar disorder. Mel and Bob would get along well when Mel was not in the midst of an episode. When they first separated, they cooperated well with one another, but 3 months later, Mel had a depressive period. Bob became alarmed and withheld contact with their children. This led to considerable conflict and ultimately an intervention in court to sort out about whether Mel could be with the children unsupervised and how much time he could spend with them.

Severe psychopathology also can impinge significantly on families. The presence of psychopathology can amplify issues in divorce or create a special set of problems that lead to acrimony, such as the question of Mel's access to the children in the case just described. When a divorcing partner is prone to depression, anxiety, bipolar disorder, schizophrenia, chemical dependency, or a variety of other specific mental health problems that affect parenting or coparenting, issues readily arise about the competency of that person as a parent. With the stressor of the divorce, parental monitoring, structuring, and warmth (challenged in most divorcing families for a time given the many competing tasks) may decline well below acceptable levels. This interpersonal dynamic is even more challenging when the individual problem is long standing, and the family has basically functioned through the overfunctioning of the second parent. Cooperative divorcing parents find ways to mitigate these difficulties (e.g., by finding ways to identify times when symptoms affect parenting and alter parenting plans in relation to those times), but in difficult divorce, parents cannot find effective ways to deal together with the concerns that accompany the specific kind of psychopathology. Even in couples without children, severe psychopathology in a partner can cause the process of divorce to become extremely complex, especially when the divorce process triggers the onset or worsening of psychopathology.

15. There are parent–child difficulties.

Harvey is a busy executive who travels the world. Distant in his personality, he never established much of a connection with his three children. When Lynne finally decided she had enough of having a partner who did not relate closely to her or the children and the parents separated, two of the three children refused to spend the assigned weekends with Harvey. Harvey began to devote more attention to this time with the children, only to find them unwilling to accompany him or speak to him on the phone or message with him. This led to further conflict between Harvey and Lynne, since Harvey blamed Lynne for what he called their "alienation" (having read about this on the Internet).

The topic of parent–child cutoffs and difficulties in divorce has received much attention (see Chapter 8). Unfortunately, the constellation in Harvey and Lynne's family is all too frequently encountered. When parenting has been done primarily by one parent, the transition through divorce must include some transition to extend parenting to the second parent (unless the second parent simply withdraws). Many families negotiate this transition (even if they have a rough patch), but some, like the family just described, do not. In other families, one parent is injured and angry and actively politics for a cut-off between the other parent and children ("I don't know why your mother abandoned us"). And, in still others, children and parents have long-standing conflicts, or conflicts about the divorce or postdivorce life, that render arriving at any working stable structure impossible. In all these instances, a difficult set of exchanges ensues in which parents, as well as parents and children, blame each other. Once established, such patterns are difficult to change.

16. Children present with special difficulties, or differences between parents are intrinsically difficult to negotiate.

Jimmy, age 15, is on the autistic spectrum. Mary, his mother, took the leadership in the nuclear family in finding special schools and treatment for Jimmy. She organized a dependable treatment system in relation to Jimmy's problem. When Joe and Mary mutually decided to end their marriage, conflict ensued about Jimmy. Joe thought that Jimmy should spend the same amount of time with him that he would spend with the other children. Mary thought that Joe's laissez-faire style would cause Jimmy to regress. When she heard rumors of how Jimmy was doing during his time with his father and saw how he appeared when he came home, Mary petitioned to have Joe's time with Jimmy restricted.

Sometimes children have special issues that present challenges for nuclear families, but those challenges of working together toward the same goals become magnified when parents divorce. The stakes are high in terms of the need to respond to the specific behavioral or health issue, and this can create the context for intractable problems between parents or between parents and children in some families.

Closely related here are situations in which there are irreconcilable differences between parents about raising children. For example, when parents with different, strong religious affiliations divorce, even points of previous agreement can dissolve (as when the parents had agreed to raise the child in one religion). Similarly, differences between highly religious parents and parents who are not religious can lead to each remaining upset about how their children are being raised. Perhaps most taxing among such emerging differences is when one parent feels a strong need to relocate far away from where he or she currently lives. In normative divorce, time with parents in the context of such moves are typically negotiated (or more simply dictated by the conservative nature of the law about such issues, which only typically allow for such moves under very special circumstances without the full agreement of the former partners). However, lack of cooperation about the relocation of children or other of such major differences readily moves toward severe conflicts in difficult divorce.

17. Issues become interminable.

Natasha and Mikhail divorced 12 years ago after 4 years of jousting in court about their divorce. They fought over a set of coparenting issues over the 4 years of the divorce and have continued to fight over the same issues that were present at the time of the divorce. Mikhail believes Natasha overschedules the children purposefully to keep his time with the children limited. They have been to court several times over the years around Mikhail's petitions that Natasha was blocking his parenting.

One of the worst aspects of many difficult divorces is that often issues that move into focus are never resolved and thus remain a part of the family's life forever. The problems here are analogous to what Gottman referred to as the "perpetual issues of marriage" (Gottman, 1999) that are the subject of disagreement over the years, but without any positive sentiment override, positive experiences, or acceptance that can mitigate that sense of unresolvable conflict in married couples. The product is almost always negative expectations about cooperation, troubled coparenting, and continuing narratives that are negative about the others involved in the interaction, along with the inevitable wear and tear on all involved. It should be highlighted that courts can mandate behavioral solutions to some of these sorts of issues (e.g., how the children's time is divided), but even when these solutions are imposed, it does not necessarily lead to a change in the broader behavioral patterns or the interactions around those behaviors.

18. Issues are never dealt with (a quiet variation of difficult divorce).

Mitch and Martha are much different from the other divorcing couples described so far. They hardly ever argued, and even now that they are divorcing, they often act in friendly ways. However, they never developed successful ways of communicating or problem-solving. Now that they are divorcing, they simply don't communicate about important issues. In their habitual sequence, not communicating is followed by poor decision-making with one or the other feeling quietly resentful.

The example of Mitch and Martha reminds us that not all divorcing people are highly conflictual. This is comforting, but this couple also points to how less conflictual is not necessarily much more functional. There are noisy divorces in which the parties do problem-solve and quiet ones that can remain mired for years while multiple problems accrue. In one striking variation, quiet parties hire highly conflictual lawyers, who do the nasty work for them. Even if everyone remains quiet, if the tasks of divorce and postdivorce life cannot be negotiated, problems typically ensue.

THE BETTER DIVORCE

There is no perfect pathway to good divorce. Instead, there are many paths to more successful adjustment (Ahrons, 1994). Successful divorce always includes pain and some problems in transition. Although self-help books and newspaper accounts of celebrity divorces are filled with "how-to" advice, this is not a developmental transition amenable to formulaic answers. Having said that, better divorces present properties very different from the difficult divorces described in this chapter. In general, they are characterized by the following characteristics:

1. A better level of communication exists through the divorce process and after between partners. There are challenges, but some effective channels of communication remain in place.
2. There is less sense of personal injury and blame for that injury than in difficult divorces. There is injury, but that injury does not run as deep. Some ability to mentalize and empathize with one another remains, at least in most aspects of life.
3. A mode of problem-solving remains in place regardless of conflict about specific issues.
4. Feelings are powerful but most times remain regulated rather than dysregulated, and thus the cascade of feelings in difficult divorce is avoided.
5. Developmental tasks are completed in a timely manner, even if slowed a bit by the stresses of divorce.
6. Family structures evolve from the two-parent family to two single-parent households (and then perhaps ultimately to two remarriage families). Thus, there is always a relevant family structure to help guide family life.
7. Children's needs are considered and prioritized, so that the children are not triangulated into parental conflict. Parent–child alliances are roughly balanced, such that there remains a parental coalition even though parents are divorcing.

8. There may be conflict in terms of issues in the legal system about children or money, but those conflicts are constrained. Typically, these conflicts are resolved with help from family lawyers or through mediation.

9. Families of origin support their family members in divorce, but do not become sources of support for destructive behavior.

10. When new partners enter the family system, they do so gradually, respectful of the role reserved for parents (Papernow, 2015). The entry of such partners is delayed sufficiently so that the family can digest the divorce.

11. Essential issues are dealt with so that the lasting impact of those issues is lessened.

12. Attorneys work toward fair solutions, representing their clients' interests but also seeking outcomes that are balanced.

Of course, a better divorce may still include, at least for a period, one or two of the problems that become reified in difficult divorce. No divorce is perfect. Some conflict is intrinsic to the process of ending what for most people is the anchoring attachment in their lives. In better divorces, there still is much pain, and few people are at their best in this time. Yet observing normative and difficult divorces, these two modes of relating look very different. For those in difficult divorce, both an individual and systemic cascade is underway, flowing toward conflict and chaos.

A FRAMEWORK FOR THERAPY IN DIFFICULT DIVORCE

The period during which divorce unfolds is a complex time with many tasks that need to be accomplished. These include modulating anger and hurt, negotiating and making the transition to a new family structure, adapting to the new circumstance, finding individual and relational resilience, transforming relationships with others in this new context, and considering what has happened and learning from this experience. In addition, there are a wide variety of practical tasks involved, such as planning for a new financial life, establishing a new home, and making changes in one's social network. For the former partners, there also are the tasks of detaching from what has been their primary attachment and considering the possibilities for new relationships. These are formidable tasks for which our society provides little preparation.[1] For those in difficult divorce, the challenges of these tasks

---

[1] In our society, there is almost never any consideration of how to divorce or how to negotiate expectations in divorce until the highly affective time of divorcing comes. How to divorce is not a typical part of relational education programs before or during marriage. This probably serves to enable more positive expectations about marriage but also leaves much to learn during the highly charged time of an ending marriage.

are potentiated in the whirlpool of the cascade occurring, where feelings are raw, and distraction and provocation are everywhere. And, typically, those involved in difficult divorces bring special individual vulnerabilities to such a cascade.

The methods described in this book seek to help family members in difficult divorce, who are vulnerable to the various pitfalls of their situation, to slow down the process and find their intentionality and resilience, to which they may have lost access at this time. The best chance for solutions lies in a steady patient therapy, strong in the common factors that enhance the change process in psychotherapy, with a therapist who is knowledgeable about this territory. The skilled therapist can, from a large repertoire of intervention strategies, selectively choose those that can help provide this set of clients with what is needed to help ameliorate the specific problem at hand. Given the complexities involved, it is best practice to involve multiple family members in therapy when feasible to be able to draw on whatever change is possible in each and deal with systemic processes. Yet, paradoxically, it is also best practice not to look to coequal change from all family members but to build on whatever change is possible in each individual. Therefore, there are important roles for therapy in a variety of treatment formats with these clients.

Having become stuck, how does therapy best help clients in difficult divorce get unstuck? This book looks to find ways to help families, and the individuals in those families, to move closer toward being more like those in more typical divorce. Yet, as we will see, in many difficult divorces, it simply is not possible to transform fully into normative divorce. What is often realistic for many of those who are mired in the difficult divorce is to help these families and individuals move toward a "not-as-bad" divorce in which the extent of the problems is mitigated, strengths are found and amplified, and at least the cascade is quieted. In this way, difficult divorce and its legacy can become less damaging for the family members, leaving them better able to function and deal with other developmental tasks.

Becoming a difficult divorce almost invariably involves the confluence of several factors. Although occasionally one individual's problematic behavior is sufficient to make for a difficult divorce (as in when a highly belligerent, out-of-control individual causes chaos), these systemic runaways in which one bad behavior begets another typically involve multiple participants and the repetition of dysfunctional sequences of behavior over time. Just as Gottman (1999) aptly described marital dissolution as the product of multiple factors leading to a cascade, here a further downward cascade occurs.

The makeup of this cascade is a complex equation that typically includes a very special instance of a cycle of mutual vulnerability (Scheinkman & Fishbane, 2004) accompanied by mutual negative sentiment override. The cascade begins in the context of a low marital bank account in which there are already low levels of trust and connection, or alternatively a sudden plunge in the marital bank account, such as one partner leaving after infidelity, that bankrupts the marital system. Given this, there is almost no positive feeling about the current relationship on which to draw. During the course of divorce, either what had already been a mutually destructive interpersonal process in the marriage is potentiated, or vulnerabilities are exposed that lead to profoundly negative exchanges. There may be positive pursuit of one partner by the other, but when this pursuit is rebuffed, it typically leads to further vulnerability. The ability to mentalize or empathize with one another is fully lost in almost all areas of life.

To cross the threshold into difficult divorce also typically requires at least one person whose personality, or at least whose temporary mental state, presents a sufficient level of vulnerability to engage in a highly provocative way. In this environment, individual dysregulation and systemic dysregulation coevolve, sometimes augmented by triangulation of children into the conflict. Typically, there also needs to be a sustaining focus to maintain the conflict. Those without children and few assets may have a brief period of "difficult," but with few ongoing issues to resolve, former partners disconnect and lose touch. In contrast, when wounded parents are defining new roles and when a sense of vulnerability about one's financial security or social status is engendered, there are endless opportunities for conflict. Most often, conflicts over children or money provide this focus. Establishing a set of expectations for child custody and time with children requires some level of realistic appraisal of various possible configurations, some level of mutual positive regard as a parent, and some willingness to negotiate. In these families, one or all of these elements are missing, replaced by negative sentiment override. Often, the gatekeeping parent, if there is one, believes in the wisdom of keeping the gate as closed as possible, while the other parent is unrealistically ambitious in his or her expectations. Financial issues are approached in a similar manner, with the negotiation framed as win–lose rather than sharing coequally in the assets and hardships. In some systems, social supports step in to calm the waters; however, in these families, such supports can also add to the provocation. Attorneys may enter with unrealistic and aggressive modes that stoke the flames, and extended families and friends can play a similar role. Once the cascade begins, like a fire in the desert, it is hard to extinguish, especially as the legal process and ongoing interactions pour gasoline on the flames. What is an intrinsically challenging task, for partners to separate from what for most is their primary attachment and establish a sufficient working relationship of a much different kind that allows everyone to move forward becomes detoured into a recursive pathogenic process.

Therapy with these systems must slowly and steadily move to control the blaze by promoting a very different, calmer perspective. The approach described in this book works to address what needs to change most to lower the temperature and slow down toxic processes. The core of the approach lies in the common factor of a grounded therapist who has a realistic vision of change that might occur, helping clients access and work with behaviors, cognitions, and feelings. Everyone is highly anxious and energized. The key lies in bringing down these levels of intense negativity systemically by monitoring and intervening with provocative behaviors and creating some positive alternatives; individually, it involves helping clients live with their felt experience. No one process is likely to have a great enough impact; change is a product of multiple impacts in these overdetermined systems. Given that this is largely a systemic problem, change in one person can have a disproportionate effect on others; thus, the approach focuses on who can change what. The specific problems involved require attention, but the resolution of many problems often come more in the form of accepting that a somewhat better version of that problem will remain (again, a parallel to Gottman couple therapy; Gottman & Gottman, 2015) and learning to live in that context. Therapy with difficult divorce is a balance of behavior change and acceptance (Christensen, Dimidjian, & Martell, 2015). There aren't easy solutions for those who have had poor marriages with little left in the marital bank account and deep senses of injury. The postmarriage bank account after the cascade begins at empty, and slowly needs to be rebuilt to have just enough in it to pay the (emotional) bills, perform the tasks needed (e.g., completing the divorce and figuring out how to minimally cooperate and, if there are children, parallel parent), and get to (somewhat) higher ground.

SUMMARY

This chapter summarized the special characteristics most frequently encountered in difficult divorce and contrasts these characteristics with how better divorces proceed. A model for conceptualizing what is occurring in these families was presented, leading to consideration of how therapy can best assist those in difficult divorce.

2

DIVORCE TODAY

Divorce is a highly controversial topic, among both the larger culture and psychotherapists. One aspect of working with divorcing families and individuals lies in having a solid foundation of understanding what is known about divorce and its impact as well as about the broader evolving conversation about divorce. This chapter reviews the substantial body of research about divorce and considers its evolving place in today's world.

THE DEMOGRAPHY OF DIVORCE

Prevalence

Divorce occupies an ever-evolving place in society (Amato & Irving, 2006). In the United States and much of the world, until the mid-1950s, divorce rates were low. This was a by-product of both the strong cultural bias

http://dx.doi.org/10.1037/0000116-003
Treating the Difficult Divorce: A Practical Guide for Psychotherapists, by J. L. Lebow

in favor of staying married and the major economic and legal constraints to divorcing. The divorce rate increased considerably between 1960 and 1980 (a 136% increase in the United States; Amato & Irving, 2006), then stabilized over the past few years[1] (Cherlin, 1992, 2009). The present divorce rate in the United States is 3.2 per 1,000 population; this compares with a marriage rate of 6.9 per 1,000 per year (National Center for Health Statistics, 2017). Translated into a more understandable metric, 43% to 46% of marriages in the United States end in divorce, which coupled with those whose marriages end in long-term separation without legal action, suggests a functional rate of the demise of 50% of marriages (Schoen & Canudas-Romo, 2006). Stated another way, over a lifetime, cohort data suggest a couple that marries today in the United States has a 40% to 45% chance of divorcing (Copen, Daniels, Vespa, & Mosher, 2012). The probability of individuals having more than one divorce also has increased substantially, with rates of divorce greater than 65% for those in second and beyond second marriages (DeLongis & Zwicker, 2017). Coupled with the declining marriage rate in Western society, this means that most children now do not grow up in a home in which two parents also reside throughout their childhood.

Several interrelated reasons have been suggested for the divorce rate reaching its present level (Cherlin, 2009). First, the general improvement in economic well-being and changes in family size have made dividing into two homes more financially feasible for many.[2] Second, Western culture has changed its attitude toward divorce. In much of the broad culture and many subcultures, the life path of marriage–divorce–remarriage evolved to become as acceptable as the single marriage nuclear family, and divorce has come to be viewed as a normal life transition (Walsh, 2012). Third, a variety of other changes in society (including higher expectations for the quality of marriage, geographic mobility, time pressure, and lower levels of community and social support) potentiate marital problems, which, in turn, lead to an increase in considering divorce as one potential solution to these relationship problems (Cherlin, 1992, 2009).

Finally, the law in all states and in many countries changed from a system in which fault needed to be demonstrated on the part of one party for the marriage to end to a "no-fault" system in which one partner's wish to end the marriage became sufficient to trigger divorce (Oliphant & Ver Steegh, 2016). In the law, expected outcomes about the division of monies and sharing the

---

[1]By some counts, there may be a slight decrease recently in the overall divorce rate, although demographers debate how much this may be due to undercounting of divorces and increasing age of first marriage. Some argue that these factors obscure what is a continuing increase in age-standardized divorce rates in this century (Amato, 2010; Kennedy & Ruggles, 2014).

[2]This macrolevel change, of course, does not vitiate the major financial concerns that family members experience due to divorce (discussed later in the chapter); in many families, one or both parents are highly financially stressed after divorce.

lives of minor children also evolved, making those outcomes more predictable. These trends have continued to evolve toward an almost universal preference for shared legal custody between parents with regard to both decision-making and significant, if not coequal, amounts of time allocated for children to be with each parent. Other laws have made it more difficult to avoid child support. Each of these changes has removed constraints to divorce, particularly for those in marriages where at least one partner experiences high levels of marital distress.

Demographic Differences

There are some differences in divorce rate across various subgroups. Level of education has a substantial impact. Those with college degrees have lower rates of divorce than those with less education (Amato, 2010; Bramlett & Mosher, 2002). The rate of divorce for college-educated Americans is declining slightly, whereas for those with high school degrees or less, divorce rates remain steady or may even be continuing to increase (McLanahan, 2004). Perhaps related to this, U.S. divorce rates in more conservative "red states" are higher than those in "blue states" (Glass & Levchak, 2014).

Rates also vary across racial and ethnic groups. African Americans have higher rates of divorce than other American cultural groups (Amato, 2010). For example, Bramlett and Mosher (2002) found that 55% of African Americans divorced within the first 15 years of marriage. Rates for Hispanics approximate those of non-Hispanic Whites but with substantial differences within this group. For example, those with origins in Puerto Rico and Cuba are more likely to divorce than those with origins in Mexico and Central America (Amato, 2010). Immigration status also matters. For example, Mexican Americans born in Mexico have lower divorce rates than Mexican Americans born in the United States (Amato, 2010).

Divorce is somewhat less frequent in older than younger couples and in those with than without children. Yet the rates of divorce in older couples and those married for longer periods of time have recently been increasing considerably. Among those aged 50 years and older, the divorce rate has roughly doubled since 1990, and it has tripled in those in 65 and over, reaching six people per 1,000 married persons in 2015 (S. L. Brown & Lin, 2012). This increase points to the emergence of a new population that divorces—one with a different set of issues than that of younger divorcing couples.

Several other factors predict higher rates of divorce. These include being poor, experiencing unemployment, marrying as a teenager, having a premarital birth, bringing children from a previous marriage into a new marriage, being in a second or third marriage, and growing up in a household without two continuously married parents (Amato, 2010).

Such trends point to the great importance of always considering context when speaking about divorce. Although there are universal aspects to divorce, the meanings in different subgroups may vary considerably. For example, older couples who divorce typically face fewer issues about the division of time with children and often focus more on meanings in terms of health than do younger counterparts.

Other Partings

It is also essential to note that the overall rates of divorce inevitably undercount the number of families in which the partners decouple because many couples now never marry, even after maintaining a relationship over a period of years and having children. That is, there are a group of partners who have significant involvement over extended periods of time who part and may not be counted in the demography of divorce because of the legal status of their relationships but who are, for all practical purposes, "divorcing" (Hita & Braver, 2016). This book includes such parting couples under the umbrella of difficult divorce when their partings are problematic. Such cohabitating units are also more likely to part than are married individuals when relationship problems arise. These transitions also may be more difficult, given that the structured mandated legal process for relationship dissolution, including questions of financial support for children and the lower income spouse, may not be relevant or involved.

There are still other nonmarital relationships of short duration that produce children. Pregnancy may occur in the context of a casual dating relationship or a more intense connection of short duration. Issues in relationships of short duration about child custody, visitation, and financial support are, if anything, more complex in these families, and they typically have fewer resources with which to seek help (Hita & Braver, 2016). Coparenting programs targeted to such "fragile" families have tried to fill some of this void (McHale, Waller, & Pearson, 2012; Waller, 2012; Wilde & Doherty, 2013). This book also speaks to such relationships when the less involved parent remains in contact and seeks a role as parent, and there is conflict about that involvement.

Remarriage

Divorce often segues into remarriage. Demographic data compiled without regard to the length of time since divorce show that 60% of men and 52% of women who have divorced remarry (DeLongis & Zwicker, 2017). Although first-time marriage rates have been dropping in recent years, the percentage of previously married adults remarrying has held steady. Overall, 40% of new marriages involve one or both partners having been married before. More than half of these remarrying adults have children from previous marriages, making the remarriage family a common family form (Ganong & Coleman, 2018). Further, almost one quarter of children whose parents remarry gain a stepsibling in the first 18 months after remarriage. Yet the divorce rate for remarriage couples is more than 60% (about 75% for third marriages and beyond), and remarriage couples are twice as likely to divorce early in marriage as first-marriage couples (DeLongis & Zwicker, 2017). The result is that half of children whose parents divorce and remarry will have their parents redivorce. When asked, these redivorcing couples point to conflicts over children as the major source of marital problems (Browning & Artelt, 2012b). Difficult divorce in stepfamilies can be especially complex, given that by law stepparents have no parental rights (and thus no mandated time with stepchildren after separation) unless a new spouse has adopted his or her stepchildren (nor do stepsiblings have mandated time with one another), adding another layer to the problems in these families (Coleman, Ganong, Russell, & Frye-Cox, 2015).

LGBTQ Relationships

Fewer data are available about the stability of lesbian, gay, bisexual, transgender, and queer (LGBTQ) relationships, given that marriage has only recently become an option for such couples. However, there is no reason to believe that divorce is any less likely among these couples, and parallel examples of both better and worse partings are as easy to find in LGBTQ couples as in heterosexual couples (Johnson, O'Connor, & Tornello, 2016). These couples often face additional difficulties (Green & Mitchell, 2015) because their relationships may fall into gray areas of the law, such as when the laws in various states about same-sex marriage differ or when laws related to adoption or complex arrangements around conception that are often involved in having children are brought into focus. Sometimes, in this legal minefield, the court can make odd decisions, such as denying parental rights to the nonbiological parent. LGBTQ couples also add whatever stigma there remains in divorce to stigma that is already in play, making for additional stressors.

WHY PEOPLE DIVORCE

Divorce occurs for a variety of reasons, and those reasons have a strong effect on how divorce is experienced. It is crucial to emphasize that divorce, like many life events, describes the outside of an event in which there is significant variability. There are common threads among divorces but also vast differences among people who divorce and how they experience this life event.

Amato and colleagues (Amato & Previti, 2003; Amato & Rogers, 1997), in a series of studies, surveyed reasons for divorcing. The most common reasons reported for divorce were infidelity, incompatibility, substance use, and growing apart (Amato & Previti, 2003) in one study; infidelity, spending money foolishly, moodiness, jealousy, and irritating habits were the culprits in another (Amato & Rogers, 1997). Interestingly, and not surprisingly, divorcing partners thought their partners were the principal reason for the divorce. The more divorcing partners thought of external factors, as opposed to internal factors (e.g., problems in themselves or their partners), as the key issues, the less difficult they experienced the divorce. This is an important finding that has great meaning for clinical practice: Externalizing helps people feel better. Bear in mind here, however, that correlation is not causation. This finding simply says that people who externalize the reason for divorce onto something other than self or partner have less of an internal sense of being troubled. Hovering here is the question of what is more important as one experiences the impact of divorce: depth of emotional experiencing or coping. The widely circulated therapeutic technique of externalizing the problem can help in reducing complex difficult feelings and thus symptoms of anxiety and depression but also may serve to reduce emotional experiencing—and with it, learning from this crucial life event.

In another study that inquired into clients' narratives of reasons for divorce, Hawkins and colleagues (A. J. Hawkins, Willoughby, & Doherty, 2012) found that the most frequent reasons for divorce were more pedestrian: growing apart and not being able to talk to each other. It is often the slow growth of distance that makes for the ending of marriages. Yet these normative findings should not obscure that, for a small but important set of people who need to be incorporated into this discussion, the impetus toward divorce comes from the presence of long-standing unacceptable behavior patterns in a spouse, such as intimate partner violence, child abuse, severe and long-term chemical dependency, and severe anger management issues. Divorce rates increase in the context of domestic violence, frequent conflict, infidelity, number of relationship problems, weak commitment, and low levels of love and trust (Amato, 2010).

Yet, broadly, it has been difficult to predict who will divorce rather than merely stay unhappily married by examining marital process, given that commitment seems to be only imperfectly related to marital satisfaction. Gottman and Levenson (1992), in a landmark study, found that the presence of a set of marital behaviors they labeled the *Four Horsemen* (i.e., criticism, defensiveness, contempt, and stonewalling) predicted divorce in couples. Gottman and Levinson's research begins to point to potential relational signs of high risk for divorce in those who are unhappily married, beyond simply the presence of chronically high levels of marital problems.

In related research, Amato and Hohmann-Marriott (2007), employing cluster analysis, identified two different groups who divorced. The first (much as in Gottman's findings) reported frequent arguments, higher rates of physical aggression, thoughts of divorce, low levels of martial happiness, and minimal interaction. However, in Amato and Hohmann-Marriott's research, a second, much different group emerged; these couples reported few arguments, little physical aggression, and moderate levels of marital happiness and interaction before divorcing. Pointing to the importance of demography, they highlighted that their two divorcing groups did share several characteristics that actuarially make it more likely to divorce: growing up in a divorced family, having low levels of religiosity, and being in a second or third marriage. The psychological availability of divorce as a life choice clearly seems to make a difference in whether divorce occurs, independent of the marital process.

Thoughts about divorce in marriages not yet in the divorce process are also commonplace. In a nationally representative random sample of couples, Hawkins and colleagues (2017) found that 25% had actively considered divorce in the past 6 months, and another 28% had actively considered divorce in the past. Thoughts about divorcing in the general population also change over time. In Hawkins's sample, 31% of those considering divorce were not considering it a year later, and 36% of those who were not considering divorce earlier were considering it a year later.

DIVORCE AS A MOVING TARGET

The findings presented in the preceding section highlight the rapid change related to divorce in our society that has occurred in recent decades. In its wake lie families and family members who conceive of the experience in radically different ways. There are people and groups for whom the upheaval is cataclysmic, not much different than it would have been 100 years ago. They often refer to "betraying the vows of a lifetime" and typically experience a great deal of shame in the experience. At the other end of the spectrum are those for whom, although they are still filled with significant feelings, divorce is experienced as one among many acceptable options available to them in 21st-century Western world. People marry less, often choosing to have children without being married, and divorce more easily than in earlier times. Books are even written about "starter marriages" (Harrison, 2005; Paul, 2002; Rothchild, 2010)—early marriages of brief duration that primarily serve as a preparatory experience for later life. And in longer lived marriages, transitioning out of marriages that may seem "good enough" in the eyes of some but not maximally fulfilling has become more commonplace. Many now exit marriages that still have positive aspects, based in a rational or emotional decision, perceiving there to be alternative, preferable lives that await. Divorce today can only be understood in relation to changing expectations about marriage (Cherlin, 2009; Finkel, 2017).

There is much debate ranging from among scholars in the tabloid press about what this means. Is this a positive or a negative change? Opinions are often strongly stated in absolute terms. Some believe marriages are scuttled too easily, emphasizing working to improve troubled marriages; others opine on the benefits of following one's feelings in whatever direction will best promote personal growth (Gallagher, 1996; Riss & Sockwell, 2016). Whatever position one holds about this cultural phenomenon, it seems that divorces in which both partners part well and remain friends are becoming more common and have far fewer negative consequences than the old-fashioned form of divorce. A widely circulated example is actress Gwyneth Paltrow and singer Chris Martin's "conscious uncoupling" (Cooper, 2014). Although there is pain in the separation, a strong connection remains. Such a connection is also evident in those divorcing partners that Constance Ahrons labeled *Perfect Pals* (discussed subsequently) in her study of divorcing couples (Ahrons, 1994; Ahrons & Rodgers, 1987) that made up 12% of the sample. Yet there also are many difficult partings that segue into continuing problematic patterns over time (Johnston, 1994).

THE IMPACT OF DIVORCE ON FAMILY MEMBERS

The history of research about the impact of divorce on family members offers a prime example of the evolution of research, where highly provocative early findings generated through questionable methodology eventually are succeeded by better research, which presents a more balanced picture. The best-known early studies about divorce were the longitudinal studies of Judith Wallerstein. In the early 1970s, Wallerstein began a study in which she interviewed a sample of 131 children and their parents from middle-class, White, urban, Northern California families that had recently gone through a divorce (Wallerstein & Kelly, 1974, 1975, 1976, 1980). In the years following, she interviewed the children of these divorces at several junctures in their lives into young adulthood (only 93 of the original 131 children were reinterviewed at the 25-year mark). In their initial study, Wallerstein and her then-collaborator, Joan Kelly, found a range of reactions of the children in their sample just after the divorce. Some seemed to be handling the disruption without major emotional difficulty, but others were struggling with depression, school difficulties, and other psychopathology.

Over the next 20 years, Wallerstein alone (Kelly had disavowed the project) conducted three additional follow-ups of the children from these divorces and came to increasingly dark conclusions about the long-term effects of divorce (Wallerstein, 1991, 1998, 2005; Wallerstein, Corbin, & Lewis, 1988; Wallerstein, Lewis, & Blakeslee, 2000). By the time she had produced her last follow-up study in 2001, Wallerstein believed that divorce was not only harmful to children when it happened but also led to what she termed a *sleeper effect* that crippled these children's ability to form romantic relationships as adults. Her view became headline news; was adopted wholesale by socially conservative, self-defined "family values" proponents; and was widely trumpeted as proving beyond a doubt that virtually all children whose parents divorce suffer traumatic and lasting emotional injury.

The methodology underlying Wallerstein's study is today considered primitive by most social science researchers, however. First, she is criticized for basing her conclusions on interviews with a small sample of divorced families representing only one kind of family—urban, middle class, and Caucasian. The study, critics contend, is thereby low in external validity, the ability to represent the general population.

A second, more serious objection is that Wallerstein's version of the effects of divorce may not accurately represent even the population she studied. There was never a control group (now virtually required for this kind of study)—that is, a set of comparable individuals at the same juncture in life who had not experienced divorce in their family. Thus, it is impossible to know how many of the difficulties Wallerstein observed in the children of divorce might also hold true for those whose parents did not get divorced.

Third, Wallerstein's data-gathering methods have been challenged. Rather than being the dispassionate observer, she clearly developed relationships with many of the children of divorce she followed and encouraged them to read her writings. Some critics suggest she actively cocreated with them the idea that they were irreparably damaged by their parents' divorce. In sum, the threats to validity render the Wallerstein reports possibly true for some, but generally poor science.

Wallerstein's study did have the positive effect of spurring some of the most prominent social science researchers in the United States to carefully study whether her findings applied to other divorcing families. Of the many projects that have assessed the impact of divorce on families, most prominent have been those conducted by Mavis Hetherington (1979, 1987, 1989; Hetherington & Anderson, 1988) of the University of Virginia, who followed divorced families over time; Christine Buchanan, Eleanor Maccoby, and Sanford Dornbusch (1996) of Stanford University, who examined the effects of divorce on adolescents; Paul Amato (2006) of Penn State University, who followed children in divorcing families; Constance Ahrons (1994) of the University of Southern California, who examined the effects on the adult partners over time; and Robert Emery (Emery & Dinescu, 2016), of the University of Virginia, who examined the feelings of young adults whose parents had divorced when they were children. What has emerged is a balanced view of divorce as a challenging life transition that most people are able to negotiate but that is marked by periods of strong emotion and retrospective feelings of pain for most, and real risk for some.

Emotional Reactions and Behavioral Problems

Almost everyone going through divorce, both adults and children, experiences short-term negative consequences. These changes are experienced in a variety of ways. One way people are affected is in their social roles. People know themselves best in their most typical roles, such as husband and father. When such central roles change, identity becomes more fluid. Although this means there is potential for growth in new roles, the experience of one's core roles changing is typically experienced as stressful. Emotion is also heightened for almost everyone going through divorce. Most experience a great deal of this emotional upheaval in which fear, anger, distress, and sadness are common. And although some, especially those who initiate divorce, may experience positive emotions, such as excitement in relation to new experiences and relief in terms being out of what was an unhappy or limiting relationship for themselves, negative emotion is frequently present even for those who feel such positive emotion. As noted in the previous chapter, Hetherington aptly described experiencing such changes in social roles and heightened emotional arousal as leading to feelings of not "being me" (Hetherington & Elmore, 2003; Hetherington & Kelly, 2002)—that is, feeling and operating in ways that are very different from one's prior sense of self.

Short-term behavioral problems are also common. Most adults and children don't develop symptoms that would meet criteria for a psychiatric diagnosis (Greene, Anderson, Hetherington, Forgatch, & DeGarmo, 2003; Hetherington & Kelly, 2002), but a substantial minority do. For example, rates of depression are much higher than in the general population. Research has shown the experience of being left in a relationship—and most especially being left for another partner—as having a strong correlation to depression in adults (Hahlweg & Baucom, 2011; Hall, Fincham, Fine, & Harvey, 2006). Notably, in a long-term follow-up of adult individuals who had suffered from depression, going through a divorce was the only variable that had clinical significance in predicting a recurrence of a depressive episode (Sbarra, Emery, Beam, & Ocker, 2014).

Nonetheless, after an initial period of 1 to 2 years, most individuals in divorcing families do well and cannot be distinguished from those in families who did not go through divorce on measures of functioning, symptoms, or happiness (Hetherington & Kelly, 2002). Rates of problems in those who have experienced divorce remain higher than those who have not, but only marginally so (Amato & Booth, 2002; Emery, 2004; Hetherington & Kelly, 2002). For example, approximately 25% of children whose parents divorce emerge with diagnosable psychopathology versus the baseline of 15% in the general population. The majority of children whose parents divorce fall within the normal range on all measures of functioning and symptoms (Hetherington & Elmore, 2003).

Furthermore, it is crucial in considering these data to highlight that when research involves comparisons of families that experience divorce and those who do not, the comparison (nondivorced) group comprises families with both happy and unhappy marriages. Thus, even the small differences in the rates of difficulties in families experiencing divorce and in those who do not may be inflated because the comparison being made is not fully to people who experience ongoing continuing relationship distress. That is, it is hard to sort out how much of what effects there are stem from divorce and how much stems from simply having relationship difficulties. There is no specific evidence that family members who go through divorce do any worse than those in families in which the marriage is unhappy but the parents remain together (Greene, Anderson, Hetherington, Forgatch, & DeGarmo, 2003).

The level of family conflict is one crucial moderator in determining which individuals emerge with serious difficulties. High conflict in marriage is a major risk factor both for children in families with marriages that last over time and those that end in divorce (Grych & Fincham, 1990, 1992; Grych, Fincham, Jouriles, & McDonald, 2000). It is not clear whether high conflict is more deleterious in nuclear or divorced families. However, in both contexts, high conflict is damaging for most everyone.

Other factors have a considerable impact on which children and adults do well or do poorly when divorce occurs. Having many overlapping life changes has deleterious effects. For example, compounding divorce with other changes such as moving several times, change in financial status, and parental remarriage within a short span vastly increases children's risk for a wide variety of health, educational, and mental health problems (Amato, 2010; Hetherington, 1979; Hetherington & Elmore, 2003). Financial strain, parental depression, and low levels of child monitoring (each of which often accompanies this transition) also increase children's vulnerability (Hetherington & Elmore, 2003). Expectations matter as well. Paradoxically, one specific path to difficulty occurs when family members hold unrealistic expectations that the postdivorce family should function like a nondivorced, two-parent family, and a sense of disappointment and deficiency emerges when those fantasies cannot be met (Ahrons & Rodgers, 1987).

The research about the impact of divorce also highlights that although the presence of massive deleterious effects of divorce on functioning is easily overstated, the emotional pain in the experience numbers among the most significant life stressors. Children and adults almost universally describe challenging affective experiences about which they often have continuing feelings. When Robert Emery surveyed college students at the University of Virginia about their experiences with divorce (Emery, 1999; Laumann-Billings & Emery, 2000), he found that even among these high-achieving young people who in life functioning would be generally regarded as highly successful, stories of family life were filled with pain. Nearly 50% believed they had a harder childhood than others (compared with 14% among adults whose parents' marriage remained intact), and 28% wondered whether their fathers loved them (compared with 10% among adults whose parents' marriage remained intact).

Additionally, Paul Amato and colleagues (Amato, Loomis, & Booth, 1995) identified a group of children who do worse when their parents divorce rather than remain together: children in families in which parental unhappiness is not transparent to their children. Their research revealed that the sense of loss for these children is particularly great, causing them to be especially vulnerable and to have increased levels of problems. They interpreted their findings as suggesting that these are children for whom it may well be wise to "stay together for the children." Although widely accepted, some (Ahrons, 2004) have challenged Amato and colleagues' interpretation of their findings, arguing that one does not in fact know how the lives of these children would have progressed if their parents had not divorced and there ensued a longer period of marital unhappiness.

Conflict

As already noted, protracted conflict between parents in divorce has a deleterious effect on all involved (Mahrer et al., 2016). Conflicts over child custody and visitation are especially harmful for all involved given that these conflicts directly involve both parents and children (Hetherington & Stanley-Hagan, 2002; Johnston, Walters, & Olesen, 2005). Further, high levels of parental conflict almost always accompany lengthy disputes over child custody and visitation. It is rare that such disputes occur in a calm atmosphere in which parents simply differ about the allocation of time with children. Those parents who do differ but can nonetheless deal well with one another almost always arrive at a solution even if they disagree—at the very least after mediation or negotiation between lawyers (Emery & Dinescu, 2016). Even for those who may start out with what simply is an irreconcilable difference (e.g., both parents want more than 50% of the time with the children), the systemic cycles that emerge in protracted legal conflicts between parents, and between parents and children, almost always transform those who formerly were somewhat cooperative into dysfunctional patterns. Such conflicts may be full of hot, angry confrontations; cold rejection and withdrawal; cycles of demand–withdraw; or triangulation; whatever the form, the effects are palpable. The child-centered conflicts that remain for parents who cannot resolve such differences are particularly upsetting for children (Buchanan et al., 1996; Grych & Fincham, 1992; Mahrer et al., 2016).

DIVORCE AS A DEVELOPMENTAL PROCESS

The research also suggests that divorce represents not so much a single event but a developmental process. Families undergo many challenges and transitions in the process of adaptation to divorce (Hetherington & Kelly, 2002). The first phase, typically lasting 1 to 2 years postdivorce, is a period of high stress and turmoil. Because most families are more distressed after 1 year than immediately after the divorce, many families come to feel overwhelmed and discouraged at that time. However, longitudinal research (Hetherington, Cox, & Cox, 1985) indicates a remarkable recovery for most families by the end of the second year. Most families stabilize in 2 years, and most parents and children are functioning well when followed up 6 years later. Still, many families undergo multiple transitions as residences and custody arrangements change over time. When remarriage of one or both partners occurs, other complexities are introduced, some that promote better coping and others that involve further challenges. Nearly two thirds of women and three fourths of men remarry after divorce (Weitzman et al., 1992). In most families, divorce and remarriage merge into a continuous process.

Added to these complexities is the ambiguity of norms in divorce regarding the degree of involvement between former spouses, between parents and children, and between new partners or new stepparents and children during and after divorce. Like other major life transitions, divorce disrupts a family's paradigm, the worldview and basic premises that underlie family identity and guide its actions. Clearly, there is no one template for how divorced families should function. There are many successful models. On one end of the spectrum are those where close connection remains between the former partners and there may even be regular rituals of connection of the "old" family as a whole and continuing connections of ex-partners alone and with their ex-partner's family of origin. On the other end of the spectrum are those families where former partners have little direct connection and times of reassembling the "old" family are restricted to the weddings of children and other similar events, if then. What characterizes all more successful divorces, however, is the emergence of some level of respect between the parties, old hurts being worked through or at least not being continually revisited, and communication and problem-solving that works with issues that emerge in the postdivorce family (Ahrons, 1994). Such processes are much different from those in the difficult divorces that are the focus of this book.

It is possible in the developmental process for families to transform from patterns of a difficult divorce to greater cooperation over time. "Difficult" patterns lie along a continuum. Almost all families show some "difficult" patterns for a time; it is the intensity and duration of the "difficult" patterns that families move into what this book is labeling as *difficult divorce*. However, once a certain level of conflict and bad or contemptuous behavior is crossed, it is rare that such a transformation occurs. Typically, the best that can be hoped for in the wake of such levels of dysfunction becoming set patterns is for the intense conflict to become less intense and less in focus, so that individual and relational functioning can be less impaired.

Financial Ramifications

Divorce represents a financial crisis for most families (Killewald, 2016). The net cost of a divorced family living in two homes is simply higher than the cost of living as a unit in one, and numerous other financial benefits of marriage are lost as well. This is a time when short- and long-term financial planning almost always must be revisited, often with considerable pain and revision of plans for the future. Retirement plans are often radically changed, the household of the lower-earning partner may undergo a severe dip in financial viability, and children may be asked to reconsider their plans for financing college.

Families in which one parent is the sole source of income are especially challenged, given that one partner often has no means of support. For many of these families, the divorce at a practical level means the partner who has been a homemaker returns to work, often to a low-wage job given the time he or she has spent out of the workforce. These families also often have child-care needs that are not easily accommodated when the stay-at-home parent returns to work, and thus money becomes a challenge to family organization in another way: how to pay for child care. Some of the most difficult negotiations and arguments that occur between former partners are about finances, both in terms of ongoing support and division of assets.

Another factor related to finances is the ability to pay for attorneys and other experts involved in the divorce. Here, financial well-being allows for good representation of each parent (and where needed, the children), but also can enhance conflict relative to those without such resources. If so inclined, those with unlimited financial resources can litigate endlessly even over small matters. Although some of modest means do squander their resources in such litigation (clearly among the most tragic of these families), most people with less income feel forced to settle legal matters because they cannot afford the time and fees involved to pursue them. Thus, having more money can lead to more difficult divorce than having less money. Yet those who are poor are at risk for numerous other problems. Divorce may move some family members well below the poverty level, and absent any prospect of good representation, family conflicts may become a free-for-all in which outrageous behavior occurs without the constraint of cases being managed by competent attorneys.

Money also often looms in the narratives people have about other divorce-related matters. For example, parents who have difficulty with one another will often believe that the other parent assumes positions about child-related issues less due to specific issues that actually matter to them, and more because these outcomes can be used as bargaining chips in financial negotiations. Where such beliefs flourish (and it must be added, even more so when those beliefs are based in an accurate assessment), resolving differences becomes more difficult.

Individual Differences in Divorce

How divorce is experienced varies considerably for different people. Most crucially, divorce is often a very different experience for the initiator of the divorce than it is for the partner less interested in divorce.[3] Foremost here is the difference between the "leaving partner" and the "left partner." For some of those who initiate divorce, it is primarily experienced as the opening of a new and happier life. Thus, Wang and Amato (2000) found that spouses who initiated divorce showed better postdivorce adjustment than those who did not. Such feelings are magnified when the divorce comes after a protracted period of unhappiness, and, most especially, when the leaving partner already has a new partner in mind. Indeed, leaving partners can describe the positive side of divorce as blissful, a period of being closer to a (new) partner than they ever dreamed possible. (It should be added that the risk for these individuals and their partners is also well known: Some fall into periods of hypomanic activity and change, followed by a realization that life may not be better; Hiyoshi, Fall, Netuveli, & Montgomery, 2015.)

How the relationship has been perceived also makes a difference. Amato and Hohmann-Marriott (2007) found that those in seriously distressed

---

[3] It is important to note here that who is the initiator is not a simple question. The concept of "initiator" is clearly distinct from simply noting who files for divorce. In the United States, 60% of filings are made by women, but many women whose partners exit relationships are nonetheless the ones who file for divorce. Further, in situations in which, for example, a partner has had numerous affairs and the other partner initiates divorce, it would be a stretch to regard the filing partner as fully the initiator. This section speaks to the common situation in which one partner is more clearly initiating the divorce.

marriages reported improvements in happiness after divorce. In contrast, partners who had felt that the marriage had satisfied their needs or had potential to do so are particularly vulnerable (Doherty & Harris, 2017).

On a continuum, the more a partner sees divorce as a desirable outcome, the more positive the experience; the more the partner sees divorce as an undesirable outcome, the more it will be viewed negatively (Black, Eastwood, Sprenkle, & Smith, 1991). Paired with this, the more the initiator experiences guilt, in relation to either partner or children, the more this positive sense is mitigated. Culture also makes a considerable difference. Typically, the less divorce is an option in a specific culture, the more negative the experience, unless the divorcing person moves into some different subculture.

There are also marked differences between marriages that end quickly once problems emerge and those that survive through a long duration of visible difficulties. There are ways in which it is easier to experience the end of a marriage in which the partners have had major issues for decades than that is experienced as suddenly imploding (as when there is an affair that ends the marriage). It is important to remember that the granting of a divorce happens at one moment in time, but that the period of marital happiness for one or both partners proceeding that moment can be of brief duration or over decades. The actual time of the divorce from the time of first discussion to the decree can also occur in as short a period as a few months, or, as in some difficult divorces described in this book, as long as 5 years. As Rolland (1994) described in the context of illness, the trajectory of this life event also has a great impact on how this event is experienced. That trajectory may also feel quite different for various family members; for example, between the partner who has been contemplating moving into action about divorce for years, and the one informed only recently that their partner is filing, who feels the divorce happened suddenly.

Commitment is a wild card in discussions of marriage and divorce. Some with low levels of commitment end marriages more readily, whereas those with high commitment may prefer to go on regardless of how the difficult the marriage has been. Mismatches in terms of how commitment is viewed are toxic in divorcing couples. Some are willing to tolerate almost any level of distress because commitment is so high, whereas others low in commitment may end what might be seen by others as successful marriages. Outside the bounds of this book's focus, but relevant in this conversation, are highly distressed–highly committed couples, who long ago gave up hope for the marriage but cannot de-couple. They cannot find a way out of marital misery but do not see divorce as a possibility. When someone in such a relationship moves to end the marriage after many years of misery, the other partner may still be outraged by this betrayal.

Linda and Phil have never had a stable happy time in their marriage. They enjoyed dating one another while Phil was married to his first wife. However, as soon as they established a life together, they became fixed in a cycle of mutual misery. Phil would seek out other women for comfort and conversation. Linda would become jealous and engage in detective work that would out Phil's behavior. A couple of times, she caught him being unfaithful. When Phil would wander, Linda would become enraged. Phil would then settle down and try to repair only to find Linda angry and rejecting. They would endlessly fight, with confrontations being especially ugly when one or the other had been drinking. Eventually, this would settle down for a time, only to find Phil extending out in ways with women that violated Linda's sense of boundaries. Linda then would go into rage/detective mode, and the cycle would go on endlessly. Each would threaten to leave, but neither ever did, placing them in the endless state of being on the brink. Yet when Phil, at a moment of suicidal despair, moved out and filed for divorce, Linda became enraged at him for his lack of commitment to the marriage.

Divorce Across the Life Cycle

There also are differences in how divorce is experienced at various stages of the life cycle. In Western society, divorce in early marriages breaks the romantic haze, but this is also the most frequent time in life for divorce. The frequency of youthful divorce, coupled with the prospect of many years ahead to re-partner and learn from the experience, render divorces for most in this time typically less traumatic than other times in life. Difficult divorces in this time frame often also involve active participation of the couple's parents, who often flame the conflict.

Midlife divorce presents the special challenge of reorganizing the family system at the point of maximum demands, with issues easily emerging about parenting concerns such as the division of child custody and time with children, as well as parenting styles. Divorce in families with young children raise all the issues of coparenting over an extended period in a context in which parents may also emphasize keeping open their individual options for the future. The presence of very young children also raises the complex issues of overnight visits with infants and toddlers, issues over which parents, and even experts, often disagree (Pruett et al., 2016).

Many divorces also occur at approximately the point at which children leave home. These divorces typically highlight issues in parenting and coparenting young adults, feelings of abandonment after marriages of long duration, and the obvious reality that the couple had been staying together largely in relation to their roles as parents to the children.

As already noted, late-life divorces are rapidly increasing. Here, the lifelong companionship that is typically developed between the couple can soften the impact, although at times the sense of betrayal in a world that is perceived as having more limited options can be considerable. Also here, as in midlife divorce, adult children can come to play a central role in whatever conflict occurs, although they also can act as a positive bridge between divorcing parents.

Some people have more than one divorce. Observation suggests practice doesn't help people divorce better. At times, earlier experience with divorce can mitigate the sense of trauma in this life transition, but it can also make for fragility or belligerence that can ensure intractable problems.

Gender Differences

In heterosexual couples, there are vast differences in how most men and most women experience and think about divorce (Bourassa, Sbarra, & Whisman, 2015; Crane, Soderquist, & Gardner, 1995; Sharma, 2015). These differences apply in emotional processing and in attitudes about divorce and about how family responsibilities should be allocated postdivorce. An especially highly gendered difference in heterosexual marriages emerges around questions of time with children after divorce. Many women, particularly those whose lives have primarily been as homemaker, have a strong belief that children are best off with their mother, seeing their bond as primary. Men often disagree and seek 50–50 split time arrangements. The normative couple may have an initial difference about such matters but figure out some less than fully satisfying solution. Yet some become bogged down in this debate, which becomes the fulcrum of a slide into difficult divorce. Blogs and websites promulgate highly gendered, radically different points of view. Former partners in difficult divorce often read and cite the arguments offered on the Internet and are significantly influenced by them. Notably, stay-at-home fathers often offer the same argument as stay-at-home mothers, as do stay-at-home parents in same-sex relationships.

Cultural Variation

Culture is also a major influence on how divorce is experienced (Bhatia & Saini, 2016). Over the past two centuries, divorce has moved from being unacceptable in almost all cultures to being one of many life choices in much of the world. Nonetheless, many cultures and subcultures still regard divorce as a violation of cultural norms, and some of the most difficult divorces involve those who come from cultures that do not accept the concept of divorce.

Culture also can be an important factor affecting how matters are perceived and negotiated in divorce. Customs in the divorcing families' subcultures may differ from those in the mainstream culture. Among Orthodox Jews, as well as devout followers of other religions, obtaining a religious divorce may be more important than obtaining a legal divorce. There also may be rigid rules, which sometimes involve the other partner, about how to obtain religious divorces. Some difficult divorces come to focus more on religious than civil divorce.

Culture also plays a significant role in divorces that involve intermarriages across cultures. Often, a source of problems in divorcing intermarriages is the emergence of challenges to compromises previously reached between partners from different ethnic/religious groups, or between partners at different levels of being devout to their own religion. A frequently encountered scenario pits a parent wanting to uphold the arrangements followed during the marriage against their former partner, who wants to now have their children practice within their own traditions.

A Typology of Divorcing Partnerships

Connie Ahrons, in her classic study in the 1980s, distinguished five types of divorcing partners with children (Ahrons, 1994; Ahrons & Rodgers, 1987; Ahrons & Wallisch, 1987). Although the frequencies of these kinds of postdivorce relationships may have changed, the types of divorcing partners today remain more or less the same. Ahrons types include Dissolved Duos, Fiery Foes, Angry Associates, Cooperative Colleagues, and Perfect Pals. *Dissolved Duos* are so distant that they no longer communicate at all. They may not even know how to reach one another in case of emergency. The product is no coparenting and loss of contact between the children and one parent. Although this situation is occasionally for the best in reducing conflict, it presents a major loss for children. (Dissolved Duos may be the norm for divorcing partners without children, however.) *Fiery Foes* are locked in deep hostility. They become involved in long-lived court battles, attempts to contaminate children's relationships with the other parent, and anger that lasts for many years. Fiery Foes rarely communicate without it turning into conflict. If they talk to each other, it is mostly through third parties, such as lawyers or other family members. This is a highly pathogenic combination for children. Angry Associates aren't as furious with each other as Fiery Foes. However, there's still much discord. These couples talk more than Fiery Foes, but they often have the same arguments repeatedly, unable to let go of past pain. They are often locked in an ongoing power struggle, and their relationship remains stuck. Children find this situation stressful, although not to the same degree as living with Fiery Foes. *Cooperative Colleagues* have had difficult times when they divorced. However, they have learned to communicate, if at a distance, and are generally able to manage their relationship with some civility. Typically, they can coparent productively most of the time, keeping the best interests of their children in mind. The emotional divorce is final with these couples; they have moved on. *Perfect Pals* get along really well. They are still in frequent contact and are friendly and positive with each other. This arrangement is mostly helpful, although children and new partners may ultimately find it a bit confusing. Placed in the context of the focus of this book, Fiery Foes and Angry Associates fall into difficult divorce in their conflict patterns, while Dissolved Duos with children present an alternative set of problems in terms of loss of contact and communication.

RESEARCH RELEVANT TO SPECIFIC QUESTIONS IN DISPUTES OVER CHILD ARRANGEMENTS

There also is a considerable empirical literature relevant to the relative merits of various solutions proposed to questions often hotly debated in difficult divorce about arrangements involving child custody and residence. Highly relevant is the vast literature that strongly supports authoritative and cooperative parenting to promote attachment (R. M. Lerner, Easterbrooks, Mistry, & Weiner, 2013). A more specific body of work examines joint custody and shared parenting versus sole custody arrangements in which children reside primarily in one home. The emerging body of relevant research here make clear that shared parenting has enormous advantages in promoting positive relationships with both parents in those who cooperatively arrive at such arrangements, but the literature is more ambiguous about the impact in highly conflictual families where the value of the increased connection that typically ensues with both parents may be offset by the negative effects of the conflict, competing parenting styles, and poor communication between parents (McIntosh & Smyth, 2012; Nielsen, 2017; Smyth, McIntosh, Emery, & Howarth, 2016). To date, the vast majority of shared parenting research has focused on cooperative arrangements.

A related research question concerns the impact of overnight visits with very young children. Here, Nielsen (2014), in a review of 11 studies, found few negative effects, although other reviews, while in support of overnight visits, have cautioned about the frequency of such arrangements in the context of high conflict and other problematic factors and have stressed the importance of building secure attachment and connection with both parents (McIntosh, Pruett, & Kelly, 2014; Pruett et al., 2016; Pruett, McIntosh, & Kelly, 2014). For each of these questions, research suggests that one size does not fit all and the overall parenting context must be considered (Smyth et al., 2016).

SUMMARY

This chapter reviewed the most important research focused on divorce. The considerable body of findings about divorce can help guide clinical practice and is especially useful to draw on in providing psychoeducation. Demography reveals divorce to be frequent in our society, as the divorce rate approaches 50% of marriages. The divorce rate is higher in less well-educated couples and potentiated by several other factors. Psychological research shows that divorce is a powerful cognitive, emotional, and social experience for almost all involved. Most adults and children experience a period of high stress during the transition through divorce that may include a variety of negative signs and symptoms. Although the rates of psychopathology and other major problems in adults and children double compared with comparable levels in all families, most successfully negotiate this time and function well when it is over. However, most children and adults also continue to have strong feelings about this experience. Divorce also represents a developmental process in which there is considerable individual difference in how it is experienced. Some patterns in divorce, such as high conflict, are especially deleterious. It is in the context of this background that the next chapter begins to consider the interface between psychotherapy and divorce.

3

CONSIDERATIONS IN PSYCHOTHERAPY WITH CLIENTS CONTEMPLATING DIVORCE

This chapter examines the ways in which contemplating and moving toward divorce may become the focus of psychotherapy. Given that divorce is a process, decision-making about whether to divorce can extend over long periods of time. That process can encompass less intense early thoughts about divorce as a life path, through getting ready to divorce, through deciding to divorce, to initiating divorce, and finally to completing the divorce process. Some decisions to divorce are made mutually, although more often, at least initially, one partner is the prime mover toward divorce, or there is a dance of problematic behavior by one partner and movement toward divorce by the other. For some, the process of contemplating divorce even extends beyond the time of filing for divorce or establishing a separate residence, as the partners keep options open for a possible reconciliation. For others, the process can be remarkably brief.

http://dx.doi.org/10.1037/0000116-004
Treating the Difficult Divorce: A Practical Guide for Psychotherapists, by J. L. Lebow

DIVORCE AND COUPLE THERAPY

Divorce occupies a special place in couple therapy, given that couples typically present with relationship difficulties. Whether explicitly mentioned as a possibility or not, divorce is frequently in the consciousness of these clients. Further, many who are actively considering divorce seek couple therapy (Crane, Newfield, & Armstrong, 1984).

The Decision to Divorce as an Aspect of Couple Therapy

Probably no issue in couple therapy is as contentious as how to deal with discussions of divorce as part of therapy and how to evaluate it as an outcome when couple therapy precedes divorce. Divorce occupies a wholly different space than other potential goals and outcomes of couple therapy. In case formulation, it may be clear that couples need help with a variety of general and specific aspects of being a couple, such as communication, problem-solving, attachment, sexuality, or relationship satisfaction, but these foci all share common ground in targeting positive movement toward a better relationship. Divorce and exploring the possibility of divorce present a different kind of journey and possible result. Divorce represents a core change in organization of the couple or family in which having a better marital relationship is no longer a goal.

From most observers' vantage points, divorce is viewed as a less than optimal outcome even when it occurs in the best possible way. Indeed, many view divorce as the worst possible outcome of couple therapy. Consider this: Even though a significant percentage of clients enter couple therapy with at least one partner well into a plan to divorce, it is rare for the ultimate therapeutic goal of couple therapy to be divorce. The major exception, when divorce becomes the primary goal of therapy, occurs when both partners agree to separate and seek therapy to help them divorce well. Even then, many couple therapists only reluctantly accept this as the treatment goal, still exploring the viability of the marriage, and actuarial systems for counting outcomes of couple therapy may treat these couples as treatment failures no matter how well the divorce proceeds.

What Is Couple Therapy?

A bit of a digression is needed here to consider the language we use to describe therapies that involve couples. The words we use to name this activity often obscure what is involved, perhaps because this area of personal relationships is so tender and perhaps because softer, more acceptable labels help encourage clients to take part in the activity (using the word *divorce* itself surely would mean many people would not participate). Thus, the words *marriage counseling, couple therapy,* and the like are used to describe help offered both to couples who are actively seeking to work on relationships and to couples in which at least one person is strongly considering exiting the relationship. Also contributing to this mix is that there is often social pressure today to participate in counseling or therapy (rather than to work toward divorce) before ending a relationship (even if someone has no energy for working at that relationship). Additionally, many well-meaning partners enter couple therapy with a primary goal of providing a place for their partners to seek help as they leave rather than to improve the couple relationship.

For couple therapists, this means that they frequently encounter clients who aren't interested in what more typically is meant by couple therapy—that is, targeting a set of relational problems and working on them. Instead, these clients present in a 21st-century ritual of coming for a session or two and then having one partner withdraw from the therapy (with many of these clients subsequently including that event as part of their narrative about the divorce: that counseling has not helped). Providing these clients the same treatment as other couples, and combining the analysis of the outcomes of these clients in couple therapy with those who are present to see whether relationships can be improved isn't fair or appropriate. These clients overtly or covertly have quite different goals.

In a recent breakthrough, Doherty and Harris (2017) described a novel way of treating clients when one partner wants to preserve the relationship and the other is leaning toward divorce, giving this activity the distinct name of *discernment counseling*[1] (discussed in greater detail later in the chapter) rather than couple counseling or couple therapy. Whether or not one follows Doherty and Harris's specific procedures for working with these couples (which are nicely summarized in their book), movement to the use of a different term for such work is enormously helpful. *Discernment counseling* describes well work with couples who differ in their ideas about divorcing, whereas *divorce therapy* seems the best label for work that explicitly moves to end marriages in partners who have decided to divorce.

Evaluating the Outcome of Divorce in Couple Therapy

More broadly, it is extremely difficult to evaluate what an outcome of divorce means in the context of couple therapy. Does this result intrinsically mean couple therapy has failed, or might it be regarded as a success? Clearly, in terms of the continuation of the marriage and the resolution of marital

---

[1]In this book, the words *therapy* and *counseling* are used interchangeably; Doherty and Harris use the word *counseling.*

issues, divorce represents a failure to move the marriage to greater relationship satisfaction. Indeed, divorcing in couple therapy outcome research is often counted as sufficient to label treatment as unsuccessful regardless of how the divorce goes in research on couple therapy (Roddy, Nowlan, Doss, & Christensen, 2016). However, from a different perspective focused on individual satisfaction, many consider divorce a positive (if stressful) outcome (Amato & Hohmann-Marriott, 2007). It also can represent a transition through which one or both partners come to feel better and improve in their individual functioning, have greater personal satisfaction and less conflict and frustration with their relationship, and ultimately achieve higher relational satisfaction if the assessment includes their next relationship and a new partner (Amato & Hohmann-Marriott, 2007). Bill Pinsof, in demonstrating his Systemic Therapy Inventory of Change system of outcome monitoring, provides several interesting clinical examples in which relationship demise is accompanied by an improvement in individual functioning (Pinsof, Breunlin, Chambers, Solomon, & Russell, 2015).

How Couple Therapists Approach the Topic of Divorce

Considering the place of divorce in marital therapy raises complex questions. One lens into these questions lies in examining how couple therapists treat divorce as a topic of discussion and possible outcome. What therapists do when one or both partners indicate a desire to divorce varies across couple therapists, yet there is shared common ground. The clear majority of couple therapists strongly support marriage; therefore, they listen carefully to the basis for the decision to divorce and almost invariably explore whether there remains any possibility for reconciliation. All good couple therapists also take seriously the wish to divorce on the part of one or both partners and work to establish an empathic connection and therapeutic alliance with both partners in the process of working with this issue. Few therapists, if any, would either suggest or indirectly imply that it would be better to remain married in the presence of certain pathogenic behaviors (e.g., severe intimate partner violence or child abuse) or to merely accept rather than work to improve highly unsatisfying marriages. There also is little debate that the task becomes to divorce well when partners agree that it is time to end their marriage.

Observation also suggests that when couples are not considering divorce as a possible outcome, most therapists do not bring this choice into the conversation as a preferred alternative (although they may bring the specter of divorce into treatment as a motivational tool; e.g., some couple therapists use the presence of the Gottman, 1999, Four Horsemen to raise couples' consciousness that they are at risk for divorce is they do not change these behaviors). Many therapists hold the belief that discussion of divorce should only enter most couple therapy when it is raised by clients. The principal exceptions are typically in the context of the most intractable difficult marriages that include particularly threatening issues such as intimate partner violence, severe substance abuse over time, or child abuse, where issues of safety are compromised.

Most good couple therapists also track (either formally through measures or informally through observation) the extent to which clients are considering divorce as one input into their assessment of a couple relationship. However, observation also suggests that many therapists may not regularly ask questions or provide questionnaires that would bring such thoughts to the surface, assuming that such discussion is counter to the intended positive flow of the couple therapy. Even texts about various approaches to couple therapy omit specific consideration of assessing how much each partner is thinking about or planning to divorce, offering instead a set formula for how to explore the marriage, based on the premise that marriages can be made satisfying by implementing the treatment protocol and that the active presence of the alternative of ending the marriage does not require special consideration. Without such tracking (described subsequently), therapists often encounter what might be the avoidable surprise of suddenly learning that someone who seemed to be working on a marriage has decided to exit it.

There has been little agreement about what therapists should say and do when one or both partners state a desire to divorce. There are agreed-on core competencies about couple therapy (Stanton & Welsh, 2011) but not in relation to this complex subject. The largest point of contention among therapists is what to do when one partner wishes to seriously consider or move forward with divorce but the other does not. Couples who come to therapy when divorce is a consideration typically present with such a split, with one partner leaning toward this transition (and often hoping to mitigate the damage to the other partner and others involved) and the other viewing it as a negative outcome very much to be avoided.

In their astute discussion of this dynamic, Doherty and Harris (2017) presented discernment counseling with these partners as an alternative, and a possible prelude, to either couple therapy in which both members of the couple have decided to actively work at improving the marriage or a more mutual acceptance of divorce as the realistic option. In discernment counseling, the *leaning-in* and *leaning-out* partners (as Doherty and Harris termed them) meet in concurrent (that is, separate) sessions with the same therapist to clarify whether they are prepared to enter a process of working on the marriage or moving toward divorce. The goal is to try to achieve agreement about direction, so that the couple can reach consensus to work on the marriage in couple therapy or both accept the reality that the marriage is ending and enter the best possible version of the divorce process and possible divorce therapy. Doherty and Harris's discernment counseling represents a new, state-of-the-art option for such couples, and it has already generated considerable enthusiasm among couple therapists. Developed in the context of couples in which one person has already filed for divorce but still has some ambivalence, it appears likely to be even more applicable to leaning-in and leaning-out couples before someone files for divorce and the momentum of the divorce process begins to take hold.

Divorce and the Therapist's Personal Values

When encountering issues involving divorce, couple therapists find themselves grappling with some combination of the highly polarized views in our society about contemporary life interwoven with the data about what is known about 21st-century marriages. Those strongly identified with marriage preservation view therapists and, for that matter, our society as too easily condoning decisions to divorce, whereas those at the opposite pole accentuate the normality of divorce as a life decision.

Debates about the meanings of more traditional and more modern values fill innumerable blogs and websites today. One tip for the readers of this book (which they may pass on to clients) is always to look at the source of information they are viewing. Often, such sources are more political than representative of the best knowledge from social science. Facts are readily misreported or reported out of context to support positions and promote certain values. At times, research is even carried out and funded by those looking to find a specific result (e.g., that divorce is inevitably harmful). Although the great majority of social science research is relatively free of such bias, the findings of some work conducted or sponsored by those with a specific agenda must be questioned. A tip-off is that such research is often published in obscure journals or not peer-reviewed.

A major divide remains between couple therapists about how much to lean in working with couples on the verge of divorce toward restoring and improving their marriages versus emphasizing individual autonomy and decision-making. At one extreme are the self-designated marriage savers and "divorce busters" (Weiner-Davis, 1992), who suggest that the therapist should strongly side against a decision to divorce or separate. Doherty (2001), in his earlier work, offered a somewhat more tempered version of this position, suggesting that therapists begin with a strong family-centered declaration on the side of marital stability, followed by a focus on reviving the marriage, and supporting divorce only if all possible efforts to produce a viable marriage are exhausted. At the other extreme are the writers of popular books such as *Creative Divorce* (Krantzler & Krantzler, 1999), who support divorce as a growth-enhancing outcome. Ahrons (1994, 2004; Ahrons & Rodgers, 1987) has presented a more moderate version of this position, attending to the reality that some marriages have never worked or lost their viability long ago, and that the only alternative to divorce for many is to remain in an unsatisfying marriage. She also has emphasized the vast differences that occur between those who divorce well and those who do so poorly, noting that the best use of therapy for many couples is to help them divorce well.

Marriage therapists also sometimes distinguish between divorce early in marriage or between those who do not have children from divorce when children are minors. Those therapists with such a developmental focus often bring much more of a marriage preservation philosophy to their work when children are in the home, especially when children are doing well and the home environment is low in conflict, emphasizing the risks divorce presents for these children as suggested in the research of Amato (e.g., Amato, Loomis, & Booth, 1995).

Between the poles of a strong emphasis on marriage preservation or personal growth and development lie most couple therapists, most of whom strongly support marriage yet also see divorce as an option that may be worth considering. Such a flexible position, truly open to both perspectives, sets the foundation for a therapy most likely to be helpful. In therapies of all kinds, fairness and balance are important common factors related to better process and outcomes (Norcross, 2011).

Further, when therapists assume polarized positions about such central issues, alliances necessarily suffer. Even if, as is often the case, the leaning-in partner can locate a leaning-in therapist and bring their partner to therapy, the chances of a good alliance forming between the leaning-out partner and the therapist are limited. Such therapies often are of short duration, marked by a final session that only the leaning-in partner attends during which the therapist overtly or covertly communicates the superiority of the leaning-in partner's position. Sometimes the leaning-out partner simply withholds how much they are leaning out until the end of therapy, lest they challenge the convention of couple therapy to work on the relationship. This is not good systemic therapy. Couples need therapists who are open to both partners' points of view. Each client is entitled to his or her personal narrative, and clients do not evaluate their marriages and divorces in relation to an objective standard but according to their own subjective experience. Many marriages that appear to therapists to have positive potential and leaning-in partners do not look that way to one or both spouses, who may well be psychologically "done" with the relationship regardless of what anyone might do.

And yet this is an area where sweeping generalizations must be qualified. Sometimes, as a therapist, one has a sense that the specific divorce in the room with you is a mistake—that is, this change will do more harm than good and that even the leaning-out partner will likely not achieve the greater life satisfaction he or she seeks through divorce. This is particularly the case when either an immediate injury is at issue (e.g., a partner has had an affair) or when it seems clear that what life after marriage is likely to be doesn't seem to have been fully digested (e.g., when the principal concern on the part of at least one partner is simply to get out) or when the obvious impact on the family may be dire (e.g., in the context of a special needs child who requires specific supports). Add to this the findings that show how fluid such thoughts about divorce may be, even when those thoughts are strong (Hawkins et al., 2017). Also, the focus in this discussion has been almost entirely on the couple. Children are significantly affected by the decisions made, sometimes for the worse, and in closely related extended families, the reverberations of divorce are also strong. Best practice is clearly to keep in mind the interests and reactions of what Pinsof (Pinsof et al., 2018) has called the *indirect patient system* (i.e., those very much involved in the situation who are not included in the therapy) and include some plan for dealing with the interests and concerns of those people.

In the context of couple therapy, it is hard to not be affected by one's personal attitude toward divorce. Therapists, like most others, have personal experiences that lead to beliefs connected to the experience. They also have personal reactions to risk-taking, and divorce is very much for most (or at least those with children) a risk-taking life decision. It is hard not to bring countertransference to divorce, particularly in those gray areas in which both the leaning-out and leaning-in partners have narratives that make sense in the context of their own lives. There are only a few situations in which specific circumstances transcend ideology and for which there is clear consensus about how to proceed. For example, it is widely agreed that severe marital violence is a circumstance under which divorce is strongly preferable to remaining married, summing the total well-being of all parties. The same may be said of unremitting unhappiness and marital conflict that affects all family members. In most situations in which one or both partners consider divorce, the shadow of the therapist's personal values is powerful in the context of such questions as how much effort to put into troubled relationships or what to do about issues that cannot be fully resolved.

It would be inappropriate to suggest that there are correct or incorrect positions relative to such personal values. These are positions that can be endlessly argued. However, there is considerable consensus among most marital therapists in favor of a both–and position that supports marriage but remains open to consideration of the life stories and feelings of the partners in treatment when divorce looms as an option. There also is consensus that a first task of therapy becomes to assess the viability of the marriage, most especially in terms of each partner's present commitment to the marriage.

Part of the skill of the marital therapist lies in distinguishing deeply held convictions that divorce represents the best option from transient expressions of emotion or tactics in communication that include raising the possibility of divorce. Some marriages clearly are highly likely to remain mired in problems, regardless of intervention (Gottman, 1999). When the sorts of patterns that have been identified indicate the complete erosion of marital connection, with low levels of positive regard coupled with contempt or stonewalling (Gottman & Notarius, 2000), serious questions surround the viability of the marriage, whatever the present positions of the partners. Furthermore, when one partner unequivocally states that he or she is leaving the marriage, there is little to be gained from anything other than exploring how absolute this feeling is and observing whether this state lasts over time. If this remains the reality, the time has come to help the couple and family cope with divorce.

A Process for Considering Divorce in Couple Therapy

The preceding discussion leads to my proposal of a process for dealing with the discussion of divorce in conversation with couples in therapy.

1. Begin with a bias in favor of helping couples work together to resolve their difficulties, yet remain open to the positions of the clients and encourage them to voice those positions.
2. Assess each partner's engagement with the process of improving the marriage and the possibility of leaving it, as well as their values about marriage and divorce.
3. When both partners want to work at their marriage to improve it, conjoint marital therapy is the treatment of choice (Lebow, Chambers, Christensen, & Johnson, 2012), except if this presents special dangers to the parties, such as severe intimate partner violence. The therapist's evaluation of the strengths and liabilities of the marriage should otherwise inform client choices about improving the marriage or divorcing. When enormously toxic signs such as Gottman's (1999) Four Horsemen are present, therapists should provide feedback about their presence and the long-term impact of those patterns, but decisions about direction to pursue remain with clients. When relevant, a couple's children should also be regarded as stakeholders in this discussion even if they are not directly involved; the potential impact on them considered in the context of a balanced view of the impact of divorce.
4. If both partners agree that divorce is the best option, move to divorce therapy.

5. In the context of one partner leaning in and the other leaning out, propose discernment counseling and use that experience to see whether the couples can agree to actively work to improve the marriage in couple therapy or find the best way to end the marriage in divorce therapy or mediation. In Doherty and Harris's (2017) discernment therapy, work is with each individual with the same therapist to help each sort through whether they want to continue to work on the marriage. Agreement about a direction is the prime goal of this intervention. If the partners still cannot agree on whether to engage in working at the marriage after discernment therapy, the principal option is divorce and divorce therapy.

6. In the evaluation of therapies, work that moves couples to agree about whether they are moving toward divorce or trying to restore the marriage needs to be regarded as a positive therapy outcome. Thus, obtaining agreement about the decision to divorce and finding ways to launch this process effectively should be regarded as a positive outcome of some therapies.

Being in the process of divorce or considering that possibility numbers among the most frequent reasons that people seek individual therapy. In Chapter 6, I describe a method for using individual sessions or individual therapies as part of a comprehensive approach to treating difficult divorce. Here, the focus is on the more typical experience of individual therapy in the context of considering divorce.

Clients seeking therapy who are considering divorce are typically in a period of great upheaval. Therapists can be of immeasurable value in helping clients explore this vital life decision, often a deep and complex question given the changing values in our society, the client's cultural context, external pressures, internal conflicts between various parts of self, and the residue of issues from early experience and family of origin. Therapists can use their various tools and methods to help clients consider this life change, while also attending to other related issues in the client's life. They can also function somewhat like Doherty and Harris's (2017) discernment therapist with only one client in helping their client examine where he or she is in relation to getting divorced. This can be a highly impactful and satisfying experience for clients (and therapists).

However, caution is warranted. There is no evidence that individual therapy improves marriages, except as a by-product in the much different context of therapies in which the client targets his or her own individual psychopathology (e.g., a partner who is depressed becomes less so and thus may be more able to participate in a satisfying relationship; Gurman & Burton,

2014; Lebow et al., 2012). In fact, many forces in individual therapy focused on relationship issues may lead down the road to divorce if the therapist does not remain systemic (Gurman & Burton, 2014). Such therapies tend to identify and emphasize a partner's negative characteristics as the primary source of dissatisfaction, which begins to dominate the client's view of his or her partner and the marriage. There is no opportunity to see the context in which a partner's behavior occurs when the focus remains wholly on the other person. This context often leads to a distorted, negative view of the marriage (bear in mind that at any given time, 25% of people have thoughts about divorce, and another 28% had such thoughts not long ago; Hawkins et al., 2017). The partner who is not in individual therapy often winds up looking much different if his or her own narrative is presented in couple therapy. Without the presence of the partner in therapy, it is easy to fall into a downward spiral.

If a marriage is to improve, both partners generally have to participate in working to mend it, and by its very nature, individual therapy does not involve both partners. When a client expresses some remaining engagement with a partner, couple therapy is the treatment of choice, and thus, the therapist should make a referral to couple therapy and continue to push the client to pursue that referral. Although being pushy is not usually an admirable therapist skill, in this case, not to push is to risk that the relationship as a whole will remain unexamined.

Consider that clients coming to therapy with questions about remaining with their partners break down into two groups. There are those who want to use therapy at least in part as a place to examine themselves and their feelings. These clients want to use therapy and this moment in life to look at themselves and perhaps deal with long-standing issues or set new directions. Whatever their struggles, they are highly motivated to change and are at one of those moments in life where change is most possible. These clients often do examine their own behavior and look to see whether change is possible.

The second group of clients seeking individual therapy in situations of this kind is different. This group, which includes the great majority of those who move into in difficult divorce, approach individual therapy primarily as an opportunity to justify their own position. They seek support with little attention to self-examination. Sometimes they look to therapy for some perfunctory judgment that, yes, the therapist agrees the marriage is over. This function can be understood as the 21st-century equivalent of seeking out clergy to confess and obtain some sort of external permission or forgiveness. Still others enter therapy as a strategic move because someone important, such as a parent or a lawyer they have consulted, has told them to go to therapy with no real motivation to do much exploration.

Individual therapy can make an important contribution in helping clients consider their marriages and divorce. It can play an essential role in working on personal dysfunctional patterns (both in marriage and in other aspects of life) and provide a place for sharing private feelings and a balanced contemplation about problems in living. It can even make the major difference between becoming a mental health casualty and a resilient survivor if divorce ensues. However, it is essential for therapists seeing clients considering or beginning to divorce to assess which kind of client is in the room. Is this a client in the action stage of change who wants to work at personal issues, or is it someone in precontemplation who sees no personal issues to work on or perhaps is there for extratherapeutic reasons?

The same sorts of intervention strategies that are helpful elsewhere (e.g., mirroring, providing unconditional support) readily offer support for dysfunctional behavior in what emerges as difficult divorce. It may require some time to truly see the difference, but the signs that go with the second type of client are clear. There is much self-justification, little questioning of one's own behavior, and lots of blaming others for the problems that occur. Also, there are other indications, which, although not 100% predictive, suggest it is more likely than not that the therapist should be cautious. These include client narratives about the absolute evil of a partner, the partner and children being angry at them for no reason, children being completely on the spouse's side, and highly edited versions of the facts available from collateral reporters. Holding a systemic view of all stakeholders is crucial to being truly helpful. Helping these clients move from precontemplation to contemplation, where they can at least see their role in the problem, is essential.

Of course, clients don't absolutely divide into the two groups; even some of the most manipulative clients may have some genuine issues with which they want to engage. Additionally, concerns with alliance are inevitably profound with this latter group of clients. Challenging them may be precisely the way to end the therapy. Still, there are few life situations that psychotherapists encounter for which "first, do no harm" applies more than in this context.

ASSESSING THE INCLINATION TO DIVORCE

Across individual, couple, or family therapy, it is crucial to have a good sense of where clients are in terms of their inclination to divorce. Assessing the degree to which one or both partners are moving toward divorce is a simple, objective task, albeit one that depends in part on a client's willingness to self-disclose. There are several components to this. First, how much is a person thinking about or contemplating divorcing? How definitive is his or her sense that the marriage is over? Many partners make such statements long before they act. Second, what emotional state (e.g., anger, sadness, excitement, fear) accompanies thoughts of divorce and that sense of being emotionally "done" that so many divorcing people describe? Third, are there behavioral signs? How many steps has the partner taken toward getting divorced? This can range from only having thoughts thus far, to interviewing lawyers, to beginning to live more of one's life alone, to looking for or obtaining a new residence, to separation, to hiring a lawyer and filing for divorce. Finally, how long have these thoughts, emotional reactions, and behavioral patterns been occurring, and have they been stable? There are marked differences between transient states and well-fixed patterns.

Some partners are in precontemplation about divorce; they haven't even considered the option. Others are in contemplation, weighing the option, and yet others are in action and taking steps within the stages of change (Norcross, Krebs, & Prochaska, 2011). The maintenance stage of change may also figure here. Many partners move toward divorce only to reconcile or simply return to the status quo of an unhappy marriage. Doherty and colleagues (Doherty, Harris, & Didericksen, 2016) found that among those in the divorce process in a judicial district in Minnesota, 25% remained ambivalent, and another 8% did not want the divorce; both of these groups were highly interested in reconciliation services.

Typically, most partners speak clearly and directly in therapy to whether and how divorce enters their thoughts, as well as how far along they are in their psychic and physical disengagement. It is especially easy to see signs of extreme disengagement and emotional unresponsiveness on one end of the continuum and of strong wishes to save the marriage on the other. Of course, not everyone directly shares his or her thoughts of divorce. Some people conceal their private thoughts over long periods of time, only to have their hopeful partners be shocked at the news that their partner is leaving the marriage. Good couple therapy as well as working with couples on the brink of divorce includes clear and pointed questions that elicit thoughts about divorce (e.g., "Has it ever occurred to you that you might be better off apart?" or, for those considering divorce, "How close are you to divorcing?"). In this way, at least the topic is brought up and private thoughts elicited, even if some clients will not share those thoughts.

It also is essential to grasp what threats of divorce mean in the couple and family system. For some, saying "I want a divorce" or "I am going to divorce you" is simply emotional catharsis; they will never act on this threat. The use of the word *divorce* may also primarily be a way of punishing one's partner, or its use may be a sign of exasperation. For others, the most quiet and occasional use of the word signifies an action plan. It is also a frequently encountered phenomenon that partners whose spouses have threatened divorce often are shocked when the spouse acts on this threat. In this case, the word *divorce*, previously understood as only a threat or emotional expression, now takes on a very different meaning.

There also are unobtrusive behavioral signs (Kazdin, 1979; Webb, Campbell, Schwartz, & Sechrest, 1966) that correlate highly with a movement toward divorce, albeit these are not perfect indices. The most obvious behaviors are engaging new partners, separating finances, or having serious discussions with divorce attorneys. A step down from these are spending great amounts of time apart, withdrawing from any physical connection, and emotionally disengaging. Some partners also show that they are considering divorce by engaging in unacceptable behavior and thereby challenging the partner to stay in the relationship. For some, actively moving to divorce is not acceptable, but provoking one's partner to divorce them is. However, such provocative, conflict-inviting, and distancing behaviors are as likely to reflect movement away from a partner in those prepared to live in protracted highly conflictual or distant marriages rather than necessarily signifying a move toward exiting. In a similar vein, Gottman (1999) pointed to precursors of divorce, such as contempt, stonewalling, defensiveness, and high levels of criticism (the Four Horsemen). These signs do not mean divorce is inevitable, but they point to couples on the relational road to divorce with whom inquiring about their thoughts and plans for divorce is especially important (and for whom progress in improving their relationship will probably depend on finding ways to change these specific behaviors and the states that underlie them, as Gottman has suggested).

Self-report instruments are also valuable for assessing readiness to divorce. The Marital Status Inventory (Weiss & Cerreto, 1980) is a brief and user-friendly instrument that assesses the presence of thoughts and behaviors related to divorcing. This is the standard measure of how far a partner is in the process toward divorce. It assesses a range of thoughts and behaviors from the frequency of thinking about divorce, to setting up a personal bank account, to contacting attorneys. The measure also assesses how much the reporter has shared these thoughts with his or her partner.

The assessment of inclination to divorce is, of course, only part of the assessment of a couple. This information can be paired with assessing relationship satisfaction, allowing each couple to be placed in an informative 2 × 2 matrix of divorce readiness by relationship quality. In such a matrix, those who fall in the cell "high divorce readiness/moderate to high relationship quality" seem to be candidates for special efforts to preserve these marriages, particularly in situations in which there are minor children, whereas those low in relationship quality and high in divorce readiness seem most readily segued into divorce therapy. Still, clients' preference for how they wish to proceed with their marriages is always more important in clinical decision-making, especially given the imperfect association between relationship quality and client decisions to pursue divorce.

Clients with low relationship quality with high commitment levels often struggle over many years with unsatisfying relationships, while clients envisioning some critical aspect of life being better sometimes make firm decisions to end relationships that others might find more than acceptable. Clifford Sager (1976) long ago spoke to the crucial importance in marriage of partner expectations being in harmony. For example, if both partners are accepting of a low-sex, companionate marriage, they may both be highly satisfied with such a relationship, whereas if one partner seeks a more sexual marriage and the other does not, marital satisfaction plummets, and the possibility of divorce increases.

SEPARATION IN MARRIAGE

Separation represents a state between marriage and divorce. It is a heterogenous collection of arrangements, ranging from a few weeks apart to a lifelong arrangement. Separation can be a joint or individual decision and can be viewed as part of a process of seeing whether a marriage can be repaired or simply as a step toward divorce. At its best, separation can allow for a cooling-off period to process difficulties while couples explore their relationships in therapy. It also provides an opportunity for partners to evaluate difficult-to-assess factors such as their underlying attachment (which may be more apparent in the absence of an environment of conflict) and how it might be to live outside of the marriage.

Although there are articles and books written about separation (Hale, 2015; Raffel, 1999), there has been almost no research about separation that is not connected to divorce, leaving little empirical data about separation as an intentional event designed to assess and possibly improve marriage. Eighty to 90% of separations do not result in reconciliation (Tumin, Han, & Qian, 2015), but the meaning of such simple statistics about separation can be confusing, given that most people separate as part of the plan to divorce.

Clinical experience suggests that separation is most useful as an agent for helping couples move toward a more positive relationship in a few select subgroups of couples. One group of couples are those for whom it is difficult to extract themselves from moment-to-moment conflict or other dysfunctional processes (e.g., demand–withdraw) but who retain some significant attachment. Here, the space allowed may help the couple grasp the extent of that connection and provide a better environment for working on communication and problem-solving skills. A second group are partners who are flooded with strong feelings of aversion or disconnection and who, in the context of separation, may be able to become more centered and experience feelings of connection, or at least weigh the costs and benefits of the relationship more objectively. A third, small group are those who are prepared as a couple to fully see what postdivorce life might be like; that is, those who agree to actively date and see how this new life will compare to the marriage. This latter choice only works for those prepared to deal with the range of emotions that such life choices entail.

The downside of separation as a planned way of trying to improve a couple's relationship is that the great majority of couples who separate ultimately divorce (Tumin et al., 2015). For most, separation becomes a step in disconnection and an interim step on the way to divorce. With the distance of separation, many couples find plans for reengagement more difficult to carry out than when they remain together. Separation readily degenerates into little contact and few real opportunities to work at couple issues, leading to further feelings of disengagement that spur even less contact. Also, new issues readily emerge, such as what partners are doing while they are apart, as well as conflicts about access to children. Further, separation often can be a smokescreen on the part of one partner to more gently move toward divorce with little actual interest in using it as a vehicle to improve or even really consider the marriage. In this way, it becomes one of the most frequent of the "50 ways to leave your lover."

Given these many possible liabilities, separation tends to be helpful in improving marriages only when partners are highly motivated and accepting of this change and when there are agreed-on expectations for the separation. Clear ground rules need to be set for relevant aspects of life, including dating, the amount and type of time expected to be together as a couple, physical intimacy, time with children (both together and alone), sharing of information about what each is doing and thinking, and shared decision-making. Couples also need to consider how they will process their difficulties and work on rebuilding their relationship during this time apart. A commitment to honesty and agreement about the level of self-disclosure during this period is also essential (couples with trust issues are particularly poor candidates for separation as a path to reconciliation). There are approaches that prescribe structured separation, following clear ground rules (Raffel, 1999), that claim great levels of success. These appear promising for a select group of highly motivated couples, but there have been no assessments of the outcomes of this intervention in terms of improving marriages.

Separation is often a structured and useful way of moving from marriage to divorce, even if it is not labeled as such. Partners have time in this context to work on uncoupling and their individual feelings about it. For many, the separation does not feel nearly as unfathomable as leaping off the cliff into divorce. Often, this is the greatest benefit of separation.

MOVING TO DIVORCE THERAPY

Once a decision is made by at least one party to divorce, therapy comes to have another role. There are, of course, good divorces and really bad ones, and therapy can play a key role in helping individuals, couples, and families move toward the less toxic end of the spectrum. Divorce almost always presents a life crisis for all involved, including children and extended family, and periods of divorce are characterized by a fragility that can move family and individual life in difficult directions. As other chapters have noted, most families stabilize and are resilient, but a small but significant percentage (perhaps 10%–15%) becomes mired in intractable conflict that is destructive for all. The remainder of this book focuses on work with divorcing individuals, couples, and families.

THE POSSIBLE TRANSITION FROM COUPLE THERAPY TO INDIVIDUAL TREATMENT IN CASES ENDING IN DIVORCE

When couple therapy ends in divorce, what is the responsibility of the couple therapist to the respective partners? This question presents complex ethical issues. From the Olympian heights of most theories of couple therapy, the couple therapist is the therapist to the couple system, with coequal responsibilities to both partners. According to this well-considered view, the couple therapist remains the therapist to the couple, regardless of how the couple relationship develops or whether both partners are willing to remain in couple therapy. Therefore, the couple therapist refers partners to another therapist for individual therapy if it is desired. Triangulation is thus kept to a minimum, and the alliances remain balanced if the couple chooses to return to treatment.

Yet, when divorce ensues, a range of situations and feelings may occur that renders such a decision clinically questionable in some circumstances. For example, when one partner abandons the other and the therapy, if the therapist is unwilling to continue to see the abandoned partner, that therapist leaves that partner subject to a second abandonment, a decision that cannot feel "therapeutic" and usually is not. Additionally, as discussed earlier, some partners enter couple therapy with a covert agenda, so that their at-risk partner is engaged with a therapist when the bad news comes. Such situations call for something more than simple, absolute boundaries around the transition from couple to individual therapy. The subsequent work in individual therapy often turns out to be potentiated because the therapist has been a witness to a major life trauma and has seen the real-life relationship. Therefore, there clearly are circumstances in which cost versus benefit comes down strongly on the side of continuing therapy with one partner.

Having said this, it is essential to be clear that not all couple therapists would agree with the wisdom of making such a transition. It should only be made with a full consideration of the ethical dilemmas of the situation. A partner who is leaving also has feelings and typically has an alliance with the therapist. It is always wise to obtain the partner's consent to this transition before making it and to be sure that consent is truly informed. This transition is ripe with opportunities for transference and countertransference. This is particularly the case here because as the demise of the marriage may be seen as the therapist's failure. Such potential transferences and countertransferences need to be examined carefully. More than a few lawsuits and ethics complaints occur around the boundaries between therapies in divorce, particularly when disputes over child custody issues follow.

SUMMARY

This chapter examined the special place of divorce in psychotherapy as typically practiced. Couple therapy is mostly conceived of as helping couples increase relationship satisfaction, and thus, couples where one or both partners lean toward ending their relationship present a quandary for couple therapists. Likewise, the topic of considering divorce in individual therapy is fraught with potential problems. In this instance, the tendency is to potentiate forces moving toward divorce. This chapter suggested several ways to find balance in work with each format—couple and individual therapy. Therapists can enable clients to make informed decisions about how to proceed, helping couples who wish to save their marriage and assisting those in which at least one person has made a clear decision to divorce to do so successfully. The next chapter begins to consider interventions for those who have made the decision to divorce.

4

INTERVENTION WITH DIVORCE

Many couples and families seek therapy to deal explicitly with the process of divorcing; other therapies morph into divorce therapy when one or both partners decide to leave the relationship. Explicit work toward a good divorce is an underappreciated variation of couple and family therapy. The differences between couples and families who divorce well and those who do not are pronounced, and effects radiate through partners, children, and extended family. High-conflict divorce is particularly toxic for all. There are numerous other high-risk scenarios, such as when children are triangulated into parental conflict; when establishing clarity about the new family structure (e.g., about where children reside when) is extended over a long period of time; when a marriage ends with little communication and much unfinished business, vanquishing any coparenting alliance; or when a family member manifests significant serious psychopathology. Complicating matters, this also marks a time during which divorcing partners are typically in the precontemplation stage of change, in which they don't recognize their own

http://dx.doi.org/10.1037/0000116-005
Treating the Difficult Divorce: A Practical Guide for Psychotherapists, by J. L. Lebow

problematic behaviors and accentuate problems in the other. This is a time for which few people are prepared and therefore a time when intervention can make a special significant difference.

This chapter sets the stage for considering the key issues and methods in therapy with difficult divorce and integrative divorce therapy in the next few chapters. It begins with a review of methods for intervention in divorce other than therapy. It then moves to consider in a broad context how individuals, couples, and families involved in divorce come to therapy and the key ingredients for successful therapy with those going through normative divorce. Differences in working with difficult divorce and the need for a special systemic approach to this problem are then highlighted.

METHODS FOR INTERVENTION IN DIFFICULT DIVORCE

There are five major methods for intervention with divorcing couples, beyond simply leaving them to either the sage or less wise advice of attorneys and family members: group psychoeducational prevention programs, mediation, parenting coordination, collaborative divorce, and divorce therapy. Although this book focuses on divorce therapy, the distinct value of the other four forms of intervention also needs to be emphasized. Significantly, prevention programs and mediation are offered in larger system contexts (school/health systems and the judicial system respectively) and therefore are more readily accessible for many than is divorce therapy. Each is frequently mandated and sometimes paid for by the judicial system.

Prevention Programs

Prevention programs teach adults and children about the process of divorce, providing guidelines about what to expect and how best to deal with problems that typically arise and sometimes also involving the sharing of personal experiences. These primary or secondary prevention programs may be offered to all divorcing families in communities, schools, or a judicial district or to those at high risk of developing difficulties. Such programs anticipate the most typical problems that arise in divorce and educate and offer practice in ways to avoid these problems. One widely disseminated set of programs relates to children's understanding and coping with divorce, providing psychoeducation and opportunities to talk about feelings. Examples are Rainbows and the Children of Divorce intervention program (Boring, Sandler, Tein, Horan, & Vélez, 2015; Cowen et al., 1996; Kramer, Laumann, & Brunson, 2000; Pedro-Carroll, 1997; Pedro-Carroll & Velderman, 2016; Pedro-Carroll, 2005; Pedro-Carroll & Jones, 2005). Other programs focus on parents going through divorce, accentuating helping children through better parenting (Arbuthnot, Gordon, & Center for Divorce Education, 2014; Becher et al., 2015; Goodman, Bonds, Sandler, & Braver, 2004; Jewell, Schmittel, McCobin, Hupp, & Pomerantz, 2017; Sandler et al., 2017; Stallman & Sanders, 2014; Wolchik, Tein, Sandler, & Kim, 2016). A subset of parenting programs concentrates on fathers, given that most parenting programs are attended by mothers (Braver, Griffin, & Cookston, 2005; Braver, Griffin, Cookston, Sandler, & Williams, 2005; Cookston, Braver, Griffin, De Lusé, & Miles, 2007). Strikingly few programs are directed to divorcing adults without children.

Many of these brief, evidence-based programs for adults, children, and families experiencing divorce have been demonstrated to have a positive impact on the divorce process and to mitigate potential problems in such areas as coparenting and child development (Braver, Sandler, Hita, & Wheeler, 2016; Keating, Sharry, Murphy, Rooney, & Carr, 2016; Pedro-Carroll, 1997, 2010; Pedro-Carroll & Velderman, 2016; Pedro-Carroll & Jones, 2005; Sandler, Knox, & Braver, 2012; Senko, 2017; Sigal, Sandler, Wolchik, & Braver, 2011; Winslow et al., 2017; Wolchik et al., 2009). A meta-analytic study of parent education programs found participants to have 50% better outcomes than nonparticipants (Fackrell, Hawkins, & Kay, 2011). As a result, parent education programs are offered as extensions of usual court process in many jurisdictions. Such programs seem especially helpful in typical divorce and as an antidote to the first steps in sliding into difficult divorce. However, their efficacy has yet to be tested in the context of difficult divorce.

Mediation

Mediation involves a formal process of people or entities negotiating differences to reach a fair and mutually satisfactory solution. In the context of divorce, mediation is intended to negotiate differences that are essential to resolve to reach a joint parenting agreement (when there are children) and a financial settlement. Topics typically include the division of assets; child support; maintenance payments; decision-making about education, health, religion, and other key aspects in the lives of children; and time children spend with each parent. However, each mediation is idiosyncratic depending on the issues that matter and remain unresolved between the former partners. Thus, the content may range freely to such topics as division of animals, children's activities, and how time in a vacation home will be divided, for example.

Mediation is a process distinct from therapy with its own specific set of methods, structures, and ethical guidelines (Emery, 2012; Emery & Dinescu, 2016; Poladian, Rossi, Rudd, & Holtzworth-Munroe, 2017). Mediators may be mental health professionals, attorneys, or former judges; whatever their profession, it is expected that they have specific training as mediators. The typical process involves initial meetings with each partner, with the partners together, or meeting in both formats to define the issues, followed by negotiation sessions. Typically, these meetings are 2 hours in length, although there are more intense, longer duration structures for mediation. Most mediations are conducted with only the partners present, although there are variations in which attorneys participate in the meetings. Children are also involved in some mediations as a source of input so that the mediator can also understand their position, although the negotiation remains between the parents (Ballard, 2014).

Mediators do not have the power to make decisions but endeavor to promote a positive exchange in the process of resolving differences. At times, they provide feedback to the parties about typical arrangements—that is, ones that work well and ones that work poorly—and about the likelihood that a court will support one position over another if there remains a dispute. Mediations can lead to agreements about all issues, leave some issues unresolved to be dealt with in the legal system, and sometimes fail to resolve any issues. Mediation is almost universally governed by complete confidentiality about the process, save for the emergence from successful mediations of signed agreements that speak to the decisions that have been successfully mediated. That document is then incorporated, either directly or as rewritten by attorneys, into the joint parenting agreement or financial settlement that are linked to the divorce decree. When mediation does not result in agreements about any issue, there is no product from the mediation, and its discussions remain confidential.

The success of mediation in promoting positive outcomes in divorce for both parents and children has been well established (C. J. A. Beck, Sales, & Emery, 2004; Emery & Jackson, 1989; Emery, Laumann-Billings, Waldron, Sbarra, & Dillon, 2001; Emery, Matthews, & Kitzmann, 1994; Emery, Matthews, & Wyer, 1991; Emery, Sbarra, & Grover, 2005; Folberg, 1983; Folberg & Milne, 1988; Folberg, Milne, & Salem, 2004; Kelly, Gigy, & Hausman, 1988). For example, Emery and colleagues (Emery & Jackson, 1989; Emery et al., 1994, 2001) have shown that 75% of couples in litigation were able to resolve conflicts over child custody in mediation versus one third of those who proceeded without it. Other research shows comparable levels of success (Kelly, 2004; Poladian et al., 2017). As Emery et al. (2005) suggested, mediation can (a) settle a large percentage of cases otherwise headed for court; (b) possibly speed settlement, save money, and increase compliance with agreements; (c) clearly increase party satisfaction; and (d) lead to remarkably improved relationships between nonresidential parents and children and between divorced parents. They further suggested the key "active ingredients" of mediation are (a) the call for parental cooperation over the long run of coparenting beyond the crisis of separation, (b) the opportunity to address underlying emotional issues (albeit briefly), (c) helping parents to establish a businesslike relationship, and (d) the avoidance of divisive negotiations at a critical time for family relationships (Emery et al., 2005).

There does remain some concern, especially in the longer session form of mediation when pressures toward resolution can be high, that resolutions can be achieved that later may be regretted. Nonetheless, it seems clear that all partners with important differences to negotiate are served by participating in mediation. Mediation now is often mandated in a brief form through court services in all disputes over child custody in many jurisdictions. It also is widely available in a more extended form through private divorce mediators.

Mediation provides something of a litmus test for defining difficult divorce. Those who fully fail at mediation and produce no product that helps move toward resolution are almost always on the road to difficult divorce. Reaching an agreement through mediation also typically suggests a divorce will not fall into being especially "difficult," although there are exceptions in which, although agreements are reached, animosity continues to run high; in such cases, mediation agreements are often not followed. For many of the most troubled difficult divorces, mediation is often a perfunctory process. A session or two occur in which the former partners hold to rigid positions, with no real speaking, listening, and responding and often great acrimony. These difficult divorces quickly pass on to the next phase in the legal system.

Parenting Coordination

As an offshoot of mediation, in many U.S. jurisdictions and in some other countries, parenting coordination emerged early in this century and, more recently, has become widely available (Demby, 2016; Higuchi & Lally, 2014; Kelly, 2014b; McKinney, Delaney, & Nessman, 2014). In addition to mediating differences and offering relevant parent education, parenting coordinators can arbitrate about issues involving children when mediation fails, thus avoiding court appearances in relation to minor disputes among those for whom the major issues have been decided (Kelly, 2014b). They also may serve as intermediaries when interparental communication is highly problematic and report directly to the court on issues of substance. Parenting coordinators are typically only appointed in difficult divorces. Many joint parenting agreements in difficult divorce mandate parenting coordination to resolve small points of disagreement. Parenting coordination can occur on an as-needed basis or be mandated at regular intervals to ward off potential problems. Parenting coordinators can make decisions about small matters of difference if parents cannot reach agreement in meetings (e.g., about which camp children will attend or about who actually has what part of the holidays this year). Parenting coordination is most likely to be employed at or toward the end of difficult divorce to avoid the high probability of new litigation postdivorce over small differences, although in the most problematic difficult divorces, parenting coordinators may be assigned during the divorce. As yet, there is no evidence on the impact of parenting coordination, although this work has come to be highly appreciated by courts around the United States and elsewhere and clearly has come to serve an important role in the management of the most difficult cases.

Collaborative Divorce

Collaborative divorce adds a mix of elements of therapy (and frequently using therapists as "coaches" in one on one relationships) to what essentially is a mediation to resolve parental differences (Alba-Fisch, 2016; Kaufman & Pickar, 2017; Mosten, 2009; Tesler & Thompson, 2006). In this extensive set of procedures, help is offered to each person in the family system. Both children and adults are seen alone by individuals assigned as their coaches, providing help with problem-solving, and sometimes other aspects of coping, in parallel with work with the parents together to arrive at an optimal resolution. Other experts such as independent financial consultants are involved as needed to offer a more objective viewpoint as input into discussion of contentious issues. Again, data are lacking, but collaborative divorce is well regarded by those who participate in it. Given the many professionals involved from various professions, collaborative divorce is possible only with families who have the financial resources to support its practice.

PSYCHOTHERAPY WITH TYPICAL DIVORCING FAMILIES

There is no single, widely disseminated method for therapy with families going through divorce, although there have been a few specific efforts that present methods for working with this population (Emery & Dinescu, 2016; L. R. Greenberg, Fick, & Schnider, 2012; L. R. Greenberg & Lebow, 2016; Isaacs, Montalvo, Abelsohn, & Isaacs, 2000; Johnston, Roseby, & Kuehnle, 2009; Johnston, 2005; Johnston & Roseby, 1997). When divorcing families seek therapy, they mostly remain subject to the same diversity and ways of selecting therapists, as do other consumers of mental health services. Perhaps an adult in the family is having difficulty and seeks out therapy from someone they have heard about from friends, through research on the Internet, or through a more careful process of selecting a therapist. Or a parent may be concerned about a child and seek out a family or child therapist in similar ways.

As in much of the therapy marketplace, many—or even most—clients wind up seeing therapists of various orientations in a somewhat random way. For example, when therapy is sought for a child or children dealing with divorce, if the therapist consulted is primarily an individual child therapist, the child is likely to be primarily seen alone. Sometimes, that therapy may even occur in the context of the child being brought to therapy each time by only one parent, and thus all consultation about the child is with that parent. In contrast, the same child brought to a family therapist is likely to have treatment involve the child, parents, and siblings. Similarly, the content of the therapy may vary considerably with the orientation of the therapist. Therapists who practice from a psychoanalytic perspective are likely to focus on attachment and underlying dynamics, cognitive–behavioral therapists on developing coping skills and more balanced cognitions, experiential–humanistic therapists on the feelings at work, and so on. Each therapist uses his or her respective toolkit.

In middle-of-the-road divorce, this system of matching clients to therapists is less than optimal but more or less does work. Therapies are usually helpful and achieve therapeutic goals through multiple pathways. Decades of research shows considerable progress in two of three cases in psychotherapy (Datchi & Sexton, 2016; Lambert, 2013; Wampold & Imel, 2015). It is likely that therapy in normative divorce has an even better success rate than this typical expected level. Many of the predictors of positive therapy outcome are present in divorcing families (Lambert, 2013). Clients are going through major transitions, and for most, even simply the passage of time helps resolve problems. As we saw in Chapter 2, the period of divorce for most is characterized be upheaval, followed by a return to feeling better and improved functioning within 2 years. These are clients for whom the generation of common factors of psychotherapy—such as a good therapeutic alliance, the therapist's witnessing the client's experience of this tumultuous time, the therapist's generating hope for the future, and the therapist's maintaining a calm empathic attitude—probably matter most (Lebow, 2014; Norcross & Lambert, 2011; Sprenkle, Davis, & Lebow, 2009). So, provide a supportive therapist, and especially one sufficiently well versed in divorce to offer some psychoeducation and help with coping skills in some way, be it challenging irrational beliefs ("my life will be ruined") or probing and accepting strong feelings, sprinkling in some useful advice, and therapy is likely to be helpful.

Thus, most therapies have a good chance of having a positive impact on typical divorcing individuals, couples, and families. Having said that, it is important to add that it is likely that not all therapies have the same degree of effect. Given challenges of this life transition, therapies are most likely to be the most helpful when they include certain ingredients, such as psychoeducation about divorce, enhancing coping skills, enhancing distress tolerance to the inevitable stressful situations that unfold, some process of growing self-awareness and introspection, and a systemic focus.

Good therapists of all orientations provide information about the typical stresses of divorce, issues likely to be encountered, and ways to minimize problematic situations. And everyone with children benefits from following the well-established body of knowledge for how to talk to children about divorce, reorganize into two homes, and coparent (Emery, 2004, 2016; Emery & Dinescu, 2016; Ricci, 2012). Most therapists also offer simple, useful advice to divorcing partners about such topics as the deleterious effects of protracted conflict, methods of reducing that conflict, and recognizing and avoiding the triangulation of children. Similarly, children can be helped through psychoeducation to understand fully that they are not the reasons for their parents' conflict, even if the conflict has at times been about them, and to help find ways to avoid being hooked into parental conflict.

Helping family members develop divorce-related coping skills is similarly important. This is a time when the ability to adapt and find both individual and systemic resilience is crucial (Walsh, 2006). With coping and adaptation come communication skills—actually a very special set of these skills. Partners who have children must figure out how to communicate well enough with what soon will be their former spouse under stressful circumstances. Children, familiar with one environment, need to figure out how to relate to their parents individually in a new context and cope with difficult feelings. There clearly are better and worse ways to do this, and therapists can help guide such coping.

Similarly, this is a time of deep feeling, and accessing and working with those feelings is also crucial. For some, this may involve finding ways to calm oneself in the context of great stress and pain; for others, it means getting better in touch with their pain and underlying emotions. Feelings can also be a guide toward better coping in the future as new life plans emerge. In tandem with experiencing and working with emotion is work with cognitions to move from the pulls of what Beck termed *black and white thinking* (A. T. Beck, 1976) to narratives that actually incorporate the gray of this time of life. And with both exploration of emotions and cognitions, this is a moment where old patterns, family-of-origin issues, and psychodynamics often assume new salience. During this transition, many clients become more aware of the problematic legacies from early life that have negatively affected them, and use this insight to transform. Still other therapy skill sets that help clients overcome specific problems (e.g., depression, anxiety, other forms of psychopathology) also become relevant as such concerns emerge in the context of divorce.

All the foregoing strategies are simply good therapy applied to this specific context. Perhaps the one special consideration for therapy in the "normative" divorce is the transcendent importance of the therapist holding a systemic perspective, regardless of whether the therapy format is individual, child, couple, or family therapy. It is essential for the therapist to keep in mind that the functioning of the system also matters—that individual and system functioning are interwoven. First, the therapist has an ethical responsibility to what Pinsof (2005) called the *indirect patient system*, consisting of those closely connected to the client. The functioning of family members is highly interwoven, and the well-being of other family members also matters. Second, therapies that promote gains in one family member at the cost of unnecessary losses for others are ultimately less likely to be "therapeutic" for the client. Such processes are laden with elements that promote a level of self-ishness and being tuned out to the feelings of others that is iatrogenic. Further, disconnected short-term gains are likely to be followed by later problems in those relationships. In fact, this can be a route for moving from normative divorce to difficult divorce, given the normative divorce depends on maintaining a "good-enough" set of working relationships to successfully complete this life transition. It matters a great deal that the therapist remains grounded in a systemic position that values the outcomes for all family members.

One well-known problematic pathway in divorce lies in the demonization of others. Divorce is painful, and one way of reducing that pain and turmoil is to externalize—to see the problem as fully resting in others. For example, if one partner blames the other for the divorce and all the problems related to it, and if the locus of control is pictured as completely external, this can help in the short term with self-blame, regret, and loss. A narrative can be constructed that "I had no choice," "I am only reacting to him or her," "Nothing I could have done would have made any difference," or "My partner is crazy, borderline, etc." All these narratives help distance, ward off dealings of hurt, and protect oneself and can help one feel better in the short term. However, such solutions do not make for a process of learning from the experience or gaining insight that can help future functioning. Further, when children are involved, such positions may promote ongoing destructive conflict and triangulation. No matter how badly someone acted in the marriage (there are a few obvious exceptions, such as domestic terrorism), there remains the often-difficult task of finding a good enough coparenting relationship to carry through the remainder of the clients' lives as parents. Such solutions predicated on demonizing the other, whether a parent or child, hamper future coping. The best therapy helps clients to move toward systemic resolutions.

To summarize, many therapeutic approaches work with the most typical divorcing clients. Whatever the therapist's orientation, effective therapy often includes a few key simple elements, and good outcomes can be expected. Clearly, this is a context in which common factor elements of therapy, such as alliance and conveying a realistic sense of hope, have great importance (Lebow, 2014, 2017; Norcross & Lambert, 2011; Sprenkle, Davis, & Lebow, 2009). Thus, even though it is easy enough to suggest key elements of an integrative therapy of normative divorce (see Chapter 10 for a more complete explication of an adaptation of the model presented in this book to normative divorce), it is typically sufficient to simply being able to listen and empathize with client feelings, provide some way of working with thoughts and emotions, offer encouragement and information when needed, and hold a systemic perspective. As we will see in the next sections, what is sufficient for good therapy changes drastically in the context of difficult divorce—most especially when there are high levels of direct or indirect conflict.

RISKS OF THERAPY IN DIFFICULT DIVORCE

Although most therapy is likely to be helpful in normative divorce, this is not the case in high-conflict divorce. This is a much different context, in which often even the most fundamental cherished ideas from "how to do therapy" guidebooks do not apply (or at least need to be considerably augmented). For example, consider the notion of the value of supportive therapy, following the constructs identified long ago by Carl Rogers (1951). In difficult divorce, support in the midst of an angry set of beliefs about a former partner can easily potentiate problematic emotions and actions. Therapists who see many cases of difficult divorce readily recall instances when what was intended as therapeutic support of a client was followed by a negative confrontational action that the client attributed to following the therapist's suggestion. This is a much different territory for therapists. Those who are going to work with these clients need to learn about and follow procedures specifically adapted to this context.

Case Examples

Consider the following examples.

Jeff, a well-known therapist with an emphasis in the treatment of trauma, begins therapy with a client engaged in a major dispute over child custody. In these meetings, Lana, age 47, looks to have all the classic symptoms of posttraumatic stress. She is highly cooperative in the therapy, which probes the depth of her feeling. The therapy appears to have a positive impact because Lana has fewer signs of posttraumatic stress disorder. However, 1 year into the therapy, Lana asks Jeff to be a witness for her in her custody dispute. Given the strong alliance he has had with Lana and a desire to be helpful, Jeff agrees. In deposition and testimony, Jeff is asked to verify that Lana has been abused in the relationship. He is asked several questions about what he understands about their relationship, to which his answers turn out on cross-examination to be factually incorrect. When asked about whether he has considered that his client might have borderline personality disorder, Jeff experiences a loyalty bind and dodges the question.

Here, as in numerous other examples, fine therapists in other contexts who have been triangulated into conflicts sometimes become coopted into appearing in court to justify a client's position in reciprocal negative conflict.

Mindy is treating a family in which there is a dispute about the access of Jack, an unmarried father, to his 3-year-old child. The work centers on helping Jack build his parenting skills, and Jack and Caroline, the child's mother, their coparenting. During a period when the therapy is progressing well, Mindy has a meeting with all the lawyers in the case (i.e., the attorneys for mother, father, and the child), during which all agree about the therapeutic goals. In relating what occurred in that meeting, Mindy tells Caroline that her lawyer is on board with the agenda of moving to greater unsupervised time between Jack and his son. This, in turn, leads to a rift between Caroline and her attorney, during which Caroline threatens to change attorneys because Caroline does not believe her son is ready for such contact. Mindy then receives an angry call from Caroline's attorney for causing a rupture in her relationship with her client.

Here the complexities of communication involving attorneys, and a specific mistake by the therapist in speaking to a client about what her attorney told the therapist, undermines the therapy.

Mark is a skilled therapist who practices in an experiential way. Typically, he makes decisions about whom to see and what to do without creating a specific plan. So, when a high-conflict divorce family was referred to him, he began the therapy with the father, the first person who called. Because the father had a great deal to say, he had had several meetings with him before the mother, Patricia, called for an appointment. When Patricia came in, she was highly defensive and reactive to the therapy because she believed Mark already had a strong connection to her former partner. Patricia dropped out of therapy soon after.

Here, practicing in the typical protocol in which the therapist has experience jeopardizes the treatment in the sensitive and fragile task of forming of therapeutic alliances in families in difficult divorces.

Connie is a family therapist with strong beliefs that changes are not hard to initiate if strengths are engaged and in the value of direct communication. So, in the first meeting with a family consisting of a mother, a father, and two sons in which the children refused to see their father and there was a history of very hot conflict, she met together with the entire nuclear family. Within 5 minutes, a heated exchange occurred between father and one of the sons that almost reached the point of violence, and the two sons and mother walked out of the meeting, never to return.

Here the therapist is following a protocol that is helpful in other contexts but in this case sets the stage for further relationship deterioration.

Tashika is a cognitive behavioral therapist, and thus when she met with two highly conflictual and detached parents, she gave them homework to follow a set structure in their communication. Despite modeling good communication in meetings and providing psychoeducation about its value, the parents simply could not follow through with the program of more positive engagement. The mother did not communicate at all with the father, and the father continued to obsessively send (and keep records of) endless texts and e-mails.

As in some other complex contexts for skill-building therapies such as cognitive behavior therapy, these methods only have value if clients follow and practice the methods. For many in difficult divorce, especially at the beginning of therapy, this expectation is unrealistic.

Harriet is a lesbian therapist with a strong personal agenda about lesbian couples being good coparents. When she met with Eliza and Ashley, a couple who were having no contact because Ashley refused (having been hurt by Eliza's withdrawal from the relationship), she implored them to show that they could be a model divorcing family. Yet, after months of meetings mandated by the court, they continued to struggle. Every time there would be progress and Eliza and Ashley would briefly coparent successfully, an issue would explode, and Ashley would return to no contact.

Sometimes therapists become stuck precisely because their intentions are so positive. Especially, when countertransference plays a role, therapy can become stuck in sequences which do not produce progress and can even lead to deterioration.

Isaac is a wonderful child therapist. He is considered skillful by all his colleagues, especially in his use of play to help children work through their conflicts. He also holds strongly to the position that young children are to be believed in almost all circumstances. So, when his client Noah, age 5, reported that "Daddy punched me," he treated this as an actual event that had occurred. He reported the event to protective services and told them he believed Noah had been abused. A subsequent investigation by child protection (initiated because of his report) assessed that this allegation was unfounded. Isaac's position caused the father to seek to remove him as Noah's therapist.

What is expected in most clients often doesn't apply in families with a difficult divorce. The construct that children report accurately and are to be believed often becomes part of the problem in so many of these divorces. Here, the therapist became an active agent in the problem sequence.

Risks of Therapy in Difficult Divorce

The principal risks in therapy with clients in the throes of a difficult divorce include the following:

1. inadvertently supporting processes that move toward greater conflict, pathological processes, and problematic situations for children;
2. becoming involved in a legal dispute between the parents as a witness or expert witness in a way that was not intended;
3. having an extremely distorted sense of the facts in a dispute when given only one perspective;
4. becoming part of the rationale for whatever poor decisions and provocative behavior is occurring; and
5. establishing therapy as a place where a client in a precontemplative stage of change is never challenged, which clients can use to suggest to themselves and others that they have worked on their issues in therapy.

The principal risks in seeing former partners together in difficult divorce, either around couple or coparenting issues, are as follows:

1. very high levels of unremitting conflict in session;
2. carryover effects from sessions that are blamed for further problems;
3. safety issues;
4. extreme difficulties in scheduling as clients engage in dances for control over when they will see the therapist;
5. alliance issues, in that any support for one partner readily becomes a rupture for the other;
6. a tendency to overpathologize everyone, or at least one partner; and
7. unexpected legal involvement when partners have conflicting views about what is confidential.

The principal risks in family therapy are

1. high levels of unremitting conflict;
2. carryover effects from sessions, which are blamed for further problems;

3. complaints from family members about being coerced into therapy;
4. safety issues;
5. extreme problems in scheduling;
6. silence on the part of family members who are mandated to attend but highly resistant;
7. alliance issues, in that any support for one family member readily becomes a rupture for others when family members are in conflict;
8. a tendency to overpathologize everyone or at least one family member;
9. detouring from exploring issues in one subsystem into complaints about another; and
10. unexpected legal involvement about conflicting views between family members about what is confidential.

Risks in child therapy parallel those in individual therapy with adults. As individual child therapy, therapists are often engaged to treat children when parents are divorcing or considering divorce. These meetings may simply occur alone with the child (or children) but more typically involve some involvement of at least one parent to orient the therapist about the issues and how the child is progressing. Such child therapies in the context of normative divorce can be a wonderful resource. Children can use a place to process their feelings, where therapists can also provide psychoeducation and other intervention strategies (see Chapter 10). Also, a parent and child(ren) can work together in therapy on their relationship and to help evolve new patterns in that parent's home as an extension of this format.

However, in difficult divorce, therapies that involve children can take on more complex meanings. Children often are engaged in therapy by parents, at least in part for reasons other than helping them cope. Although the ostensible reason for the therapy may be a concern about the child (e.g., anxiety or depression), it sometimes soon becomes clear that there are other reasons for the treatment. For example, a parent may want a child to tell the therapist how much they disapprove of the other parent. This may serve to reinforce the "us versus them" mentality in the divorce, provide support for the idea of their taking draconian measures because of the problems of the other parent, or cue up a future professional witness who will report to the court or the custody evaluator about how much the child has contempt for the other parent. In a similar fashion, family sessions with a parent and children may come to focus primarily on difficulties in and with the other parent. In such situations, therapists should be cautious, obtain releases from others involved with the family to gain alternative perspectives, be sure to involve the other parent, and move away from the first parent's agenda in therapy. Maintaining systemic understanding here is essential to being truly helpful.

A Basis for Competent Practice in Difficult Divorce

Therapy with high-conflict, court-involved, and other difficult divorce and postdivorce families is littered with stories much like the case vignettes presented in this chapter. Otherwise fine therapists, used to being mostly successful with their cases, find themselves in a much different territory, where their methods do not work nearly as well. Sometimes the very patterns that are helpful in other therapy backfire in this context, resulting in an increase in problems and deterioration in the family process.

Two antidotes for these problems are suggested for this all-too-often encountered circumstance. The first is that working with these individuals, couples, and families is truly a special expertise. Therapists who see more than a few of these cases and truly develop an expertise in this area do better with these clients (although there also remains the liability of seeing too many of these cases, promoting burnout; see Chapter 9). The second antidote is understanding the need for special therapy approaches to working with this population—that is, having a road map for working on this terrain. (Such a road map is presented in Chapters 5–9.) These antidotes are not so different from those for other difficult-to-treat problems. It was once thought, for example, that clients with borderline personality were impossible to treat. Then came dialectical behavior therapy (Linehan & Dexter-Mazza, 2008) and a cadre of therapists who specialize in treating this population.

To some extent, both these principles sum to the ethical guideline present in the codes of ethics of most mental health professions of working within the boundaries of one's competence (American Psychological Association, 2013; Knapp et al., 2012). Working with difficult divorce is a special competence. Beyond becoming acquainted with therapy with divorce in graduate school, reaching a level of competence requires mentorship and considerable practice. The best route for the practicing clinician or student wishing to acquire this expertise is to do extensive reading about practice in this area, attend relevant workshops, and locate and meet with an experienced mentor who can supervise early work. Cotherapy with a therapist more experienced in this work also is enormously helpful. Inevitably, this work leads to various contacts with the legal system, which, especially in the context of working with a mentor, can lead to mastering that interface (see Chapter 7).

THE CHALLENGE OF HOLDING A SYSTEMIC
PERSPECTIVE IN DIFFICULT DIVORCE

As I've already noted, holding a systemic perspective is crucial to success in working with difficult divorce. This remains true regardless of the specific role of the therapist, whether it is treating the entire family, divorcing partners, or an individual child or adult. Information unfolds in bits, and the punctuation of information may mean early in therapy that the therapist is invited into a very biased perspective, most especially with a damaging perspective about a client or someone in the family.

Risks are greatest here when there are constraints to gaining access to other perspectives, as when, for example, a child is brought to therapy by only one parent. Such a limited perspective may not necessarily be incorrect, but it is always incomplete. That is, the impression from a child and one parent may be confirmed over time, but more often in difficult divorce, what initially is presented as the unfolding of one kind of situation turns out to be far more complex as more is learned.

> Consider Amy, a very well-regarded child therapist. When Heidi called for a first appointment for her daughter, Sydney (age 7), she did her normal intake. During that appointment, Heidi emphasized Sydney's anxiety, also reporting that she and Sydney's father were separated and that Sydney was not seeing her father. Amy had a first appointment during which she saw Sydney alone and met separately with mother. Both Heidi and Sydney described father as having a major anger problem and said that Sydney was very fearful of seeing her father, among her other anxieties. Amy proceeded to work primarily one-on-one with Sydney on her fears (other than the fear of her father, which she thought was probably warranted), using primarily a combination of play and exposure techniques. After seeing Sydney for 2 months during which they made considerable progress with her generalized anxiety disorder, Amy received an urgent call from Heidi that the father was attempting to stop the therapy through the court. When she entered a process of talking to the attorney who had been recently appointed to represent Sydney, she learned that father was regarded as the more reasonable of the two parents and as not at all a threat to his daughter and that father was concerned that the therapy was supporting her cutoff from him.

The point here is that even good, thorough therapists readily fall into such traps if they do not pay attention to the special signs. Amy thinks of herself as an anxiety therapist, and her client clearly has anxiety. She has a manualized way of working with anxiety, and it is helpful in certain ways. However, when she does that work in her usual way, using one parent as the source of information and as the responsible adult with whom to discuss progress, and ignores the difficult divorce occurring, she falls into a trap. Having no contact with a parent when working with a child is a marker for likely trouble in these sorts of families—one that most appropriately requires further investigation.

So being systemic begins with a fair and balanced view. However, it also means probing to learn more about family dynamics and how they relate to both the maintenance of the present problem, but also to the politics of working with it. Sometimes, getting that information isn't easy, as when one parent is eager for the therapy to proceed and the other is not. As we will see, assessment in these cases must be ongoing and is best always regarded as being "in process." Multiple perspectives need to be engaged before even forming a working plan.

Holding a systemic perspective amid strong pressure from a client is also difficult. Clients often want what they want, covertly looking to the therapist to provide active or passive support for their position. Whether the presenting client is an adult, a child, a disconnecting couple, or a family, there is often strong pressure to support a specific position about the divorce. Indeed, some clients even directly tell therapists that they are only willing to be in therapy or form an alliance if the therapist supports them in their position; such clients will quickly withdraw from therapy that does not support their position. The therapist working in such a context must have a strong ethical position in support of maintaining balance. Better for the client not to continue in therapy than to have a therapy predicated on a pathogenic foundation.

AN INTEGRATIVE MODEL FOR INTERVENTION IN DIFFICULT DIVORCE

The clinical methods described in this book are the application to difficult divorce of a broad integrative way of working I have described elsewhere (Lebow, 2014). With several colleagues, I also have described a related method of therapy called integrative systemic therapy (IST; Breunlin, Pinsof, Russell, & Lebow, 2011; Pinsof, Breunlin, Russell, & Lebow, 2011; Pinsof et al., 2018). However, the nature of this population and problem set requires several major changes of a few of the basic principles of IST. For example, IST begins with a premise of health in all parties. In difficult divorce, beginning with a more balanced view of health and pathology is necessary. It remains possible that systemic factors overwhelm good judgment, but other pathological forces are often involved. The intervention strategies used in the context of difficult divorce also are wider ranging, somewhat different, and use unique terminology compared with IST.

The foundation of this model for working with divorce lies in a developmental systemic integrative framework. The approach is developmental in that it views the time of divorce as a time of individual and collective instability and of structural reorganization of the family into separate households. This is a vital life transition for those for whom marriages end. Even in normative divorce, this is a challenging process. In difficult divorce, one or more family members remain stuck in ways that prevent completion of this life transition, often fixed in an emotional–behavioral–cognitive state featuring problematic responses to the changes occurring such as denial or rage. The model emphasizes steady progress over time in establishing and adapting to the new family structure.

The approach is systemic in that it views the family as a system and the action of each person as having important meanings for the others in the family. *Systemic* here does not imply that the origin and maintenance of all problems lies in circular arcs of causality. As in the latest versions of systems theory, systemic in this context includes both linear and circular arcs of causation (Carr, 2016; Lebow, 2014). That is, although it always is important to examine sequences of behavior and there often are circular effects in which the behavior of two or more people inevitably affect one another, sometimes the most important sequence is simply one person engaging in some negative or positive behavior to another. Flowing from this core vision, concepts and interventions from individual psychology, personality, and psychopathology may be the emphasis of therapy, as well as what are typically thought of as system-focused concepts and interventions. A treatment plan emerges through setting goals in the context of case formulation that includes the systemic and individual inputs into the problem.

The approach is integrative in that it draws from an understanding that there are many effective therapy strategies and highlights the selective use of a wide range of relevant conceptualizations, strategies, and interventions to address the problem in focus. Strategies of therapy are employed as they are useful, drawn parsimoniously and selectively from various evidence-based methods of therapy. Individual, former partner, and family subsystem (e.g., parent–child) formats are all used in the service of treatment goals. Therapy may be delivered by one or more than one therapist depending on the circumstance and resources available. The approach described in this book can be used in a comprehensive way with one or more therapists treating the entire family system but is also intended to help orient therapists who work with a subsystem (e.g., a parent and a child) or individual (e.g., an individual ex-partner) that is part of difficult divorce, working from a systemic perspective. This work is very much the art and science of the possible, with each therapy or therapy format providing an opportunity to advance a systemic focus and mitigate individual and systemic problems.

Working with a core set of concepts and strategies, the therapist (or therapists) looks for those methods that are most applicable and likely to be effective with the case at hand to work as parsimoniously as possible with the difficulties that have emerged. This leaves room for a wide range of specific interventions toward similar goals. The vision is that there is never only one path toward change but multiple paths among which the therapist can select, informed by the particular problems presented, the strategies most useful for those problems, what is most acceptable to the clients, and what the therapist is most skillful in doing.

In less difficult divorces, the full gamut of intervention strategies that have been developed as ways of doing psychotherapy are readily applicable (see Chapter 10). In the context of difficult divorce, there still are several roads to working with the issues in these families. However, with difficult divorces, paradoxically, although there is a need for more extensive intervention, there are fewer and narrower pathways to success. Most effective strategies move toward similar ends in helping clients to slow down their internal process and the systemic cascade underway. These strategies include finding ways to pause to consider in a more balanced way what is occurring and the costs and benefits of their actions, to soothe themselves better so they can settle down emotionally, to identify and work with thoughts and feelings that underlie problematic behaviors, to build basic relationship skills or restore a version of those skills appropriate in the context of divorce, to distinguish what can change and what cannot, to work to change that which can be changed and accept that which cannot, and to identify and work with internal and external blocks to engaging in these processes.

In difficult divorce, doses of treatment need to be longer than with many other problems, and typically several intervention strategies need to be used. Further, the strategies for intervention need to be much more carefully considered than with less disturbed systems. Some therapy strategies such as therapist passivity and the client being the best expert about his or her own life simply don't work. More generally, risk of problematic outcomes may be great when the "wrong" intervention strategy is chosen. When the therapy begins to go badly, recovery seldom occurs. Thus, the therapist needs to carefully and methodically make and carry out complex clinical decisions, involving who and when to see and when to do what, informed by what the clinical and research evidence suggests is the most likely path to success. This, in turn, depends on good assessment, careful case formulation, building on client strengths, and having a flexible therapist with a wide range of therapeutic skills. Both knowing what to expect in terms of impact from a specific intervention strategy and being able to adapt in relation to the feedback that comes in the way of clients' responses to intervention are essential. As a whole, therapy with difficult divorce needs to be highly coherent, emphasize a few key foci of intervention, and steadily and deliberately (often with much repetition) move toward designated treatment goals.

SUMMARY

This chapter began with a review of various structured ways for helping divorcing families, including prevention programs, mediation, parenting coordination, and collaborative divorce. This was followed by a consideration of the numerous ways members of divorcing families enter treatment, and the reasons most therapies prove helpful in normative divorce. In contrast, risks in therapy with difficult divorce present many distinct challenges that lead to the need for special methods for intervention and considerable specific skill development in working with this population on the part of the therapist. The chapter concluded with a presentation of the central importance of a systemic perspective to the treatment of difficult divorce and an overview of the integrative treatment model. In the next chapters, specific attention is focused on the various aspects of this model, beginning in the next chapter with the structure of treatment.

5

STRUCTURING TREATMENT
IN DIFFICULT DIVORCE

Structure is important in any therapy, but in difficult divorce, the importance of creating a structure that can serve as a stable base for therapy cannot be overemphasized. This chapter considers several key elements of structure in therapy with difficult divorce: the therapy contract, forming and maintaining therapeutic alliances, assessment, case formulation, setting goals, and treatment planning. There is a circular process between these elements of therapy structure. Progress in each informs the other elements of structure. It is not possible to do one of these tasks well without doing the others; problems in one invite difficulties in the rest. This chapter concentrates primarily on therapy in which the therapist has access to the entire family system and thus has choices about whom to include in treatment. Because clients in these systems present in other ways, such as referral from the court for treatment of one individual or subsystem or where only one client seeks help, some therapies are intrinsically limited in who will participate. In those contexts, the therapist can work to expand who is included or work within

http://dx.doi.org/10.1037/0000116-006
Treating the Difficult Divorce: A Practical Guide for Psychotherapists, by J. L. Lebow

those constraints, but even if this is not possible, attending to these elements of treatment structure remains equally important.

CREATING A THERAPEUTIC CONTRACT

The first step in working with difficult divorce is to establish a clear therapeutic contract. The therapeutic contract includes several crucial ingredients: who will participate, who will pay how much, what therapists will be involved, and who will have access to the information from therapy, plus the elements of a standard Health Insurance Portability and Accountability Act (HIPAA)–compliant mental health consent. When the court is involved, specific elements of the contract (e.g., who will participate, the frequency of sessions, confidentiality/privilege, payment) are ideally incorporated into whatever court orders are issued about therapy.[1] Even without court involvement, clarity about the therapy contract is essential.

The key message here is to have a clear verbal understanding of the essential ingredients in therapy and a signed document that reflects those key ingredients. In difficult divorce, the involvement of lawyers and the court in almost all aspects of clients' lives brings additional importance to a clear, agreed-on contract. Some argue for signed consents of many pages that cover nearly every possible eventuality in language more of the court than a therapy practice with families involved in the legal system. In the context of this model, which aims for parsimony and looks to minimize constraints to alliance, the discussion and documents address the legal necessities, as would any consent to mental health services, but remain user-friendly, jargon-free, clear, and concise in content. The central question is one of cost–benefit: How much specificity, documentation, and legalistic sign-offs are required of all clients to rule out the possibilities of problems arising in the legal context with a few? This model of working suggests that optimal balance lies in being thorough about designating and documenting the key elements of the therapy but not be unduly burdensome to clients or run the risk of unintentionally creating a frame of a legal rather than a therapeutic encounter.

Specifying Who Will Participate in Therapy and How Often

The therapeutic contract clearly specifies who will participate in therapy. In this way, it is an evolving document, given that this may change over the course of therapy.

---

[1]Greenberg, Fick, and Schnider (2012) provided a concise list of elements to go into such a court order for therapy in high-conflict parenting disputes.

The specific kind of problem, the focus of the referral for therapy, the makeup and culture of the family, and the willingness of family members to participate all inform who will be involved. Difficult divorce has massive effects on extended relational systems. A social network therapist (Speck & Attneave, 1974) readily could involve, with justification, dozens of people in some of these therapies. However, given that a major principle of the model described in this book is parsimony, deciding who to include in what sessions is a complex equation, driven by the assessment of the case, the specific goals of a therapy, the nature of the referral, and the willingness of clients to participate. As Pinsof and colleagues (2018) suggested, such choices should primarily be driven by who can best help to resolve the problem in focus (discussed subsequently).

Ideally, in most instances, the partners who are parting and any children living with them are involved to some extent in therapy. How much each family member will participate varies with the problem and can only be stated as the therapy progresses. For example, in a family with high conflict between all parties, all family members would likely to be involved to a similar degree. However, where the primary problem lies in a relationship between two people (former partners or parent and child), those individuals would be present in more of the therapy. Who is included and how much is a product of what is assessed to be the most efficient pathway to change, and, to a lesser extent, client preferences. At the same time, systems are systems, and thus some involvement of others in the dissolving nuclear family is always advisable when possible. Other significant family members such as stepparents, stepsiblings, or grandparents may be included later as well for some meetings, as it emerges that they may be useful in problem resolution as articulated in the assessment.

Sometimes the therapist treating a part of a family system in difficult divorce is not able to assemble all of the most relevant family members. Only one person or a subsystem may be seeking therapy for a specific purpose, or the court may make a specific referral of a person or a subsystem for a targeted goal. Being effective as a therapist in such a circumstance lies in working in the context of what is possible, reaching out to attempt to incorporate other family members as that seems helpful, staying systemic regardless of who is being seen, and coordinating with other professionals involved. Pragmatically, this often means working with who is available. Still, at times, an essential ingredient to treatment success may lie in assembling the needed family members who might best help with the problem, and this may vary from who is referred. A frequently encountered example is when there is a problematic relationship between a child and parent, the court may mandate the child and that parent into therapy but not the gatekeeping other parent, who may be instrumental in resolving the problem. In such an instance, working with those in the legal system to help them understand the importance of the participation of the other parent, support that involvement, and sign off on their inclusion (see Chapter 7), and using family therapy skills for extending out to incorporate family members who are not initially identified as part of the therapy (Pinsof et al., 2018) is best practice.

Although there can be many permutations on who is involved in therapy, typical first sessions in this model of working are with each divorcing partner in individual meetings. These meetings allow for an opportunity to gather history without being sidetracked by arguments or different versions of what has occurred, as well as a less stressed context to share and explain the therapy contract and have it signed. Where appropriate, initial permissions include parental consent for the involvement of children as needed (specific consents for treatment from adolescents are presented at the time of their first appearance in sessions, as are consents for treatment to other family members who may join the therapy). Matters not fully specified at this time (e.g., who else will participate) are added to the verbal and written contract as those become clear.

Frequency and duration of sessions varies, but experience suggests that typically families in difficult divorce seen less than once a week tend to fare poorly, and these rarely are affected by a very few sessions. The helpfulness of therapies with these problems are a direct function of the dose of therapy; high doses work better than low doses for moving difficult problems.

Payment

In difficult divorce, couples often disagree about who is going to pay for what. This tends to be true when it comes to other expenses, and this also applies to the cost of therapy. Even those who have great financial resources argue about such matters. Typically, each former partner pays half of the treatment fees, or payment comes from some account of marital monies (amounting to a 50–50 split). Arrangements may vary somewhat from this, especially when the treatment is offered postdivorce after monies are divided when one former partner has far greater financial resources than the other.

Therapists can work with a range of financial arrangements if they are not influenced by who is paying. If one party is paying the fees, it should be made clear that this will in no way effect the course of treatment, and the therapist must remain alert to the possibility of unconscious bias related to this.

What is essential is to have each former partner's financial responsibility spelled out before treatment begins and for this to be part of the therapy contract. This also should involve what role insurance reimbursement is to play in the expectations for payment for the therapy. What happens with the reimbursement and its ramifications often become another area of contention between these highly contentious former partners (who often have other similar financial disputes that they bring to court). Because of the complexity of such issues, it is usually best to allow attorneys (when lawyers are involved) to work out the arrangements concerning who will pay before the first session. This both saves the time to negotiate this and removes a major constraint to moving on with the therapy. One major consideration here: The therapy must be affordable. Where financial resources are limited, the therapy must find the best way to work within those limitations, lest the therapy itself creates additional financial problems or becomes untenable due to cost. The good news here is that, with court-involved cases, therapy will almost always be less expensive than litigation, and a by-product of therapy may be reducing the need for litigation (and thus fees).

Therapists

The model presented in this book is a comprehensive systemic model. Either one or several therapists can be involved in the execution of the model. In the multiple-therapist version, one therapist may meet with the partners, while another may meet alone with the children or with children and a parent. There are equal arguments in favor of having one therapist or multiple therapists. When there is only one therapist, that therapist comes to know everyone well, and coordination is simpler. Yet this also presents multiple tasks for the therapist, some of which may be incompatible (e.g., confronting a parent and having a warm connected relationship with the child connected to that parent). Additionally, the one-therapist model challenges therapists to be skillful at very different activities (e.g., child therapy and former partner therapy) and thereby may extend a therapist into formats in which they have less competency. Multiple therapists mitigate some of these challenges but necessitate a fairly high level of therapist coordination and create the possibility of conflicts between the therapists emerging that are isomorphic with family conflicts. Given therapists with multiple competencies, one or multiple therapists are equally likely to be successful. The question of which will be best in a specific case is more a product of the treatment goals in focus (some problems are more amenable to a single therapist working basically in one format) and the resources available (multiple-therapist involvement is inevitably more expensive and demands time to coordinate) than the innate superiority of having one or multiple therapists.

Sometimes divorce therapy is an evolution from marital therapy with the same therapist. More often, it is a task with a new therapist prompted by the emergence of a new set of issues (e.g., coparenting, child arrangements). There is no evidence that one or the other is more helpful, although the marital therapist moving to divorce therapy has the difficult task of making sure both partners (and children, if involved) attend to the same revised goal of successfully moving to a new postdivorce life.

What therapists are to be involved in what roles should clearly be stated in the therapy contract. When multiple therapists are involved, the contract, and the process of creating the contract, becomes more complex. In this context, there would typically need to be multiple written contracts specifying the key parameters with that therapist, accompanied by a verbal understanding of the work family members would be engaging in with other therapists. (When all therapists work for the same entity, this can be done through one shared document.) When therapy is initiated in the context of a legal dispute, expectations about which therapist will perform which function are often specified in court orders.

Again, for some therapy with these systems, referral only involves one person or subsystem. Those therapists either work to expand that mandate or remain crisply anchored in a clear therapeutic contract within those parameters with their clients. Either way, it is essential to hold a systemic perspective and to communicate and coordinate with other therapists involved with the family (see Chapter 7) with appropriate releases obtained. Although less efficient than one coordinated therapy (as when one therapist or a team of therapists treats a case), multiple coordinated therapies can be quite effective in these cases.

Confidentiality

Maintaining confidentiality is a cornerstone of almost all psychotherapy and constitutes an important ethical responsibility for therapists. It might go without saying that in the sorts of intense, painful dramas that unfold in these families, confidentiality would be even more important. Thus, a central, stated provision in the therapeutic contract is that conversations with clients are private and confidential, unless there are named exceptions to confidentiality.

However, issues surrounding confidentiality in difficult divorce are complex, particularly in cases with court involvement. Although participants may have the technical right under the law to confidentiality, there are necessary exceptions that should be clearly articulated (e.g., a court ruling that some aspect of the therapy is not confidential). Further, clients who are involved in the judicial system are in a special bind in these cases. Although confidentiality of psychotherapy is a right protected in laws and professional ethical codes of practice, pressures within the legal system sometimes make it damaging in that venue to insist on confidentiality in some circumstances. For example, custody evaluators, who are often involved in disputes surrounding child custody and visitation, look askance when clients refuse to allow their therapists, or their children's therapists, to be interviewed as part of an evaluation, leaving the client without much functional choice about granting permission. Even more clearly, attorneys for children typically have the right to discuss treatment occurring with the children they represent, regardless of the wishes of parents. Indeed, L. R. Greenberg and Gould (2001) and others have persuasively argued for the important function of therapist as treating expert whose feedback contributes within the legal system, a function beyond that served in the therapy room (see Chapter 7, this volume).

Therefore, there are special constraints to confidentiality that need to be acknowledged in the therapy contract in difficult divorce. First, it essential for there to be permission for sharing among the mental health professionals involved. It is simply unwise to conduct these therapies, when there is more than one therapist involved, without there being sharing between the therapists. Clients can work with their own therapists to decide what will be shared (e.g., some aspects of relationships, such as lives with new partners or family-of-origin experience may be set as off limits), but there needs to be a basis for a coordinated therapy system.

Second, when cases are court ordered or referred by judges or by attorneys who represent children, it is vitally important to maintain a level of open communication with the court through the child's attorney. As already noted, many clients enter these therapies at a precontemplative stage of change: They do not think what they do has any relevance to the problem. Sharing about treatment progress with the child's attorney and the court not only serves the function of keeping the court up-to-date so it can make informed decisions, this sharing also can enable leverage that can be engendered in which the attorney for the children or the judge puts pressure on clients to participate and work toward the goals of therapy. At the very least, simple reporting on attendance promotes attendance, and, more broadly, attorneys for children and the court are often helpful in promoting therapeutic goals. Third, it also is essential to lay the groundwork for reporting on progress to other key professionals who are or may become involved, such as custody evaluators. Fourth, occasionally it may be useful with specific permissions for each contact to engage in conversations with client lawyers about their own clients (as opposed to about the other family members). In general, such sharing is typically most useful when it speaks to motivation, effort, and progress as opposed to specific details about the life of the family.

Family members also inevitably discuss therapy with family and friends, which is not easily constrained. Thus, although it remains useful to call attention to the value of keeping conversations that occur in therapy in the room, it should be understood this is a useful aspiration rather than an expectation among family members in these cases. Otherwise, needless conflicts occur about who told whom about what.

Given the clear advantages of such sharing, it is important to have whatever ground rules there are for confidentiality be clearly stated, with written consent for any exceptions to confidentiality from adults involved, and from children old enough to be able to give consent, that allow conversations or written communication about the therapy with select others named. Some waivers to confidentiality are central to effective treatment (e.g., with other treating therapists and the attorney working with the children), and thus if clients are not willing to allow treatment coordination, it is far better to choose to not be involved than to conduct the therapy with such a major obstacle.[2]

> Celia has been in a custody dispute with her husband for 2 years. Several times during the conflict, she became highly dysregulated. She was warned about stalking her husband, and when she would not stop, she was arrested for violating an order of protection. She subsequently stalked the attorney for the children. However, when a court order was issued for her to receive therapy, she told the therapist at the first meeting only that she was in a dispute with her husband and that the court was against her, taking on the position of a victim. When the therapist obtained a release of information to talk to the attorney for her children, that attorney explained the context for the referral and facts of her and her family's situation. This allowed the therapist to begin to better understand the reason for the referral and work with Celia to explore whether she could be moved further along the stages of change to at least recognize her problem. When Celia stopped attending after three sessions because she saw no point in the therapy, this was reported to the attorney for the children, and she was redirected by the court back to the therapy. Eventually, the focus was able to move to how she might cope with what she saw as an unfair situation.

The Nature of the Activity

Clients in difficult divorce also often bring inappropriate frames to therapy, especially when they are highly involved with the court. Frequently, they believe the therapist will act as a moral judge, cajole others to support their position, or even act as custody evaluator in mandating changes in behavior and reporting the need for such changes to the court. A clear explanation of what therapy involves and how it differs from

---

[2]Not everyone agrees with this perspective. There is much to be said for the tradition of the totally sequestered relationship between a client and therapist. This holds both for contacts with family members and for contacts with others. For children in the midst of interparental conflicts, it can provide an island for differentiation and coping with the conflict. However, in difficult divorce, these benefits are massively outweighed by the risks entailed in the therapist being out of touch with the relevant social systems, the advantages that accrue through having leverage from representatives of the court, and the important function that can be served by being a treating expert whose report can have an impact in the legal system.

evaluation needs to be a part of the therapist's orientation of each client into therapy. Some brief general statement about this in the contract also helps make certain this has been clearly communicated. Notably, with those clients involved in litigation, given their many overlapping priorities and involvements, no matter how clearly this is stated, at times confusion can remain. Reiterating and clarifying any misunderstandings as therapy goes forward mitigates the possibilities of problems arising in this regard.

Timing of the Contract

The preceding expectations, as well as any others more specific to the individual case, should be outlined clearly in the contract presented before the beginning of treatment. Whatever the terms of the contract about who will participate, payment, and confidentiality, these parameters should be clearly stated and approved with a signed consent at the beginning of therapy. This contract is revised as needed as the therapy progresses and consents from any additional participants obtained before participating in the therapy.

Interface With Codes of Ethics

Therapies in this domain always need to be structured in ways that are consonant with professional codes of ethics and laws in the state or country where service is rendered (Campbell & Arkles, 2017). Even if a divorce presents apart from the judicial system, there is a high risk in difficult divorces that someone will at some point consider linking the therapy to the judicial system. Therefore, beyond the obvious needs to provide ethical service governed by applicable laws and codes of ethics to all clients, these are cases in which to be sure to adhere to the letter of such practices given possibilities for procedures being examined by others.

There needs to be a clear understanding of who the client is in each case, and who has privilege in terms of the disclosure of what information is a closely related question. These can be complex matters in families with varying goals and where there is judicial involvement. For example, a child with two disputing parents may be referred to therapy by the child's attorney. Given the systemic understanding at the center in the approach described in this book, the child and each parent all would be regarded as clients (and that would be the case even if this were a "child" referral that was primarily about the therapist spending time with the child). Thus, each would be entitled to the rights of clients, but the extent and content of the sharing of information between family members and, most especially, the child and the parents, would be clearly delineated at the beginning of treatment.

In the United States, HIPAA and state laws are also germane. Complicating matters in cases referred by the court is the frequent presence of an attorney having some role in relation to the rights of the children. Those roles may grant them say about such matters as consent to treatment and privilege, or they may more simply represent the children.

The structure of the treatment also needs to be situated in a way that anticipates issues that may emerge. For example, record-keeping needs to be conducted in ways that speak to the separate rights for confidentiality of various parties in therapy from each other. This is especially important in so far as there is communication with one family member apart from the others. Records also need to be written keeping in mind that they may be subpoenaed.

FORMING AND MAINTAINING THERAPEUTIC ALLIANCES

It is widely understood that a therapeutic alliance is a necessary condition for successful therapy (Lebow, 2014; Norcross, 2011). Some even hold that the alliance is the most important active agent in psychotherapy (Wampold & Imel, 2015). The therapeutic alliance is no less important in these families than in others. It is vital to create and maintain a good working alliance with each person in treatment.

However, the challenges involved in doing so are considerable. First, there are all the complexities that are involved with alliance in any couple and family therapy (Friedlander, Escudero, Heatherington, & Diamond, 2011; Friedlander, Heatherington, & Escudero, 2016; Lebow, 2014). The presence of more than one person makes alliance more precarious, with more opportunities for ruptures in alliance and split alliances, in which one client is more positively connected to the therapist than are others in the family.

Second, there are additional constraints in the form of the animosity and opposing positions between clients, and the frequency with which clients present in the precontemplation stage of change, rendering it more difficult to engage clients in the change process. In these cases, building an alliance with one client can easily be interpreted as forming an alliance against the other family members. Adding to the problem is that some clients, especially those referred through the legal system, have little choice but to participate in the therapy and thus feel coerced. Further, there often is no *within-client alliance* (Pinsof, 1988) about therapy; that is, the clients may have no positive connection with one another about the treatment. The major exception occurs when alliances between some family members (e.g., a mother and child) are rigid and overly close and may present yet another obstacle rather than a positive factor in the pursuit of change.

Therefore, alliance is a project in these cases. A major task lies in building alliance with all participants. Given the competition—and often enmity—between family members, Boszormenyi-Nagy and Spark's (1973) concept of a multipartial alliance is particularly relevant. In a multipartial alliance, clients have a sense of fairness and balance on the part of the therapist and a sense of connection with various clients. In successful alliances, the therapist conveys a sense of nonjudgmental understanding with each client. The therapist is also experienced as creating an environment in which each party feels able to express his or her thoughts and feelings, while feeling safe and respected.

To some extent, successful alliance depends on the therapist's creating the classic therapeutic conditions, suggested by Carl Rogers (1951), of empathy, congruence, and positive regard. This, in turn, depends on therapists finding a way to bring a sense of positive concern to each family member. This is not to ignore the difficult behaviors that are often in the therapy room and being described as occurring elsewhere, but rather to find a sense of how this particular client got to this position and empathize with the underlying hurt that almost all the clients in these families feel and exhibit. Staying empathic with all members of these families is not an easy task and typically calls for therapists to work with and monitor their interaction with each set of clients (see Chapter 9).

It is also essential to monitor how particular family members take sides. Therapists in conjoint therapy inevitably must side with specific clients at times, but there needs to be an overall sense of balance across the totality of this, with a sense that the therapist is helping the family as a whole, rather than acting as the agent of one individual. A multipartial alliance is an aspiration in these cases, given that they are so fraught with possibilities for triangulation. Successful alliance inevitably consists of a dialectic in which balance needs to be continually assessed. The therapist may purposefully need to move from such balance at times, while clients may at other times experience a shift, despite the therapist's best efforts to balance client–therapist connections.

Therefore, monitoring alliance becomes an essential aspect of therapy, so that the therapist can understand how the therapy and therapist are being experienced. Carefully examining signs of alliance in sessions is one means to this end, as are direct inquiries about the status of alliance. Use of brief alliance scales, such as the Integrative Psychotherapy Alliance Scales (Pinsof, Zinbarg, & Knobloch-Fedders, 2008) or Session Rating Scale (S. D. Miller, Duncan, Sorrell, & Brown, 2005), can also be enormously helpful. Given the many issues at hand in these families, for some, the presence of alliance issues can be obscured, and alliance scales can bring such issues to the surface. When the alliance scale indicates a problem with a client or a problematic pattern such as split alliance, it can serve as a cue to the therapist to deal directly with the alliance issue.

Given the dominance of the highly controversial issues in these cases, it is immeasurably helpful to seize opportunities to build alliances around other foci, when such opportunities are available. Personal connection about the smaller aspects of life helps, as does human relating. The first meeting is an especially good place to build an alliance, given that those meetings in this model provide opportunities to meet with clients alone. Sometimes, even if the task for therapy is primarily about settling about child arrangements or issues around coparenting, clients feel a desperate need to share other parts of their lives (often traumatic), such as their narratives of the demise of the marriage. Although such narratives may have only marginal value in planning how to achieve the key goals of therapy, listening and empathizing may be crucial to building alliance. Although the therapist must avoid cues that might suggest he or she is siding with one client over the others, these are opportunities for one-on-one connection. Whatever the basis, everyone in these difficult divorces carries a great deal of pain and trauma.

Because of the very charged nature of the issues with which these families are grappling and the therapist's need to balance the well-being of all involved and move toward therapeutic goals, alliance ruptures occur and are often an inevitable part of these therapies. Ruptures are moments when clients lose the sense of having a bond with the therapist (Falender & Shafranske, 2012). Ruptures occasionally occur in most therapies, but in this context, they are more frequent and probably unavoidable if therapy is to be effective. When they do occur, the therapeutic plan needs to be put aside momentarily and the focus moved to repairing the rupture, which is not an easy task, especially given that the rupture may not have stemmed from a therapist error but from a need for the therapist to work on a difficult issue with a client. If this repair work cannot easily be done in the conjoint context and the rupture is acute, individual meetings can be a place to explore the rupture and rebuild the alliance.

The need to deal with alliance ruptures in these families is as strong as it is in any psychotherapy. Alliance ruptures that are not successfully dealt with generally result in failed therapy. However, the notion of repair is a bit different here than in other couple and family therapies. Especially if the court is involved with its external pressure to continue (exiting a court-ordered therapy is an invitation to trouble in court), repair does not need to be complete. It only needs to be good enough for the therapy to continue with sufficient alliance to allow some chance of success. In other words, the bar for repair is lower than it is in other therapies. Getting to the point where the issue is acknowledged and having the therapist take some responsibility for his or her part in the problem may be enough.

Marjorie had met with Laura and Betty, who were former partners, for 3 months, focused on issues of coparenting. During that time, Laura was a strong proponent for therapy and communicating, thus establishing a connection with her was easy. In contrast, Betty only felt a sense of alliance with Marjorie when she felt actively supported around her wishes for having almost no contact with her former partner. When conversation turned to any version of seeing one another, especially any time the therapist spoke positively about the value of contact for the children, Betty would become dysregulated, and verbally attack Laura or Marjorie. She would then speak angrily of Laura, the court, and the therapist—all of whom she pictured as demanding too much of her and as wrongheaded. Each time this occurred, Marjorie would stop the conjoint session and meet alone with each client during the remaining time. She would then concentrate on rebuilding her connection with Betty during their time together, always emphasizing her understanding of how hard it was to be separated and have to meet with her former partner. She also made it clear that the only goal of the therapy around connection was for there to be just enough communication to be functional for the children. Each time, with such a process, Betty would move back into a workable (if always fragile) position toward the therapy. The treatment moved in and out of rupture and repair until the therapeutic tasks were accomplished.

Following are a couple of additional observations about the alliance in difficult divorce. Alliance and promoting behavior change in these cases are often yin and yang. Most clients experience some sense of pressure to change, and that is useful. However, this must be balanced with conveying acceptance to the client as a person—that old truism about having positive regard for the person but not for a given action. Erring at times on the side of behavior change or acceptance is inevitable in working with the more difficult of these families. Ideally, the therapist brings attention to problematic behavior and provides honest, direct feedback and paths to behavior change, while acknowledging the positive intent of each client and highlighting client strengths without pathologizing family members. Issues about alliance arise in good therapy with these families, whatever the role of the therapist may be—individual counselor to a parent, child therapist, divorcing couple therapist, or family therapist.

William M. Pinsof (1994) presented an extremely helpful vision of alliances in couples and families. He envisioned not one but several alliances that contribute to a good outcome. The first type of alliance is the self–therapist alliance that exists between each client and the therapist. A second kind of alliance represents the connection between significant others (either participating directly in therapy or not) and the therapist. To the client in family sessions, the other–therapist alliance is the alliance between the individual's family and the therapist. In therapy with only one client, the other–therapist alliance is the alliance of the others in the client's life (who are not in therapy) in support of the therapy. Although others are not present when meeting with an individual or subsystem, those people still are involved indirectly in those meetings. If a meeting occurs that moves a client further to a pathological relationship with other family members, that change has systemic meaning; this is also the case when a session helps minimize problems. Families in difficult divorce are families in which the indirect client system matters a great deal because are the alliances with those individuals, even if the therapist never meets them. Pinsof's third form of alliance is the "within-system" alliance that family members have with one another while they are in therapy together. The within-system alliance is inevitably a problem in these cases. It is best approached by finding common ground (e.g., the underlying welfare of children or getting divorced) and ways to work with the families in the context of low within-system alliance.

The principal ingredients in successful alliance in most cases lie in conveying a nonjudgmental connection with each client, creating a holding environment that allows a sense of safety in which to share thoughts and feelings, having a plan of intervention that protects therapy sessions from becoming pathogenic, and finding ways for meetings to be useful in moving toward treatment goals. Given the frequent narratives of victim and victimizer, of behavior viewed in radically different ways by the partners, and of questionable behavior on the part of at least one party (e.g., extramarital involvements or triangulation of children into marital disputes), working with alliance remains a major challenge to keep in focus throughout therapy with these clients.

For those who meet with only one family member, alliance issues still remain complex. In some instances, establishing the primary alliance with the client may be easier, given that there is less competition for attention and taking sides in sessions. However, if clients are mandated into therapy and have low levels of motivation, it is generally difficult to engage them because such clients often only recognize problems in others. Additionally, even when clients are not mandated, systemic therapists still struggle to find a balance between promoting a secure attachment and not crossing the line to tacitly support problematic behavior toward others. Being a voice for systemic solutions is often challenging for the individual client (child or parent), who may look to have his or her (often pathogenic) position toward others simply be mirrored. Further, when the primary client is a child, parents need to have some involvement with the therapist, and that interface may be a special challenge, either in the alliance with the child or in maintaining balance in alliance between two parents (especially given that one parent is often more supportive of the therapy than the other).

Adding to the complexity of alliance in therapy with families in difficult divorce is the substantial minority of families in which no effort by the therapist will engage certain family members in anything other than perfunctory attendance (if that). In these families, the therapist is left with complex decisions about when to move to the alternate frame of focusing primarily on work with those family members who have some motivation to change to see whether this might benefit the system as a whole. Here, first efforts should be to determine if there are ways to build alliance (e.g., around the client's anger or sense of helplessness in the context of the dispute) or at least mandate attendance (through intervention of the court or attorneys), but when this does not succeed, the therapy algorithm must inevitably move to how best to help the system while seeing whether there is some way to limit the extent of the negative alliance in the resistant client.

INVOKING OTHER COMMON FACTORS IN THERAPY

Much has been written about the importance to treatment success of invoking common factors shared by therapies of different orientations and focus, including creating a steady holding environment for the therapy, generating realistic positive expectancies about outcomes, building a sense of optimism, invoking resilience, attending and adapting therapy to client stage of change, reading feedback, and adapting therapy in relation to that feedback. Common factors remain perhaps the most essential elements in successfully treating difficult divorce (Lebow, 2014; Sprenkle, Davis, & Lebow, 2009) but are especially hard to engage, steadily and reliably, in these cases.

Each of these common factors is discussed further in the Chapter 6. The therapist's primary challenge in difficult divorce is to enter a flow that is cascading in a direction that promotes psychogenic experience and blaming others, and yet set a frame that can steadily help move clients forward toward better coping and therapeutic goals. This requires continual work by the therapist to help the therapy remain therapeutic, and not have what might be therapeutic overwhelmed by the saturated level of family problems and individual dysfunction (see Chapter 9).

ASSESSMENT

Assessment and case formulation are integral to therapy in difficult divorce. Parsimonious intervention is predicated on evaluating each family member's behavior and how it contributes to the problem, as well as circular processes that occur among family members and others related to the problem. Usually the problem is not due exclusively to either circular process or individual behavior; assessment allows the therapist to explore the role of each. Assessment can be enigmatic in some cases, given conflicting accounts and the constraints in terms of time available to assess and formulate that inevitably occur when a family is referred for intervention instead of evaluation.

In court-involved cases that center on issues around determining issues of custody and time with each parent, sometimes a separate child custody evaluation is ordered (Ackerman, 2001; Ackerman, Kane, Gould, & Dale, 2015; Benjamin, Beck, Shaw, & Geffner, 2018; Galatzer-Levy, Kraus, & Galatzer-Levy, 2009; Goldstein, 2016; Gould & Martindale, 2007; Hynan, 2014) and can be made available by obtaining appropriate releases. Custody evaluation is a highly specialized task, conducted by those with specific expertise. It centers on offering recommendations to the court about specific questions related to contested issues, such as who should make decisions in the lives of children, whom children should live with and when, and whether there is a need for a supervisor in contact between a parent and child. In such custody evaluations, a trained evaluator spends 20 to 40 hours (usually at a considerable cost to the parties) assessing families similar to many of those described in this book and writes what typically is a voluminous report. In that time, the evaluator can gather all relevant information, assess records and reports, hear at length from each person in the family, see family members together in various configurations, and talk to any therapists, counselors, physicians, teachers, and other professionals involved. There also is likely to be some psychological testing in the evaluation. Sometimes there also are more focused evaluations of specific clients, usually when there are questions about their functioning. Both child custody and individual evaluations, when available, should be requested with appropriate releases of information. Although these evaluations focus on questions different from those central in therapy (e.g., which parent should have decision-making authority about children and what is the optimal division of time between households), they contain a great deal of information about families beyond speaking to the central questions in focus. Typically, that information is enormously helpful in creating a case formulation, treatment plan, and a road map for the changes needed in therapy. When available, such evaluations often allow therapy to begin with a briefer assessment phase, focused principally on what clients want to accomplish in therapy.

A caveat here is that there are two routes to custody evaluations. Generally, evaluations in most jurisdictions are initiated by the court or the attorney working with the children or through cooperative arrangements between the attorneys representing the parents. Such evaluations are conducted by a neutral evaluator, who is almost always unbiased and typically can be trusted (even though, depending on the evaluator, these evaluations may be imperfect). However, there also is a second kind of evaluation in most jurisdictions that is initiated by only one party in divorce. In these instances, that party or his or her attorney selects the evaluator. Those evaluations may be unbiased (if one wants to question an evaluation initiated by the court through a second opinion, one route is to select an expert who is well known for being difficult to manipulate), but, more frequently, these evaluations reflect the bias of the party who initiated the evaluation. Thus, the origin of an evaluation needs to be considered in considering its helpfulness for treatment planning.

It is more typical for therapy to begin without the aid of an independent child custody evaluation. Here, therapy must begin with a still brief but more extensive assessment period. During this time, the therapist learns about the issues in the case, the perspectives of the family members, the opinions of those who are most likely to have the most useful information, and the goals of various stakeholders (including the clients, but also possibly the court and an attorney for the children) have for the treatment.

Let's clearly state the problem here, one that is crucial to keep in mind: Assessment, which a custody evaluator may take 20 to 40 contact hours to do well, needs to occur in a brief time early in therapy to allow for at least a working case formulation for the plan of therapy. One might say this is an impossible task, but, although difficult, it is not as impossible as it may sound. The problem is mitigated somewhat because typically in these cases, there is a focal concern that needs to be at the center of the formulation and intervention. For example, it is much simpler to assess the individual and systemic processes in coparenting than all the intricacies of the life of a family. A good-enough solution to a coparenting problem is to find a way to help parents coparent. Second, the purpose of this assessment is to create a foundation for therapy, not providing this assessment for the court. Therefore, the concentration on small detail (e.g., When did mother first move out of the home? How many times did father drink to excess?) that a custody evaluator must keep in focus to eventually write a thorough report and be ready for cross-examination is of less importance here. It is the big arcs of life, and what might be done about them, that matter. Ultimately, the purpose of assessment here is to not write a comprehensive treatise on the problems in this family (in a difficult divorce, such a treatise would require many pages) but to parsimoniously consider the main problems in the family and what underlies them to develop the most efficacious treatment plan. Third, assessment in therapy is always a work in progress. Unlike a custody evaluation, there will be more meetings after the initial assessment and an opportunity to see what happens when various intervention strategies are used (Pinsof, 2005; Pinsof et al., 2018), which provides a continuous flow of further assessment information about the family. Thus, initial assessment does not need to provide a final determination but simply be good enough to move on with the beginning of treatment. The key elements to such a working assessment are described in the text that follows.

Problems in Focus

The first and foremost question is what is the problem for which the clients are seeking help in therapy. It is rare that these client systems have only a single issue; the question is what is most salient and essential to resolve? This question should be asked of each client directly. However, bear in mind that the most frequent answer in difficult divorce to "What problem is bringing you here today?" is some version of "Someone else in the family has a problem." Thus, it requires some shaping with each client to arrive at his or her view of the primary problem in the family that might be labeled in some way than simply to change someone else.

It also is essential to gather various versions of the key problems that require attention from not only various family members, but also other major stakeholders in the treatment, such as attorneys for the children and the court in court-ordered cases. When the referral is from the court or from attorneys, their input is particularly important. Many clients are referred for very specific reasons. There may be a special concern about parent conflict, parents' lack of coparenting, a child–parent conflict or cutoff, or an individual problem in functioning in a parent or a child.

Perhaps the most frequent problem in focus in these cases is a breakdown in communication and problem solving in divorcing parents. For some, this manifests in a failure in the major task of coming to agreement about the post-divorce family structure (especially where children will be and when) despite efforts by attorneys and mediators to reach agreement. For others, communication problems manifest as insufficient positive communication to allow for sufficient coparenting. Often as well, high levels of conflict block communication and problem-solving; these are the highly dramatic cases, rife with stormy, overt conflict, that are the bane of family court judges and family attorneys.

Another frequent concern is problematic parenting. One parent may show sufficient issues in parenting that this becomes a concern to the other parent and the court, or one parent may allege behaviors on the part of the other, which the second parent denies. Closely related are cases in which a parent has a major mental health problem (or one parent perceives the other to have such a problem), and the concerns of the other parent flow around that problem.

A third set of frequently encountered problems focuses on the relationship between a parent and a child. Sometimes there is a cutoff between and parent and child, which the cutoff parent attributes to parental alienation on the part of the other parent (Johnston, Roseby, & Kuehnle, 2009; Kelly & Johnston, 2001; Templer, Matthewson, Haines, & Cox, 2017), while the other parent attributes it to a lack of parental skill or connection or to bad behavior on the part of the other parent.

In other situations, divorce (or a temporary arrangement leading up to divorce) can mean that a parent is assigned time with a child without much experience in parenting such that they barely have had a relationship previously. This may trigger very different beliefs about the parental competence of the less involved parent; such issues are most acute with very young children. Even two competent parents (and for that matter, experts about parenting) can argue about how much contact for how long should occur between an infant and each parent (Lamb & Kelly, 2001; McIntosh, Pruett, & Kelly, 2014; Nielsen, 2014; Pruett, McIntosh, & Kelly, 2014). In difficult divorce, such differing viewpoints mushroom into major conflict. A subtype within this presenting problem involves parents who have children but have never had much of a relationship with one another, or one of very short duration[3] (see Chapter 8). Here, the child is likely to have had limited experience with one parent, and the less involved parent looks to the court to grant more involvement.

Finally, in many difficult divorce cases, the principal reason for the referral is because of a child problem. Major difficulties in children, such as bipolar disorder or oppositional defiant disorder, necessitate more than the average amount of cooperation between parents, and the acrimony of divorce engenders additional concern for the welfare of these children. A child may also have particular difficulty dealing with divorce.

Whatever the problem, the therapist seeks to get a clear statement about what are the central problems that need attention from each family member and from other stakeholders involved with the family, such as the court. These perspectives are then brought together into the best reframing of the problems in ways that help with buy-in from all stakeholders (discussed later in the chapter). For example, if mother thinks father is incompetent at parenting and too harsh, and father thinks mother is withholding and too lax, this can be framed as looking to find some level of working agreement about what their goals are for their children and how best to achieve those goals.

---

[3]Given that there never was a marriage or anything close to one, the term *divorce* does not apply to arrangements between the parties in such conflicts, but the issues between these virtual strangers with children are closely related to those in divorcing couples, without any of the history of positive connection. Because of this similarity and because a remarkable number of these situations do wind up in family court, they are included in the context of "difficult divorce."

Danger

Assessment of danger is another crucial aspect of initial assessment (Jaffe, Johnston, Crooks, & Bala, 2008; Johnston, Lee, Olesen, & Walters, 2005; Rossi, Holtzworth-Munroe, & Rudd, 2016). Difficult divorce numbers among the experiences in life with the highest levels of physical danger, physical confrontations, and other threatening behavior such as stalking (DeKeseredy, Dragiewicz, & Schwartz, 2017). In many instances, this follows physical abuse during the marriage, although in other instances, the physical confrontations are unprecedented. The level of risk must inform all the therapist's actions. Therapeutic plans only make sense if they ensure safety. Risks are clearly higher for women, given that men comprise the great majority of batterers, but physical confrontations in which women are the perpetrators are also frequent.

To assess this as thoroughly as possible, therapists should meet alone with each client at least once and ask about past and present violent or harassing behavior. If someone says that a situation is unsafe, this must be followed up and attended to. Collateral reports are helpful here, as are decisions made about these matters in court-involved cases. Those decisions (e.g., orders of protection) may turn out to be overly expansive (courts tend initially to err on the side of protecting people) but should always give pause about connecting people where risk of violence has been confirmed.

Using a standardized screening questionnaire about family violence such as the Conflict Tactics Scale—Revised (Straus, 1979, 2004) or Detection of Overall Risk Screen, a screening instrument developed specifically for divorcing families (McIntosh, Wells, & Lee, 2016) can help. Yet, when using such self-report questionnaires, as with other self-reports, it also is vital to keep in focus that difficult divorce also often involves false allegations. Reports should trigger some further process of follow-up. One perhaps useful side benefit of litigation is that in the context of the court process, such allegations are often fully vetted.[4] Absent that, the therapist must use his or her assessment skill to differentiate between situations that are dangerous and it is best that there is no contact, from those experienced as dangerous without much direct cause, and from those situations in which allegations are made for other reasons.

There are families in difficult divorce where it is far better not to bring various clients together than to run the risk of danger or, even after ensuring safety, retraumatize the victim of violence. Where there is such a history,

---

[4]Although this is in marked contrast to the vast underreporting of family violence in other contexts, it remains important to remember that it is still possible family violence has not been reported, especially in those instances where litigation is less active.

extreme caution is indicated. A closely related assessment task for therapists is tracking levels of more extreme psychological abuse that may have occurred or may still be occurring. The presence of such behaviors must become an immediate target for intervention.

Severity

In divorce, level of difficulty falls along a continuum. It is helpful to have a sense of how near or far this specific family or individual is from normative behavior in divorce. One relevant dimension is in how pervasive the problem is. Does it center on or affect one or many aspects of living? How many family members are involved in the problem, and to what extent do various family members display pathological patterns? A second dimension is how extreme the pattern in the specific area of difficulty is. A third dimension to consider lies in how fixed and long-standing the pattern is. Such a three-dimensional view (how pervasive, how extreme, how fixed and long-standing) of severity helps orient therapy in terms of creating projected realistic goals and how much movement is needed.

Closely related is the question of the relative contribution of family members to the problem. Families vary widely between ones with coequal participation of family members to others in which some family members heroically try to function and retain balance in the wake of egregious behavior by another family member. This aspect of assessment in some substantial sense will drive the focus of the therapy. However, it is important to highlight here that this question is often more complex than it may seem at first glance. Very noticeable dysfunctional behavior is sometimes a response to more subtle provocation.

Multilevel Assessment

Families function at a variety of systemic and psychological levels. The integrative model for working with difficult divorces assesses across these multiple levels of experience, looking to uncover what intervention strategies are most likely to be effective and acceptable. This is a biopsychosocial model of assessment that incorporates dimensions that are emphasized across the major models of psychotherapy.

This section highlights the key dimensions of assessment relevant to intervention. Because each of these dimensions of systemic and psychological functioning is described at length in the context in which it was developed (e.g., there is an extensive literature describing functional and dysfunctional cognitions), rather than duplicate here a primer that thoroughly describes each dimension, the reader is referred to the relevant primary sources for each molecular concept. Discussion here focuses instead on the specific relevance of each dimension in the context of difficult divorce.

At one level, families are a system (Carr, 2016). Systemic understandings substantially focus on the cybernetic interaction patterns and sequences that occur between individuals (Breunlin & Schwartz, 1986). In assessing, notice the sequences of behaviors, thoughts, and emotions. What leads to what? Are there patterns that frequently result in manifestations of problems? Are there other sequences that move in a more positive direction? The former will be targets for intervention, and the latter provide clues to what might help. In difficult divorce, families often feature one person's bad behavior inviting another's bad behavior in what is termed a *systemic runaway*, moving toward chaos (Watzlawick, Bavelas, & Jackson, 2011). For example, an angry outburst on the part of one family member may lead to an angry outburst on the part of the other, and so on, in a process of symmetrical escalation. Demand–withdraw cycles (Christensen & Heavey, 1993) and sequences of aggression and passive-aggression are also common in these families, as are cycles of one partner posing a sense of physical or psychological threat and overly strict gatekeeping by the other parent.

Systemic assessment also focuses on identifying processes that characterize the family as a whole, and its subsystems. These may be global processes, such as the level of cohesion or adaptability in the whole family or in subsystems (Olson, Russell, & Sprenkle, 1983). In these families, subsystems such as coparent, child–parent, and so forth are often quite distinct in their properties. There is a quality to these families of not only going through a transition but of being fragmented. For example, a father–son dyad may be overly close, as may be a mother–daughter dyad, but the two dyads may largely be at odds with each other, such that there is little overall family cohesion. Frequently these families feature what once were called *perverse triangles* (Haley, 1963) in which children join with one parent against another. Coalitions are often powerful, and with them may come other problems in relationship or individual psychopathology. Thus, the therapist must notice how the family is organized in terms of the core aspects of family structure: boundary, alliance, and power (Minuchin, 1974).

Beyond attending to systemic issues, assessment extends across the dimensions of the biopsychosocial continuum. Biology speaks to major biomedical factors. Included here are family health issues that may impact the divorce process. The level of behavior includes the actions of individuals and their behavioral exchanges (Dattilio & Epstein, 2016). Here, the focus moves to who does what and to the most important evident behavioral patterns, accentuating interpersonal behaviors. Common behavioral exchanges in these families include confrontation, conflict, and withdrawal. At the level of behavior, observe the reinforcement contingencies in place and the social exchanges made. Negative reactions between family members in difficult divorce readily become conditioned behaviors; that is, beyond being negative interactions, family members show signs of classical conditioning. Family members learn to have visceral negative reactions to one another and then avoid one another, with enough ongoing conflict to never change that pattern. As in all such conditioning on variable reinforcement schedules, such conditioning is often hard to reverse, even when information inconsistent with that conditioning paradigm becomes available (Goldfried & Davison, 1994).

Communication and problem-solving are also an important focus of attention in assessment. If functional communication and problem-solving ever existed in these relationships, these processes often have dramatically eroded. Communication may be cutoff or highly confrontational. It also is important to observe who brings what to the communication. Often one person wants to improve communication, but others do not. Family members frequently participate equally in pathological processes, but sometimes they do not. Difficult divorce is still difficult with one unremitting combatant but not nearly as challenging as when there are dysfunctional patterns in multiple family members. Nonverbal communication is also important to observe. Members of these families often demonstrate all of Gottman's (1999) Four Horsemen—contempt, stonewalling, defensiveness, and criticism in their nonverbal behavior.

Another level of assessment focuses on cognitions. Dysfunctional cognitions are typically easy to find with the core cognitive errors described by Aaron Beck (1976) manifested in pervasive ways in relation to family process. For example, a frequent occurrence is maximization and minimization, in which the importance and salience of troubling patterns in other family members are maximized well beyond objective rendering, whereas the importance and salience of positive behaviors are minimized. Similarly, catastrophizing the effects of what are objectively small problems is common, as is overgeneralization from small samples of behavior. In assessing, look at what cognitive sets and errors are established and in place that look to be obvious targets for change. Also notable is that for all the blog reading and Internet searches that many of those in difficult divorce do, looking for like-minded support, this tends to uncover surprisingly little in the way of objective information about divorce and the tasks needed in working through it. Thus, many in difficult divorce deal not only with their own cognitive distortions but also the collective distortions of prominent fringe websites that focus attention on topics such as borderline personality in divorce or how men or women are treated unfairly. These inputs further color dysfunctional cognitions about other family members and present another obstacle to recognizing one's own problematic, individual patterns.

Emotion is another level for analysis (L. S. Greenberg, 2015). Given that divorce is intrinsically loaded with emotion, affect for many is also fraught with problems that extend well beyond the normal pain of divorce. Most frequently, this entails emotional dysregulation in one or more individuals, although parents and children emotionally shutting down is also common (Fruzzetti, 2006). Underlying pain also easily transforms into rage. Emotion may be passed between family members—that is, projected from one onto the other by taking provocative actions that invite problematic emotional states in others (Siegel, 2010). This can readily morph into an interpersonal game, frequently seen in the legal forum, in which the person who responds looks emotionally fragile, but the provocation of the other family member is equally important in the sequence leading to that behavior (Berne, 1964).

Even with brief interviewing about early experience, it is relatively easy to find massive family-of-origin issues in most adults experiencing difficult divorce (Wanlass & Scharff, 2016). Early experience tends to create vulnerabilities that emerge under the stress of divorce. Often, these center on early attachment issues, issues surrounding parental divorce, or dysregulation in family of origin. However, what is most important here is not so much to look for specific sets of family-of-origin problems but instead to understand what this particular difficult divorce means in the context of each specific client's early experience. Sometimes the fact that divorce was never part of one's family of origin can make the experience particularly tortuous, whereas multiple generations of divorce in other families can have a similar impact on others.

Assessing each individual's stage of change is of perhaps greatest significance in planning for therapy and the most likely path toward changing present patterns (Norcross, Krebs, & Prochaska, 2011). Some clients are in precontemplation, unaware of having any contribution to the problem at hand. Others are in contemplation, aware of some personal difficulties but not ready to act on them. A few are in action, having grown tired of the effects of these negative interactions. As we will see in the next chapter, therapy very much needs to be geared to each client's stage of change.

A multilevel understanding of the family and the individuals in it is crucial to devising a case formulation and treatment plan. This does not mean that every case needs intervention on every level, but understanding how the problems reside on each level, and how problems manifest across levels, is at the core of effective treatment in this context. Such an understanding is no less important for those treating individuals or subsystems (e.g., two parents). In these circumstances, drawing on information from other therapists and professionals involved with the family can be immeasurably helpful in gaining a systemic viewpoint.

DECIDING WHETHER TO TAKE THE CASE

One important initial decision before proceeding to case formulation and goal setting is whether to treat the specific family, or the part of the family, that has been referred. In the context of these agonizing family problems in which clients are often at their worst, this is a more significant question than in other therapy. First, the therapist should ask whether she or he has the necessary experience with this kind of problem to work with this case. These clearly are not the cases with which to gain early experience without a structure that supports a more gradual entry into working with these cases. Even experienced therapists in this context should be wary of practicing beyond their range of expertise (as already noted, this would be a violation of professional ethical guidelines). Learning to work with difficult divorce ideally includes some didactic training, extensive reading, being mentored in this work by someone skillful in it, functioning as part of a team working with such cases, and acquiring enough experience to move on to become more broadly competent in this work.

Part of the decision about whether to treat a case also focuses on the family. There clearly are families in which some members might request therapy or whom the court may refer to therapy, for whom, at least in the configurations they present, therapy is highly likely to be harmful to at least some of those involved. For example, there are well-established parameters for working with abusive parents and children, typically predicated on there first being individual work with the abusive parent, that can help move them to a point where conjoint therapy might be helpful. As the maxim goes, "first do no harm." If the concept for therapy is dangerous or unrealistic, it is far better to identify this upfront than have the family engage in what inevitably will be both difficult emotionally and ultimately almost surely a failed therapy experience.

> John, a father, has had no contact with his 17-year-old daughter, Sylvia, for 5 years. She has been in individual therapy over that time. John petitioned the court, which referred John and Sylvia to family therapy with Wendy to begin reconciliation. At the first meeting with Sylvia, she described a long-standing history of violence by her father. On contacting Sylvia's therapist, she strongly supported Sylvia's view as fact based, and this history was confirmed in discussions with the attorney representing Sylvia. In meeting with John, he denied any violence and simply wanted to restore normal visitation with his daughter. After an initial period of assessment, Wendy contacted the attorney for Sylvia and recommended that the plan be rethought for John to be in individual therapy with someone skillful in working with abusing parents and that he show insight into his behavior as a precondition of beginning sessions together. If this was not possible, she made it clear that she would need to withdraw as a therapist for this case.

In a similar vein, there are often referrals for parents to work together or for parents and children to reunite when an initial assessment shows little if no basis for reconciliation. For example, a parent may want contact with a child but have no insight about the impact of his or her earlier or even current behavior and its effects on the child. There are families in which children are doing well in their current lives with no contact with a parent. Would it be better in such instances for therapy to work to create parent–child contact? Sometimes the answer to this question is provided by lengthy litigation in which the court orders some degree of contact (which may be supervised or unsupervised contact[5]), often informed by a child custody evaluation concerned with precisely this question. Other times, referrals are made on more limited information and authority. Either way, the therapist must make a determination of what is feasible given the referral, and most especially how therapy might be best staged; that is, whether it begins with contact or with work with the individual clients separately until a point is reached that conjoint work is indicated. A wise response in many cases is to ask a parent and child to do preparatory work individually and, when the therapist feels there is sufficient progress, to begin conjoint meetings.

In other instances, a referral may be made for only one part of a family system, leaving out someone who is clearly essential to problem resolution. For example, a mother–child dyad may be referred with no willingness on the part of the father to participate. Here again, the therapist must decide whether this is a possible route to success. Certainly, in such a situation, effort should be made to involve the other parent in some session format, but what if he or she will not participate and no one mandates that participation? Here, most often, the therapist works as well possible with whoever is available. It is essential in this work to remain pragmatic and provide what help can be provided. However, in some instances, the therapist may decide that without the presence of key family members, the therapy is not viable.

Finally, one must consider the mix of therapist and clients. Are the resources sufficient for some reasonable chance of progress? Does the therapist have too many similar cases to take on another, given the demands of these cases? Again, better to answer these questions before beginning treatment. Having said this, there is much a therapist can do in these cases, and the positive outcomes probably have impact beyond almost any other kind of psychotherapy, given the many risks involved for these families.

---

[5]There are also cases that the court deems too complex to have ordinary supervision of parenting by a social service agency, and parent and child are referred to therapy instead, which serves as the contact between them.

CASE FORMULATION AND GOAL-SETTING

From assessment, the therapist emerges with a working case formulation that includes the problems in focus, the sequences in which those problems emerge and the effect of those problems, how various individuals contribute to those problems, and the systemic processes involved. There are multiple layers of individual and collective experience to consider. What problem needs to be addressed? What principally accounts for the problem? How much do systemic or individual factors appear to be involved? Ideally, who might best change what? Pragmatically, what are the possible and most likely pathways to resolving the problem? (There is a difference between these last two questions, given that the second also asks "who is motivated and able to change what?") Again, the assessment and case formulation are not about creating a treatise but a parsimonious understanding that can lead to a treatment plan. This case formulation then directly migrates into what is perhaps the center of this work: arriving at achievable, realistic treatment goals.

In difficult divorce, goal-setting becomes perhaps the most crucial aspect of treatment. Goal-setting is always important in psychotherapy (Norcross & Wampold, 2011), but several factors contribute to its importance here. First, these are families in which multiple problems are present and in which the problems have roots at almost every level of a multilevel analysis. The sheer number of problems, and the pain and "stuckness" associated with these problems, can be discouraging. So, where to start? It is unsurprising that many therapists avoid work with these families.

A second factor that makes goal-setting so essential is the presence of radically different views of the presenting problems among various stakeholders, which include family members but also the court, attorneys, and others who refer these families. There are variations on these differences. Earlier, we spoke to the common predivorce dynamic in which one person presses for divorce while the other resists. At this stage, there may remain remnants of this dynamic, although well after almost all others would have accepted (perhaps unhappily) their fate. Some resist no matter how clear the handwriting on the wall is. Here the therapist's initial task is apparent: to help clarify that the goal now can only be to divorce as well as possible, with as little harm to everyone as possible. Most of the work here must be with the "leaning-in" partner, who may be admirable in other ways but remains stuck. That partner is entitled to his or her worldview but must adapt to the reality that divorce does not need to be a mutual decision.

In a few cases, there may be significant ambivalence about the marriage on the part of both partners. Here, if an interest in reconciliation is more than a passing thought, these families are best referred for discernment therapy until this possibility is fully explored, unless there is an urgent family agenda to sort out, such as where children will reside while discernment counseling is continuing. However, bear in mind that in this circumstance, we are talking about difficult divorce, not the middle-of-the-road variety. Although rates of ambivalence in divorcing partners run higher than might be thought (Doherty, Harris, & Didericksen, 2016) and many divorced people even remarry each other, experience suggests that those in difficult divorce almost never reconcile even when they do try, given the typical volatility in these relationships.[6] Often, such efforts involve a split-off part of self or a manipulative effort due to the fatigue of the fight on the part of at least one partner.

Most difficult divorces feature other prominent differences in goals across family members. There may be differences about who needs to change what, what postdivorce family life might look like, how acceptable conflict is as a life path, how much coparenting will be involved, and a bevy of other issues. There are typically many overt conflicts and issues to be worked out and problems evident at multiple levels of the assessment.

The question of who is at fault often looms as central in the narratives of family members. One question for the therapist is how much behavior change needs to occur versus more simply moving (although with difficulty) to greater mutual acceptance. Here, assessment plays a crucial role. When there is behavior that is essential to change, it is much different from a situation in which there is simply a power struggle about some difference of opinion about how to best live one's life or parent. Is there behavior that simply is not acceptable? If so, what kind and with what meaning? The therapist here must be able to appreciate the source of powerful feelings that are occurring on the part of every family member and be understanding of each of their narratives (all of which have validity in the eye of the beholder), yet also be able to sort through how essential it is for various behaviors, cognitions, or emotions to change. Sometimes there is a clear need for behavioral change.

> Don, a father who had almost no connection to his son, David, age 4, engaged in behavior after separation that would qualify as neglect with him, leaving the child alone for long periods.

Clearly, for therapy to have any chance of working (if Don were to have unsupervised time alone with the child), Don needed to change.

> Contrast this with Julia, who is furious at her former partner, Tony, for having left her for another woman. She is clearly justified in her feeling, but the solution she might seek of barring her children from having any relationship with Tony, although understandable, is simply not possible.

---

[6]These are former partners for which one partner saying he or she still wishes to remain married often betokens a statement of the disagreement at the core of their conflict rather than a hopeful sign. Given the typical degree of the conflict about the divorce, such thoughts also fade over time.

For Julia and Tony to reach a resolution, the most direct key to helping the family move forward is to explore whether Julia can work with her deep anger sufficiently to accept this life circumstance and find a way to share a postdivorce life with Tony that does not imperil their children. Of course, it would help immeasurably in that pursuit for Tony to move from righteous indignation at Julia's position to empathy for her pain and acknowledge his contribution to the problem. Almost always, the chances for change in difficult divorce are massively enhanced with some mutual ownership of the problem and work to resolution. In couple therapy with those working on relationships, the most comparable parallel lies in the balance between work toward behavior change and work toward acceptance in integrative behavioral couple therapy (Christensen, Doss, & Jacobson, 2014). For some, behavior change emerges as the principle target; for others, it is acceptance; and for still others, it is a mix of what is possible and what can only be better tolerated. Here, it lies principally with the therapist to help clients sort out what is possible and most likely to prove helpful.

With a good-enough assessment and case formulation, naming a set of useful goals is relatively simple. The problems occurring in these families are typically not subtle. A key therapist skill lies in framing goals in a way that speaks to the diverse needs and narratives of the various family members. At the forefront of such simple goals, families in which there is no communication most usefully target good-enough ways to communicate without becoming entangled. Families in which there are threats of violence or explosions of anger target how to manage affect and come to feel safer. Families in which there are patterns of demand–withdraw target developing other patterns. Families in which interactions are laden with drama about pain, guilt, hurt, and punishment target finding other ways to relate. Families in which there are cutoffs between parents and children or other triangulation target moving beyond such cutoffs. Families who cannot figure out how to divide time with children or their monies target finding a way to do this. Those in families with individual psychopathology relevant to the problem target working at that psychopathology and finding ways, if it is a more permanent fixture in their lives, to adapt to it. And those whose strong affect around the demise of the marriage becomes a block to other necessary operations target finding ways beyond such blocks. In the context of each such goal, the therapist needs to find ways to frame the specific issues in a form that can promote mutual agreement about treatment goals but also be able to take on the difficult conversations about individual changes that are needed. Fortunately, it is much easier to engage such conversations about individual change in the service of already agreed-on superordinate goals, such as getting along better in the best interest of the children.

In difficult divorce, therapists must be pragmatic, focusing on what will be good enough to help the family move past its present block in family development to become a more functional postdivorce family, rather than envisioning ideal goals. This is not to say that movement beyond this may not be possible. Divorce is a tumultuous time, and more than a few families with major issues reorganize and do far better later in life. It is to say that for now, goals in difficult divorce need to be to get to "good enough," and therapy first needs to establish a proximate target that is just the other side of functional.

It is fairly easy to name the most difficult, and ultimately pathological, variations of pathways to divorce. In the high conflict variation, practical matters that need to be resolved cannot be negotiated without extreme conflict. A subset of these couples moves to complete avoidance because levels of conflict are so great. In another variation on the same theme, family and friends are triangulated into the conflict and become active combatants; this is particularly problematic when children are triangulated. A different variation is the couple with much unfinished business that is never processed and for whom there never can be any sense of understanding or resolution about what has occurred. In each case, we might best ask what would be a better version of these problems—one that has less negative impact on everyone—and how might that be achieved.

Couples with children are in a much different situation than childless couples. When there are no children, the period of dealing with one another is typically delimited, followed by little or no contact. Couples with children need to engage in some degree of coparenting for the rest of their lives, perhaps ultimately presenting greater opportunities for mutual acceptance, but for the present in difficult divorce, there is simply endless conflict. The challenges for couples with children also vary between those with minor children and those whose children are adults, although both groups face challenges. In therapy, the key relevant questions surround what goals will serve each family system at its particular point in development. For the young childless couple, the best solution likely will be to help them move out of this stage to a future of little contact. For those with many years of coparenting, finding minimal ways to coparent well enough becomes crucial.

Whatever the therapist's thoughts about potential treatment goals, shaping and negotiating treatment goals between family members remain crucial. For therapy to have any chance of being effective, there needs to be some working consensus about some state toward which the parties will attempt to move (Norcross & Wampold, 2011). Contributing to this problem is that clients in difficult divorce often see therapy as a win–lose activity, much as the vying for power and control elsewhere. If they are involved in the jousting of the legal system, this tends to be even more the case because they probably already have had considerable practice at escalating to solve problems, rather than finding a shared viewpoint. And although a good post-divorce life and the best interest of children are easy enough to hold out as a positive end, such thoughts (typically familiar to those who are in the legal system because they have heard such thoughts from frustrated judges and attorneys for the children many times) are readily overrun by intense feelings of betrayal, hurt, fear, anxiety, revenge, and anger and by patterns of cognitions and behavior that point to this being an idea that may not be worth trying to achieve.

So, what does the therapist do? First, the therapist works as he or she might in any other family therapy to find superordinate goals that incorporate the specific vantage points of multiple stakeholders. Often, for example, even in the worst of circumstances, parents will agree that sharing information about children is useful—if for no other reason than such sharing tends to rarely occur in one direction if there is no sharing in the other. Calming the fray also often stands out as an overarching goal. Finding a position that at some deep level acknowledges everyone's hurt and weariness and building on the many negative statements most make about the legal system helps. The hope is to see whether there is a way to collaborate toward some other end, albeit one that will not be ideal for anyone.

With such superordinate goals in focus, the therapist works to see whether the focus can be moved toward such goals, rather than following the easy digression into fault and blame. This is an operation that therapists in difficult divorce engage in many times over in any treatment. This shift in focus happens not by a therapist brilliantly framing an obvious goal to which everyone eagerly works as in a demonstration video but by an iterative process of moving to collaboration, falling back, and the therapist remaining centered and invoking the value and spirit of collaboration again, if for no other reason than to get out of the present situation and perhaps help children. Always hovering are the questions of what is essential to change (and can it be changed) and what is most pragmatic to approach as a target of change, informed by the ongoing feedback from the success of various intervention strategies employed in relation to the various problems.

An important therapist skill lies in finding ways to work with family members to agree about goals and collaborate. Sometimes, given the clear, direct, and conscious benefits of collaboration (if families communicate well, they are likely to fight less and know more), simply developing mutually stated goals can become the agent of progress.

> Pierre and Michelle had a tumultuous marriage of 15 years. They separated after Michelle had an affair with an old boyfriend from high school. When they first moved to divorce, they argued about with whom the children should reside. While they began litigation about this, the court

imposed a temporary split-time 50–50 arrangement. Michelle immediately introduced her new partner, who had relocated to live close to her, into the children's lives, resulting in further anger for Pierre. When referred for therapy by the court, Pierre framed the entire difficulty as due to Michelle's acting out and what he called "borderline personality disorder." Michelle similarly framed the problem as about Pierre's rigid personality. Both certainly were correct in naming problems in the other (especially Michelle's impulsiveness), but the task remained to come up with a shared agenda. One common ground was that each could see the conflict was taking a toll on the children, especially their son Jacques, age 7, who was having trouble sleeping and was very anxious. Therefore, despite their vastly different views of the problem, the therapist was able to help steer the conversation toward the mutual goal of being able to see if there were ways to work together better for their son's welfare. They agreed to target reducing their arguments about these matters in the presence of the children.

Despite the strong preference for arriving at agreed on goals, for some of these families, some goals that speak to the important issues only can emerge for treatment when voiced and moved forward by the therapist.

With Pierre and Michelle, it was clear that there could be little long-term progress unless Michelle identified her pattern of impulsive action and found some way to slow down the impact of this on the children. Similarly, Pierre clearly had a former partner much different from himself, had no control over her behavior, and needed to find ways to live with her lifestyle. The therapist brought each of these agendas into focus in individual meetings not to accede to the complaints of the other, but as something that would enable good parenting and a better life for their children. In a process that took some time, each moved to understand that their own behavior needed to change and was able to target this change.

In the most difficult divorces, it is enormously challenging to arrive at agreement between family members about anything, and family members are stuck. When those cases are court involved or when extended family has influence, there may be other stakeholders to whom the clients will respond. That is, it may fall to the therapist to involve others in arriving a treatment goals and problem resolution in the most stuck cases.

Negotiation of the content of sessions that follow assessment and initial goal-setting is much like the negotiation about content in any other difficult couple or family therapy. Each family member lists his or her goals, and an agreed-on agenda is generated for each meeting. Larger goals are revised as relevant as the therapy moves forward. In the best case, over time the goals can be more ambitious than they were earlier in therapy.

Part of the problem in therapy with divorcing systems is that there is a core paradox in this work. Divorcing couples and families are reorganizing their lives; one task in divorce lies in transmuting whatever core attachment remains in the relationship into something else. Therefore, each aspect of the therapy must be considered against this lens. How does a couple and family share with one another in therapy, yet work toward separating their lives into two units? Couples range enormously in their ability to engage in these two very different sorts of tasks simultaneously. For some, sharing vulnerability with a partner who one feels has betrayed the relationship is the opposite of therapeutic, but for others, it is a useful step in parting.

There are many ways partners divorce, and no one ideal one-size-fits-all way partners are with each other. For some, creating a great deal of distance works best; for others, a sense of resolution following intense processing feels most helpful. Notably, partners may be mismatched in how they best envision this event occurring, adding to relational difficulties. Former partners (and children as well) may have very different ideas about what life should look like during and after the divorce. Such differences cue up the possibility of considering those perspectives, determining how many are realistic and possible in the specific circumstance (close, happy connection between former partners if one has been traumatized is typically not possible), and negotiating such differences. Both proximate and ultimate therapeutic goals need to be set with the specific family and its individuals in mind.

PLANNING TREATMENT

Assessment of and negotiation about treatment goals lead to the formation of an initial treatment plan. This treatment plan outlines a starting view of an efficient path for the formats and focus for the therapy. As noted, all family members are viewed as part of the client system, but who participates in specific sessions will vary according to how the treatment is organized and what will be most helpful in accomplishing proximate goals at that specific point in treatment. The number and type of sessions also depend on several other factors, including participants' willingness to participate in therapy and monetary and time constraints. Depending on the willingness of all parties and the nature of the referral, sessions may include family therapy with parents and children, sessions between parents, or individual therapy sessions for each family member.

In these cases, collaboration often depends on therapists' active leadership and reframing of the meanings of behavior in helping clients move toward constructive goals. A central tenet of this approach is to set realistic, attainable goals. This involves holding a clear picture of what needs to change (or a set of options for what might change) to allow the family to more closely resemble normative divorcing families. Typically, this also involves moving away from idealized views of divorced family life and toward a vision in which there is minimal coparenting and thus little contact, but also little conflict. The first proximal goals are almost always about calming what has become either a runaway conflict or embattled, chronic hostility. Once these goals are accomplished other, more ambitious goals, such as engaging collective problem-solving and improving parent–child and parent–parent relationships, move into focus, but for most of these families, the approach still looks to an ultimate goal of parallel households with respectful detachment rather than close interconnection between households.

Always also in focus is who has what energy to change what—the question of stage of change. Pragmatic work with these families looks to resolve the problem by engaging all family members in their best effort to change what they can. Assessing, working to enhance, and adapting to each client's stage of change is an essential part of therapy with difficult divorce (see Chapter 6) Sometimes this means that certain family members take on more goals and are more impactful than others in the resolution of family issues.

It must be added that this is therapy that also considers the resources available. In situations where there are considerable resources, multiple therapies and therapists can be involved in a range of treatment formats to maximize the comprehensiveness of the work and the chances of success in accomplishing a variety of treatment goals. For example, having individual therapies with all parties is often helpful if this work can be coordinated toward treatment goals. When resources are more limited, choices may need to be made to distribute resources more sparingly across therapy formats, necessitating either–or choices between the number of treatment sessions across various treatment formats and thus offer the best chance for a positive outcome given the limited resources.

SUMMARY

This chapter focuses on the core structural elements of integrative therapy for difficult divorce. First, a clear contract for therapy is established that deals with such issues as who will participate, confidentiality, and payment. Second, building a multipartial alliance is a constant focus of the therapy. Third, other common factors are invoked in support of the change process. Fourth, assessment builds a multilevel understanding of how problems come to occur and maintained. Fifth, a case formulation is created based on assessment and goals for therapy are negotiated consistent with this case formulation, leading to treatment planning. Therapy then segues into the focus of the next chapter: the use of specific treatment strategies in integrative therapy for difficult divorce.

6

SPECIFIC TREATMENT STRATEGIES IN DIFFICULT DIVORCE

Therapies employ a number of distinct treatment strategies. Schools of psychotherapy name these ingredients in idiosyncratic ways, but a limited number of core interventions are used in good psychotherapy (Lebow, 2014).[1] Integrative therapy for difficult divorce draws on the range of those intervention strategies and techniques, incorporating them selectively in relation to the most crucial targets for intervention from the case formulation. Also, following a premise of integrative systemic therapy (Pinsof et al., 2018), given the short-term nature of this work, brief direct interventions are given central place, unless the need for longer term intervention is demonstrated. Preference is also given to intervention strategies with demonstrated evidence of being effective in the process of ameliorating related problems in other contexts. As in the discussion of assessment in Chapter 5, this chapter focuses on the application of specific treatment strategies for difficult divorce.

---

[1]See Lebow (2014) for a complete discussion of how therapies can be deconstructed into sets of common factors and treatment strategies, that can be used and reconfigured in the context of integrative therapies.

http://dx.doi.org/10.1037/0000116-007
Treating the Difficult Divorce: A Practical Guide for Psychotherapists, by J. L. Lebow

For a more basic primer in these treatment strategies, consult the key texts cited for each in their respective sections.

TREATMENT STRATEGIES

Many effective treatment strategies have been developed for working with various aspects of human problems that are becoming well established in transdiagnostic, evidence-based treatment (Barlow et al., 2011). Integrative therapy for difficult divorce draws from treatment strategies that have been widely disseminated and shown to be helpful in other couple and family situations in which there is high stress and high conflict. This chapter reviews such strategies, divided as follows: broad strategies that set the stage for more specific interventions, behavioral change strategies, third-wave strategies, psychological strategies, and other strategies. It then continues to consider therapy formats, sequencing, and other issues in the implementation of these interventions.

Broad Strategies That Set the Stage for More Specific Interventions

Several broad sets of interventions set a frame for the use of more specific intervention strategies.

Guaranteeing Safety

Guaranteeing safety is not so much a treatment strategy as a wild card in the treatment of difficult divorce. Although it is different from the other strategies summarized here, guaranteeing safety is presented first here because, given the high actuarial level of relational violence in this population, first and foremost safety needs to be ensured (Rossi, Holtzworth-Munroe, & Rudd, 2016). For many of the highest risk families, legal measures, such as orders of protection may already be in place, and there may be only minimal opportunities for violence because there is minimal actual contact. However, where there are concerns about potential violence, these concerns must take precedence over other goals. Further, orders of protection don't fully protect; these orders only provide a mechanism for punishing people who violate such orders. As already noted, the time of divorce is among the highest risk times for relational violence in the life cycle.[2]

---

[2]As already noted, there also are many more false accusations of violence in difficult divorce than elsewhere. Thus, risk assessment is crucial. Nonetheless, whenever there are allegations of abuse, structuring in therapy should proceed with safety in prime focus. In instances of false accusations, this also serves the client accused, since it reduces their exposure to further allegations.

People who may be violent should only be brought together with other family members with great care. Sometimes therapists need to inform the court (which may at times have a high threshold for tolerating contact and make referrals that may not be appropriate) that conjoint therapy is contraindicated until various conditions are met and move the initial treatment format to individual sessions (i.e., those with the violent person will focus on anger management). When violence is less likely but remains a risk or a cue to traumatic memory, or where there is risk of harassment or angry outbursts before or after meetings, having clients arrive and depart at different times is necessary. In terms of the content of therapy, when there is special risk of relational violence, treatment begins with management of emotional regulation, de-escalation techniques, and anger management (discussed subsequently). Beyond attending to physical safety, certain family configurations may be psychologically injurious to some family members, and similar safety planning and work with them is needed as a prelude to conjoint meetings.[3]

It needs to be added here that, albeit rarely, a very few of those in difficult divorce can also become threatening to therapists. When such situations develop, therapists should assess the level of danger (some very angry people only give the appearance of something to fear and don't pose a threat) and whether there is danger consider terminating the therapy.

Witnessing

Witnessing consists of being an empathic listener with client(s) as they share their narratives and move through troubled times (Weingarten, 2010). In difficult divorce, it is an inevitable launching point for therapy, given how incredibly saturated family members are with their problems related to the divorce. These problems take up almost all the life space, and narratives are always filled with trauma. Having a place to speak about those feelings can be an entrée into developing a therapeutic alliance. Witnessing itself here, however, has little impact, save for helping build alliance. The frequency with which people in difficult divorce share their unprocessed feelings with others, coupled with thick defenses of those in difficult divorce, render simply creating space for speaking one's truth and feelings only minimally impactful. While in the witnessing mode, the therapist must also remain aware of the risk that the client may take silence and support in response to the presentation of a one-sided narrative about the sequences of events as a further justification for dysfunctional thoughts, emotion, and behavior.

---

[3]Especially in the context of psychological safety, the therapist must be able to distinguish what truly is damaging from what is experienced as damaging. The therapist works to minimize real threats while also helping family members distinguish between what they don't like and what is actually threatening.

Providing Psychoeducation

Psychoeducation about divorce, and about better and worse ways of divorcing, is a cornerstone intervention in divorce. Inaccurate information proliferates (fueled by divorce-related websites and blogs), most especially about normative feelings and behavior. This inaccurate information filtered through high emotional arousal, and carried through distorted cognitions, can then become a major ingredient in the process of systemic runaway featuring reciprocal patterns of problematic interaction. The information from psychoeducation can then be used in other intervention strategies (described subsequently) in providing a context for considering behavioral, cognitive, and emotional patterns (e.g., as objective data to place behavior in context).

One important focus for psychoeducation is on the range of feelings and behaviors that typify families going through divorce. As noted in earlier chapters, Hetherington (1999) succinctly described a core aspect of divorce for divorcing partners as being what she termed the "not-me" experience—the feeling that "I am not feeling or acting in the usual way I experience myself." Divorce and separation is a time of numerous overlapping changes. Beyond the ending of what is the core anchoring relationship in our culture, there also are changes in living arrangements, finances, daily routines, relationships with extended family (some of whom technically are no longer family), and innumerable other factors. Helping clients understand that such feelings of disequilibrium are typical and yet do, for most people, resolve over a period of 6 months to 2 years helps promote a sense of balance. So can helping clients understand that in such a period of high emotional arousal, it can be difficult to objectively view situations, especially in the context friends and family who provide supportive (and thereby perhaps provocative) feedback. It is difficult for clients to deal with their own distortions, but this becomes easier in the context of an enhanced, broader understanding of this life transition.

Closely related is helping clients develop a sense of how symmetrical escalation develops. Presenting a basic primer in this aspect of systems theory is helpful, accentuating how conflicts can escalate given certain responses, or not escalate given other responses. The clear message is that one person can make a major difference in difficult situations in how they go about dealing with it, even if that person is not able to fully resolve the problem.

Another important emphasis of psychoeducation centers on the typical reactions of children to divorce. Perhaps most crucial here is to help parents re-envision the common fear about inevitable damage inflicted on children by divorce. The take-home point is that children survive and thrive after divorce but can be thrown off course by precisely the kind of interactions that occur in difficult divorce. It is important to stress that children almost invariably have strong feelings and considerable pain about their parents' divorce and are vulnerable to the way parents deal with divorce. Psychoeducation can also help orient parents to the ways children feel and how to communicate about those feelings—feelings these parents often decode poorly. Additionally, psychoeducation can help parents better understand the likely short-term impact on their children of various events in divorce and orient them on how to monitor for the emergence of problems while remaining hopeful about children's resilience in the wake of this life stress.

The range of idiosyncratic concerns that parents bring to what they see as the "best interest of their children" can be astonishing. Small differences in the timing and frequency of contact (often hours or even minutes) or changes in routine can seem of great importance to parents and induce states that do not promote cooperation or negotiation. Psychoeducation that anchors parents in what is truly important for children (e.g., having a good relationship with each parent, avoiding triangulation, being able to develop their own lives without feeling they need to care too much for their parents) can help parents work toward how to be better parents. A central message to underscore is the harmful effects of family conflict or setting up triangles on children, as well as the importance of avoiding persistent, acrimonious conflict, especially those that include the children. A second key point for psychoeducation lies in the value of maintaining as much stability in the children's lives as possible. Considerable research has shown that multiple changes increase risk for children (Hetherington & Kelly, 2002). A plan for a stepwise process of absorbing change is preferable to having a child suddenly coping with a remarriage, a stepfamily and a new house and school. A third key point is about the need for structure, yet providing some room for flexibility. Both too fluid and too rigid expectations set the stage for conflict, especially given the challenge presented to both children and parents of the children living in the varying contexts of two homes. Additionally, for some parents, psychoeducation is needed about how to parent when deficits in parenting skills are due to lack of experience or other issues that can be addressed in therapy.

Another frequent focus of psychoeducation lies in helping parents understand how to talk to their children about the divorce. In the context of most difficult divorce, this psychoeducation centers less on presenting the ideal script for such sharing and more on how to correct errors already made in earlier conversations. First on this list are the destructive effects of inappropriate sharing with children about the divorce and either directly involving or inducing children to become involved in the fray. Second, parents in difficult divorce often fail to recognize that children process divorce through the lens of their developing understanding. Therefore, it is valuable to help parents understand ways of talking with their children that may best speak to the age and particular characteristics of their children. Third, it also helps to emphasize the ways children decode various messages and the sorts of messages that help to steady them. For example, children often tend to blame themselves for their parents' divorce, especially in families in which there is much fighting about them. An antidote lies in reassuring children, explicitly and often, that the parents are not divorcing because of them. Children also fear that divorce will mean drastic and awful changes in their own lives, and perhaps in their connection to one or both of their parents. In difficult divorce, it is easy for the message to be conveyed that catastrophe is around the corner. Parents should thus provide reassurance that, although there will be changes, life will go on. Somewhat paradoxically, it is also important in some families to help parents who downplay such concerns to understand that children tend to become upset about parents' too-strong assurances that life is not changing. Such messages minimize the disruption that is occurring and fly in the face of the obvious understanding that close relationships and other aspects of life are in the process of evolving. The best communication between parents and children both empathizes and reassures. There are terrific books here to consult written for all divorcing families about how to best talk to children (and more broadly about parenting in divorce), such as those by Emery (2004), Pedro-Carroll (2010), and Hetherington and Kelly (2002). Certainly, the expectation here is not that such psychoeducation will lead to sudden transformation in parenting, but instead to lay the groundwork for better communication with children to be explored further as therapy moves forward.

Another focus of psychoeducation centers on typical feelings that partners have toward soon-to-be former partners. Divorce is unique among human challenges: to disconnect from the person, still living, to whom one formed (at least at one time) a primary bond. Feelings such as anger and contempt are helpful in this radical act of excising such a core attachment, yet such feelings, especially when accompanied by hostile actions, readily lead to a symmetrical sequence of escalating conflict that is bad for everyone. Thus, therapy in difficult divorce should support the exploration of feelings (in an appropriate format for such exploration, most likely in individual sessions), yet also uncover ways for clients to manage these feelings.

Psychoeducation also has great importance in work directly with children in therapy. Typically, children have nowhere to learn about divorce other than from their parents (who in difficult divorce probably haven't offered the most useful messages), peers (who may not know much either), or the Internet (where finding the distress-producing sites is easier than the useful ones). Messages that suggest strong feelings are normal, that sadness often underlies anger in these situations, and that both the child and his or her parents will recover if they can follow a certain path are helpful. For young children, illustrated books, such as *Dinosaurs Divorce, Two Homes*, or *My Mom and Dad Don't Live Together Anymore* that carry useful information about coping are a wonderful adjunct to therapy (L. K. Brown & Brown, 1986; Masurel & Denton, 2001; Rubin, 2002).

The key question about psychoeducation is not its place in this work but how to deliver it in a way that it might have some effect on these clients. This is crucial information to absorb, but many of those in difficult divorce do not or cannot attend to it. Those adults who are in the legal system have probably been told many times about deleterious effects of difficult divorce, especially on children. Indeed, some involved in intense legal processes repeatedly hear the same lecture from judges about the "best interest of their children." This is a classic example of clients in the precontemplation stage of change who are distracted by many other factors and tuning out relevant information. Furthermore, good psychoeducation in these cases often touches on issues about which clients may be highly reactive.

The answer is not about looking to create a precise moment of miraculous recognition, but instead an evolving process of opening clients to relevant information. Some of this lies in finding the right way to share information. It is better to share information in digestible doses and move back to specific psychoeducation when it becomes relevant in therapy (and when other intervention strategies such as Socratic questioning can be paired with psychoeducation). It is also essential to remain aware of possibilities for triangulation of the therapist. For example, presenting the sort of information discussed in this section may be very political in the context of bad behavior on the part of one parent. The material needs to be presented, but the format and how it is presented matters. Some psychoeducation is best reserved for individual meetings that do not serve to triangulate before moving discussions of a topic into the conjoint format.

Stories about similar families and how they have succeeded or failed often engage clients. So can pointing to sequences in the family where good intentions lead to bad results, mirroring properties in other troubled families. Finding engaging media, such as films that demonstrate good and pathogenic patterns, helps as well.[4] It is usually fairly obvious who is taking in information and who is not. For those for whom the information does not seem to be processed, the therapist needs to look for different ways to present it, engage motivational interviewing (described later in the chapter), or begin to assess where the blocks are to incorporating this information into individual meetings.

---

[4]*Kramer vs. Kramer, The Squid and the Whale, Blue Valentine*, and the *War of the Roses* are all moving and provocative stimuli for conversation for adults, as is *Don't Divorce Me* for children.

Maintaining a Solution-Oriented Focus

Families in difficult divorce are caught up in problematic sequences in which feelings are strong and fault-finding is constant. One remedy for this lies in adopting a solution-oriented focus. Best represented in solution-oriented therapy (De Shazer, 1982, 1985), such a focus continually moves attention from dwelling on problems to considering possible solutions. To do this, the therapist first explicitly describes the value of concentrating on solutions and then actively and persistently intervenes in ways that recast problem statements into possibilities for working toward possible solutions. Drawing on strategies from cognitive and narrative therapies (discussed subsequently), the therapist reframes statements about problems in forms that are less provocative and that can be addressed through action. For example, when one former partner obsessively centers on the other's behavior (an almost constant in difficult divorce), the therapist refocuses attention onto what might be done to mitigate those concerns or how to better live with them in a way that is less damaging. Often this involves explicitly refocusing attention from past complaints and the losses that have occurred in the divorce to what might be done to make life work as well as it can under the present circumstances or to determining possibilities for the best, most positive future.

Each time problem language is encountered, the therapist reframes the problem as a target for potential solution. Thus, for example, a statement such as "He is always out of control" is followed by an effort to shape some question, in relation to that perspective, that might lead to some useful action. The therapist might ask, "How might we work toward there being fewer angry outbursts?" or "How might you find a way to not have it effect everyone as much when he gets angry?" In delivering this treatment strategy, it is essential for therapists to keep their attention on impact over the long run, rather than expecting such a simple attempt to refocus will result in the client successfully altering his or schema or lead to a quick and easy resolution. The best of clients in difficult divorce continually—directly or indirectly—keep returning to a problem focus, with the problem usually being the "other." The therapist introduces the idea of looking to solutions and persists in returning to that idea, session after session. In the context of a steady, purposeful, empathic redirecting of focus, clients can move over time toward more useful pathways to change.

> Already well versed in the legal process after a year of meetings with lawyers and a child custody evaluation, Travis and Emily, and their teenaged children, Maxine and Mario, came into meetings with a litany of complaints about each another. Mario and Maxine, following their father, complained about Emily's returning to work and having too many rules at home. Travis complained about Emily's decision to divorce him, and

Emily complained about Mario's drinking to excess and undermining her parenting. Although acknowledging these complaints and working to resolve some of them, the therapist continually reframed such complaints in terms of what might be done to help or cope with the problem rather than simply reiterate complaints. For example, she worked with Emily and the children to establish agreed-on rules in her home and for there to be clear expectations what would happen if rules were followed or not followed. Slowly, the therapist was able to move through the key issues in this family, one at a time, bringing a frame of solving problems. Family members never stopped complaining about each another, but a sense of being able to cope and solve problems developed.

It is important to note that there are exceptions to bringing a solution-oriented focus to difficult divorces. In those rare circumstances in which there is very real danger or no intervention is likely to help, other frameworks are needed, such as coping as best as possible or simply relying on the court to establish boundaries through supervision or orders of protection.

Orienting to Client State of Change and Motivational Interviewing

Given the massive issues in terms of motivation in almost everyone involved in difficult divorce, orienting, adapting, and working with the stage of change of clients is a necessary second overarching strategy in working with these clients. Clients in difficult divorce largely begin in precontemplation about their own potential role in problem resolution. In a striking variation on the concept of stages of change, they do see problems but have no understanding whatsoever in their role in the problems or that they might be able to have some role in resolving those problems.

Prochaska and colleagues have written extensively about recognizing and working with clients at various stages of change and helping them move through a sequence from precontemplation, where they don't see problems; through contemplation, where they see problems but are not ready to do anything about them; to action, where they are actively ready to work at problems; to maintenance, where the task becomes maintaining the changes gained when in the action stage (J. M. Prochaska & Prochaska, 2014). Toward this end, they highlight the need to adapt treatment to the clients' stage of change and to concentrate on helping clients move one stage of change at a time. In difficult divorce, the focus early in therapy, for most clients, needs to be on moving from precontemplation, in which they cannot see their role in problems, to contemplation, where they at least recognize a potential role for themselves in problem resolution.

Techniques from motivational interviewing are immeasurably helpful in working with clients in precontemplation to help them notice problems and to weigh the pros and cons of working at them (W. R. Miller & Rollnick,

1991). These are methods that, after establishing empathic connection, look for ways to engage the client's own motivation. Motivational interviewing techniques include inviting clients to consider the differences between their values and their behavior, examining their views of what the future will be like if things continue as they are, and questioning whether there might be value in not changing. Later in therapy, it is similarly beneficial to concentrate on helping clients move one step from contemplation to action and from action to maintenance.

> Margarita became enormously depressed when her husband, Pedro, filed for divorce. She sat home, letting her teenaged children do whatever they wanted and rarely leaving her room. Pedro cited her depression as a reason that he should be the principal parent to the children. At the beginning of therapy with this family, Margarita was unable to see any problem in her parenting, mostly defending herself against Pedro's attacks, and attacking Pedro for his undermining behavior. In a series of sessions with Margarita alone, Martin, the therapist, posed several motivational interviewing questions: "What's the best thing that might happen if you changed this?" "If you do change, how might your life be different?" "Is there a downside to changing this?" "What might happen if you don't change?" In this way, Martin was able to help Margarita experience that there might be some benefit to herself in explicitly acknowledging her depression and that her stonewalling this accusation seemed to be enabling Pedro's position rather than helping her in her legal process. Once she acknowledged this, Margarita entered separate therapy with a different therapist for her depression and was then able to establish a much better working relationship with her children.

Behavior Change Strategies

Several strategies involve direct efforts focused on behavior change. These have origins in a range of theoretical orientations, but all attend to changing behavioral patterns.

Behavioral Strategies

Behavioral strategies are among the most evidence-based interventions in psychotherapy (Dattilio & Epstein, 2016). Drawing on principles from classical conditioning, operant conditioning, and social learning theory, therapists help structure family contingencies to shape behavior toward treatment goals. One crucial set of interventions drawn from classical conditioning is based in the principle of exposure: Anxieties and fears are overcome most expediently simply by exposing clients to feared stimuli under the right conditions. Operant conditioning paradigms use reinforcements, both positive and negative, to shape behavior toward positive goals. Social learning interventions build on operant conditions that use modeling, vicarious learning, and principles of exchange to shape more effective and constructive behavior. All the behavioral strategies, when effective, also lead to the increased possibility of more positive exchange and cycles of behavior moving toward problem solution rather than problem maintenance.

These strategies are applicable in multiple ways in therapy for difficult divorce. In terms of classical conditioning, repeated exposure, paired with negative experiences, has left many in these families with conditioned fight-or-flight responses. This may be true of two former partners with each other or of children with one or both parents. Providing opportunities to have more positive experiences and reducing negative experiences, if this can be successfully executed, may promote reconditioning of expected responses at the level of neural pathways. One strategy in families with this kind of problem is to create exposures that initiate a different sort of relationship (e.g., finding a way to have highly conflicted former partners enjoy a moment together about some shared interest). However, bear in mind that if the exposures simply result in fearful or otherwise unpleasant experiences, the conditioning will further deepen, so these exposures must be carefully structured (and be safe, not retraumatizing).

> Four-year-old Timmy was very fearful of his father, with whom he had spent almost no time. His mother and father had been in a dispute over father's access to Timmy since his birth. As part of a multicomponent treatment of this fear, Timmy and his father spent sessions with the therapist playing and getting to know one another. As his father turned out not to be scary, Timmy settled into enjoying time with him. After a few meetings, the contact was moved to sessions held outside the therapist's office, and then extended to meetings without the therapist, providing opportunities for Timmy to alter the conditioning that had occurred.

There also are numerous places where therapists can help invoke operant conditioning and social learning that moves in a positive direction in difficult divorce. People in these families are often in processes of punishing one another for their behavior and participate in cycles of exchange in which one negative behavior begets another. Therapy can help clients become more aware of these cycles and experiment with seeing whether they can be altered. It often takes perseverance to develop a new, improved behavior when such cycles are in place, given the expectation (like a mouse in a Skinner box) that punishment awaits. The therapist's encouragement can help shape better exchanges, particularly if one client can engage in the experiment with enough perseverance to continue positive behavior even in the wake of some negative feedback.

In difficult divorce, parenting practices also are often fragile. For many of these parents, good parenting practices never developed, providing some of the impetus for the concern many express about how their former partner interacts with the children. For others, authoritative parenting practices—especially monitoring, predictable contingencies, and parental warmth—have been lost in the chaos of the transition to divorce (Hetherington & Kelly, 2002). Therefore, in many families, helping parents create a sense of reliable monitoring and rules, with dependable reinforcements in relation to those rules, becomes a crucial step toward cooperation (A. Kazdin & Rotella, 2013). Establishing a good enough set of working parenting practices in each household can calm arguments and provide a basis for discussions of visions of coparenting. How much parenting practices will be the same or different across households in this context can then become a matter of negotiation, rather than a trigger for fault-finding. In this, as in other elements of social learning, teaching and modeling good parenting practices is sometimes a necessary first step to practicing.

> After a dispute with the mother of his teenage son, Dmitri developed a very laissez-faire style of parenting. He would leave his son for extended periods of time, not monitor him, and then become angry because his son rarely completed his homework. This led to further conflict with mother, who ran a tight ship in her home. Using motivational interviewing, the therapist succeeded in getting Dmitri's buy-in to try out his own version of a more authoritative parenting style. The therapist modeled these behaviors, had Dmitri read a parenting book focused on contingencies, and then Dmitri practiced them in conjoint sessions with his son and at home. Dmitri succeeded in improving his parenting skill. After a period that included a few errors on Dmitri's part and a few misunderstandings about what had occurred on mother's part (changes in belief on the part of ex-partners about such behaviors in difficult divorce rarely come easily), one source of conflict with mother was mitigated.

Those in difficult divorce readily all become trapped in endless exchanges about the divorce and its vicissitudes. Helping each client enact a behavioral plan for developing their life outside the family drama is often beneficial in reducing the intensity of these negative interactions. Sometimes, like Occam's razor, such a development in a particularly vulnerable party can have remarkable effects on the interaction.

Systemic Strategies

Sometimes behavioral strategies need to be extended to a comprehensive effort to alter family structure. Again, distressed divorce often features family units that have been arrested in moving to new (typically single-parent) family structures and identifying what role coparenting will play in those structures. Intervention that directly targets and moves toward establishing more functional boundaries, alliances, and the distribution of power (the key elements in family structure) prepares the new family units to be more functional in the present and into the future. This involves identifying structural problems, such as too rigid or too flexible boundaries between parents and children or between parents, dominant child–parent alliances, or one individual holding too much power. Efforts are then directed to sharing this view of family structure with family members and working directly and through motivational interviewing to see whether there can be buy-in toward the goal of improving the family structure. The hard work follows of seeing whether there is some version of functional structure with which family members can experiment. If ideal constellations are not possible, can the family at least move to a place in which, for example, exaggerated parent–child coalitions are replaced by parallel parenting across households in which children have appropriate roles? Changes in family structure are difficult to achieve, and thus, these are changes that come only with an iterative process of problem identification, noticing consequences of the problem, and trial and error around experimentation over time.

> Hugo was a very dominant father in the nuclear family. His wife, Suzanne, and their three children looked to his approval for every decision made, whether trivial or important. After Hugo and Suzanne separated, Hugo looked to maintain this level of power and decision-making authority, in both his home and Suzanne's. This led to a great deal of conflict and anger on everyone's part, including Hugo's because he no longer had the authority he enjoyed in the past. The therapist directly suggested to the parents that they needed to take leadership in deciding what the new family organization would look like and provided psychoeducation about how families like theirs make such changes. In individual meetings, the therapist helped Hugo consider not only how his attempt to maintain decision-making authority wasn't functional anymore, but also how it was resulting in a pattern of Suzanne coming out ahead in every dispute in court. With that feedback and other motivational interviewing, Hugo came to realize that it was futile for him to try to make all decisions in the family. In meetings with each parent and the children, and with the two parents together, a new plan evolved in which each parent was in charge of his or her own household, although the parents agreed that Hugo would continue to manage Suzanne's investments.

Establishing Reliable, Rule-Driven Methods of Communication and Good-Enough Coordination

As families go through divorce, ground rules change. There are many essential matters to be negotiated. Expectations need to evolve about many aspects of life, including financial responsibilities, time together, and coparenting. Communication is the vehicle for such negotiation, but the level and type of communication itself must be negotiated.

For childless couples who do not fall within the group Ahrons called Perfect Pals (Ahrons & Rodgers, 1987), the task is simpler. Poor communication patterns and conflict are typically replaced by no communication, and partners disengage. However, when couples have children and both parents choose to continue to be involved as parents, a vehicle for communication between former partners needs to evolve that can work well enough to allow for sufficient cooperation to adequately support children in their lives. In more typical divorce, this may simply involve trying out possible formats for communicating and finding what works best. However, in more difficult divorce, finding good enough communication is a challenge, and a crucial task becomes creating reliable, safe, and agreed-on methods of communication and coordination.

The most realistic goal in difficult divorces is that the two households will function independently, with only minimal communication and coordination except in circumstances that necessitate interaction. In particular, where there is high conflict, more contact typically makes for greater problems. Ordinary notions of processing easily degenerate into arguments, explosions, or nonverbal expressions of contempt. Here, it is useful to teach and practice a variation of the familiar speaker–listener technique, involving only a few crisply delivered, rule-governed exchanges (Diamond & Lebow, 2016; Stanley, Markman, Blumberg, & Eckstein, 1997). This technique helps ex-partners hear each other and stay on track rather than digress into argument. The therapist will instruct the first speaker to focus on one issue related to only one specific topic. The speaker will speak directly on this topic without switching to other topics or prematurely attempting to problem-solve. This is done in briskly delivered, short speech turns so that the listener can understand the message at hand. The therapist can stop the speaker if something is unclear or if the speaker goes off task. The listener's role is to listen without interrupting and then to paraphrase what the speaker says without including personal thoughts or explanations. Once the listener paraphrases what was said, the roles are switched.

Discussion of communication in therapy also explores various modes of communication, such as text, e-mail, mail, and phone contact, to find the ways that are least likely to result in problems. Typically, in difficult divorce, written forms of communication, such as texts or e-mails, are preferable because they are more easily managed in terms of affect, require minimal contact, and present trace materials that can be looked at if there is controversy. Hosted communication sites for divorced parents, such as the apps Our Family Wizard (http://www.ourfamilywizard.com) or Two Happy Homes (http://www.twohappyhomes.com), provide a highly structured venue for such communication, including a shared children's schedule and a channel for sharing information. Such communication also can easily be monitored with the agreement of the parents. The therapist can use these samples of communication to provide feedback, teach how to skillfully work in the format, and explore what interferes with this process when there are problems in this special kind of communication training. The downside of such written methods also lies in the trace material available. Those deep in litigation readily pass on endless e-mails and texts to their attorneys to become part of their cases, undermining any sense of safety in the process of communication. For those who have had their prior written communications used against them, establishing trust around the future uses of written communication is by necessity a slow, evolving process that begins with setting ground rules and follows up with maintenance of those ground rules.

Ideas about when and under what circumstances to communicate also often need to be negotiated, particularly when parents have very different ideas about these matters (e.g., one parent wants to be informed whenever children have a cold; the other sets the bar at going to a hospital). Whatever has been decided in sessions about communication is practiced in homework. In session follow-up looks to build on what works and to learn from what doesn't.

When differences between households present special difficulties (e.g., about radical differences in family rules), or when children present with issues that render coordination imperative (as in childhood diabetes or attention-deficit disorder, for example), more communication may be needed, but the therapist still aims to create just enough coordination for children to go on with their lives successfully. It is often best in these families to leave processing of larger differences to meetings with the therapist about the specific matter.

Sometimes families improve in these abilities over time. Difficult divorce can be a time-limited problem, but for many families, problems in communication extend forever. For those families, having a place to return to over time where they can discuss larger differences is prudent.

> Melba and Rick were a couple who argued often and vigorously. These exchanges were a downward spiral that culminated in Rick screaming and slamming doors. Even text exchanges could wind up in vicious attacks. Therefore, after Melba filed for divorce, she shut down all communication with Rick. This left them with no mechanism to exchange information about what was happening with their children or decisions that needed to be made, such as which weeks they would choose for summer vacation or whether to have their son see a tutor.
>
> In conjoint therapy sessions, Melba and Rick were taught and practiced rule-governed exchanges. After practicing this mode of communication in the office over several sessions, it was extended as an experiment to text exchanges between them and monitored by the therapist. They then moved on to try OurFamilyWizard again, which Melba had initially refused to do when this was proposed by the attorney for the children.

Initially, OurFamilyWizard, and the discussions around it, were a disaster, as Rick obsessively completed his part while Melba sporadically completed hers, leading to hostile criticism from Rick. However, the therapist proposed completing a pared down version of schedule information in sessions, with a parallel focus on remaining calm and respectful. In this way, they slowly developed a just good-enough level of communicating.

Negotiation and Problem-Solving

Negotiation is the central intervention in divorce mediation, but it is also a crucial ingredient in divorce therapies. The challenges in negotiation in difficult divorce are clear. Partners, who often have not negotiated well in marriage, are now called upon in the context of a stressful, highly emotional transition to settle many issues, some of great import, such as dividing time with children.

Mediators use a highly structured process for negotiation between partners (Emery, 2012). Negotiation in therapy mirrors many of the same processes in mediation. The therapist collaborates with the clients to list the issues that need to be discussed and creates dialogue about the partners' positions in a context of fairness and balance. The therapist alternates time with both partners together, and with each individual when an impasse appears. During the individual work, the therapist also provides clear feedback to each client about how reasonable his or her position is, what the norms are about the specific issue, and how a court might regard the specific difference. A calm and positive frame is brought to negotiation.

Yet there are some differences between mediation and negotiation in therapy. Given therapy's broader mandate, more time can be devoted to enhancing the skill of negotiation of the partners than in mediation, allowing for the creation of a process that can last into the future. There also is greater opportunity to explore blocks to resolution using other strategies in psychotherapy (e.g., exploring underlying psychodynamics, cognitions, and emotion), rather than simply keeping the behavioral exchange at the fore. Also, at times, the negotiation may be between a parent and children, rather than simply between parents. Yet mediation is also simpler and more straightforward in having a set agenda for what needs to be negotiated that, when completed, ends the mediation in most cases. Learning this skill in therapy can be more challenging than simply reaching an accommodation to a set of issues in mediation.

Denise and Monte had arrived at a plan to have the children spend 2 weeks with each parent during the summer. Given that they had a difficult divorce, they even had it written into their joint parenting agreement who had first choice each year for vacation weeks. However, when they reached the first year that one of the children would go to summer camp, they also needed to decide when camp would occur in relation to their respective vacation weeks. Denise, who had first choice that year, asked for the weeks that would cause Monte to be unable to take his 2 weeks consecutively. Monte objected. The court, having heard from them previously about a series of similar problems in coparenting, referred them for therapy. The initial phase of the therapy focused on self-regulation (discussed subsequently) and practice of the rule-governed speaker–listener technique. Using these skills in the context of this issue, the two were able to clearly state their positions and, with help of the therapist, hear the position of the other. Monte seemed willing to compromise, but Denise remained rigid.

During individual meetings with each client, Denise's old sense of powerless and rage with Monte emerged. Fortunately, she was willing to explore this, and with the therapist was able to speak to her rage over many years of having felt like she was under the control of his obsessive ways. The therapist then was able to help her differentiate between what might actually be in her own best interest and the children's (who would benefit from a long-term cooperative relationship) and identify what affectively engaged her (Monte's personality and her past trauma with him). She then was willing to agree to a plan, as long as a principle was established in it that would also apply for her in future years and if there was a process that would ensure that principle would be followed. The ex-partners then were able to reach an agreement on this issue.

Third-Wave Strategies

Third-wave strategies, such as mindfulness and acceptance, now occupy a prominent place in the world of psychotherapy (Hayes, 2016). These strategies have special value in the context of difficult divorce, helping soothe dysregulation and working with behaviors in family members that look as if they cannot change. They are also especially helpful in protracted legal divorces, where specific coping skills are required to avoid falling prey to an interpersonal cascade that often includes attack and defense over long periods of time in court wrangling.

Mindful Practice

Like those with borderline personality disorder, those in difficult divorce (whether or not they have a personality disorder) benefit from mindful practice (J. Kabat-Zinn, 2012, 2013; M. Kabat-Zinn & Kabat-Zinn, 2014).[5] These

---

[5] Although this section focuses on mindful practice, other similar methods such as relaxation training (Hazlett-Stevens & Craske, 2009) can be similarly helpful.

methods help with several frequent key targets in difficult divorce: calming self, self-soothing, and anger management. Mindful practice also lays the foundation for more effective application of other helpful skill sets in difficult divorce, such as communication and cognitive self-examination. It further is central in helping clients move toward acceptance of what can't be changed (which in difficult divorce begins with the therapist helping the client understand what can and can't be changed; these clients are typically poor judges about this distinction).

Mindful practice has the advantage of being disseminated in many venues, at least in a basic form. Therefore, with a brief introduction in a therapy session, it can often be usefully fostered by attending a few classes outside of therapy or by following the procedures on an app. The work in therapy involving mindful practice emphasizes learning to remain mindful in a state-dependent framework in the context of relational upset. Many yoga instructors and longtime meditators lose their mindfulness in the context of difficult divorce.

> Divorce in the Newcomb family was particularly stressful for everyone. The parents argued with one another a great deal, as did each parent with the children and the children with each other. In beginning work with each unit in the family, the therapist introduced a mindful calming exercise. She followed up with a short mindful moment each session and prompting family members to pursue mindfulness in various ways (e.g., yoga and using mindfulness apps). Most did, and this small intervention added considerably to the ability of several family members to remain calm and mindful in the midst of the stresses of the divorce. Given that those family members engaged less in fruitless tactics when arguments were initiated, the overall level of conflict in the family decreased.

Disengagement Skills and Anger Management

In high-conflict situations, the ability to disengage is as important as the ability to engage. Given the powerful underlying affects in these families, coupled with personality traits that cause individuals to be prone to rage, sequences of small disagreements that lead to affective discharge and angry outbursts are common. The effect of such patterns is pernicious. Not only do they end constructive conversation, they also contain the sort of pathogenic toxin that potentiates the chances for the emergence of other deleterious effects, such as psychopathology in children.

Thus, anger management skills training is a crucial strategy in high-conflict divorce (Karam & Lebow, 2006; Reilly & Shopshire, 2015). Clients are taught and then practice how to respectfully disengage from conflict, which includes ways of responding to challenging behaviors and statements, as well as selective and appropriate (as opposed to provocative) use of taking time-outs that pause the conflict. This work on anger management also often involves learning to understand the meaning of and control indirect forms of provocation such as passive-aggressive action, as well as the more obvious angry outbursts.

Although occasionally angry outbursts in difficult divorce exclusively have to do with the self-regulation of a single individual, far more often, these dances of anger involve multiple individuals each having a role (Lerner, 2005). It is far easier to work with these issues in the context of all parties working on their behaviors in the specific sequences leading to angry outbursts. Angry outbursts often follow provocative quiet statements that may be judgmental, guilt-inducing, or present one person's selective punctuation of a problem. Assessment very much informs this work, in terms of following the sequences leading up to angry outbursts, to evaluate the role of each person in the conflict. Even if one person seems wholly the source of the angry outburst (e.g., in mishearing and being dysregulated), there remains much to be said for identifying tasks for the others when such an outburst occurs.

However, it also is essential for the person or persons who are most subject to angry outbursts and other manifestations of aggressive behavior to complete a module of anger management in some individual format. Those with such anger problems in difficult divorce typically require considerable work to master these tendencies in the context of the sorts of easily provocative issues that appear in difficult divorce. Because anger issues often arise in conjoint meetings in those vulnerable to these problems, there typically are many opportunities for in-session practice of these coping skills, which can be paired with a suggestion to practice these skills the next time conflict arises out of session.

> Olga and Gregory were a couple who argued regularly. Their neighbors would often have no trouble hearing every detail of their arguments. When Gregory filed for divorce, the heated arguments escalated and came to occur frequently at exchanges of the children and school events. At the beginning of therapy, the therapist, with the help of the attorney for the children, began with strategies for minimizing contact, such as reconfiguring exchanges of the children in ways that meant they had no contact (e.g., the picking-up parent staying in the car; exchanges happening at the beginning and end of school). Having established this as a helpful way of reducing conflict, the therapist moved to work with Olga and Gregory in alternating individual sessions focused exclusively on anger management. Both were taught to track their emotional activation (e.g., by noticing heartbeat and other indications), so that each could become more self-aware of how their anger developed. Mindful practice and relaxation exercises were introduced, first to learn these

methods, and subsequently to be able to use them during energizing situations. Both were helped to use their self-monitoring to learn how to remove themselves from situations in which there was a high likelihood of exploding before such a discharge occurred. Self-talk from cognitive therapy was also introduced to help with self-regulation.

Having some success with each with these methods, the therapist began meetings with Olga and Gregory in which the first target was forming agreements to work together to reduce the angry outbursts. Although in these meetings each quickly fell back into blaming the other, the therapist was able to refocus on practicing anger management. When an angry exchange began, the therapist declared a time-out and worked with each partner individually to use their skill sets to become more settled. After several weeks of these meetings, the frequency of angry conflicts decreased considerably.

Radical Acceptance

Difficult divorce often presents the ultimate in family members trying to control the uncontrollable, whether it is the wish to not be divorced or that one's former partner would behave differently. Although, appropriately, there is much emphasis in working on that which needs to change, much of what is found most objectionable in families in difficult divorce cannot be changed. Life has developed in a way that was far removed from earlier life plans, damaging behaviors have occurred, and family members are witness to the damage that has already occurred. Further, the act of trying to control the uncontrollable inevitably leads to internal frustration and external conflict. Therefore, strategies that concentrate on radical acceptance, using techniques from acceptance and commitment therapy (Hayes, Strosahl, & Wilson, 2012) and integrative behavior couple therapy (Christensen, Dimidjian, & Martell, 2015) toward the end of living with that which cannot be changed (while changing the changeable) is a perfect match with many of the situations in difficult divorce.

Psychological Strategies

Cognitive, emotion-focused, and psychoanalytic strategies concentrate on thoughts and emotions in ways that are highly useful in difficult divorce.

Cognitive Strategies

Cognitions have an important role in relational functioning. Particularly relevant in difficult divorce are negative attributions about others, in which one family member interprets the actions of another in the worst possible way. Negative sentiment override is frequently dominant (M. W. Hawkins, Carrere, & Gottman, 2002), resulting in the reinterpretation in a negative light of even the best intended behaviors. Thus, family members often readily assign the most negative possible meaning to the another's behavior. Actions are also typically viewed as intentional, indicative of a personal defect, and the product of the other's internal locus of control.

Most benignly, in more typical divorce, such attributions help create distance, reaffirm the positive meaning of ending the relationship, and mitigate a sense of loss. However, in difficult divorce, such cognitions become an essential aspect of intractable conflict. Each person comes to view most of another's actions through a negative filter. Thus, problematic actions by one parent are invariably viewed as evidence of character flaws or hostility, whereas constructive behavior is seen as transitory, disingenuous, or manipulative. For example, a mother, faced with evidence that her separated spouse had become abstinent in the use of alcohol and a faithful attendee of Alcoholics Anonymous, attributed these changes to his desire to win his court case, and remained convinced that the alcoholic behavior would return as soon as the court proceeding was completed. Children, extended family, and friends in high-conflict cases also often easily become caught up in similar patterns of selective attribution (Johnston & Campbell, 1986).

Strategies from cognitive (J. S. Beck, 2011), rational-emotive (Ellis, 1962), and narrative therapies (Freedman & Combs, 2015) specifically target such problematic attributions, as well as related thoughts that extend well beyond any factual basis and act to energize conflict. Challenging beliefs and comparing those beliefs to the relevant available evidence, creating new narratives that emphasize a more positive view of the family situation, and testing the evidence for attributions provide antidotes to such cognitions that engender difficulty. An active style in challenging such beliefs is usually required in difficult divorce. Homework involving thought records that compare thoughts to the more objective evidence for the validity of the thoughts supplements practice in sessions.

> Kenji and Miyoko are in the midst of a difficult divorce. Miyoko complains that it must be that Kenji is handling things badly with the children because every time she picks up the children, from their father's home, they are upset. Ann, their therapist, in meeting individually with Miyoko, works through a thought record that examines Ann's beliefs about Kenji as a parent. In that process, they examine the evidence that Kenji is not providing a good environment for the children. When Miyoko considers what she sees of his recent parenting, she says that he does seem to relate with them well enough and manage the children adequately when in her presence. She also concedes that she sees progress on his part from the work Kenji is doing with Ann about parenting skills. However, she remains convinced there must be a problem because

of how the children act when they return home and what they say to her about their time with their father.

Ann asks Miyoko to consider that there may be other possible sources for the children's distress and points to the commonplace problem that young children, until they are well into a new routine, have powerful feelings about separation and the new environment in the home of the parent with whom they spend less time. In completing a thought record in relation to this together, Miyoko continues to express complaints at Kenji but is able to consider the possibility that it may be other factors, such as the children's strong affection for their mother, that might be resulting in their upset at transitions. Over time, as Kenji shows responsible parenting behavior, and as Miyoko continues to examine her thoughts about Kenji through thought records, she is able to shift into a more neutral view of him as a parent.

Especially in a context away from the other parent, where such examination is less likely to promote a sense of defensiveness, the generation of similar thought records and the use of Socratic questioning in relation to the basis for beliefs can help family members extract themselves from rigid dysfunctional attributions (J. S. Beck, 2011). The therapist can further challenge the core dysfunctional schemas that can pervade life in this family (e.g., "We are ruined," "Divorce will inevitably permanently damage our children," "There is no life after") by framing new, larger narratives that are more positive and resilient (e.g., "We are going through what has to be a rocky process of establishing two separate households, but this challenging time will pass"). Troublesome schemas most often underlie specific dysfunctional cognitions (Young, 1990; Young, Klosko, & Weishaar, 2003). Specific dysfunctional thoughts in difficult divorce are hard to change, and underlying schemas even harder, given the frequent appearance of "proof" that a dysfunctional schema actually has some basis in reality (as might occur if Kenji left the children alone for an afternoon on his parenting time). Challenging dysfunctional cognitions and schemas is a process, one that requires work over time and parallel work to ensure that catastrophic behaviors do not occur that undo the work done.

Bear in mind, as stated several times in this book, that moving clients to more positive reattribution is not therapeutic in circumstances when the negative attribution accurately reflects the facts, such as when the parent about whom the attribution is made continues to present danger to children. In that case, the focus must first center on that parent becoming more appropriate in his or her behavior.

Exploring Underlying Emotion

Family members in divorce typically feel traumatized and injured. Therapy can be a safe place to share such strong feelings. This is a way therapy is often helpful in divorce. Clients are hurt; they share their pain and feel heard; the therapist helps the client get in touch with underlying emotion that can not only help heal, but also make for personal growth.

Such sharing can have considerable benefit, particularly in individual meetings with the therapist. For example, when an ex-partner is leaving for another relationship, the "left" partner often feels relieved and supported when sharing feelings that are witnessed by the therapist. Similarly, when old powerful emotion is a factor, being able to engage with that emotion with the therapist and identify the underlying deeper emotion (as when dealing with a sense of abandonment from childhood) can allow for a block to be ameliorated (L. S. Greenberg, 2017).

In more functional divorces, the sharing of emotion in conjoint meetings also can be beneficial. For partners who have not been able to express their feelings about divorce, such expression may be a key event in working through those feelings. Some parting couples can even connect around their shared sense of sadness.

However, the sharing of deep feeling in difficult divorce among family members is punctuated by a sign that says "danger." By the time these clients come to therapy, there has been a long series of injuries, in most instances, moving in all directions. Clients are highly sensitive to the expression of feelings by others. The Four Horseman described by John Gottman (1999) as signs of relationship dysfunction—criticism, defensiveness, contempt, and stonewalling—are now fully on display in these couples. Added to this are high doses of belligerence, rage, martyrdom, and passive-aggression. Therefore, catharsis in these families in the conjoint context is likely to be unhelpful and damaging to any sense of progress. In difficult divorce, such feelings typically have already been expressed many times over and often devolve into increased conflict and despair.

Therefore, the sharing of affect between those who have trouble with one another in these families in therapy must be carefully managed. In such families, exploration of deep feeling is better reserved for separate, individual sessions where the agenda, at least in part, is to express, understand, and work through feelings of hurt and anger. As such feelings appear, typically the therapist does best to refocus, manage the feeling in the moment, and set individual meetings to follow up and work with what underlies. Techniques such as those used in individual emotion-focused therapy (L. S. Greenberg, 2017) for accessing underlying emotion lying behind the emotional patterns presenting, or Bowen (1978) therapy coaching in which the therapist helps access underlying feelings and then helps the client differentiate from the aspects of the feeling fused to family-of-origin issues, can be useful in helping clients move out of dysfunctional emotional processes.

Leona would often rage at Quentin during the divorce process. The inter-actions were striking. Although Leona was the one who had moved for the divorce, she would become dysregulated in Quentin's presence about minor grievances with him. Quentin would sit quietly in the face of these attacks. In individual meetings, the therapist explored these feelings with Leona. Through this exploration, she was able to uncover deep hurt; focus on her disappointment in Quentin, whom she had found too passive and unavailable; and then attend to even deeper, underlying emotion about her sense of having been ignored within her family of origin. Even initi-ating the divorce did not get much of a response from Quentin. Now in touch with her deeper sense of not mattering to him, Leona was better able to work with herself on self-care and be less rageful at Quentin about his small lapses with the children.

Exploring Individual Psychodynamics

Addressing the individual internal processes and personal histories of family members and their internal conflicts represents complicated ter-ritory in divorce therapy. Few clients enter such a therapy looking to do this kind of exploration; other issues predominate. This work is typically easier to initiate when a marital therapy has morphed into divorce therapy and the precedent and alliance for this kind of work is already established. In high-conflict situations and many other variations on difficult divorce, the context of this therapy is not likely to feel like a safe place for such exploration.

Having said this, the transition of divorce is a time in which reflection about self is almost always valuable. And, at times, deep-seated individual issues with strong roots in early experience are so dominant that having a for-mat for such work is essential. The dyadic and family contexts often provide places where early object relations are vividly manifested and become trans-parent. The question becomes whether there can be a way, during difficult divorce, to focus clients' attention away from others—and for that matter, from the practical exigencies of the moment—and on to old forces working inside them.

Following the integrative systemic therapy guidelines (Pinsof et al., 2018), integrative therapy with difficult divorce first attends to the sorts of direct behavioral and cognitive interventions that can be delivered in various contexts. Sometimes this is not enough, and a shift to exploration of "deeper" individual feelings about self and personal history is necessary. When this is the case, that work is best done in a format that allows for it, usually indi-vidual sessions or in a concurrent individual therapy that ideally is informed by what the conjoint therapist observes. Those in difficult divorce almost always have profound problems in mentalizing one another (Allen, Fonagy, & Bateman, 2008). Often the ultimate source of such blocks lies in early experience, and such individual work can hold the promise of helping find empathy, an antidote for some of the problems of difficult divorce.

> Freda was adopted as an infant into a home where no one cared much about her. She experienced an insecure attachment and remained highly anxious as a child and into early adulthood. When Sal entered her life, she thought he was different and truly loved her, but he turned out to be unreliable, and she became insecurely attached to him as well. When after 10 years, Sal, weary of her worries and complaints, filed for divorce, she was furious. They continued to reside together for a time, a period punctuated by terrible fights that often directly involved the children. Therapy with Freda and Sal had little success, given Freda's core dysregulation and Sal's powerful ways of withdrawing and counterattacking. However, with a separate individual therapist, working in coordination with the other therapists involved with the family, Freda was able to get in touch with the impact of her core early issues on her present life. In the context of feeling held and supported, she was able to understand and experience how the anxiety of her early self stayed with her and invited others to act in ways that she dreaded. This insight served as a fulcrum in work to steady herself, engage in self-care, and improve her individual and relational functioning. Although she continued to move in and out of feeling unsteady, this allowed work with the family to empathize, problem-solve, deescalate, and establish new ways for the family to move ahead.

Other Strategies

Spiritual Solutions

Spiritual solutions and resources can provide a major protective factor during the time of this transition (Breunlin, Pinsof, Russell, & Lebow, 2011; Walsh, 2009). Although there is no Alcoholics Anonymous–type mutual aid group for divorce, finding a higher power in working through this experience one day at a time can still have great importance. So can finding a spiritual framework for transcending this experience.

Religious communities can also be valuable in helping clients find hope and steadiness, and sometimes even acceptance and forgiveness. The social support available also can prove invaluable as an antidote to the swirling forces moving toward bad behavior and hopelessness. However, sometimes religious institutions and communities can spur conflict, devalue former partners, and use terms such as *broken families* that lead to feelings of alienation. Such messages from religious institutions add additional constraints to resolution. Thus, these are wonderful resources to help clients connect with the right people in the right communities, but can also be sources of additional difficulty for others.

Biological Solutions

Biological solutions are mentioned last in this listing of interventions because this is principally a psychosocial treatment. However, when the case formulation points to a key role of biology in a case, either in relation to a health issue or a mental health problem amenable to treatment with medication, appropriate referral is essential. Sometimes an intervention as simple as starting an antidepressant medication or paying better attention to one's diabetes can make for a major change in functioning and radically improved family process. Further, psychopharmacology also has the advantages of being fast-acting, and thus helpful in slowing down reactivity in the time before other solutions can be implemented. Thus, psychopharmacology can be particularly useful in the context of difficult divorce, given that the sooner change can occur before negative cycles are well established, the better the chance of avoiding traumatic experiences and repetitive problematic sequences, which ultimately make it less likely that clients will move into the normal range.

> Rudy and Patrick had a quiet parting at first when Patrick informed Rudy he wanted to divorce. However, when Rudy had a hypomanic episode, both coparenting and Rudy's parenting completely broke down. Rudy became argumentative and provocative, and Patrick engaged his lawyer to restrict Rudy's time with the children to supervised visits. In approaching this case, the therapist in the first meeting alone with Rudy explored whether he was willing to see a psychiatrist about medication for what he himself described as distressing symptoms. He had similar episodes in the past that were helped with medication. Given the various pressures on him, most especially wanting to see his children more often, Rudy agreed. The psychiatrist started Rudy on medication for bipolar disorder, Rudy quickly settled back into his more normal self, and most of the conflict subsided.

IMPLEMENTATION

Combining and Ordering Strategies in Treatment

Combining and ordering the strategies I have described with divorcing couples is the art of working with these cases. Divorcing families are alike only in that they are experiencing divorce. They come to treatment as very different people with a wide array of issues, difficulties at several systemic levels, and vast differences in the acceptability of various kinds of intervention. A number of factors can suggest that one intervention strategy is likely to be most impactful or acceptable to the family. The choice and ordering of interventions in this model of working is always related to the specific case formulation and treatment plan. Further, people respond better and worse to different interventions; the therapist always has to see how an intervention strategy is experienced and how much of an impact it has. Who the therapist is and the context for the therapy also matters, given that different therapists have different skill sets and preferred methods, and who is in treatment and the reason for referral may vary. Thus, treatments differ enormously in the strategies employed and when they are used in treatment.

However, a few generalizations are possible about the typical course of therapy. The first interventions employed during and after the initial alliance-building period are almost always psychoeducation about the deleterious effects of such conflicts and the typical experiences of families engaged in these sorts of conflicts. This psychoeducation points to the most obvious places where a specific family typifies such patterns and where the deleterious impact is occurring. This is usually followed by direct efforts to identify and modify the most problematic behaviors, through raising awareness about the presence of those behaviors, engaging client self-monitoring about them, and recommending direct behavioral efforts to change them. In parallel with these efforts, cognitions are identified and explored, as are methods for increasing emotional regulation in the context of family issues. As progress is made with these strategies, methods for improving communication and problem-solving are typically introduced, first limited to a few topics and forms of communicating, with this base expanded as these skills are mastered. When considerable dysregulation is present, mindfulness-based, cognitive, and emotion-focused strategies are emphasized to help enable responsiveness. Radical acceptance is brought in focus in relation to problems that appear unchangeable. Understandings from systemic and psychodynamic methods are also incorporated into intervention as needed, when relevant in the case formulation. Deeper emotional experiencing and psychodynamic exploration are generally reserved for situations that are particularly relevant, and then typically in individual meetings.

In each case, the formulation is used to organize the treatment; at times, that formulation can result in much additional attention to a specific problem or intervention strategy. Whatever the sequence of interventions, it is essential to keep these treatments simple and straightforward. Integrative practice offers many options. Skillful practice lies in applying those options parsimoniously in a form that is easily followed, where clients can master the skill sets involved against the background of the noise of family conflict. Therapy in difficult divorce is less about writing an essay on how various interventions might be valuable (all bona fide intervention strategies are relevant), but in finding a few clear foci that can help guide the family to a less difficult divorce and following through.

It must be emphasized that the therapist is also a major factor in the treatment (see Chapter 9). The integrative treatment model described here draws on an expansive therapist toolkit. Therapists are likely to be much more familiar and adept with some treatment strategies than others. A tenet of this treatment model is that there are always multiple (if complex) pathways to change. Thus, although therapists are encouraged to master multiple treatment strategies, the skill set of the therapist must in part be a determinant of the pathways chosen.

Therapy Formats

This therapy with difficult divorce selectively uses all potential therapy formats as they appear likely to be useful, given the goals in the case and case formulation. Most therapies include more than one format, with one or more therapists participating, depending on the resources available. Still, most cases have a "go-to," most frequently employed format that best speaks to the most central issues and goals in the case, with only occasional sessions involving other formats.

Working With Families Together

Perhaps ironically for a model with origins in family systems theory, therapy sessions with the entire original nuclear family represent only a small part of this treatment model. Although there remains an important place for such work in less difficult divorces, there are too many possibilities for therapy moving in dysfunctional directions in typical therapy settings with everyone involved to make such meetings advisable except in special circumstances.[6] The times such meetings are most helpful are when there are problems for which parents agree on a plan, such as when children have difficulties and parents have a working alliance to work together to ameliorate them.

Family meetings are used more often in subsystems, particularly those in which there are problematic relationships. Thus, there may meetings between a parent and children, especially when these relationships have been identified by one or more stakeholders as needing to be improved, as impinging negatively on other relationships, or there are child-related issues that require greater focus. In these conjoint sessions, the therapist draws on the traditional set of family therapy skills in terms of such goals as working to create a safe space, open up communication, enhance attachment, advance family structure, or find the best ways for family members to work together.

---

[6]Such sessions can also be less risky in the context of intensive programs for treating difficult divorce where, for example, a family is in residence for a period with the sole purpose to work at issues surrounding divorce and there are immediate options for follow-up.

Working With Ex-Partners Together

Because coparenting problems are so frequently the central reason for referral in these families, this is perhaps the most frequent format used in this treatment model. The task here is challenging. Parents who are hurt and angry and in a process of disconnection are brought together in the name of the task of coparenting. The therapist looks to set a frame for these sessions as task oriented, continually returning to the topic when ex-partners digress or insert other agendas, such as criticizing or wounding their former partner. In this context, the multilevel toolkit of intervention is used to work toward good-enough, minimal coparenting.

Working With Adults Alone

Individual work, either through a separate coordinated therapy with a separate therapist or in a brief series of meetings with select family members, when there is a single therapist, occupies an important place in this model. Given the conflict and other trust issues in these families, therapy processes that are about internal processes (e.g., cognitions, emotions, psychodynamics) can be engaged well only rarely in conjoint formats. Meetings alone with a therapist are the place that these inner processes can best be engaged and altered, with that progress then brought back to enhance the conjoint work. A specific marker indicating the need for this work is when clients struggle with simple, direct interventions presented in conjoint formats. Individual meetings allow for more room for patience, remedial skill development, and exploration of underlying issues that have a prominent place in blocks to progress.

When one person is identified as in need of such sessions more than others, there is a complex political issue to deal with about why this person has been so singled out and whether the individual therapy takes place with the relational therapist or another practitioner. It is important for this to be done in a way that does not overpathologize or triangulate and everyone is helped to grasp that meetings with this individual alone promotes the collective good, including that of the person being offered the individual meetings. Given the level of pain typically present in individuals in need of such meetings, this addition to the therapy is surprisingly often processed as reasonable. When issues of triangulation are most likely and there is an especially strong reaction to the notion that one person needs something special, a simple alternative is to have all parties take part in individual meetings. There is no shortage of work for everyone, and it is rare that there isn't some value in individual meetings.

Paradoxically, individual sessions are also the place where the greatest progress may be possible with the most motivated family members. Change in difficult divorce is often not a coequal process but instead the product of one or more family members differentiating themselves from the problematic sequences and helping move the family process to be more on track. Although the conjoint format has the great strength of optimally promoting collaborative processes between family members, the individual format is the setting in which the therapist has the best opportunities to help family members cope with their feelings toward the less motivated, more stuck family members. Specifically, the therapist can work most effectively in individual sessions to promote that client's behavior change and radical acceptance strategies (Hayes, 2016) to help the more motivated family members accept and find better ways to live with the problems in the others, toward the best possible individual and collective outcomes. More broadly, for all family members, individual meetings are also the best place to help each family member consider what is changeable in self and others and what is not, to learn to accept this as much as possible, and to better work within these limits.

Working With Children Alone

Divorce is an event that affects not only the divorcing couple but the family as a whole. It is common, but unwise, to fully separate divorce therapy from therapy that simultaneously occurs involving the minor children whose parents are divorcing. That is, these are family systems, and work with children in divorce is always best related to work with the others in the family. There are several ways that this can occur. Children may be brought directly into sessions with parents or family, they may be seen alone or in a sibling group by a therapist connected to work with the parents, or they may be indirectly the focus of coparenting meetings with only the parents. What is most essential is to emphasize that children are very much part of most divorcing systems. Whatever the therapy format and whether the children are present or not, they are inevitably affected by and a part of divorce therapy.

The need to involve minor children directly in therapy is greatest in high-conflict situations or when the children themselves manifest strong signs of problems in relation to the divorce. By meeting alone or as siblings with a therapist, children can be helped to find ways to differentiate from the parental difficulties, adapt to their circumstance, avoid the pitfalls that might emerge in their life situation, and continue to develop their own lives.[7] As highlighted elsewhere in this approach, stabilizing one part of the system in

---

[7]The choice of whether to meet with children in a sibling group or in individual meetings is also important. With many families, this is primarily driven by the children's preference and by efficiency. Perhaps most important in this choice is that in difficult divorce, there is often contagion in families from the strong feeling of one child (often a parental child fused with one parent) to the others. That circumstance indicates that children should meet individually with one or more therapists.

this way has benefits for the rest of the family system as well. And in those systems where difficulties among other family members cannot be changed, individual therapy meetings with a child may be the sole force protecting that child from the cascade of emotional and structural chaos in the family. Sometimes, steady therapy that helps a child differentiate from the family conflict and find a pathway to coping is what makes a difference in the life of a child.

Each of the core strategies of intervention described in this chapter can be, and usually are, part of work with children. Psychoeducation is enormously helpful. It is perplexing for children to understand what divorce is in the context of parental actions in difficult divorce. They may be privy to more information than most children, but often it is biased information from the perspective of one parent that has been presented out of any consideration of the developmental abilities of children to process this information. Psychoeducation can also help children better grasp that they are not at the center of divorce, even if they seem to be. Simplified versions of working with cognitions and emotions, as in other child therapies, can also have great value (Szigethy, Weisz, & Findling, 2012), as can coaching children in differentiating themselves from the conflict. Often, it is most simply the common factor aspects of attachment with a therapist acting as a steadying force that can help a child in difficult divorce feel anchored in a stormy world. For some children who have been highly politicized in the divorce, differentiating self from the positions of parents and siblings can be a demanding task, requiring considerable work using motivational interviewing and challenging solidly held beliefs.

Work with children must always be framed in the context of the child's stage of development (L. R. Greenberg, Fick, & Schnider, 2012). Explanations and understandings appropriately vary with age, as do the materials used (e.g., toys, books). In meetings with children, there also are opportunities to deal with any major mental health concerns that have historically been present or that have emerged during the divorce (e.g., depression, anxiety). In the context of such problems, one part of the therapy is the application of evidence-based methods for helping those specific problems (e.g., working toward activation, challenging depressive thoughts).

Working With Extended Family

The families of origin and new partners of parents in a family also are strongly affected by and influence the level of conflict in divorce (Johnston & Campbell, 1986). It is important to hold on to the systemic understanding that divorce may affect and be affected by extended family, not just the nuclear family. Involvement of extended family in difficult divorce can be intense, especially in certain cultural contexts. I have heard more than a few times that "this divorce will kill your father/mother" when speaking of extended family. Extended families are typically very loyal to their blood relative, at times showing even greater intensity than those in the nuclear family. Yet there also are situations in which extended family, perceiving a great loss, join with the partner of their relative against their blood relative. There are other situations, particularly with young couples divorcing, where most of the executive decision-making is actually done by extended family members Thus, there are many scenarios in which extended family members are extensively involved in the most problematic sequences.

The question then becomes when and under what circumstances to involve extended family in the direct client system (i.e., in treatment sessions). In this model of working, direct involvement of extended family is reserved for those situations when they are truly intrinsic to problem resolution. This is simply a matter of trying to remain parsimonious in the treatment. It is those families where the kin wars are occurring, or where decision-making is strongly influenced by extended family, that their involvement in conjoint sessions with their own family member (not with the former partner) becomes essential. Otherwise, the work with the nuclear family is readily undone. Such involvement is most beneficial when partners who are subject to conscious or unconscious pressure from families to remain in conflict are unable to deal with such pressures and when extended family members have the personal resources to bring a calming effect to the conflict. It is helpful to frame bringing in the extended family as potential sources of help for settling difficult matters in the nuclear family. The effort is to determine whether they can be engaged in some new, more helpful role. This work is inevitably brief (typically one to three sessions) and highly goal focused to see if extended family can become part of the solution. Again, the toolkit for intervention here is much as in the rest of the model: primarily direct efforts at behavior change and a mix of psychoeducation and cognitive and emotional processing.

Assessing Progress and Feedback

Regularly assessing progress and then providing feedback to clients is a key aspect within this treatment approach. A great deal of research has shown that in psychotherapy broadly, assessing progress and providing feedback about it is an important factor in the service of change (Carr & Stratton, 2017; Halford et al., 2012; Lutz, Stulz, Martinovich, Leon, & Saunders, 2014; Wampold, 2015).

Monitoring progress is even more important in difficult divorce than in other cases. There are several reasons for this. First, in difficult divorce, a bad start often means a bad outcome. Early alliance data in the measurement of progress is invaluable in helping recognize which clients are unlikely to connect in any useful way. Important to note here is that alliances in difficult divorce (save for those with individual therapists) are lower than in almost any other kind of therapy, and positive outcomes typically evolve slowly; the question is how a specific case's alliances and progress compare to norms in such cases. Given negative early ratings, can enough of an alliance be created that the therapy might ultimately succeed? Don't expect too much too quickly, but look for some positive alliance to form in three to five sessions and signs of progress by five to 10 sessions. Don't assume poor early alliances can't be salvaged or that no progress after 10 sessions means progress is not possible, but be sure to attend to such emerging problems. Second, small, difficult-to-achieve changes that do occur can be used as further impetus for change. Success in these cases primarily lies in building on small changes, which often begin in one person. Third, the risk of an "off-track" path of many sessions with little change can be reduced with regular measurement of alliance and progress using scales for monitoring these variables that cues the therapist to this sad fact, allowing for a reconsideration of the therapeutic plan (Tilden & Wampold, 2017).

Standard good alliance and outcome measures can be used in such ongoing assessment, adapted to divorcing systems—for example, measures of individual functioning include the Outcome Questionnaire (Lambert, 2015), Clinical Outcomes in Routine Evaluation (Barkham, Mellor-Clark, & Stiles, 2015), or Systemic Therapy Inventory of Change (Pinsof, 2017) or for children, the Child Behavior Checklist (Achenbach, 2000); the Family Assessment Device (Mansfield, Keitner, & Dealy, 2015) is a measure of system functioning; and the Parting Parent Concern Inventory (Sanford & Rivers, 2017) provides a measure of coparenting. Even if measurement on a regular basis is difficult in the setting in which the therapist practices, the therapist can, more simply, inquire each session about the therapeutic alliance and individual, subsystem, and system processes in a way that allows determination of whether clients are forming satisfactory alliances and making progress.

Impasses and Resistance

Change in these cases does not come easily. There can be considerable resistance, especially in response to directives. Engaging in therapy in the context of difficult divorce is stressful, and the changes needed are often hard to make, even when there is full cooperation. Clients often fall prey to focusing their energies on their distress about what is occurring, and especially the behavior of others, instead of on how they might best promote better individual and systemic functioning.

The therapist must tune into and monitor emerging client resistance and deal with it in a timely fashion (Beutler, Harwood, Michelson, Song, & Holman, 2011). One common way resistance is manifested is to make scheduling unusually difficult, so that there will be as little therapy as possible. Such an issue must be dealt with as it emerges, lest the therapy lose any chance for impact. In the context of issues about scheduling, therapists can use their broad skills for improving alliances; in court-referred cases, therapists can simply let the client who is making scheduling difficult know that this will be reported to the court.

Other common forms of resistance include clients working from their own agendas, such as continually returning to the notion of "fixing" some other family member, or attempting to minimize the impact of forces moving toward change. Again, therapists should use their considerable toolkits to deal with this resistance, turning to motivational interviewing when needed and patiently staying with the frame of a slow, evolving process moving toward change to help clients stay on course. Other paths to reducing resistance include reemphasizing the solution-oriented focus, reframing therapy tasks to make them more acceptable, trying to understand and deal with the sources of resistance, or changing the intervention strategy to better match what clients may be ready to do.

Having said all this, resistance is a constant companion in therapy with difficult divorce. It is to be expected at each step in the process. The key questions surround differentiating when resistance necessitates a major detour in the therapy rather than steady, persistent efforts to move ahead that may involve some pushback about that effort. Early in such work, the therapist also almost always gains a good sense of how much engagement toward therapy goals each client will show and learns to work in the context of helping those who are motivated to move as far as they can and to push those who are less motivated to at least get to a place that is "less toxic."

Ending

It is hard to know when it is best to end therapy in difficult divorce cases. Clearly, difficult divorces feature many problems that in theory might be helped by ongoing work over the long term, and nobody should be discouraged from continuing to work on themselves. And there are some families for whom it would be beneficial for therapy to remain a part of their lives over many years. For example, continuing in therapy may be the only way in the context of ongoing family tension that a parent can continue to have successful interaction with a child or that two hurt and angry parents with different parenting styles can resolve evolving issues around coparenting.

Having said this, the model presented here suggests doing as much as is needed, allowing some time to see whether change can be maintained, and then ending therapy. Families themselves typically will stay in therapy for only so long. Furthermore, families are in a developmental process of reorganizing into two families, and ongoing therapy, even with subsystems, moves in a direction of making for more contact and connection than may be ideal between parents. There typically are too many problems in these families to solve them all. The goal of this therapy is simply to get the family system running well enough in its new context so that it is at least functional, although it may still be far from ideal.

Endings should be planned and celebrated. However, bear in mind the context. Families are often in treatment in difficult divorce not because they want to but because they are so mandated. It is not unusual for a therapy to end simply because the court is no longer pressing for the therapy, something that often happens when litigation about divorce ends when it has been finalized. In such situations, special efforts with the clients are warranted to see if they will agree to extend the therapy for a short time beyond the time the court has mandated to help the family digest the results of the court process.[8]

All this speaks to the importance of ongoing monitoring of treatment, so that progress or deterioration can be clearly recognized and processed as it occurs, as well as of being prepared to quickly put together an ending for the therapy when external forces prompt it. Follow-up plans should include referrals for those who are ready to continue their personal work and suggestions for future work for those who currently are not in individual therapy. An open-ended strategy that creates a frame for returning to therapy after termination if future problems arise is also part of this model (Lebow, 1995). Those in difficult divorce remain at high risk for the return of problems as stressors accrue and life progresses.

EMPIRICAL SUPPORT

There have been no studies on the impact of divorce therapy, including the model described in this volume. This stems from a combination of a climate that renders government funding of research on the treatment of divorcing families (Lebow, 2015a) and individuals virtually nonexistent and the complexities for research presented by the frequency of ongoing litigation in difficult divorce (making such questions as informed consent more complex than elsewhere). However, there is indirect evidence in support of this method of

---

[8]Even for those not mandated by the court, the point at which the divorce is formalized is often a time when many stop treatment.

intervention. Research on psychoeducational prevention programs (Pedro-Carroll, 2005) and mediation (Beck, Sales, & Emery, 2004) have shown a considerable impact in those participating in these interventions. More closely connected to this approach, each of the specific strategies in this treatment model have been shown to be highly effective in the context of other problems. Some of the problems helped by these strategies involve similar goals of reducing conflict, anger management, emotional regulation, and improving communication and problem-solving. Perhaps most important in the evaluation of divorce therapy broadly today is that judges and attorneys typically see it as essential and almost always refer family members in difficult divorce for therapy.

SUMMARY

This chapter has reviewed strategies for intervention that are helpful in intervening in difficult divorce. Broad strategies include guaranteeing safety, witnessing, a solution-oriented focus, psychoeducation, and motivational interviewing. Behavior change strategies include behavioral, systemic, and communication and problem-solving procedures. Third-wave strategies include mindful practice, anger management, and radical acceptance. Psychological strategies include cognitive strategies, exploring underlying emotion, and exploring individual psychodynamics. Other strategies include spiritual and biological methods. Issues around implementation were also discussed, including the sequencing of interventions, and choice of therapy formats. For many cases of difficult divorce, treatment occurs in the context of a pervasive dealings with the legal system, and working in this context is the focus of the next chapter.

7

INTERACTING WITH THE LEGAL SYSTEM AND OTHER PROFESSIONALS

This chapter explores the issues that may emerge in difficult divorce when interacting with the legal system and other mental health professionals. The judicial system is unfamiliar territory for most therapists, and therefore how to work with lawyers and the court are typically not well-developed therapist skill sets. The first part of the chapter provides information about the ways courts approach divorce (most especially, difficult divorce with extensive legal involvement) and the various roles different professionals fill. This is followed by a section focused on how therapists can proactively interact with the legal system and deal with special problematic situations that arise. The final part of the chapter focuses on the more familiar, but often equally complex, interactions with other mental health professionals in this context. A proactive systemic approach to treatment that brings together various professionals working toward joined goals, as much as possible, lies at the center of this discussion.

http://dx.doi.org/10.1037/0000116-008
Treating the Difficult Divorce: A Practical Guide for Psychotherapists, by J. L. Lebow
Copyright © 2019 by the American Psychological Association. All rights reserved.

THE INTERFACE OF DIVORCE THERAPY
AND THE JUDICIAL SYSTEM

Divorce occurs in various venues, one of which is the legal system. For many of those in difficult divorce, dealings with the judicial system are significant, particularly when legal matters over child custody or finances become intense or stalled. The impact is considerable and experienced in multiple ways.

Most important, the adversarial context of much of the judicial system provides endless opportunities for confrontations in pleadings, subpoenas, depositions, and court appearances, which frequently engender conflict at a personal level as well as within the legal system. Statements made by attorneys, text in pleadings, and behavior around such issues as the sharing of financial information or a parent's conduct readily become the focus of arguments and bad feeling.

Second, the time involved and nature of the involvement with the court can be a major additional stressor, amplifying the tension in the interpersonal environment. For more than a few of those in difficult divorce, attending to the details of the legal divorce becomes a full-time preoccupation. This can be no less true for those with few assets and one child as for those with many assets to track and five children. All the elements are in place for this to be a highly stressful experience: the high emotional engagement, the adversarial context, the high stakes involved, the requests for litigants to gather a great deal of information about their own cases (often involving literally keeping a diary of bad actions or a backward search for faults), and the frequent provocative actions of attorneys.

A third source of difficulty is that what transpires in court, between attorneys, in depositions and testimony, and in court documents readily becomes evidence for further negative attribution about motivation. Many months of cooperative behavior can easily become undone in the context of disconnected behavior initiated by attorneys in court (sometimes the timing of issues moving into action in the legal system can mean that even "old" issues can come back to interfere with progress). Presentations in the win–lose environment of litigated divorce may be much different and more provocative than in daily life, even among those who already are having trouble with one another.

Fourth, in the context of interviews with judges and attorneys and parents coaching them in relation to such meetings, children can become highly polarized about their best interests and may become provocative themselves. This engenders further bad feeling not only between parents and children but also between parents, who almost always blame one another for the children's bad feelings.

In the best divorce therapy, therapists work closely with lawyers and the court to help clients understand and work with what is transpiring within the judicial process and help the court understand the therapy process. By working in concert with the judicial system, the therapist can anticipate court appearances and related legal events, such as depositions and pleadings, and develop ways to deal with these events to minimize the trauma that may occur and mitigate additional conflict. Most especially, attorneys who serve the children typically welcome such a proactive stance and are prepared to intervene actively to support the therapy process. Attorneys for the parents and the court also are frequently fully committed to providing support for the therapy process.

However, bear in mind that although attorneys and judges often do intervene to mitigate conflict, such measures in difficult divorce can be met with resistance by one or both divorcing partners, sometimes even leading to the engagement of new attorneys or petitioning for a change in judges (the latter rarely succeeds). Clients sometimes select attorneys because of their reputation for moving toward resolution or toward more aggressive lawyering. Others make this selection based on other factors, such as reputation or, more simply, their accessibility (e.g., someone they know has used that attorney). When there is a mismatch in style with an attorney, particularly if the attorney is less aggressive than the client desires, clients often change attorneys. Ultimately in difficult divorce, this "selective mating" means that attorneys are often of the more aggressive kind (as more balanced attorneys are discarded), moving the divorce toward greater conflict. Although the great majority of attorneys working in family law look to resolution and equitable and fair outcomes, a significant minority are more aggressive in solely pursuing the best possible outcome for their client at whatever cost in terms of raising painful issues, making provocative and often distorted allegations, and fighting a war of attrition that may move the other side to settle for less than it might otherwise.

ROLES AND PROCESSES IN THE JUDICIAL SYSTEM

Therapists treating families in difficult divorce need to become familiar with the judicial process and the various roles of those involved in it. Divorce law varies from state to state in the United States and across various countries, and thus these roles (including what the people in these roles are called) and the typical course of the legal process may vary somewhat across jurisdictions. Therapists should familiarize themselves with the specific roles and the relevant laws involved with divorce in their jurisdiction. In what follows, I review typical processes and roles in the United States, which apply in some similar form in many other countries.

A limited set of issues about divorce is within the purview of the court, although there are endless variations on this small set of issues. All divorce must involve a decree obtained from the court, so all divorcing couples have some contact with the court. The process of getting to such a decree and its related agreements can range from complete cooperation with almost no court appearances and limited attorney involvement to hotly contested litigation over many years. Matters essential to obtaining such a decree are primarily financial or related to minor children. Agreements related to divorce must divide the couples' financial life, including financial assets, debts, and property, and also set expectations for any future exchanges of money (e.g., child support or maintenance). A joint parenting agreement accompanying the divorce allocates decision-making and time with the children between the parents and may include other stipulations (e.g., about health care, religion, times of exchanges, dispute resolution). Decision-making authority (often termed *custody*) concerns large, specific areas of decision-making such as religion, health care, and education. This can be structured as joint (shared) or sole (one parent has decision-making power over these decisions) custody (Folberg, 1991). Although courts generally favor joint decision-making in most divorces, in difficult divorce, the contested nature of family life often leaves the court favoring sole custody arrangements.[1] Arrangements can vary from 50% of time with each parent to 100% of time with one parent.[2] In some cases, one parent may allege that the other is unsafe for the children and therefore that their contact should be severely restricted or some form of supervision be mandated in which the parent is continually observed during his or her parenting time. Court-involved difficult divorce typically includes a major dispute between the parents about at least one, and typically more than one, of these fundamental issues. In difficult divorce, there often also are a plethora of legal complaints over time, ranging from emergency petitions for orders of protection, to urgent financial disputes, to who will turn over what records, to arguments over who is supposed to have the children when, or who can have the children during what school vacation.

Judges and Court Processes

Judges are public officials with the authority to hear and decide cases. They may be elected or appointed. Typically, no specific background in terms

---

[1] This is consistent with research findings indicating there are more difficulties in arrangements and negative outcomes for children when there is high conflict and joint or coequally shared residence versus sole custody and one primary home (Steinbach, 2018), although some argue that maintaining the importance of both parents in the child's life makes this worth this cost (Warshak, 2015).
[2] Typical arrangements are rapidly changing. In one American state, Wisconsin, the rate of joint custody and shared parenting time (defined here as 25% or greater with each parent) increased from 12% in 1986 to 50% in 2010 (Meyer, Cancian, & Cook, 2017)

of family knowledge is required for being charged with overseeing divorce cases. The extent of that knowledge usually is a function of how long they have filled this position and the judge's interest in becoming more informed about family law and family processes. In most jurisdictions, judges are assigned a large number of cases, and thus they are likely to have various cases at various stages of development at any time. In smaller jurisdictions, handling family law cases may be only one part of a judge's caseload. In larger jurisdictions judges are assigned to a division that only handles family law matters and may even be divided between those assigned to cases moving to trial and those who handle other aspects of divorce.

Judges become involved more intensely to the extent that cases are brought to their attention because there are conflicts. Thus, in an uncontested divorce, appearances in court are kept to a minimum, confined to what are called *status calls*, in which the lawyers inform the judges how well the case is moving toward divorce (or reconciliation if that is occurring). Discovery between the parties here is essentially simply sharing information. In many jurisdictions some form of mediation is mandated if parties have trouble getting to a resolution of differences, especially if those differences are about custody of children. In most divorces (but not most difficult divorces), mediation resolves remaining differences over the key elements that go into a divorce decree: finances and arrangements about children.

In highly contested cases, there typically are many more appearances in court about specific matters having to do with both short-term and long-term arrangements. On these occasions, judges may hear evidence and make decisions about these specific matters. Almost universally, judges use such appearances in court to strongly emphasize the value of ending divorce litigation and resolving the differences between the parties. Occasionally, some matters may be brought to the court on an emergency basis, necessitating a decision by the judge about whether what is being put forward constitutes an emergency (examples include requests for orders of protection when there are allegations of violence or for cessation of visitation). Given that such emergency motions are fit into a judge's already-busy schedule, this often necessitates the judge making an initial decision based on little available information. In such circumstances, judges often err toward being conservative and guaranteeing safety and set a time to hear the matter more thoroughly at a later time. Whatever decision is made, emergency motions inevitably potentiate conflict in difficult divorce.[3]

---

[3]Thus, it may be that by the time clients enter therapy, significant and sometimes traumatic interactions have already occurred, followed by similarly traumatic legal decisions, although these decisions may be temporary.

Discovery is a process in which each side in the divorce learns more from the other side. In difficult divorce, there often are many intense requests for very specific information during discovery, which again tend to be emotionally challenging for the parties. Turning over information in difficult divorce is rarely simple, so such requests often occur over several court appearances over an extended time. In the most highly contested cases, a range of experts in areas such as child custody or finances may be involved either by the court or attorneys; again, this is accompanied by strong emotional reactions in the family.

As a difficult divorce progresses without a legal settlement and begins to move to a trial about the remaining issues, there may also be depositions of witnesses and the former partners. During depositions, attorneys for one party ask questions of those connected to the other to learn what potential witnesses have to say about various matters. Depositions are principally intended to learn about the other side's case and find ways to challenge it should the case move further though the legal process. Litigants sitting through these depositions often experience further traumatic stress as they hear worst-case presentations of who they are and what they have done.

In most jurisdictions, in contested cases, there is some pretrial process during which the judge offers some notion of the likely outcome if the case is to go to trial. This often is a decision point when compromises are reached in the wake of the judge's thoughts about the case, given that the likely outcome is now known. However, such last-minute legal agreements do not necessarily mean that families are out of the zone of "difficult divorce." Many feel coerced into these agreements because the alternative is the great expense of a trial (and often the reluctance of their attorney to go to trial, given that for attorneys, trials are an extremely intense and time-consuming activity).

Despite typically extensive efforts of the court to find alternative dispute resolution, some cases move on to trial, which, as already noted, is an expensive and time-consuming process. At trial, the judge hears all the relevant evidence about the case (typically over a few days, although the days may be spread out over a few months). Typically, litigants testify (with cross-examination) and sit through the presentation of witnesses; these may ignite further trauma and acrimony. When there are disputes over child custody and visitation, children may meet with judges or occasionally even offer testimony; these are almost inevitably highly triangulating experiences (most courts typically look to minimize children's direct participation in the legal process in such cases, often appointing an attorney early in the process to represent them, as discussed later in the chapter). After a period of considering the evidence (often a few months) the judge writes an opinion that is binding about the contested matters in a case. The judge's decision can be appealed, but it is rare that appeals courts overturn judges' decisions in divorce cases.

Altogether, the process of legal divorce can take as little as whatever the minimum waiting time for getting divorced is in a particular state in those who are highly cooperative (in some instances, partners don't even file for divorce until there is agreement about all postdivorce arrangements) to what can be 3 to 5 years in the most difficult divorces. Difficult divorces that play out as conflicts in the legal system also are almost always prolonged, leaving families in limbo with the partners totally estranged yet still married for an average of 1 to 2 years. For many, this means not only that there is extended time for conflict but also that at least one partner has moved well into a new relationship before the legal divorce. Remarkably, some nuclear families live together through this period, guided in part by advice to each parent that their legal case for their version of child custody will be weakened by moving out of the marital home.

Whether simply arrived at through eventual agreement or handled more complexly at trial, all divorce cases eventually result in a decree that ends the legal marriage. This decree either includes or speaks to in separate documents the division of monies (including assets, child support, and maintenance payments to the lower earning partner), and, if there are children, a joint parenting plan that includes how decision-making is divided and shared, how time with parents is divided, and numerous other details about parenting arrangements. In difficult divorce, wise resolutions result in long, very specific documents that cover even smaller issues about finances (e.g., who will pay for camp) and about the lives of children (e.g., what is the precise list of school holidays; what are the specific times for pickups and drop-offs of children). The more such matters can be covered in the documents that are part of the divorce, the less there is to argue about later.[4] Most cases terminate the legal process with the divorce decree (i.e., the divorce ends the case), and further court involvement only occurs if new complaints are filed.[5] Still, there is a limit to how specific such documents can be, and those in difficult divorce have plenty of room for future disputes about matters that are not covered or about failure to comply with the details in the documents. The completion of the legal case in difficult divorce typically does little to increase cooperation or resolve problems other than the most concrete matters covered in the specifics of the divorce decree, such as when which child is with which parent. Contention and lack of cooperation in difficult divorce typically do not end with the divorce decree.

---

[4]Those who have less money for lawyers often wind up with what are boilerplate agreements that do not speak to the unique issues in a given family, which often leaves much unspecified and significant room for ongoing conflict.

[5]Courts often have a period during which they will not hear certain kinds of complaints (e.g., reassignment of child custody).

For a few very difficult divorces, attorneys that serve the children remain in place and the case may remain open in court for follow-up. Individuals or the family may also be mandated to continue in treatment after the divorce (with some provision suggesting how a new therapist will be chosen if the therapist is no longer available). A significant percentage of cases relitigate matters about children or money later.[6]

There is second set of cases in which divorce is obtained without much difficulty but the former partners later enter into similar postdivorce litigation about divorce-related issues. For example, issues about the parent schedule, a parent wanting to relocate at a considerable distance, the fitness of a parent, the exchange of monies, or the action of a stepparent may arise at a later time. There are still other cases in which partners never married and so do not go through divorce but in which there are similar conflicts over custody and visitation with children; such cases go through a legal process similar to divorce litigation.

Attorneys and Their Roles

Attorneys represent the parties and sometimes the children in divorce. In many instances, these attorneys specialize in family law, although in others they may simply be lawyers with heterogenous practices and only limited experience in this area. They range widely between the attorney who is minimally attending to the legal aspects of a divorce at low fee in limited time, to those who are part of expensive teams specializing in family law who spend many hours over years working on contentious cases. Attorneys fall on a continuum in terms of how they approach divorce. Although attorneys almost always act to support their client's interest, most attorneys also work to promote resolution and resolve differences Others are more aggressive, and a few are hyperaggressive and attacking. Such differences are clear in their private conversations with clients, which for some move toward realistic resolution and with others encourage unrealistic expectations, as well as motions filed and arguments made with the court. In the context of difficult divorce, attorneys range widely from calming to starting and stoking the fires of conflict.

As already noted, attorneys are also appointed by the court to serve children. These attorneys tend to be appointed when there are special issues that involve the children (e.g., a major mental health issue), there are questions about the parenting children receive, or there are disputes over child custody, residence, or access to children. Although the law is written in different ways

---

[6]Relitigation rates can be as high as 40% (Koel, Clark, Straus, Whitney, & Hauser, 1994), although most of these contested cases have to do with financial arrangements, particularly nonpayment of child support.

in different jurisdictions, these attorneys basically serve in one of two roles. Either they are attorneys for the children (meaning that they represent the children in the legal process) or they hold a guardian role (serving the children's interest rather than representing them). Either way, these attorneys intervene in various ways on behalf of children in contested cases, attempting to help parents arrive at good solutions and serving as an important voice to the court. They often actively coordinate services for children. Judges frequently follow their advice about contested matters. Typically, these attorneys have acquired a good working knowledge of these roles and about family processes in divorce. Most attorneys working with children promote resolution and fair and balanced outcomes. Nonetheless, many parents in difficult divorce develop a contentious relationship with them when they do not share their view of the case and come to view them as one-sided.

Limitations of the Judicial Process

The legal process is ideally set up for both partners to have an attorney who represents them well and works with them toward an equitable resolution. When there are children, the legal process is explicitly intended to serve and emphasize their best interest. In this ideal vision, children are represented as needed when there are disputes about what would be in their best interest, alternative dispute resolution such as mediation is encouraged (discussed later in the chapter), and the process moves to a calming and fair resolution.

Unfortunately, the legal process often falls short of this ideal. Some attorneys may be adversarial, moving in directions that look to use whatever tactics favor the best outcome for their client. Other attorneys sometimes do not fill their role well, either because they have limited time available for a specific matter or due to their ability and skill. Some divorcing partners cannot afford attorneys at all, leaving them to find a resolution to differences without help of counsel. This plethora of possibilities can leave both partners poorly represented or create a mismatch in skill and availability in the judicial process between representation for the respective sides, thus favoring one partner. This also means in many cases that there may be no one representing the children or their best interest, even though that is greatly needed. Any of these possibilities can move the process toward greater acrimony and increase the possibility of less fair, balanced, and wise outcomes. Families in difficult divorce also are particularly vulnerable to acrimonious legal processes, both in joining them (as already noted, those in difficult divorce when mismatched with a less aggressive attorney often simply move to a more aggressive attorney) and being sensitive and reactive to the legal process.

Therefore, it is perhaps good news that many cases reach an end point and an agreement about divorce simply because no one can afford the attorneys to further litigate the case. The bad news is that in the territory of little or unbalanced attorney involvement, awful resolutions often occur, especially when clients represent themselves in court.

It should be added that the judicial process can only reach a decision about the matters it is asked to consider: generally, the division of monies in the form of assets, child support, maintenance, and the division of time and authority about minor children. It cannot make people cooperate or act in positive ways toward one another during litigation or postdivorce. Indeed, the more difficult the litigation with its mutual accusations and the more one-sided the decision, the more likely that postdivorce life will still be fraught with difficulty. In addition, the law is clear about what constitutes a minor child—in almost all jurisdictions, someone under 18 years of age. Disputes about those in late adolescence who are over 18 are not adjudicated by the court. This sometimes results in the court making a decision about only two of three teenagers in a family; leaving the family without a plan for the third. Disputes about those in late adolescence–young adulthood who are over 18 fall into a gray area governed only by the willingness of parents to work together. In typical divorce, parents continue to coparent these emerging adults. In difficult divorce, there may be no vehicle to carry such coparenting forward.[7]

The Role of Mediation

Mediators engage in a formal process of alternative dispute resolution designed to help parties reach mutually acceptable resolutions of their differences (Emery, 1994). In the United States and many other countries, mediation and other methods of alternative dispute resolution are highly encouraged. Mediation is often a mandatory part of the legal process where there are initial disputes about child custody and sometimes about assets. Mediators may be lawyers, but they may also be mental health professionals or former judges. In mediation, an agenda of issues about which there are differences is set, and these issues are then negotiated in meetings between the former partners that include breakout time with each party to help move to resolution. Mediators also bring an actuarial sense of the sorts of decisions

---

[7]In therapy, given the agreement of the various people involved (parents and the young adult), the therapy can widen to include these emerging adults and coparenting in relation to them. That work, however, is outside the bounds of any court order or court-mandated recommendation for therapy. One therapist skill in such cases lies in working to see whether the logic of addressing the broader problem—coparenting—can extend to nonminor adolescents.

judges make in similar situations to these conversations and share that view with the partners.

Mediation can be conducted in the context of a government-funded alternate resolution program connected to (and often mandated by) the court or a private fee-for-service activity in which there typically may be more time involved. Mediation may be conducted in very long sessions or in shorter time blocks (2–3 hours). The longer, more intense meetings have a pull toward achieving resolution, which has its merits (resolution is good) and demerits (parties can feel they made less than optimal decisions in an emotional moment). Children also at times meet with mediators in a less typical version of this process (Rudd, Ogle, Holtzworth-Munroe, Applegate, & D'Onofrio, 2015). Other mediations include attorneys who are present to represent the parties in the mediation process. This latter alternative seems to be especially useful to balance a perceived difference in power when one partner perceives the other as more knowledgeable about the matters in the negotiation or more skillful at negotiating.

Mediation is frequently written into divorce decrees as a means of future resolution of disputes. In many cases, it is stipulated that the court will not hear further disputes without first bringing those differences to mediation.

Mediation is highly effective in reducing the frequency of difficult divorce. Randomized clinical trials show that the percentage of those who go on to litigation is reduced by approximately two thirds (Emery, Sbarra, & Grover, 2005), and with that the major trigger for further ongoing conflict is removed. One way to envision the impact of mediation is as helping most families with conflicts about divorce to recover some balance, decide the most important matters about future family structure, and thereby not fall into the cascade of difficult divorce. Yet for those fully engaged in difficult divorce, mediation typically offers little help. Given the frequency of mandates for mediation, most difficult divorce already includes a failed mediation. It may not even be fair to label these outcomes of mediation as failures because often one or both former partners only perfunctorily participate in a few meetings.

The Role of Parenting Coordination

Parenting coordination is a process developed early this century that is designed to help parents who have problems in joint decision-making or coordinating and communicating (Emery, Rowen, & Dinescu, 2014; Higuchi & Lally, 2014). Parenting coordination fills what was formerly a gap in the legal system, providing a mechanism for decision-making about small matters during and after divorce, and a person available to monitor communication. Parenting coordination is principally mandated for those who have completed a difficult divorce as a means of alternative dispute resolution but may also be used during the divorce process as an adjunct to the legal process. Parenting coordinators also work to minimize the points of conflict, enable better communication, provide relevant parent psychoeducation, and troubleshoot during crises (e.g., father is at the door and mother says it is not his day).

Parenting coordinators meet with parents, together and alone, and at times may meet with children to inform their work (Kelly, 2014a). They mediate, but they also can arbitrate differences; that is, they are empowered to make small decisions when parents disagree. Absent a parenting coordinator, what to others may be small differences (e.g., who gets what weeks in the summer in an agreement that specifies each parent will have 2 weeks with the children) can become intractable conflicts in chronic difficult divorce and might needlessly return the former partners to court. Parenting coordinators also can serve as bridges for communication for those who cannot communicate without acrimony. Parenting coordinators, like mediators, may be lawyers or mental health practitioners and thus tend to bring the special skill sets of their respective professions to this activity.

WORKING WITH THE COURT AND ATTORNEYS IN DIFFICULT DIVORCE

The court is an important stakeholder in therapies for difficult divorces that are court involved. Therapists interact with the court or its representatives in several ways: helping promote positive goals suggested by the court, using leverage from the court to further therapy goals, and reporting to the court to inform the judicial process.

Building Alliances With the Court

Working well in the context of the court is immeasurably easier in the context of becoming familiar with and known to the various participants in the legal system: judges, attorneys, mediators, custody evaluators, and parenting coordinators. Building relationships over time has substantial benefits. Much of this process is indirect. Good work on one case invites referral and closer collaboration on another. Meeting at venues where topics of mutual interest are discussed (e.g., laws concerned with mental health practice) help as well. Developing a good working relationship case by case and through other informal channels enhances the possibility of positive collaboration.

Further, therapists having contact with the court can also serve a public health purpose. Attorneys and judges may grow very skillful in family psychology, child psychology, and understanding mental health, but these are not the areas of their training. Therapists, in contact to the court, can help those trained in the law better understand the world of therapy. Therapists who work in this context often are asked to participate in educational activities for the court, and this in turn further solidifies relationships.

Becoming Familiar With Court Procedures

One crucial aspect of doing therapy in court-related cases is learning about how the court operates, expected points of interaction, and how to best function at that interface. First, one must become familiar and comfortable with the massive differences in culture between the judicial system and the world of psychotherapy. Whereas cooperation and establishing comfort are foundations of successful therapy, the legal system evolved with a foundation of opposing sides vigorously clashing, vying for victory. Although the culture in family courts has evolved toward greater emphasis on searching for solutions, many elements of the older, combative culture remain. Thus, therapists must learn to live with and adapt to these aspects of the legal system.

The legal system is also highly rule governed, and it is therefore essential for therapists who interact with it to learn the rules and procedures of the court that are relevant to clinical practice and how best to work in the context of those rules. One example lies in learning how to communicate and with whom about cases in relation to the customs of the specific jurisdiction. Another is in establishing a reliable way to learn about court developments involving clients, especially those that affect the therapy. One important example is that for court-involved cases, there often are court orders appointing the therapist to serve a role as therapist. In the best case, an attorney sends that order to the therapist; in the worst case, the therapist does not even know there has been an order and what it specifically says. When beginning work with court-referred cases, the therapist specifically needs to ask the clients and any referring attorneys for copies of any such relevant order. Occasionally, the content contains some surprise, such as the specification that a report will be generated to the court after a period of time.

The court and attorneys in the court in most instances are supportive of therapists, and judges and attorneys for children, in particular, will tend to protect therapists and their work. Having said that, there are exceptions. A crucial fact in the judicial system is that the therapist is not represented by an attorney (except in the rare instance when therapists hire an attorney to protect their own or their client's rights). Attorneys may be friendly and helpful, but their client is someone other than the therapist, and they may, when there is a conflict about whose interest predominates, jettison their support for the therapist in relation to what will help their case. Therefore, it is essential for therapists practicing in this area to develop knowledge and assertive skills about how and in what way they are willing to participate in the judicial process (see the subsequent discussion about functioning as a treating expert). It also is vital to have, either personally or through one's organization, a working relationship with an attorney who can consult about matters and intervene as needed.

When making referrals, the court and attorneys typically also have clear agendas in mind. Whatever the therapist chooses to do with that agenda (usually it is worth following), it is essential to actively coordinate with the court about it, lest the court envisions one set of procedures while the therapist follows another, leading to misunderstanding about who and what is involved in the therapy.

Drawing on Leverage From the Court and Attorneys in Therapy

Ideally, therapists and the court have similar aims in difficult divorce where there is court involvement. Fortunately, this is often the case, given obvious goals, such as resolving differences, limiting conflict, reducing psychopathology, and improving communication and connection.

Leverage from the court can prove to be the key ingredient in a successful therapy with court-involved difficult divorce. As has already been described, many clients in difficult divorce are in a stage of precontemplation in terms of understanding any role they may have in ongoing problems or any sense that they could play a part in problem resolution. To mitigate this problem, therapist skill in alliance-building is essential, but when therapists alone are working to build an alliance and promote change, they are swimming upstream against a powerful river. The judicial systems' involvement can help reverse the river's flow.

First, the court and attorneys are often the primary reason that those in difficult divorce seek treatment at all; not only do they suggest it, they often mandate it. They often can see that the sorts of remedies available through the judicial system (e.g., decisions about who has custody, division of assets, or whether a parent should have time with a child) are not able to touch the more basic difficulties in the family system.

Second, the court and attorneys can help cement therapeutic alliances by being strongly supportive of the therapy. Clients largely put their trust in their attorneys, and when the therapist is identified being helpful and working toward the right goals the therapy (and perhaps even that cooperation will in fact help their case if it does come down to a decision by the court), the therapeutic alliance can piggyback on client–lawyer alliances.

Third, the involvement of the court and its representatives can help mitigate the effects of clients' reactivity at those moments when clients are being challenged by the therapist and therapy. For example, if clients know the court will not tolerate their ending therapy prematurely, this can provide the buffer needed to allow for repair and the processing of steps toward change that may initially have seemed unapproachable to clients. In the same spirit, attorneys can help encourage a more open attitude toward the intervention strategies being used. Here, the responses of the attorneys involved is a vital wild card. If the parents' attorneys or the attorney representing the children provide supportive messages in terms of what is being done, this can have an enormous positive impact. However, if attorneys join against the intervention (e.g., "It's too early to bring the children into therapy"), this adds an additional constraint in the treatment. Indeed, even moving an attorney from opposing the flow of therapy to a neutral position can have a substantial positive impact.

Collaborating With the Court and Attorneys

Direct communication about what is transpiring in a case with the court and lawyers can be useful in a variety of ways. Best practice here varies with various roles filled by judges and attorneys. As already noted, judges rarely directly communicate with therapists, although they may occasionally ask for updates about progress, usually responded to in writing or through reports via attorneys representing children. Judges can be particularly helpful in ensuring that attendance follows agreements made and in providing feedback to litigants that is consistent with therapeutic goals. Typically, they only become involved with the therapy to the extent that issues are conveyed to them by one of the attorneys.

Attorneys representing children are the most common collaborators with therapists in the judicial system. Typically, attorneys for children function as important stakeholders in helping set and support therapeutic goals, communicating the key issues that they and the court view as in need of attention. It is important for therapy goals to fit with the overall goals of the attorney for the children.[8] The goals of the attorney for the children and the therapist ideally inform one another. Typically, these attorneys also share important information with therapists about the legal process and how it is progressing. They almost always strongly support therapy and typically actively intervene to preserve it when a client either stops attending or stops bringing children to therapy, or petitions the court to end therapy or change therapists. They also are the best conduits of information from the therapist to the court.

---

[8]Rarely, the attorney for the children may have a much different view of a family than the therapist. These are occasions for processing those differences and represent another place that therapy and the judicial process can collaborate to improve services to families.

Coordination and communication between attorneys for adult parties and therapists involves the greatest complexity. In the legal process, these attorneys represent only one person in what is a largely adversarial process, and therefore sharing with them about the content and progress of therapy needs to occur with caution. Some therapists, for this reason, have a rule barring any communication with these attorneys. However, there are special circumstances when such communication can be extremely useful and well worth the risk involved. This is principally in the context of clients who are less motivated; support of their attorneys can be instrumental in moving their clients toward pursuing therapy goals. Lawyers for various parties are often keenly aware of their clients' problem areas, even if in the adversarial process they may argue vociferously on their behalf. Attorneys may want to be helpful in moving their client to work at important issues, even as they represent their positions in disputes, and can be important allies. However, when involving attorneys for the parties, there need to be clear ground rules and an explicit understanding that sharing will involve only information about their own client, not the others in the family. Further, if the therapist is to share information from therapy with one attorney, it is vital to develop a similar interaction with the other party's attorney so that the process remains fair and balanced and has every appearance of being so.

Using the leverage of the court and attorneys does involve risks, and these must be considered and anticipated so that the cost–benefit ratio remains slanted toward benefit. Such reporting, even with the clearest communication, entails risk for inaccurate transmission, which can lead to alliance ruptures. Additionally, even accurate reports of negative information being conveyed, if not handled well, may lead to problems in alliance. Further, the mere sharing of information can engender a pattern of seemingly overt cooperation on the part of clients (i.e., following the rules) that covers a covert lack of cooperation. At other times, reporting can produce a symmetrical escalation of conflict between the therapist and one client. If the possibility of such sharing is not clearly indicated in the initial conversations and contract with the clients and made well known during the therapy, there is also potential for ethical problems related to confidentiality and privilege (L. R. Greenberg, Gould-Saltman, & Gottlieb, 2008). Yet even if this list of potential problems, working actively with attorneys and the court is almost always more useful than not in these cases.

Potential problems can be mitigated through transmission of crucial information in clear, concise, nonpathologizing language and by having clients fully understand the information that is being shared about them and with whom it is being shared. Also, it is important to bear in mind that some lawyers collaborate and use such information in better ways than others. Over time in working in this role, a sense evolves as to how information is likely to be used by different attorneys. The possibility of support for the therapy and the result of sharing is far more likely to be positive in dealing with attorneys for children or with the court (often through the attorney representing the children given that court etiquette does not allow for many ways to directly approach judges). Involving attorneys for the partners entails greater risk and should be reserved for situations in which some specific goal with a client can be served by bringing an attorney into the solution. Even in that circumstance, this is likely to be productive only with attorneys with whom the therapist already has a good working relationship and when similar sharing with the opposing attorney is not contraindicated.

A final word here: Efforts to work with attorneys, even those representing children, can have a potent positive impact but are fraught with potential difficulties. Working in this systemic way is a process to grow into through experience with these cases. Once a therapist is well grounded in working with the legal system, the potential for enabling positive outcomes is greatly increased through such collaboration, but while learning how to work with cases in the legal system, it is better to remain conservative about sharing. And even for the most experienced therapists in this work, sharing with attorneys for the partners in a case needs to be strictly limited to feedback to those attorneys about their own client and eliciting their support for the therapy goals for that client, not cross the boundary into disclosing information about others involved in the case.

> The Doherty family came before the Court with multiple problems. During the process of divorce, Siobhan, the mother, and Dan, the father, fought about almost every issue. When their son, Connor, age 15, refused to go to school for several days, this only served to heighten the level of arguments between the couple. When they presented in court, with the lawyers arguing why each parent should be the parent with primary authority about and have the most of the time with Connor, the judge appointed Isabella as Connor's attorney. Isabella immediately involved Vincent as an individual therapist to see Connor, and Noreen as a family therapist to see Connor and the parents. Connor was willing, if reluctant, to participate in these therapies, as was Siobhan, but Dan refused.

Thus, the individual therapy with Connor began, centered on overcoming his school refusal and helping him differentiate from the parental fight; the family therapy did not commence, however. When Noreen informed Isabella about Dan's refusal to attend family therapy, Isabella called Dan and let him know why she thought the therapy would help and said that she would have to let the court know if he did not attend. Dan then attended an initial meeting with the therapist but would not schedule further appointments. When informed of this, Isabella brought an order before the judge that Dan attend the therapy, which the court approved. That order specified that Dan's access to his son would be radically reduced if he did not attend therapy. Dan then began to regularly attend the sessions that were structured with Siobhan and Connor, providing an opportunity to deal with coparenting and father–son issues. As the case proceeded, Noreen and Vincent kept Isabella informed about the progress of therapy, and helped Isabella differentiate between times when court intervention was needed versus times when the conflict was more ordinary, and Isabella kept Noreen and Vincent informed about developments in court.

The Therapist as Treating Expert

The preceding considerations apply to collaboration of therapists and the judicial process toward the shared goals of improving the lives of those in difficult divorce. There is a much different way therapists can become involved in the legal process. This is when the court or attorneys seek information from the therapist beyond who has attended what sessions to inform judicial decisions. Therapists may be asked to file reports or may be subpoenaed as witnesses in legal matters. L. R. Greenberg and Gould (2001) described the special role for what they term the *treating expert*, who collaborates with the judicial system in divorce cases, serving both as therapist to the clients and as a reporter to the court in service of the goals of the judicial system. This is an important role, but it is one best reserved for special circumstances. Therapists participating in judicial processes can easily undermine any sense of a multipartial alliance and result in damage to any possibility of progress. The cost–benefit ratio of engaging in such a role is largely on the cost side, given that the therapy is likely to suffer and that there are more nuanced ways that have been already been described that therapists can work in tandem with the judicial system.

There are three principal exceptions to this caution. One is in the role therapists can play in informing custody evaluations, where they can be informative without unduly disrupting therapy (discussed in more detail shortly). The second is in therapies that are not making progress, where there are clear constraints to progress to which the therapist can speak. In such cases, there can be value in having the constraints to progress inform the judicial process. The third, closely related to the second, are in therapies that have concluded and are not likely to resume in which the therapist might be able to share ideas that inform the judicial process. Always, costs and benefits of offering this information need to be weighed. There are other cautions as well. Clearly, therapists should remain consistent with the level of confidentially and potential reporting to the court described at the beginning of therapy.[9]

Additionally, to effectively function in court-involved cases, therapists need to develop good toolkits for being in charge of their own participation in the judicial process. Although there is no way to perfectly achieve this goal (judges are by law granted authority to make decisions about such matters), skillful, experienced therapists learn to work effectively and assertively in the context of the judicial system. They come to know what are typical and reasonable expectations for their participation in judicial procedures. For example, dates of service and records are typically expected to be delivered when requested (this is even a client right guaranteed by the Health Insurance Portability and Accountability Act). Knowing such expectations, records are kept with the possibility that they might be subpoenaed in the legal process. Experienced therapists also learn to distinguish between requests for materials and testimony and when participation is mandated. Further, they acquire a set of ways for discouraging attorneys from calling them as witnesses, either in hearings, depositions, or trials, when they believe it unhelpful to participate in this way in the legal process. For example, letting the attorney who wants the therapist's participation know that it will not be helpful to their client's case for the therapist to be called usually is sufficient to minimize that possibility. Further, they come to understand when they need to consult their own counsel about matters and use such counsel when needed.

More broadly, experienced therapists who work in this area with practice become familiar over time with the environment and approach the judicial system as another arena in which to work, rather than a place to fear. Such experienced therapists cooperate with the judicial system, finding it primarily an ally. Occasionally, the judge in a case may be left to decide whether a therapist needs to testify, but either way, the therapist knows how to minimize any threats. In most jurisdictions, assertive therapists, even with the most contentious cases, exercise a good deal of control over how much they choose to directly participate in the judicial process.

COORDINATION WITH OTHER HELPING PROFESSIONALS

Coordination is also critical between therapists and other helping professionals in difficult divorce. As already noted, difficult divorce can become a therapist's Tower of Babel, inviting conflict in goals and strategies across professionals.

---

[9]"To the extent possible" must be added to this sentence given that the court may have ultimate say to override the therapist's position about such matters. This only happen rarely but is a possibility that must be considered.

Working With Child Custody Evaluators

Child custody evaluations centered on issues of child custody, time with parents, or access of parents to children has already been discussed in this book in the context of evaluations completed before treatment begins. In that context, these evaluations can be an enormously helpful tool in assessment and setting treatment goals. Here, the focus is on child custody evaluations that are being conducted during treatment and the therapist's role in informing those evaluations. These evaluations are likely to have a vital role in the judicial system in the process of arriving as at a resolution for cases, either as a factor in negotiation (child custody evaluations carry a good deal of weight if there is going to be a trial and therefore are a strong force to resolution) or in judges' decisions after trial.

In integrative therapy for difficult divorce, following L. R. Greenberg and Gould's (2001) notion of the treating expert, therapists are viewed as having a responsibility to cooperate with custody evaluations. Therapists have unique information relevant to the questions in focus for the custody evaluator. The alternative of withholding that information leaves the possibility that this crucial aspect of the judicial process will proceed with incomplete information.

The key question becomes how best to share information with the custody evaluator without setting back the therapeutic process substantially. Once the report is issued, clients often have access to the report, which includes what the therapist has said, and this may be interpreted as a major breach of trust by some clients.

The first step in the process is to be sure clients sign appropriate releases.[10] With such releases signed, the therapist is left to work out an equation of how much to share with the evaluator versus promoting the best chance for treatment success. As a practical matter, this is typically less a problem than it might be theoretically. Most evaluators are respectful of the therapist's position in these cases and want to be supportive of therapy. They also have other sources for most of the information they need about the clients. The unique information from the therapist is about participation in the process of therapy. Most evaluators are satisfied with sharing the facts of the treatment (e.g., how long treatment has gone on, who has been involved, therapy goals, progress made), coupled with any observations the therapist may think are important to offer. In some instances, where the therapist judges external reporting is more important than maintaining alliance, he or she can choose

---

[10]Bear in mind here that, unfortunately, in this context, clients are in a bind. They have almost no actual room to refuse such a release. Not letting one's therapist or one's child's therapist talk to a custody evaluator is not a good way to win favor in an evaluation.

to say more. Given that the custody evaluator is performing an assessment task that involves forming an opinion on a few very concrete decisions, such as how custody and time with the children are divided, the failure to include the therapist's softer observations in a report are of less importance.

It should be added that many difficult divorces that reach the point of a child custody evaluation go on for extended periods and segue into post-divorce problems; thus, some of these therapies become long-term propositions. In these cases, the eventual emergence of the custody report can prove an additional resource for assessment and for reconsideration of therapy goals.

Working With Parenting Coordinators

Parenting coordinators are almost always strong allies with the goals of therapy (Greenberg & Sullivan, 2012). They also are, in most instances, a postdivorce legacy of difficult divorce (although they can be appointed for emerging difficulty later), left with the task of helping poorly cooperating parents avoid gridlock after all of the lawyers involved are out of the picture. When therapy and parenting coordination are going on in parallel, a simple division has the parenting coordinator involved in parent communication and negotiation, while the therapist pays more attention to the cognitions, emotions, and psychodynamic and historical factors that are more psychological and systemic in the clients the therapist sees. That the parenting coordinator can arbitrate small differences also enhances the possibility for progress in therapy, as at least short-term solutions are imposed about intractable conflicts, allowing more space to consider larger issues. The "bad-cop" presence of the parenting coordinator in the role of decision-maker can also free up space for greater cooperation in the safer context of therapy.

Working With Other Mental Health Professionals

Whether or not the therapist follows the model suggested in this book, treatment of difficult divorce requires a systemic approach to the coordination of treatments. To fail to grasp the systemic nature of the therapy system leaves therapists responding to the experiential world of their clients (which is often quite distorted). The old truism of supporting the client in his or her experience is a risk factor in these cases (as already noted, this is even the case in the treatment of children). And there is always the potential for the emergence of an isomorphic disagreement between therapists that parallels the disagreements between their respective clients.

Thus, difficult divorce is a therapy context that necessitates collaboration with other therapists involved in a case. The therapist treating a case may be the only therapist, but when other therapists are involved, there is a need for mutual sharing of information, consultation about goals, and follow-up about progress. Successful systemic therapy begins with obtaining a complete list of therapists involved in the first session (some therapists may not be mentioned if this question is not specifically asked). This needs to be followed by an explanation of the need for collaboration and obtaining the necessary releases of information to contact those therapists (including from children when their release is needed under the law). The good news here is that almost all clients, weary of the legal process and conflict, readily agree to such releases. Those who do not agree necessitate a digression into an individual meeting to discuss why they don't want to sign such a release. Here, typically, the therapist can agree on including some limitation about sharing that allows for contact (e.g., not to include information about a new relationship or other off-limits topics). Clients who won't agree to such sharing, even on a qualified basis, are best left to find another therapist. Insisting on this restriction is like asking a surgeon to proceed without an MRI scan.[11]

Beyond sharing, there is value in some organization to the therapies. Who will carry the task of sharing across therapists? Someone has to take on the role of being the central hub for moving intertherapist communication. It is natural for the therapist treating the largest system to have this role; thus, the family therapist takes on this responsibility in the model presented here. Nonetheless, if you are the therapist in such a case, volunteering for this task is suggested, whatever role you play in the broader picture; this ensures that someone will consciously take on the responsibility of organizing communication. The key issue is not so much who does this task as that someone stays on top of the coordination (Pinsof et al., 2018).

The most important specific aspects of sharing are communicating client perspectives, therapist perspectives, the most relevant information (this is a landscape of "alternative facts"), and therapy goals. Arriving together at a metalevel set of therapy goals is enormously helpful. For a team working together, this is relatively simple (even though the pulls of countertransference toward one's own specific clients remain). Working within the model presented here, if the therapists draw from the same integrative framework, work in one therapy can orient toward the same goals as in another, and extend the work in the other context. This also enhances the possibility that positive movement in one subsystem will lead to positive movement in

---

[11]Of course, never say never. Sometimes such insistence is the product of long histories of trauma around issues of trust. There, a "no" might invite conversation to ensure safety. Nonetheless, the end point remains the same: Therapies in difficult divorce are very much at risk unless there can be sharing among therapists.

another. To be clear, the specific content of the work in each therapy may vary across formats and therapists, but the overarching metalevel goals are coordinated to move toward the same ends (as when one parent works toward better self-control and the other on his or her anxieties about the other's dysregulation).

The task becomes more complex when the therapists are not part of a team but work in different environments. They also may have differences in their therapeutic orientation or very different histories with the case. Some may be recently involved in relation to the divorce, whereas others may have worked for many years as therapists to specific individuals in the family. In such instances, the goals in coordination may necessarily be more modest—less to introduce a master therapy plan involving everyone, and more for there to be just enough coordination and sharing. These goals of coordination become to be sure that therapists aren't pulling in opposite directions and to serve broad, metalevel goals of better cooperation; moving through the divorce; and having the least harm to everyone. The good news here is that, although therapists take very different directions in their work, it is typically fairly easy to engage them in a joint task in the name of the greater good for all when there is coordination of efforts. It is also important to be realistic about a plan for coordinating. It is unlikely everyone will physically get together or talk once a week. The question is whether there can be a few timely conversations, especially at moments when constraints seem to be getting in the way of progress.

ETHICS AND THE LAW

Difficult divorce is a territory in which ethical and legal quagmires are omnipresent. A good working knowledge of the applicable ethical code for one's specific profession (e.g., the *Ethical Principles of Psychologists and Code of Conduct*; American Psychological Association, 2017) as well as the multidisciplinary Association of Family and Conciliation Courts (2011) guidelines for court-involved therapy are essential as a foundation of this therapy.[12] Similarly, knowledge of relevant law matters a great deal. Laws across the various jurisdictions in the United States may be similar, but minor distinctions in the legal arena make a significant difference. Matters of ethics and law about issues such as consent to treatment, privilege, parental rights, and what constitutes dual relationships are essential aspects of good treatment.

---

[12]Greenberg, Gould-Saltman, and Gottlieb (2008) provided a particularly instructive analysis of best ethical practice in several case examples of typical problems that emerge in disputes about child custody.

SUMMARY

This chapter examined interactions between therapy in difficult divorce and the judicial system. Although therapy and the judicial system represent very different cultures, in difficult divorce, therapy goals and those of the court typically coincide in seeking problem resolution. Yet therapy must also interact with other forces in the judicial system that move toward conflict. Therapists who work in this environment need to become familiar with the judicial process, overcome any anxiety in working with this process, learn how to speak in language that is understandable in the legal environment, cooperate with those in the legal system while asserting themselves when needed, and develop their skills in selectively using support from within the judicial system to further therapy goals. A systemic approach to working with other helping professions is similarly emphasized. The next chapter considers therapy with some of the more specific problems that most often appear in difficult divorce.

8

SPECIAL CHALLENGES AND PROBLEMS IN DIFFICULT DIVORCE

Difficult divorces all have their own unique lives, but several special issues frequently arise that call for specific adaptations of therapeutic strategies. This chapter considers several common specific points at issue. In each situation, the discussion of treatment focuses on the specific application of the integrative model of working with difficult divorce to this problem set. That is, the focus is on what is special, specific, and most pertinent in the applications of the model in the context of this kind of case, rather than reviewing again the full range of possibilities for intervention within the treatment protocol (all of which may be employed in a specific case depending on the case formulation). Therapy with any of these types of cases draws from the core set of intervention strategies identified in Chapter 6.

These core strategies are supplemented with evidence-based strategies for specific problems encountered (e.g., relational violence, dysregulation, depression), which typically apply similar interventions as in the model to

http://dx.doi.org/10.1037/0000116-009
Treating the Difficult Divorce: A Practical Guide for Psychotherapists, by J. L. Lebow

other specific problems and disorders. As elsewhere in this book, in describing how treatment proceeds for each of these specific variations on difficult divorce, the most typical course of treatment is presented. The makeup of any specific treatment varies with the case formulation, treatment goals, therapist skills, clients, and context.

Whatever the type of problem encountered, it is essential to rein in goals to ensure that they are attainable, so that the treatment can remain cost-effective. In these difficult divorcing systems, it is rare that conflicts are ever fully resolved. Goals that involve creating greater distance between parents, minimal communication, quieter exchanges, and better individual functioning are most easily achievable. Attaining even these ends typically requires considerable change at many levels, and the use of a variety of treatment strategies.

ISSUES CENTERED ON CONFLICT

One set of issues centers on overt, pernicious conflicts. This section considers issues ranging from custody and time allocation with children, situations in which former partners must live in the same house during divorce proceedings, violence, and extreme disengagement, among other particularly difficult conditions in difficult divorce.

Difficulties Over Child Custody and Allocating Time With Children

Conflicts over child custody and visitation number among the most pathogenic situations families face. This problem combines several stressors: the family structure is unclear; children are triangulated between parents; and others (including family, friends, and lawyers) readily become involved in these disputes. This subset of divorcing parents remains mired in intractable conflict over extended periods. Given the way such conflicts are interwoven with the legal system and the concern of the court about children's welfare, these families or some subsystem within the family (e.g., a child or the parents together) are often mandated by the court or through arrangements between attorneys to seek treatment.

The lack of agreement about family structure coupled with high levels of direct conflict or frustrating sequences marked by passive-aggression and demand–withdrawal are special characteristics of these families. Such patterns can make for great volatility around the establishment of norms that fit with postdivorce life. When is each child with which parent? What kinds of flexibility is there around rules regarding exchanges and scheduling patterns? How much information is appropriate for parents to want children to share across homes and for children to share? There is little agreement about such questions in these families.

In the midst of issues, major goals of therapy become helping family members find positions from which they might better resolve differences and evolve a new family structure and finding better ways to live in limbo until these questions are settled. One critical aspect of assessment in these cases lies in evaluating how readily attainable a resolution between the parents may be. Part of the problem is that the level of acrimony and drama in these cases may or may not be related to the ease of reaching a resolution. For some highly entrenched families, reaching a resolution is only possible, if it is at all, after a long series of interventions that can move toward greater cooperation. For others, even with high acrimony, resolutions can be more readily achieved, insofar as resolution simply means the family can reach an agreement and reorganize in the context of that structure. Sometimes, the only way to differentiate between families that can reach and support agreements and those that cannot is to track the success or failure at efforts to resolve differences. Those families that perfunctorily move through mediation, have extensive support from lawyers and families for the conflict, carry the weight of other agendas in these conflicts, and argue over even the smallest points of disagreement are ones for whom only a very slow evolving process will succeed.

Each of the core intervention strategies in the model is shaped to this specific problem in the treatment of these cases. Psychoeducation emphasizes raising consciousness about the many problems that arise from the lack of developing a new structure, the natural difficulty in moving from one type of structure to another, and the reality that almost all families adapt to new structures over time. Helping family members become knowledgeable about the merits and demerits of various structures for child custody also has considerable value (Ackerman, 2008; Emery, 2016; Kelly & Lamb, 2000). Even if the negotiation is occurring in a parallel mediation or through lawyers, it is valuable to ensure that parents understand the various options that they are considering for custody and time with children.

In many of these families mired in being unable to agree on a new structure, the factors that make a difference can be minor. Families can be stuck over how many days children will be apart from one parent or over differences over 1 day in 2 weeks in parenting. This is not to discount the crucial quality of larger difference in time with children for parents, but it is often helpful simply to walk clients though how much actual time the differences between the former partners might be. For others, the difference between parents stems from one parent looking toward a totally unrealistic solution (the parent more involved with the children wanting almost all the time with the children, or a minimally involved parent envisioning a 50–50 split arrangement). In those instances, therapist feedback about what has been actuarially realistic for similar families is generally experienced as painful and questioned, but it can be helpful as part of an overall process of getting to a resolution of the dispute.

As in much of this work, these are cases to emphasize calming acceptance-oriented interventions, such as mindful practice, reattribution, radical acceptance, narrative change, and exploring underlying emotion, to help clients find a steadier place from which alternatives can be explored. It is one thing to have a difference of opinion about how to divide time; it is quite another to be caught up in a downward spiral around these issues. Families can live with uncertainty about structure for a time (albeit this is less than optimal) if family life can remain steady and secure. Even if differences cannot be negotiated, intervention that helps stabilize life for that time makes a huge difference. Although other parties may handle the negotiation, therapy is the only place where stability during this time is likely to be enhanced (both in interactions and internally within the clients), and thus this is a vital proximate goal.

These are also cases in which it is helpful to locate the block to negotiation and see whether strategies of intervention targeted at that block might prove helpful. For example, if the primary issue for one parent is hurt (discussed subsequently), the process of negotiation may be limited until that hurt is further processed. Similarly, if the primary issue is a fear on one parent's part about the competence of the parenting of the other parent, that fear can be addressed by working directly on the parenting of the second parent.

Cases in which such disputes center on allegations about troubling behavior by parents (e.g., violence, substance use) differ from other such conflicts in that the linchpin of these conflicts are about a vital factual matter: whether a child is safe with a parent. Here, finding ways to sort out those allegations, usually with the help of fact-finding done by the court as related by the attorney for the children, plays an essential role in how to proceed. In these families, the most useful emphasis of therapy depends on evaluation of the complaint and how it is regarded in court. When individual problems are found in a parent, focus moves to emphasis of work with him or her on that problem and helping others in the family find constructive ways to deal with it (e.g., see the subsequent sections on parental violence and psychopathology). When such concerns turn out to be exaggerated, more attention focuses on other family members' perceptions and reactions. However, in many cases, and almost always especially early in therapy, the picture is far from clear. In this circumstance, best practice incorporates work with the parent alleged to show the troubling behavior (either specifically on the behavior or to minimize the perception that the behavior is severe) and with the remainder of the system in finding ways to find steady responses that do not overpathologize.

Almost inevitably in disputes about child custody or time with children, the work in therapy is interwoven with negotiation in other forums, perhaps mediation or meetings or other exchanges between attorneys. When this is the case, it is best to leave the actual negotiation to others. The therapy task is principally to enhance openness to possible solutions and negotiation, rather than to negotiate in therapy. Given the many forces moving toward reaching an agreement that include monies spent on the legal process, time expended, and the wear and tear on all involved, enhancing such openness can lead to agreements even in what look to be intractable disputes.

Therapy with children in the context of these disputes can also have profound positive effects. Although in the best of circumstances, children can be insulated from these disputes, most are not, and the natural inclination to speak one's feelings can be coopted into triangulation about taking sides. The therapist can help support children in understanding their feelings and opinions but also help coach them in remaining from taking on a role in the conflict and keeping their focus on their own lives and well-being. A paradox about these cases is that even though everyone speaks the legal talk of the "best interest of the child" (which is written into every state law in the United States about child custody), children are often collateral damage in these conflicts.

Just as maintenance follows behavior change in the stage-of-change model, when agreements are reached in these cases, it is helpful to continue therapy long enough to help the family accept and adapt to the change that has occurred and find positive ways to engage with the new family structure with a minimum of conflict. Many small behavioral exchanges go along with a new family structure (When is homework done where? Where does stuff go?), and anticipation and an ounce of prevention can help during this delicate transition. For court-ordered cases, this concept moves against the natural tendency to discontinue treatment when the court case ends and court orders for therapy no longer apply. Motivational interviewing to raise awareness of the value of continuing therapy through the transition is helpful in mitigating this problem, as is obtaining agreements with the lawyers for the therapies to continue for a time after the litigation ends.

> Ling Chen and Feng Wu were referred in therapy during a custody dispute. Ling Chen, a stay-at-home mother, thought that the children should be with her all for except an occasional dinner with father on Saturdays. Feng Wu believed he should be a major part of the children's lives and had filed for a 50–50 split time arrangement. They had moved through mediation with no resolution about custody and visitation. When the

family was referred for therapy, the therapist quickly assessed that there was little chance for resolution of these issues. He provided some basic psychoeducation about child custody: Fathers are always granted more than an occasional dinner, and mothers and fathers with their histories rarely have 50–50 splits in time. However, even these thoughts were met with doubt from both former partners.

Therefore, the therapist moved the focus away from the conflict about child custody to learning to live through this period of transition. Ling Chen and Feng Wu also had considerable conflict, secondary to their major differences about child custody. The provocative ways each acted toward the other were in marked contrast to their usual ways of acting. Focus first centered on using meditation techniques, with which both were familiar from their families of origin, to calm themselves and then be intentional in not creating a "warlike" environment. This was followed by simple efforts at communication and problem-solving about everyday life. With this new frame in focus, considerable progress ensued.

When conflict reemerged, the therapist met with the ex-partners together, and each alone to learn from that experience, emphasizing how to stay steady, so as to live successfully in this gray zone of life in a way that was best for them and the children. Eventually, after a trial about custody, the court ordered a traditional split of the children, with father having them every other weekend and an occasional dinner during the week, and joint custody about decision-making.

High-Conflict Cases

High-conflict families have frequent intense disagreements marked by angry exchanges and outbursts. High-conflict cases are often thought of as synonymous with disputes over child custody and visitation. However, families can be stuck in terms of resolution about custody and time with parents without high levels of conflict, and for other families, high conflict occurs even if they reach agreement about the few simple structures involved in deciding child custody. A variation on high conflict is the demand–withdraw pattern, in which there may be fewer outbursts, but high levels of anger and little in the way of problem-solving. The research literature shows that in both families who are divorcing and those who are not, each of these patterns has negative effects on all involved. High acrimony in divorcing families numbers among the most pernicious factors in the mental health of child and adults (Drozd, Saini, & Olesen, 2016).

Therapy in the context of high conflict prioritizes strategies of anger management and emotional regulation. Fortunately, there are evidence-based methods for reducing conflict and anger management in couples and families in systemic therapy (Karam & Lebow, 2006), cognitive behavior therapy

(Reilly & Shopshire, 2015), and dialectical behavior therapy (Fruzzetti, 2006; Fruzzetti & Payne, 2015; Fruzzetti, Santisteban, & Hoffman, 2007).

When conflicts are primarily between parents, the first strategy is to create structures that minimize the interface between parents. There are simple behavioral ways to do this, yet these are ways in which volatile couples often do not engage. For example, forming simple agreements around points of contact, such as drop-offs, that ensure there will not be direct contact, reduces the possibilities for conflict. Closely related is creating a mutually agreed-on time-out procedure for when anger begins to escalate. A second strategy, applicable to both interparental conflict but also to high conflict involving children and others, lies in presenting and practicing a simplified version of mindful practice and emotion regulation. Teaching and practicing self-monitoring, breathing, and self-calming, and using thought records targeted to reducing emotional arousal have extensive evidence for helping with emotional dysregulation (Karam & Lebow, 2006). A third set of strategies lies in practicing rule driven ways of communicating. This most appropriately begins with establishing simple rules for texting and e-mail, refraining from verbal communication until after these lower intensity forms are well managed. Often, even keeping texting or e-mailing modulated requires considerable practice, invoking thought records to slow down and making the process of communicating more intentional. In both electronic and personal interactions, a procedure of taking time-outs when the conversation begins to go badly should be incorporated.

In terms of the format of treatment, high-conflict families most successfully begin treatment with several individual meetings focused on self-regulation skills. After a few such sessions (how many is best judged by skill development, not by a set number of sessions), conjoint sessions that involve the angry dyad or larger subsystem are introduced to build on these skills together and begin to see whether there might be ways to problem-solve about differences.

High-conflict divorce is almost invariably thought of as conflict between former partners. However, children also participate in high conflict by either entering into parent arguments or in having arguments with parents or siblings about various issues. When children are involved in conflict, part of assessment focuses on the important differential assessment of how much the conflict is the result of triangulation in the divorce compared with other factors Whichever is the case (and sometimes it may be a combination of these ingredients), work on self-regulation and problem-solving is indicated for both parents and children. Between parents and children, the planned mutual avoidance that might be sought in former partners becomes untenable, and thus drawing on each conflict as an opportunity for further practice at anger management is essential. When triangulation is involved, additional focus needs to move to helping the child differentiate from the parental conflict. Strategies here include speaking directly to the child's role that has emerged, using motivational interviewing to determine whether this problem can move into focus, and examining the merits and demerits of a child serving (or being willing to serve) this mission from a cognitive standpoint. Work with the parent who is not involved in the conflict focuses on helping him or her understand ways that child loyalties can emerge, the destructive impact on children this situation, and working to explicitly and implicitly help the parent challenge the child about these behaviors rather than support them.

Although not as pernicious as direct high conflict, the quieter demand–withdraw version of high conflict deserves a similar level of attention. Here, the intervention focus is less on self-control around explosive behavior, and more on finding ways to notice the emergence of this state and find ways to stay in contact or take a mutually agreed time-out and return to conversation. Key strategies here lie in self-regulation, teaching and practicing direct communication and problem-solving skills, becoming aware of when emotion distracts from these tasks, and working on self-talk to be able to stay in connection long enough to complete the business required.

> Theresa and Ted were well into the process of divorcing, yet every time they came into contact, a heated argument would occur. Each would become dysregulated, and they came to be well known in their children's school for screaming at one another during children's events. Therapy began by arranging, with the help of the attorney, an alternating schedule for attending child events and for pick-ups and drop-offs so that only one parent would take care of each event. In separate meetings, Marcelo, the therapist, worked with each of them on behavioral, cognitive, and dialectical behavior therapy anger management skills. They each practiced these skills in situations that did not involve their former partner, and in separate sessions with Marcelo, they role played the sorts of situations that triggered their angry fights. An intentional choreography was created with each of them about how they might best interact with the other, with considerable practice with breathing, relaxation techniques, mindful practice, noticing signs of getting angry, and bringing their developing toolkits to those emerging feelings.
>
> Marcelo then brought them together in session with the first meetings framed as further opportunities to practice their new skills. In the first meeting, they agreed to a time-out procedure to follow, in sessions and in the future, when someone became overly angry. With practice, both greatly improved in their anger management, and although one or the other might become angry in session, they followed the "fire drill" for what to do when this occurred; after this, they never simultaneously fell into a dysregulated state. This then allowed for a plan, again shaped with the attorney for the children, for them to try being in the same place

around their children. Although they often had complaints about each other, and their differences did not fully subside, the dramatic incidents did not happen again. Marcelo continued to work with them to further develop detached coparenting.

Residing in the Same House

One of the most problematic situations encountered in divorce therapy occurs when a couple shares a single household over a lengthy period, while in the active process of divorcing. The legal system often encourages such tortuous family arrangements. Lawyers frequently advise their clients to remain in the marital home until financial matters, what will happen to the family home, and child custody are resolved.[1] Residing together over time, while one or both partners are exiting the relationship, sets a uniquely unstable and agonizing frame for family life. Arguments about who is leaving whom for what reason, division of assets, who has what children at what time, whose lawyer has filed what motion, who is dating outside the relationship, and a bevy of other issues await the inevitable spark, as do endless opportunities for triangulation of children. As John and Julie Gottman (2015) highlighted, so much of the success of couple relationships depends on positive sentiment override. This arrangement almost guarantees a total absence of positive sentiment override and a giant dose of negative sentiment override, as well as many simultaneous problems to process.

As with other central negotiations in difficult divorce, there is little likelihood that therapy will result in a breakthrough in negotiation, such that someone will move out. Occasionally, in meetings alone, in weighing the actual pros and cons of this arrangement, someone will find the wisdom in a decision to move out, but more of the value of therapy in this context lies in promoting better living through wartime. One thread lies in negotiating clear expectations for behavior exchanges in the home, such as how time with children will be divided while parents reside together, who will be responsible for what, and what coparenting will occur. Another lies in basic training in anger management, even for families who have not yet displayed anger issues. Creating a simple structure for communication also is helpful, as are third-wave methods, such as radical acceptance, for helping clients live with problematic situations. In these ways, expectations can be clearly specified, and points of contact and conflict between the partners kept to a

---

[1]Unfortunately, this isn't the worst of advice in terms of the legal outcomes. Courts tend to take into account the status quo in making their decisions, and thus, if one parent exits without an arrangement with their former partner for time with the children that they find acceptable, he or she is at risk for being at considerable disadvantage in future legal wrangling about this matter.

minimum. As in all types of cases, specific intervention strategies vary with the case formulation.

> Evelyn filed for divorce after 11 years of marriage and asked Moishe to move out. Moishe refused, responding that if Evelyn wanted a divorce, she should move out. For a month, they both continued to sleep in the master bedroom in their home. There was much arguing and little sleep, and Moishe finally moved to the basement. Evelyn traditionally had driven the children to school and picked them up. Moishe began to drive them to school and take the children to activities on random days. The children, who were more attached to their mother, would spend more time with her. Moishe would become hurt and angry and argue with Evelyn about this and make critical remarks to the children about their not caring about him. The children became very anxious in relation to the tension in the home and their father's reaction.
>
> When the family was referred for therapy, the first agenda was to find ways for Evelyn and Moishe to live together through this time that did not continue the "accident waiting to happen" that the case history entailed. The therapist negotiated a plan for dividing time in the home that allowed both parents substantial time with the children. An arrangement was also negotiated for other ground rules in the marital home, such as each parent's responsibilities. A schedule was arranged that had each parent in the other's presence for a minimal time.
>
> In individual meetings with Moishe, the focus moved to his desire to restore what had been a positive relationship with his children. Cognitive techniques were employed to work with his powerful feelings, so that he could stay connected with them even when distressed. The case proceeded with the attorneys over time through the process of deciding custody and time for each parent with the children. During the year this required, tension remained, but at a lower level, and there were no more angry confrontations.

Violence

When a family has a history of relational violence, special measures must be taken. This truly is a situation in which the primary consideration must be to first protect the clients. The good news here for therapists is that issues of family violence in difficult divorce are likely to be evaluated and closely monitored within the judicial system. This means that typically the therapist has more to work with in these cases than simply the clashing reports of various family members. In this world of multiple realities, it is enormously helpful that someone is assessing evidence (not just reports) and has the ability to restrict access to children and set orders of protection for those showing violent, threatening, or harassing behavior.

Nevertheless, when there are allegations of violence, therapy should, as always, first be structured in ways that minimize any possibilities for future violence (Rossi et al., 2016). Conjoint meetings in the wake of such allegations are contraindicated until allegations have been investigated and determined to be without merit or there is assurance that sufficient work has been done with the perpetrator(s) in individual meetings so that sessions and their aftermath can be safe. Even then, under such circumstances, therapists should ensure that clients come to and leave sessions at different times to further ensure safety. It is important to bear in mind that divorce is often a time when even persons with no history of violence engage in violent confrontations and that rates of such marital violence are typically underreported (O'Leary, 2008). Further, in high-conflict child custody disputes or when there is a prior history of couple violence or child maltreatment, the therapist must plan for safety even when clients have not raised such issues.

Where there has been a history of violence, therapy begins with work with the perpetrator in individual meetings drawing from relational protocols for treating domestic violence (O'Leary, 2008; Stith & McCollum, 2009) and parallel meetings with others in the family to help them deal with their traumatic experience. Therapy with the perpetrator features evidence-based methods for dealing with relational violence, such as mindful practice, self-monitoring of arousal, time-outs when becoming dysregulated, and calming self-talk. There also is a focus on helping clients find a position in which they can take responsibility for their prior behavior in subsequent meetings. Therapy with the other family members focuses on safety planning and speaking to the complex feelings that inevitably come to be involved. Once progress has been made with these targets (and any related targets, such as substance abuse), the therapist can segue to meetings that include the formerly violent person and other members of the family. Work between parents and children includes opportunities for children to voice their experience and helping the once-violent parent take full responsibility for his or her behavior. Typically, additional work is needed to help one former partner overcome anxiety about the other's parenting, which almost invariably accompanies an ex-partner's contact with the children. Here, cognitive–behavioral methods for dealing with anxiety, combined with positive feedback about the parenting that is being observed, are the most direct routes to reducing these fears.

The focus is to slowly work to develop more predictable and calm exchanges, such that safety needs are satisfied and new experiences do not retraumatize. If retraumatizing experiences occur in therapy, even without violence, therapy should be paused until it can resume being therapeutic.

It is important to add here that family therapy is often proposed by courts as the place for violent parents and children who are out of contact to get together, so that there can be some connection. Wisely, the court in these cases can see that merely having contact occur in a supervised setting with what typically might be an off-duty police officer, negating the possibility of violence in session, is not enough in such cases, and therapy is viewed as a crucial adjunct or alternative to supervised visitation. In such circumstances, the therapist should be even more careful to ensure safety. Beyond working with the abusive parent, it is best to pursue these therapies in stages. The first stage emphasizes ways to calm any interactions through mindful practice and related techniques so that family members can be in each other's presence. The next steps works toward the child feeling able to voice grievances, with an apology from the abusive parent. Only then will parties be able to explore other aspects of the relationship.

It must be added that there are differences in violent parents, both in the degree of violence and the possibility of change (Holtzworth-Munroe, Meehan, Herron, & Stuart, 1999). Domestic terrorists, for example, are not candidates for conjoint therapy.

Other parents, although not physically violent, are psychologically abusive, but contact may be just as traumatic for children. Much of the same considerations and methods apply in treatment with those individuals and their families.

ISSUES INVOLVED WITH DISENGAGEMENT

Although conflict is the first problem most people think of in difficult divorce, variations on radical disengagement can be just as problematic.

Extreme Disengagement Between Parents

A very different set of problems comes with extreme disengagement. Although it is normative for married partners without children to fully disengage from one another, such disengagement in families with children between parents, or between parents and children, lead to difficulties in communication, problem-solving, family structure, and any healing process that might occur over time. The key word here is *extreme*; families can function with minimal contact between former spouses and even with a sense of distance between a child and parent, but not so much as to be dysfunctional. Extreme disengagement can come as a mutual process between parents but can also occur when one parent refuses contact with the other. Sometimes parents hold very different views of these interchanges, with the distancing parent believing the other is a conflict waiting to happen, whereas the other parent emphasizes the distancing behavior, and they remain locked in an endless circular process.

In the context of such disengagement, efforts should first focus on psychoeducation and behavioral experiments to explore greater contact. Psychoeducation stresses the inevitably strong feelings that accompany divorce and how these can readily move toward fairly complete cutoffs, which have negative effects. Carefully planned behavioral experiments focus on bringing the disconnected parties together and seeing whether contact and dialogue about contact can make a difference. Sometimes the problem is simply avoidance, and the cutoff can be negotiated with minimal guidance from the therapist. Here, exposure in the classic sense is enough to allow some useful conversation to begin between two people who have become estranged. A slight variation on exposure is to create ground rules for the content of conversations (e.g., for a cutoff between parents, that the conversation remains focused on the children and how there needs to be agreement about the agenda for the conversation). Adding the various conflict-reducing techniques and anger management techniques that have been described elsewhere in this text is also useful to ensure conversations do not degenerate.

Such cutoffs between parents may require dealing with deeper hurt and other feelings in the name of functioning adequately as parents (given that cutoffs negate the possibility of coparenting). With parent–parent cutoffs, it is important to emphasize the importance of being able to function together well enough to coparent and for children to be able to witness parents in each other's presence without feeling unduly uncomfortable. As part of psychoeducation, it is helpful here to invoke the image most people can recognize of divorcing parents at a child's sports event, whom everyone can see are very uncomfortable in one another's presence. For many, feelings run very deep, and for some, more functional behavior can only come through significant individual work targeting greater acceptance of their former partner as a coparent, through third-wave behavioral acceptance-based strategies. Again, the specific method will vary with the case formulation to arrive at an as "good-enough" minimal coparenting arrangement as is possible.

Difficulties Between Parents and Children and Parental Alienation

Disengagement also occurs between parents and children, and parental alienation also occurs between parents and children in divorce. Such disengagement often overlaps with accusations on the part of the distant parent that the other parent is engaging in parental alienation—that is, active or passive efforts to create a rift between a child or children and the other parent. Parental alienation is a hotly debated topic. Some have written diatribes about alienating parents, singling out those who work assiduously to undermine the position of the other parent. They point to a set of behaviors that often stand out in the children subjected to parental alienation: children having contempt for a parent; refusing contact; failing to maintain even minimal levels of phone, text, or e-mail contact; refusing presents; consistent oppositional behavior; lack of any ambivalence; and, in more extreme cases, even changing their names to be less identified with the parent (Gardner, Sauber, & Lorandos, 2006; Warshak, 2015).[2] Those highlighting parental alienation as a syndrome also strongly hold the other parent responsible for these child behaviors, programming their children through an ongoing series of complaints about the other parent, inappropriate sharing of information about the divorce, and active coaching in rejecting the other parent.[3]

Others have questioned whether there is a reliable category of stable symptoms that constitutes a syndrome labeled *parental alienation syndrome*, and suggest that invoking this "syndrome" often becomes a way for parents who have difficulty with children to externalize and blame others for these problems (O'Donohue, Benuto, & Bennett, 2016). Although put forth for consideration in fifth edition of the *Diagnostic and Statistical Manual of Mental Disorders*, the American Psychiatric Association (2013) did not include it as a reliable valid diagnosis.

Moving beyond this vociferous debate about diagnosis and jargon, there is no doubt that some parents very actively work to move children against the other parent. It is also clear that many parents who have difficult relationships with their children for other reasons fall back on blaming their former partner for them. Yet, which is which? Sometimes there is no doubt, as when a parent frequently tells the children that the other parent ruined all of their lives ("Dad left us") and actively avoids allowing contact between parent and child. Other times, in the wake of egregious behavior, what one parent calls "parental alienation" is clearly the failure of his or her own parenting. Other cases are more ambiguous, as when parents do not strongly support the other's parenting when there are significant challenges from the children.

Kelly and Johnston (2001) provided a more refined way of understanding the territory of parental alienation. They envisioned what is typically termed *alienation* as almost always some combination of a problematic relationship between a child and parent and some behavior on the part of the other parent that invites the child into a more troubled relationship with the parent. In this formulation, which is far more helpful for therapy than the black or white "is it occurring or not" question popular in the courtroom, the issue becomes what can be done with the entire system rather than the individual. How can we best help the parent with the problematic

---

[2]Instruments have been developed to measure the extent of parent rejecting behaviors in children including Gardner's eight-symptom checklist (see Saini, Johnston, Fidler, & Bala, 2012) and denigrating behaviors in parents including Rowen and Emery's (2014) Parental Denigration Scale.
[3]There also are measures of alienating behaviors in parents (Johnston, Roseby, & Kuehnle, 2009; López, Iglesias, & Garcia, 2014; Saini, Johnston, Fidler, & Bala, 2016).

relationship to parent more empathically and authoritatively? How can we help the other parent notice and alter the ways he or she undermines or does not fully support the other parental relationship? And how can we work to reduce anxiety in the child and to build or rebuild the bond between parent and child? Clearly, there are exceptional cases in which wonderful parents are totally rejected or individuals parent so badly that anyone would withhold contact with children until such a time as the specific behavior in concern has changed. However, the vast majority of cases that involve parent rejection show both elements of Kelly and Johnston's mixed model.

So how, then, to work with these families in the context of Kelly and Johnston's (2001) formulation, when almost every such family has a parent who blames the other parent entirely for the problem, and children who blame the parent with whom they are having difficulty? Here, the assessment and case formulation guide the degree to which each component is in focus in intervention. How intense is the gatekeeping by one parent in relation to the participation of the other (Ganong, Coleman, & Chapman, 2016; Saini, Drozd, & Olesen, 2017)? How many overt alienating messages are there and about what? ("Mother is an alcoholic," "Mother had an affair," and "Mother broke up our happy home" are three very different messages.) How bad is the parenting behavior in question, and how strong has the historic link been between parent and child? As just noted, even without "alienation," there are parents and children who do not do well with each other through this transition. Another focus for assessment is how much child psychopathology plays a role. The third leg of the stool of alienation is often a vulnerable child, who readily moves to extremes and dysregulation, including around this extreme behavior. These children may do well in school and other social roles but have special vulnerabilities (Johnston, Walters, & Olesen, 2005). Often one child in a family is the most active "alienator" of other the children.

Work in the context of this problem is necessarily intense. Brief therapies are typically of little use in rebuilding relationships in this context. One prominent exception is that at times, when the parent–child problem is recent and tied to the divorce, and the child previously had a strong attachment with the parent, exposure in a secure place with a parent who can parent well can result in change in a brief period. Beyond this, the fears engendered and problems in attachment run deep, and only a process over time can build or rebuild connection. What follows describes strategies for working with these families, but specifics of procedures are transcended by the need for patience and steady direction on the part of the therapist.

The plan for therapy evolves from the case formulation but almost inevitably ideally involves work with the child alone, each parent alone, and with each parent and the child together. Therapy (with one or more therapists) begins by taking additional time to build strong alliances with each family member through meetings alone. As the case formulation unfolds, behavioral goals that would help with the problem emerge for each person in the family. Given the lack of insight that is typically prevalent, goal-setting is left to the therapist to suggest reasonable proximate goals, accompanied by motivational interviewing to see whether there may be a way to create greater buy in about those goals.

The major strategy directly involving the children is to use positive exposure to overcome what has essentially become a conditioned fear. After building rapport, therapy with the children begins with psychoeducation, adapted to the age of the child, about how these specific fears evolve and how they can be changed. It is emphasized that the plan is for everyone to work together to make this better and that the parent about whom they are concerned is also receiving help for the difficulties about which they are most concerned. A mindful practice relaxation training module provides a mechanism for reducing anxiety. This is followed by introducing thoughts and pictures about and messages from the parent, again in the context of anxiety reducing strategies. Inevitably this is highly arousing for the child or adolescent, who is almost certain to be reactive and may not even be willing to do this. However, these serve to begin a process of exposure, and the responses to these materials provide an entrée into examination of cognitions and emotions in relation to the parent.

What needs to change, and what can be tolerated? Children with this problem have strong thoughts and fears and remind the therapist of those at every turn. The task becomes to stay the course in helping these children increase their repertoire of coping skills, while reassuring them that work is also taking place for the parent to change. Framing this process as helping them develop further strengths of courage and tolerance helps. So does differentiating their right to decide who they like and don't like from their ability to cut off contact. Such conversations often segue into motivational interviewing about what might be gained from forming or reforming some sort of connection. The proximate goal is not so much to change inner feelings, as much as to open the possibility that life might be simpler and easier, and perhaps even better in some ways if this problem was solved.

In conjunction with these meetings with the children, meetings with the disconnected parent (with the same therapist or a different one working in close coordination) focus on that parent's own behavior and what might be changed about it. Psychoeducation here presents the frame of slowly evolving from a highly anxious relationship to a steadier one and the need for that parent to become a model of steadiness to challenge the child's belief system (i.e., that parents in their position have work to do even if the specific allegations are confabulated). Specific foci toward this end emerge from the case formulation. For example, parents susceptible to anger need a module in self-control. Those who are easily distracted by the other parent need a module in keeping a calm and steady focus. This is often a matter of the therapist suggesting areas of parenting that need work. If nothing else, these parents must target the difficult task of remaining steady and empathic after rejection. In these meetings, the groundwork is also laid for taking responsibility for earlier behaviors in eventual meetings together.

Simultaneous work with the other parent (again, either with the same or a different therapist) begins with explaining the systemic plan. Having heard their complaints about the other parent, a frame is set to work on what they can do to make the problem better. The therapist explains that there will be work with the other parent to be a better parent, but the therapist also needs help from this parent in assisting the child overcome his or her fears. Psychoeducation is employed to challenge parents' belief that their actions are serving their child. The therapist highlights the very negative outcomes for children who become cut off in this way from parents. Ways that parents, who worry about their children, can unintentionally make children's tasks more difficult by raising concerns with them are emphasized. The therapist suggests language to use with the child that can act as an antidote to his or her belief that the parent supports rejecting the other parent. Having set this frame, over time, the therapist challenges those behavioral patterns that convey a much different message, working to increase the parent's awareness about the presence of these behaviors. A goal is to lower this parent's arousal in the context of parenting so that he or she can be more relaxed in the gatekeeping function.

From the responses to such early exploration, it soon becomes clear whether this parent can be an ally or whether the work will need to be done exclusively between the other parent and child. For those parents who can be brought into the collaboration, the therapist works to monitor behaviors that might encourage disconnection and coach positive alternatives when a child expresses disdain or disconnection from the other parent. Parents who allow children to take the lead in being alienated often do not see how they respond in ways that increase problems because they see themselves as simply responding to their children's complaints and requests. Consciousness raising can help these parents grasp the impact of their actions and model alternative responses. Given some collaboration, there are numerous opportunities to explore the feelings that underlie various alienating behaviors, which can be examined through the lens of mindful practice, challenging distorted cognitions, and the parent's emotional history. When successful, these meetings can segue into a few meetings between the child and parent, centered on the parent taking an active role in promoting a better relationship with his or her former partner.

The culmination of this work lies in sessions between child and the distant parent. Initially, consistent with the conditioning focus, attention is primarily focused first on getting through a few sessions without conflict or disengagement. Activities are helpful to this end. Progress or lack thereof in these meetings is followed up in individual meetings, examining blocks to progress that might have occurred and what might be done about those blocks, using the various core therapeutic tools. In later meetings, conversing moves to sharing feelings, following a speaker–listener format (Stanley, Markman, & Blumberg, 1997). Conjoint sessions almost always begin with difficulty and tension. Children protest, and their behavior is often extremely provocative. The important message here is that the sessions will go on until the goals of therapy are reached. Steadiness is the key. Whatever direct support from the other parent can be generated is a bonus. In some sense, the underlying message is to make reconnecting the simpler alternative for everyone.

Other family dynamics also play a key role in how treatment progresses. It is quite different to have one parent–child dyad disconnected, from a parent being disconnected from multiple children who have an alliance with each other about the disconnection. Indeed, the power behind the disconnection (and in the jargon the "alienator") can be one of the children who has a vested interest in the disconnection. In those instances, individual work, work with the siblings together to differentiate from each other (through cognitive and emotion-focused techniques), and parent–child meetings with only one child at a time can help free at least the other children from this position.

Given the difficulty of this problem in almost all cases that reach the point of referral to therapy, the goal of simply reestablishing the relationship and maintaining it is foremost. There will be many opportunities over a lifetime to improve the parent–child relationships; here, we merely seek to restore minimal connection. It must be added that these are often the most intractable of situations. Progress needs to be continually assessed as therapy moves forward. With those for whom there is no progress, consider the alternative of simply using the sessions as a place in which there is some contact, with the goal of some minor connection possibly growing slowly grow over time. With the most stuck cases, the alternatives are limited: either maintaining difficult contact or suggesting a hiatus in contact. One option is that there are several programs designed for such stuck families in which, over a week or so, they work exclusively on such issues (Warshak, 2010). Courts will sometimes make a radical change in the custody arrangement in this circumstance, severely limiting the alienating parent's access to children to force change. Often, however, this risks children becoming even more disturbed, as they now struggle with being separated from their preferred parent. This solution, although advised by some in extreme cases (Gardner, Sauber, & Lorandos, 2006), should be viewed more as a legal action to achieve justice through the court (punishing the parent who will not support the other's parenting) than a therapeutic solution.

James and Sheila had a tumultuous marriage of 14 years. They had conflicts about many subjects, including the parenting of their children.
Sheila very much took charge of parenting, micromanaging every aspect
of the children's lives. This was accompanied by conflicts between James
and the children; when he thought they were acting in a disrespectful
way toward him, James became enraged and yelled at them. When Sheila
separated from James, she moved as far away from him as the court would
allow. When the children told her that they didn't want to be with their
father because he was mean and they were afraid of him, she supported
them in their wishes and withheld contact from James. Over time, at
a distance, the children grew, if anything, more anxious and distressed
about contact with James. At school, they began to use their mother's
last name. They also refused any gifts James might send them for birth-
days. Each time a decision came up about the children's lives, Sheila
would make the decision on her own. When the decisions were about
events that involved James and his family, she would always defer to the
wishes of the children, which were inevitably colored by their cutoff with
James. At various points in the divorce process, James brought the issue
of contact with his children to court. He was able to obtain an order for
supervised visitation, but these visits basically consisted of the children
remaining silent. A child custody evaluation was ordered, which found
that the children were genuinely fearful of their father without much in
the way of "smoking-gun" abusive behavior on father's part. It was also
determined that Sheila had been engaging in alienating behaviors. As
the litigation moved forward, the family was mandated to therapy to
restore contact.

Therapy proceeded with a team in a format of multiple sessions per
week. Work with the children began with building rapport, so that they
might feel comfortable with the therapist in discussing their father.
In the first meeting, and most meetings thereafter, the children felt
intense pressure to tell the therapist how awful their father was. Each
time these feelings came up, the therapist took a deliberate position of
hearing the children but not supporting their father-rejecting beliefs.
With time, the therapist began to question how much these beliefs
needed to remain, especially with them already well into their new
lives. Although these inquiries were always first met with fixed negative
responses, over time the therapist was able to help the children question
some of their beliefs about the present and the future (moving away from
focusing on the past) and to consider the possibility that a different
future might be possible if dad could change.

In parallel meetings, a second therapist worked with mother and
father alone and together. With James, the work almost exclusively
focused on moving him away from his stuck position of blaming Sheila
for the issue. While showing empathy for how difficult the problem
was and how Sheila had contributed to the problem, the therapist
unremittingly refocused James on what he could do to make things

better. He would have to find a way to act that was more empathic and in touch with his own children and in which there were no behaviors that would confirm their belief that he might get out of control. Anger management, cognitive restructuring, mindful practice, and parent psychoeducation were used to help him work toward these goals. With James, as with all family members, this was frequently met with his refocusing on his complaints, but in the process, he developed his skill set for parenting and for coping with the situation.

In the sessions with Sheila, she, too, was empathically heard but also directly confronted about her problematic behaviors. Specifically, the therapist challenged her idea that she was supporting the children by following their lead in relation to James. She mostly acted in proactive ways that managed her children's lives but had chosen this one area to defer to them. How did that make sense in terms of her values? Would it be possible to rethink what being supportive to her children about their father would look like so that they might have a more normal life and get out of their endless legal wrangles? As with the others, her first response to such questions were to return to her stereotypical thinking. Steady reexamination of the data, especially that from the custody evaluation, was brought in to challenge her beliefs. As with the children, a further focus moved to trying to imagine a better future, rather than litigate the past. It was also made clear that James was working on his issues, inviting the question of whether she might become more open to considering how he functioned now.

A few meetings with the parents together focused on trying to build on the individual work to create some new vision of how this interaction might improve. Detouring comments by each parent about the other were met by the therapist refocusing on what could be done to make the situation better. Having obtained a minimal agreement about a shared vision for progress, the therapist suggested it was time for meetings with James and the children, and with Sheila and the children, to move the relationship between James and the children along.

The meetings with James and the children began with the children's same silent behavior as occurred in the supervised visitation. With the therapist's help (and some individual time together), the children began to speak about their complaints with James. Now, rather than argue with them as they did in the past, James said he thought that they all could do "being together" better now. The therapist suggested that in the next few meetings they try just that—being together in a more normal way. Those meetings had remarkable success. The children were able to maintain their calm most of the time, and James acted well. In the meetings with Sheila and the children, Sheila stated her support of their reconnecting with their father. They also discussed how they might find ways to have dad relate to the children in a more typical way for divorced families. Ideas were generated and brought back to the meetings with James and the children.

At this point, it was time to see how time away from the therapist might go between James and the children. As expected, this thought raised alarm in the children. In following up, the children's therapist worked with them on specifically how they might calm themselves on such visits, using anxiety management techniques. All the parties participated in discussions across settings about how these meetings might best be structured. A plan for short visits, and for communication by phone and text with father between visits, was established and signed off by the court on a trial basis. Slowly, more normal interactions emerged during the visits. Inevitably, there were moments of anxiety and setbacks, but the therapy was successful in moving to a good-enough working relationship between the parents and the children and little interference from Sheila. No one would characterize the relationships that emerged as ideal, but functional dinners with father and a weekend day each week were restored by the court.

Parents With No History of Coparenting

There are special cases in which parents have no history of coparenting, typically related to extreme role differentiation while in the relationship. Here, one parent parents, and the other does not, leaving the less involved parent with minimal parental skills and a limited child–parent bond, and the more involved parent and the children are used to that parent making all child-related decisions. A variant on this type of case occurs when a brief fling leads to a pregnancy, so that the parents have essentially no relationship, and one parent begins raising the child. In many such situations, the less involved parent vanishes, leaving a bevy of issues for therapists to help children deal with in constructing a positive narrative for their lives in the context of this abandonment.

It is a perplexing aspect of the transition through divorce that past behavior is often not a good predictor of future behavior. Totally uninvolved parents in the process of divorce often want to become more involved in their children's lives (likewise, some involved parents surprisingly withdraw from them). Thus, suddenly parents who never have coparented need to coparent, parents with minimal parental skill sets need to learn how to parent, parents and children need to strengthen bonds that previously have been poorly developed, and the more involved parent needs to develop trust in the other parent's parenting—all in the context of the charged environment of divorce. Given the number and complexity of the tasks, this is a breeding ground for difficult divorce.

Work with such families begins with specific psychoeducation with the parents about what is typical and most beneficial in these kinds of families. This includes promoting the value in having both parents be involved with children, but also the need for agreement that most of the time will be with the more involved parent, and for remedial work on parenting by the other parent.

Early in the process, one focus is to help the less involved parent develop the needed skill sets, usually a combination of discussing parenting practices in session, attending parenting classes, and bibliotherapy. A further goal is to work with these parents to become comfortable with finding a role that is complementary to that of the other parent, rather than competing for control and challenging thoughts and behaviors that push against the other parents' solid parenting practices.

Therapy with the more involved parent centers initially on working with narratives and cognitions that enable accepting the value or necessity of the second parent's having a more constructive role. Fortunately, most more involved parents can see the benefits of having the other parent in their children's lives (as a practical matter there is the reality that most children in such families seek out their other parent at some point) but are anxious about both the competency of the other parent and giving up control. Much of the meetings with that parent, informed by the progress of the meetings with the less involved parent, focus on examining those thoughts and either challenging them or responding to them by assuring them that building the specific competency of the other parent will remain a focus of therapy.

As progress occurs in these meetings, sessions are scheduled with both parents to focus on building a vision of how they will work together. This is framed not as a coequal conversation but one between a principal parent, who sets most of the plans, and the second parent, who is a strong force in their execution and has an important additional perspective to share. Parallel sessions are held as needed between the more distant parent and the child or children to help create a framework for building greater attachment and establish clarity about expectations. By the end of therapy, it is expected that each parent will have his or her own unique relationship with the children, accept that there will be differences in those relationships, and agree that the children will mostly be grounded in the parenting of the more involved parent but that the other parent has a significant role in the children's lives.

> Dina became pregnant during a one-night stand at Comic-Con, where Seth was a presenter. When Dina discovered she was pregnant, they briefly explored a long-term relationship but this quickly broke off. When Seth learned of the birth, he sued for access to his son. The court ordered access at Dina's house, which was fraught with the obvious difficulties. Seth had no experience as a parent, no relationship with the baby, and could only come for occasional visits. In its brief dealings with this case, the court made it clear that Seth was entitled to contact with the child and needed to pay child support. They kept the visits as

originally ordered but referred the parents to therapy to help Seth learn to parent better and for both to overcome blocks to coparenting.

Therapy began with meetings with each parent, who, as expected, focused on their own narratives of the situation. Seth genuinely expressed his desire to be a father, as well as his frustration with Dina for blocking his access to his son. Dina expressed her fears about Seth handling a baby. Meetings with Seth began by creating a plan for him to develop competency as a parent. He would take classes at his local health department, agreed to read and talk about two books the therapist suggested on parenting infants, and a cousin with parenting experience who lived in the area was located who could be of help when he was with his son. With Dina the issue was primarily her anxiety about her baby. She was told about how Seth's skill-building was being monitored and progressing but remained highly anxious about catastrophic events that might occur. Therapy with her shifted to work on these anxieties using cognitive behavioral techniques, especially thought records to explore catastrophic cognitions.

Initial meetings with Dina and Seth together were marked by drifts into argument, which the therapist refocused as topics for problem-solving. Following the rule-driven speaker–listener method, they conversed about in which skills Dina thought Seth had grown competent and what needed more work. The therapist reframed these concerns as everyone wanting Seth to do well with their child and that the specific concerns Dina had raised needed to be followed up with work on Seth's part. Plans were also arranged (with stated worries on Dina's part) for Seth to take their child on his own for an afternoon with his cousin's help. Follow-up meetings with Seth continued to focus on responsible parenting and for Dina about her anxiety.

Seth and Dina then began to discuss the need for a dependable schedule for Seth's parenting. Seth agreed to come to see his son on such a schedule. Dina, seeing the progress made and weary of the stress and expense of court, agreed the schedule. Visits then proceeded with only occasional conflict.

When Divorce Prompts the Withdrawal of a Parent

There also are quieter cutoffs between parents and children in which there has simply been a drift of a parent away from a child. Here, there may be less interparental conflict, but a parent may have entered into a new life with little or no interaction with children. Less likely to be referred through the court, these life stories are nonetheless painful for children. Where there are opportunities to work with such situations, therapy is equally important.

The special aspects of treating these divorces pertain to the absence of one parent. Therapists help children make sense of this loss, to process their feelings, and to challenge cognitive distortions (e.g., "I made Dad leave").

Work with the remaining parent centers on the difficult task of dealing with his or her own inevitable anger and helping construct a narrative for the children that can speak to the reality to the situation yet not lay down tracks for a self-fulfilling prophecy toward ruin ("When Mom left, everything fell apart"). In these situations, parents, now at a distance, may be approachable. Occasionally, a bit of outreach can lead to at least a minimal level of reconnection.

PAINFUL EXPERIENCES

Difficult divorce is often accompanied by stories of enormous pain and betrayal. In the Western world, there are few competitors to the feelings engendered by the demise of a relationship presumed to be "'til death do us part." The stronger the commitment and belief, the stronger the emotional pain. We live in an age of paradox, with the coexistence of notions of lifelong commitment and fidelity inherited from earlier generations, coupled with a divorce rate hovering at 50% and an ethos that often promotes seeking what Finkel (2017) called the "all or nothing marriage."

Thus, dealing with pain is intrinsic to working with divorce. Therapists have enormous value for most divorcing clients simply in witnessing that pain, and providing a space to work through it and experience some hope (Weingarten, 2010, 2012, 2015). Therapists also bring an array of more active tools to help clients ameliorate and even grow through pain, such as mindful practice, cognitive restructuring, emotion-focused exploration, and psychodynamic examination of self.

The Vicissitudes of Marital Infidelity

Pain experienced in every divorce is unique, and of the "50 ways to leave your lover," none is quite like being abandoned for another person. Raw and powerful feelings emerge. This creates soil in which many of the other problems discussed in this chapter can readily grow. Strong negative feelings can propel cutoffs, high conflict, or triangulation.

There are two ways that affairs morph into difficult divorce, depending on which party initiates the end of the marriage. In the first variation, the affair is an exit route from the marital relationship for the unfaithful partner. Here, for the partner who has been left, the upheaval of learning about the affair, the lack of the comfort and support of a new relationship that one's former partner is enjoying, and the speed with which transformation occurs in the family make for endless challenges. The leaving partner typically has a variety of strong feelings as well. There are decisions about how far to pursue the new relationship (with the inevitable reactivity of the former partner), the wish to keep the parenting connection stable amid marital chaos he or she has introduced, and, frequently, feelings of ambivalence and guilt. In the second variation of this situation, the discovery of an affair becomes the precipitant for the betrayed partner to end the marriage. Here, feelings may be even more complex, as the partner who had the affair also feels injured by his or her partner ending the marriage.

In both situations, there is the question of how much sharing about the infidelity occurs with family. Some operate in the hothouse of a closely held, emotionally energizing secret, while, at the other extreme, others readily engage family in the conflict. In either scenario, it is a struggle to stay on course through this turbulence to get to a reasonable postdivorce life. In fact, it is debatable what a reasonable postdivorce life might look like; that question is informed by personal values.

So how to work with the difficult divorce that contains such stories? First, these are cases where the multipartial alliance, and the therapist's strong ethical anchoring, is crucial. The multipartial alliance must include efforts to hear and understand the perspectives of all parties. In the wake of trauma, feelings are strong and need to be heard, and stories of affairs are narratives of personal trauma. Ethical anchoring comes in the form of the therapist bringing an ethical stance toward the patterns of behavior involved. For example, without being judgmental, there is a difference, in my moral universe, between the position of the partner who has had the affair for which he or she is leaving the marriage and that of the partner. Fairness is served by directly speaking to that difference, even if there is also empathy for the leaving partner (the leaving partner often has a narrative of many disappointments and sometimes of efforts to remedy those issues). From this perspective, focus can remain on helping the family move through difficult divorce.

It is best to begin such cases by simply witnessing each client's experience (Weingarten, 2012) to hear their story in separate meetings. This segues into psychoeducation about marriages that end with affairs, interwoven with listening (client narratives in these situations typically feature frequently encountered themes). An important aspect of psychoeducation is that there are families that can be thrown fully off course in these circumstances, yet others may experience difficulties briefly then recover; it is as the proverbial dust settles that patterns are set. A frame for therapy is that it is better, if difficult, to become the latter kind of family.

The case formulation then centers on what is needed to help the family move beyond the specific troubled place it is in. In this difficult life space, what differentiates those who have ordinary anger, rage, shame, guilt, and pleasure from the processes of divorce at work in this family? Often it is falling prey to the discharge of the faithful partner punishing the other while remaining unaware of the collateral damage done to others—most especially children. At other times, it is the lack of acknowledgment, taking responsibility, or empathy from the person who had the affair. At still other times, it is whatever emotional dance occurs between the former partners that makes it impossible to coparent in the minimal ways needed to move forward.

So how might such a family be helped to move into the normal range? Framing the narrative as being about the long-term best interest of children, anger management, challenging the partner who had the affair to own up to his or her responsibility and increase empathy, and helping the other partner deal with the loss are often ways of helping the family move ahead. In these difficult divorces, mixing conjoint and individual meetings with the former partners can promote emotions being experienced and processed, and self-talk examined, that allow for the necessary conversations about moving on with the divorce on to remain productive. Both adults are entitled to their own feelings and to hold whatever point of view they have about their former partner. The key in these difficult divorces is for those feelings to not bleed over into the other operations needed to get to a successful postdivorce life.

Work with children in the context of affairs that end marriages, when they have been brought into the partner drama, can be difficult. Typically, these children, intentionally or not, have been put in the middle of marital difficulties at a point in life when adult wisdom has not yet developed. Here, helping children and adolescents differentiate from the parental drama, and find their own narratives for their lives, controlling what they can best control, is the key. To the extent that parents can give children room to do this, this task is much easier.

And then there is the special case when the affair partner becomes the new spouse, and thus stepparent. This circumstance is fraught with even more complexity. Here, key elements include work with the new couple to encourage sensitivity to the feelings of the former partner and children and to have realistic expectations, as well as work with the former partner to focus on mitigating the potential disaster for the children by working on his or her own feelings that allow the children some space in which to develop. In addition, negotiating between former partners about a realistic set of arrangements and work with the children that acknowledges their feelings, but that looks to help steady them in their new family life, is important.

The Partner Who Will Not Give Up

A somewhat less pathological but vexing situation occurs when one partner will not accept the end of the marriage. Early in the process of divorce, partners who want to preserve their marriages are common, and, as already described in Chapter 3, such couples are most appropriately referred for discernment counseling (Doherty & Harris, 2017). However, here the situation is different: One partner will not accept the changes occurring long after there clearly is no chance for reconciliation, and the divorce has proceeded well down the road to completion. Such situations are intrinsically painful and readily morph into some of the other special problems described in this chapter, as cycles of pursuit and avoidance and conflict and triangulation secondary to this leave everyone exhausted.

Therapy in relation to this problem primarily centers on helping the pursuing partner accept the reality of his or her life situation and refocus on finding the best possible outcome in what is not the preferred solution. Parallel work with the former partner centers on helping him or her stay steady in responding, try not to be avoidant or conflictual, and avoid sending mixed messages. Psychoeducation about such situations, along with cognitive and emotion-focused strategies, can help such clients explore alternatives that are more likely to be successful in the long run. It is particularly helpful with the pursuing partner to acknowledge positive feelings about his or her core values (e.g., the sanctity of marriage), yet also to weigh the costs and benefits of the present position, to challenge beliefs about how divorce will be catastrophic, to mourn the loss, and to experiment with behavioral changes that might make for a more satisfying future life. For some, only probing deeply for the sources of pain, in relation to powerful, long-held ideas and feelings, can provide relief.

It should be added here that some children take on this mission as well, doing so even when both parents have moved on. A similar empathic but challenging stance, using behavioral, cognitive, and emotion-focused interventions, can help them move through such stuck points, working with the life they have rather than the lost one they seek to preserve.

Children and Adults With Severe Psychopathology

Severe psychopathology is a wild card in working with difficult divorce. Sometimes its presence is the reason for the original referral to therapy, whether the concern is about a child or an adult. And, even if this is not the case, psychopathology causes other change processes to be more tenuous and problematic. Problems such as chronic depression, borderline personality disorder, bipolar disorder, and generalized anxiety disorder can significantly slow progress in difficult divorce because intervention strategies are impaired when a client cannot successfully engage in them. Further, divorce is a major trigger for the emergence of psychopathology. Research shows as many as one third of divorcing partners have some significant psychopathology during and shortly after divorce (Chatav & Whisman, 2007). It may be clear that a mother needs to improve the home environment and refrain from placing children in a caretaking role, but what if severe depression is the constraint to better care-taking? Similarly, having a child reunite with an estranged father may be a universally agreed-on goal, but what if the child's anxiety extends not only to being with her father but also to being anywhere other than in the psychological safety of her home?

Given that what is in focus here is major psychopathology, there is also a good chance that some therapy may already be underway for the problem. If so, coordination with that therapy is essential. If not, appropriate referral is warranted for psychotherapy, psychopharmacology, or both whenever possible.

The integrative therapy model presented here draws on many of the same intervention strategies that are used in evidence-based treatment of various forms of psychopathology, such as mindful practice, the application of principles of learning, cognitive restructuring, and emotion-focused therapy. Thus, these methods are also readily extended to dealing with the specific psychopathology in the context of treating difficult divorce in a way that supports concurrent individual therapy for the specific disorder. The presence of significant psychopathology calls for an emphasis on the application in the relational context of those methods most helpful in therapy for the specific disorder (Barlow, 2014). For example, a depressed mother, who is not taking her child out to play or offering the child opportunities to socialize, can be helped to challenge that pattern through working with the behavioral activation techniques and self-talk that are part of cognitive-behavioral therapy for depression. This is a place where the therapist having a broad therapeutic palette is especially useful. In the relational therapy context, the goal is not to end the psychopathology, but to find ways of working with it in the context of the relational problem to enable moving forward and minimize its deleterious effects.

Some referrals in the context of divorce occur because the court seeks information about a parent's possible psychopathology. In this situation, the goal is to find some agreement among family members that a psychopathology is present, leaving the parent with the psychopathology to work on it and the other family members to have empathy in his or her struggle. Motivational interviewing can help the parent with the problem acknowledge it. Parallel work with family members can help them reframe accusations as concerns, so that there may be a greater possibility of working together rather than at cross purposes. If there can be a shift in how the problem is seen, families can often find ways to help those with psychopathology during challenging times. Although it is not always possible to have parents with psychopathology seek appropriate and effective treatment, better solutions are nonetheless available. For example, family members can learn to appropriately label and accept the problem and find the most effective ways to work with it.

Often, one resolution of divorce conflicts secondary to the psychopathology is an agreement to temporarily suspend some aspects of parenting during times of maximal dysfunction, to be reinstated when the parent's mental status improves.

When a child's psychopathology is the focus, much of the challenge is to bring the family together to deal with it (Birnbaum, Lach, & Saposnek, 2016; Kerns & Prinz, 2016). Again, detours into conflict can easily occur in difficult divorce. Whose fault is the psychopathology? Can we blame the divorce if it was a trigger? Good therapy helps everyone focus on the reality that much more can be accomplished by working together to help the child return to his or her normal level of functioning than by blaming one another. Among the therapist's tools here, psychoeducation about the deleterious effects of conflict on children who are already displaying difficulties and determining what might be most helpful in dealing with the problem, rather than falling prey to ongoing dysfunctional sequences related to the problem in the family, is particularly valuable.

An additional problem for these families is that in cases of significant child psychopathology, the "mom's house, dad's house" way of having two homes with very different rules and ways of dealing with the child's problem rarely works and needs to be replaced by efforts toward more coordinated parenting. Establishing the framework of the family by developing steady, consistent parenting between homes, despite whatever differences the parents might have, in the name of helping their child is critical. So, too, becomes developing some method of communicating and processing of rumors passed on about the other parent by the child, who likely will distort reports about life in the other household.

SPECIAL CONSIDERATIONS IN CERTAIN FAMILY CONTEXTS

There are special considerations is working with various presenting family forms as well. The following sections consider couples without children, chaotic families, and involvement of extended family.

Couples Without Children

Much of the writing on divorce is about families with children, but some thought should be given to those without them. Often these divorces occur early in life in couples who would have had children later, although some are long-term marriages. These are supposed to be the easier divorces, yet feelings remain strong. For younger couples, it may be the first major dose of disappointment in their lives. For older couples, there is often the additional factor of not having the comfort of ongoing relationships with children to fall back on in this difficult period. Therapy proceeds in these couples, as in others, by following the case formulation and drawing from the standard set of intervention strategies, but the unique sense of loss in these couples needs to be considered.

Families in Chaos

One of the well-established findings about divorce is that parental monitoring declines during the period of and just after divorce (Hetherington, Stanley-Hagan, & Anderson, 1989). Some families going through separation (or, as already noted, living in the confusion of staying together in one home) completely lose any steady sense of reliable parenting and consistent family structure. One parent may have little structured parenting experience, life stress may be so great that parenting skills atrophy, or messages from the two parents may clash dramatically.

In this circumstance, the case formulation must focus on the constraints to a stable home environment and good parenting, leading to a plan for establishing consistent parenting. What supports may be engaged toward these ends? Some of these may be structural, in the sense of finding more realistic child-care arrangements. Other changes needed may involve better self-care for parents, teaching parenting skills to those with limited repertoires, working on differences in parenting between homes to make them less radically different, or focusing on parent–child communication and cooperation. Given that such circumstances invite interparental conflict, there is everything to be said for very active intervention when parenting and stability in a residence are inadequate.

Extended Families Involved in the Problem

When we think of divorce in the West, we think of the impact on nuclear families. Even here, however, let alone in more tightly connected cultures, extended families often feel strongly about the divorce and may influence the situation. In the integrative approach described in this book, extended family members are almost always in the indirect client system and are not part of the therapy. Yet the impact on these others should be considered. Bowen-style coaching with clients can help in their interactions with extended family, appreciating that for them, divorce may represent a loss as well, while differentiating themselves from pathogenic feelings and suggestions that family may offer.

In this model, extended family members are only included directly in therapy when they present a major obstacle to progress. This is most often the case when the divorcing partners are young, and their behavior is directed to a large extent by their own parents. Extended family members are invited to a few sessions of therapy to help the younger clients find ways to steady their lives through the divorce. A central goal is to have them do that by becoming a more positive influence in the conflict. Initial contacts with extended family inevitably center on the competing task of making sure the therapist knows how bad their child's former spouse is. However, after this first phase, the therapist can experiment with seeing whether the same intervention strategies used with the parents can help extended family settle down—to breathe, accept the present circumstance, and become agents of how to live best within it.

Other extended family members are unlikely to be brought into therapy, but their needs should also be considered. This is a time in which relationships of decades with in-laws generally end completely, and for some grandparents, contact with grandchildren may be more restricted. A consciousness toward preserving whatever continuity in relationships is possible can be a remedy for future problems.

ISSUES THAT EMERGE OVER TIME

Some issues evolve over time into postdivorce conflicts or those concerned with lives with new partners.

Postdivorce Divorce Issues

Therapy in a postdivorce environment, where difficult divorce issues carry over well beyond the time of divorce or where coparenting issues are triggered some time later, is substantially like working with divorcing families. Intervention strategies are similar and organized in much the same way. However, there are some clear differences from therapy during the divorce.

First, many problems are by this time old, deep, and relatively intractable. When this is the case, a more radical version of separate households and a more rigid program for how communication and problem-solving will work are indicated. Typically, goals need to be kept in the more limited frame of mitigating the damage that is occurring. Yet, there are exceptions. Occasionally, a family that has not been in the "difficult divorce" range encounters problems postdivorce. There is less cause for pessimism about the prognosis in those cases.

Second, the task of setting the new structure for the family has, by definition, been completed by this time. There may be further challenges in court to that structure, but such changes are only rarely granted, and then mostly in special circumstances. Third, the court tends to be less involved in these situations. Parties can bring complaints, but the judicial system is focused much more on resolving issues in divorce than postdivorce. This often means less direct court involvement and more of the court looking to therapists and parenting coordinators to work with these cases. Occasionally, these cases do find their way into consuming much time and energy in the court system, most often stemming from either some allegation of endangerment, or someone's desire to have the children relocate with them to some place far away from where they currently reside. Fourth, being divorced for most is a time-limited state. The further developmental transition to issues of remarried families looms for most only a few years after divorcing (which we discuss next). If problems are not revisiting old complaints (much as in Gottman's, 1999, perpetual problems in marriage) or about relocation, they are likely related to the effects of the entry of new partners into the lives of the now-binuclear family.

All of these factors argue for a patient attitude toward these families, allowing for the creation of a holding environment, and work toward specific goals using the strategies in the model, but where goals are always narrowed to move more toward certain ends. Keeping the system as stable as possible is particularly important because these families are the most at risk, given that the problem state has now extended for most over a long period of time. The special aspect of therapy postdivorce is that it may involve the addition of work with new partners, especially when their behavior is a focus of the conflict.

Remarriage and Its Vicissitudes

Remarriage is a topic worthy of a book in itself, and there are several outstanding volumes and chapters about therapy with stepfamilies (Bray, 2008; Bray & Kelly, 1998; Browning & Artelt, 2012a; Emery & Dinescu, 2016; Papernow, 2013, 2015). This short consideration only focuses on the ways that remarriage can extend and renew divorce conflicts and how to work with these issues.

The major way remarriage affects how divorcing systems operate is that it introduces new, more permanent figures into the earlier set of relationships. Mostly, this is a positive factor among former partners who have had difficult divorce and are repartnering. Long-standing disputes often move well into the background as one begins to feel better, which often happens for divorced adults as they enter new relationships. Indeed, one frequent resolution of problems in difficult divorce comes with the tempering effect of a well-balanced new partner. However, other, less positive processes can occur.

In one dynamic, the new partner or partners join into the conflict, making for an extra degree of difficulty. In a second dynamic, the alliance between two former partners, who have managed reasonably well with one another, is ruptured by the new relationship, either because of the threat of the old relationship to the new partner or of the new relationship to the old partner. A third scenario introduces someone with problematic characteristics into the mix, whom the children or the other parent find difficult and threatening. More broadly, there may simply be a major developmental hurdle to negotiate, which rather than evolving in a more normative way evolves badly, as when a child and a stepparent get on poorly.

Thus, remarriage can set off new conflicts and result in the need for therapy that involves the older family constellation and new family members. Intervention in this context is essentially as described in the general model, tailored to the circumstance. A major theme becomes adapting to stepfamily life. Much of the work of therapy has to do with digesting the changes that have occurred, adjusting to them, and finding ways to work at the interface of the various relevant parties in the remarried family system.

Psychoeducation in this context centers on the norms of stepfamily life (Papernow, 2013). Part of the message is that there are ways that work better and ways that work worse in building connections between parents and children, and a knowledge base exists to guide action here. Some stepparents enter in an emotionally unwise way, trying to parent their partner's children as if they were their parent without first allowing time for children to feel engaged. Other stepparents bring a different cultural context and style to their parenting, engendering conflicts. For some original parents, the primary issue may be about learning to accept any role for a new parent figure in the child's life.

Meetings with various subsystems are the major vehicle for resolving these issues. Sessions with the parent–stepparent–children unit where issues have emerged are the best venue for working on processes in a stepfamily home and finding ways to integrate different perspectives. Meetings between the former partners or all the parent figures are the best venue for dealing with interparental conflicts and negotiating differences. These meetings are supplemented with meetings with individual family members, as blocks within those individuals are uncovered that slow progress.

It should be added here that second marriages often result in divorce, and these divorces present special issues, with complexities of difficult divorce even beyond those in a first marriage. What are the relationships to be like between former stepparents and stepchildren? Or between stepsiblings of now-divorced parents? Part of the problem-solving and work with structure in these families must be about these complex relationships. Many gravitate to the simplest splitting of these stepfamilies into the original parent–children units, but this is often accompanied in these families by an enormous sense of loss as parent figures and children part who may have been in contact for many years. Additionally, bear in mind that the law in remarriage family divorce provides no parental rights for the stepparent unless they have adopted a stepchild. In the best case, thoughtful planning in therapy can find a place for continuing some basis for these often important relationships.

ISSUES SURROUNDING PARTICIPATION IN THERAPY

Family Members Who Don't Want to Participate in Therapy

Sometimes adults or children don't want to participate in therapy. There may be an aversion to therapy in general, to therapy in this context of known difficulty in the family, to simply being in therapy with someone else, or to meeting with specific family members in this context. For both children and adults, a reluctant client calls on the therapist to summon up his or her best alliance-building skills. If adults don't participate or if parents don't bring children, in court-involved cases sometimes the therapy pauses for a time until the judge or attorney for the children once again makes it clear that therapy is essential. When even this doesn't lead to engagement, the therapy necessarily segues into working with those who are willing to participate (see the following section) or taking on more of the role of treating expert (L. R. Greenberg & Gould, 2001) in providing feedback to attorney for the children or the court in court-involved cases so the therapy can inform the court's decision-making.

With children who are reluctant, finding a frame that can lower reactivity is essential. Sometimes any progress toward goals must simply wait for sufficient alliance-building meetings for a child to become comfortable with the routine of coming for meetings or for it to emerge clearly for the child that the way to have fewer meetings is to cooperate. Other times the help of a connected parent helping to increase motivation, or sessions focused on motivational interviewing, can be the key. Some children in this context do better in the conjoint therapy, where a parent can help make them feel safe to be in therapy. Again, there are no sure answers here, but building an alliance typically ultimately pays off.

Radically Different Levels of Engagement With and Responsiveness to Treatment Between Family Members

Sometimes there are radical differences in engagement, willingness to work toward therapy goals, and success in changing over time during therapy between family members. When such differences occur, as already described, early efforts are aimed at increasing alliance and motivation in the less engaged clients. However, in some difficult divorces, this difference is intractable.

When this occurs, the therapist is left to work with the system to make as much progress as possible. Typically, this evolves to efforts to engage with the more involved clients to continue to work on their potential contribution to a solution and find an optimal steady response to difficulties in the other family members. Although one person can create havoc, this will have less impact if the others can move to a differentiated stance. Difficult divorce is ultimately about the family system, and although the system cannot change a person's behavior, it can change the context for that behavior. This model focuses on working with each part of the system (each subsystem) to make the most progress possible, and in that way to change the system overall. Radical acceptance (Hayes et al., 2012) of problematic behavior may be a key ingredient here in work with motivated family members.

It also is essential for the therapist to continue to work toward remaining empathic and connected as possible to the less involved and more resistant family members, lest a circular process develops that ensures their continued decline in participation and responsiveness. Remaining systemic becomes even more important here, lest the therapy comes to serve the interests of only those family members who are more willing to engage deeply in the therapy. This inevitably becomes more difficult when the therapist must appropriately serve as a "treating expert" (L. R. Greenberg & Gould, 2001) and report the uncooperative behavior of one or more family members with the therapy.

SUMMARY

This chapter examined how to intervene in the context of several special presenting problems that frequently appear in difficult divorce. Although this model follows the same paradigm of case formation and treatment planning as described earlier in this text, special adaptations are suggested in the context of specific problems. Having focused in the last two chapters on strategies for intervention, the next chapter moves to a much different focus: the person of the therapist in relation to working with difficult divorce.

9

THE THERAPIST'S INTERFACE WITH DIFFICULT DIVORCE

This chapter explores issues for the therapist as a person encountering difficult divorce cases. Therapists are more than emitters of strategies of change (Aponte & Kissil, 2016; Rober, 2017). They are people, usually with well-developed abilities to feel.

DEALING WITH DARKNESS

Therapists have much to deal with as they encounter overpowering affect, trauma, and crises in difficult divorce. The combination of ingredients may be unique among the kinds of problems therapists face. Other situations may have similar, perhaps even higher, levels of trauma and pain, but almost no situation in therapy combines trauma with the presence of the basest parts of the human experience. Sometimes as a therapist with these cases, it seems as if you have forged your way up the river into what truly is the *Heart of*

http://dx.doi.org/10.1037/0000116-010
Treating the Difficult Divorce: A Practical Guide for Psychotherapists, by J. L. Lebow

Darkness (Conrad, 1999), as themes of hurt, rage, vengeance, manipulation of facts to fit one's narrative, and narcissistic self-interest dominate. These are not typically cases that engender good feelings about the human condition. Even children often act badly, and parents, lost in their own emotions, often treat children as self-objects rather than truly considering their needs. There may ultimately be resilience and growth (and in fact, therapy seeks to locate that resilience; Walsh, 2006), but it is usually obscured by primal negative emotion. Inevitably, therapy begins with clients sharing their experience, in part because this story occupies the center of their consciousness. Rarely are those stories told with any objectivity; issues are seen as black or white. And the stories are often filled with people behaving badly.

CHOOSING TO WORK WITH THIS POPULATION

Given this context, therapists inevitably deal with what gets stirred up in working with this population. Some wisely decide early on that this work is not for them, preferring to see clients with other kinds of problems, where alliances are easier to form and less volatile, clients are more motivated, and goals and outcomes can be more ambitious. Many fine therapists find these cases are not for them. I had a brilliant, mature, highly skilled colleague who after two of these cases never took a similar referral for the rest of her career. Some therapist characteristics do not fit well with this population. These include those who have a strong preference for less structured treatment, cherish having positive emotional connections to all their clients, frame all therapy as about growth, or primarily focus on raising clients' level of emotional experiencing. This work also necessitates a somewhat stronger boundary between therapist and clients than with other clients and inevitably includes challenging clients who are likely to respond with mixed reactions. In addition, there is the need to attend to legal system involvement, which presents both a skill set to be honed and a form of interaction with which some therapists are innately more comfortable than others.

Thus, before beginning work with difficult divorce, therapists should ask whether they have a personality that fits with this specialty. If so, they should learn more about how to treat these clients, and then move on to treat a few of these cases in a supervised context. Extend the use of therapeutic strategies with which you are familiar into this arena, and engage in an experiment to see how well you do, both technically and emotionally, in working in this context. Through such a process, therapists self-select for work with these cases. It is a specialty that almost inevitably entails the expansion of technical skill sets, including having a range of intervention strategies as suggested in the model presented in this book. It also involves further developing the parts of self that are most needed in this work, such as patience, a sense of optimism, staying mindful, finding ways to stay empathic with all clients, drawing satisfaction from small changes that do not resolve problems but ameliorate difficulty, maintaining one's sense of personal boundaries, and being aware of and working with countertransference.

ELEMENTS OF AN EFFECTIVE THERAPEUTIC STANCE

There are personal elements essential to successful therapy with this population.

Finding a Helpful Position

The key element in effective practice with difficult divorce is less about a formula of which intervention to use and when (although many suggestions about this have been offered in this volume) and more about maintaining a therapeutic attitude amid the behaviors, cognitions, affects, and systemic patterns in these clients. These are usually dispirited and angry people, mystified about how their lives have turned out. This readily transmutes into the problematic behaviors and systemic processes described here. Most crucial is for the therapist to come to this work with a sense of positivity and realistic optimism, that this is indeed a transition, one that can be negotiated no matter how it seems now. Holding that feeling is challenging in the face of the strong feelings and problematic behaviors evident in these cases, particularly at the beginning of therapy. This also is not a place for Pollyannas, however. The therapist's sense of optimism must be anchored in a realistic appraisal of the changes needed that can occur and a systemic, patient perspective that can enable movement toward this change. The task then becomes to hold that realistic optimism, even among competing viewpoints from clients and within the legal system, and to take satisfaction in the gains made. Even if these are small gains, they can have enormous impact in the future lives of these clients.

Remaining Empathic but Strong

Therapists generally need to adapt their typical interpersonal stance in these cases. These are situations that require the therapist to be very much in charge of sessions and to establish and maintain control of the treatment process. Getting ready for these sessions often involves "pulling in" to be less vulnerable and stronger in this context. Yet therapists paradoxically must simultaneously work to maintain their empathy amid provocative and "reality TV" behavior. Underneath, most everyone involved is hurting, even while acting from their most primitive parts, and those therapists who work well with difficult divorce empathize with the underlying pain these clients feel, even as they provide structure in response to the bad behavior. When I notice my empathy flagging, it is time for a mindful moment to find it.

Being Decisive When Necessary

Therapists who work well with these cases also need to be able to differentiate from the fray and hold and communicate positions that help move toward the resolution of problems. In this world of clients, many of whom see therapy as another contest in which to compete, maintaining such a position is challenging. This is no less true when meeting with an individual client who may look to the therapist to mirror his or her view of the problem.

The same can be said about dealing with pressures to prematurely end therapy on the part of either parents or children. For example, if restoring a child–parent relationship is a goal, children, the other parent, and that parent's attorney may push for the premature end of the therapy. This is a form of therapy in which therapists must be able to hold a strong, systemic, and balanced stance and work from that position amid pressure from clients and attorneys, and sometimes even from the court.

Sometimes the therapist even needs to decide about the viability of the therapy or offer a highly impactful recommendation as a treating expert. Not all coparents can coparent, not all divorced partners should be allowed to have contact with each other, and not all parents should be allowed to be in contact with their children. When encountering such challenging situations, the therapist needs to be prepared to end therapy if it has been demonstrated not to be workable or has moved in directions that are destructive. Similarly, therapists need to be able to offer their opinion as treating experts about the viability of relationships after efforts to resolve problems have failed (L. R. Greenberg & Gould, 2001).

Finding Progress a Sufficient Outcome

These are almost never therapies in which endings occur with a great sense of transformation or full resolution of a problem. It is essential for therapists to have realistic expectations and to recognize and take satisfaction in movement that would not have occurred without therapy. In the worst divorces, even merely avoiding significant deterioration is an accomplishment. These situations readily move into downward spirals with massive negative effects on everyone. The differences between ongoing, severe conflict and something better than that are profound.

Those who work with these families frequently see the differences therapy can make, even if problems remain. Asking oneself, "How would this divorce be without the therapy?" is important both for reasons of accountability and to mark and recognize the gains and continue the work with the positive spirit it requires.

Additionally, even in cases in which there hasn't been progress with the presenting problem, there remains value in helping identify what happens when an effort is made to address it and what aspects of the situation don't improve even with significant help. These realities can help to inform future decisions of family members and the court, if it is involved, about how to approach these family problems in the future. Additionally, more than a few families subsequently progress significantly better because a single child or adult has found a way to better differentiate from the conflict, even as more provocative, difficult behaviors remain.

Becoming Comfortable With the Judicial System

As already noted, in many cases of difficult divorce, the judicial system is very much a part of the family system. The business of the court and work with attorneys is a, or perhaps the, central focus in the lives of many clients. As described in Chapter 7, therapists working with these cases need to be able to understand the workings of the court and coordinate with those processes, yet remain fully anchored as therapists. The pull may be enormous to transmute psychotherapy into rendering a verdict about the case and to take on the winner–loser paradigm of much of the legal system. Yet for the activity to truly be therapeutic, the therapist must find a way to avoid this temptation even as others in the court and the family try to pull the therapist into this position; the therapist must remain systemic in focus and search for solutions. As also noted earlier, there is a role for the therapist as a treating expert who can, when needed, share his or her opinion (L. R. Greenberg & Gould, 2001), but this role best remains secondary, used only selectively to influence the system as other, more cooperative solutions fail.

THERAPIST'S PERSONAL REACTIONS

Therapists inevitably have strong personal reactions to these cases. They must be aware of those reactions, be sure they do not contaminate their work, and stay personally in balance in relation to this stressful context.

Countertransference

To stay systemic, balanced, and helpful, therapists must be keenly aware of countertransference as it occurs. Difficult divorce places the therapist in situations that pull for countertransference. First, there are the therapist's reactions to the complex and shifting attitudes in the culture toward divorce, described in Chapter 2, and how much each client mirrors the therapist's own position. How does one hold balance with the family when the therapist strongly believes in commitment to marriage, and one client's problematic rage centers on his or her former partner's lack of commitment? Similarly, for the therapist who views divorce more as a normal transition in life and a life option, how can he or she find the part of self that can respond to such a partner's deep hurt? Working with this population depends on being able to understand and empathize with those who have various perspectives, working from a foundation of seeking to help all family members find more satisfying, and yet also accountable, lives.

Second, therapists must not become overwhelmed and disheartened by the conflict and continual problems that so often are present. Experiencing the "heart of darkness" can bring up a sense of hopelessness, particularly because some of these situations are so sad and stuck. At such moments, the therapist's work with self to hold in focus what may be possible to accomplish is crucial. Maintaining flexibility in treatment helps here. Sometimes a conjoint meeting goes so badly that it is far better to use the time to meet serially with two partners and reassemble the group on another day.

Third, there are the pulls from the primitive object relations often manifested in these families. Others, including the therapist, in contact with members of these families are strongly invited to have powerful feelings. Some of these feelings, such as anger at specific clients, are not helpful to progress. Therapists need to remain aware of processes such as projective identification that frequently occur in this work and differentiate themselves from them. It is always helpful take a few minutes after each session to attend to not only what has happened in terms of the treatment plan but also to what the therapist has experienced personally. With that knowledge, the therapist can work with self to stay empathic with all clients and not get caught up in his or her feelings.

Fourth is the therapist's reaction to the continual pull for the therapist to side with each client's position. Does one client seem more appealing, perhaps because he or she presents better to the therapist? Does the therapist carry attitudes about gender or culture that make it easier to identify with some family members rather than others? If the therapist treats only one subsystem, do they become prone to privileging their version of the narrative over the narratives of others? Again, these are feelings that each therapist can surface in self-examination alone or in consultation with colleagues as these therapies move forward, so that further work regain balance can ensue.

Fifth are the therapist's reactions to the oscillating rhythms in these cases. Progress can slowly build, only to be undone by a single event. Sometimes the trigger for regression lies in a force external to therapy, such as an action in the judicial system. Doing therapy with these families and individuals is about learning to live with such oscillations, taking comfort that some positive change is possible and recycling back to work through an issue repeatedly, as necessary.

Finally, there is the wide range of the therapist's personal experience in relation to the specific problems that play out in these families. Do issues from the therapist's adult relational life or family of origin about divorce or related issues impinge on this work? Those experiences may be directly about divorce in the therapist's family of origin or adult life but may also relate to other dramas, such as high conflict or using children as self-objects. "Know thyself" is essential advice here. Having related experience does not disqualify therapists from doing this work. Some of the best therapists working with this population are children of difficult divorce, who have dedicated their lives to helping other families suffer less with these problems. However, countertransference must be recognized and processed so that the therapist can appropriately maintain balance.

Antidotes for Burnout

Compassion fatigue and burnout are ongoing risks for therapists in difficult divorce (Norcross & Drewes, 2009). The levels of conflict and trauma, the continual possibilities for triangulation, the high pitch of emotion, and the long periods over which treatment may be needed in these families can be wearing, particularly when progress is slow. It is important for therapists to monitor their burnout in relation to specific cases and find ways to recover and stay helpful.

There is much tension in treating these cases, and therapists must have a way to live with and mitigate this tension.[1] Sometimes a long run or a mindfulness class can help. Certainly, some therapists can treat too many of these cases at one time. To keep in balance, the therapist seeing more than a few of these cases should make sure to have several other clients with less agonizing problems who are likely to have less ambiguous positive outcomes. Therapists also need to find ways to celebrate, alone and with clients, the small victories that can occur in these cases. For example, a topic that inevitably led to an

---

[1]There are fine books about therapists dealing with burnout in work with traumatic situations that are well worth consulting (Barrett & Fish, 2014).

argument may be managed without one, a child begins to relate to a father again in a small way; or two previously antagonistic parents manage to attend a conference together with a teacher at school. Often in these cases, it is the small changes that can make a difference over the long run. Minimizing the collective damage over time can have a crucial impact, even if many problems remain. Such a point of view also helps maintain one's sense of optimism and helpfulness—key factors in all therapies that are especially important among the hurt, angry, and depleted clients who are members of these families.

The Therapeutic Toolkit

Augmenting one's therapeutic toolkit is also enormously helpful in the treatment of difficult divorce and in a therapist's general sense of effectiveness. Therapy must be kept simple and straightforward, but the more tools one has from which to draw, the more the tool chosen is likely to be acceptable and effective. Further, a larger toolkit augments one's sense of being able to adapt to the various blocks that occur during a treatment. Intervention is always a matter of using a strategy based in the case formulation, seeing how clients respond to the strategy and what kind of impact it has, then revising as needed. Therapies in difficult divorce often call for shifts in strategy to see if a second way of approaching a problem works better than the first one tried.

Work in this area fits well with a therapist who has many skills and applies them as needed. In shaping this toolkit, therapists must also find which methods best fit with their personalities and preferred ways of working and how to shape the special skills called for in working with this population (Lebow, 2014). This isn't meant to suggest that those who practice in the context of a less wide-ranging toolkit cannot work effectively with difficult divorce. There are always multiple pathways toward change, and skillful therapists of most orientations can have considerable impact if they are well versed in the territory of difficult divorce and attend to the larger systemic meanings of their work. The therapist is an important factor in any treatment, and therapists are most effective when they are enthusiastic and skillful in offering a treatment strategy. The key is to find an effective pathway given the case formulation, rather than to rigidly follow a prescribed set of interventions. Typically, there are several options to reach the same ends. Nonetheless, working with difficult divorce is an advertisement for the value of expanding one's therapeutic palette.

Benefits of a Team Approach

The sense of having a team working together in difficult divorce also reduces a therapist's sense of pressure and isolation. There is special value in having others with whom to connect who have also come to know members of the family system with its specific dilemmas and problems. First, a team provides multiple perspectives about the case and possible solutions from the vantage points of working with different family members. This can be immeasurably helpful in therapy for making major decisions such as when to bring a parent and child together.

Second, there is something special in simply sharing the experience of working with these families and feeling a collective sense of social support. As in any work with trauma, therapists benefit immeasurably from social support from colleagues and elsewhere (Boss, 2006). A difficult narrative about the events of the week (all too frequent in these families full of "breaking news"), when witnessed by a team, becomes different in a context where it can be shared and better understood rather than simply absorbed in isolation. This camaraderie also affords opportunities to share and work through reactions that could be counterproductive to share in an unprocessed form during a therapy session. A team can also help therapists with the vital task of remaining empathic and connected to these clients, both those whom they are seeing and others in the family, while working with problematic, polarizing, and stuck behavior. Teams working with these cases can provide most of the benefits once found in cotherapy in a less cost-conscious age when multiple therapists could participate in the same sessions (Napier & Whitaker, 1988).

ADAPTING TO CLIENTS

Other factors for therapists lie in adapting to the cultures of clients and their ways of participating in the therapy process.

Race, Culture, Gender, Sexual Orientation, and Socioeconomic Status

Difficult divorces occur in every culture and across the complete range of socioeconomic status. Surprisingly, narratives are much the same across these divides, even though cultures may have very different rules and customs in terms of ending relationships (the one major difference is that poor people must make do with less in the way of input from attorneys).

Nonetheless, therapists must expand to engage with, understand, and work in the context of customs and expectations about divorce within different cultures and subcultures and the diverse typical process for how divorce unfolds across economic groups (Bhatia & Saini, 2016). Different ethnic groups, particularly for those strongly rooted in their traditions, may have distinct customs that are foreign to the therapist and require special consideration. When doing therapy with these families, it is essential for therapists to move outside of their own frame and into the context of the culture in which the family is nested (or cultures; many times, different family members may be anchored in very different places).

Similarly, both the very rich, with their many lawyers, and the very poor, who may barely be able to participate in therapy because of costs (while possibly spending more money than they have on their litigation), present special subcultures with variations in how the divorce proceeds. For the rich, conflict about locating assets is a common complaint, as is flocks of lawyers billing large sums for their services. The impact of this is such that anger at the opposing attorney is often greater than anger at a former partner. For the poor, the issues may be quite different, emerging as chaos in the setting of not receiving much help from attorneys or others to provide at least minimal structure to contain conflicts. Therapists must expand their horizons to understand the mechanisms and issues in both these kinds of divorce. One or both former partners may feel far afield, as though in a foreign land. Both rich and poor clients need the same empathy; they generally all feel lost in this difficult period of life. Therapists often have to work at their interactions with such families, which may be so different from their own.

Another challenge for therapists comes along the fault line of gender in heterosexual couples, given that therapists are of some gender and thereby are likely to bring some unconscious bias to work with divorce. There are huge historical differences across the dominant Western culture in ideas about gender and divorce that often play out prominently in difficult divorce. Women often assume, according to the custom of the mid-20th century, that they will continue to have the major responsibility of child rearing, whereas men often come with a 21st-century view of completely coequal parenting. A parallel set of gendered conflicts occurs about finances, where higher wage-earners, often men, may feel that they are "losing their money." Therapists need to notice any biases around highly gendered issues that they may hold. It is vital for therapists to anchor themselves in their personal values but to be open to diverse viewpoints.

It perhaps goes without saying but is addressed here lest there be any question: Same-sex divorcing couples clearly deserve the same attention that opposite-sex couples do, whether or not they are regarded as married under state or national law. The law informs treatment, but in some states and nations, the law includes antiquated ideas about marriage (e.g., many nations do not recognize same sex marriage, and in many American states, laws about children in same-sex marriages, who often result from new reproductive technologies or legal adoption by one parent, may not speak to the complex realities of family life). These laws should not govern therapy, although if there is unresolved conflict at its conclusion, then families of course remain subject to such law. Additionally, even though same-sex marriage is now legally recognized throughout the United States, legal procedures are only beginning to catch up with this change in law. Here, local law should not be the only factor in helping families to arrive at the best postdivorce resolution. In the case of lesbian, gay, bisexual, transgender, and queer (LGBTQ) families, best practice is for therapists to be able to hold to the same processes that they would bring to a heterosexual divorcing family. Again, with LGBTQ families as elsewhere, therapists should examine their interactions. The best case is to treat these families as they do others, with the work informed by the special challenges LGBTQ families face (Green & Mitchell, 2015).

Arrangements

Beyond the more complex issues involving the therapist's interaction with therapy, therapists face a series of simple frustrations in these cases that they must process and work through. One example lies in scheduling. Although there may be forces that encourage ease of scheduling (many clients want good reports to reach the courts about their participation), family dynamics sometimes trigger chronic scheduling problems with one or more clients. One frequently encountered sequence is the fight for control between parents around scheduling. Here, the former partners may insist on a symmetrical balance between the parents in scheduling, even though one parent may have a much more flexible schedule than the other. A variation on this is the scenario in which one parent cancels a meeting, so the second parent cancels the next one. Similar questions of power and control may also appear in scheduling of children, which often is tightly controlled by some parents, making it difficult to arrange any regular meeting time. Control is so powerful that some parents always want scheduling with children to be when the children are with the other parent, whereas others seek to always bring them to therapy (i.e., clients' control often seems to trump whether it is more or less advantageous to bring the children during one's own time with them). As elsewhere, remaining flexible but firm is the therapist's best remedy for these problems, so that each event can be processed in terms of the overall goal of keeping the therapy steady and moving toward treatment goals, undeterred by the various tactics employed by either side. Arrangements are often a matter of compromises between family members, which also allow therapists to feel their time is being used well.

A related consideration in terms of scheduling is that these families are frequently in crisis. It is a sad reality that they often have more traumatic events occurring during the time of the therapy than those who come to therapy for other reasons. These may range from expected traumas, such as children completely rejecting a parent with whom they have had a bad relationship, to less expected ones, such as violence or arrest. This work requires therapists to be ready to respond to such challenges when they arise (both in therapy and as treating experts) and ideally to keep the work moving in a constructive direction, when this remains possible.

Effective treatment involves being available for crisis management when a traumatic event emerges. In the short term, this is usually through phone contact, with meetings scheduled for the most relevant subsystems as soon as possible. Therapists need to consider such disruptions as part of the work with these families.

SUMMARY

Therapy with difficult divorce is not just about choosing intervention strategies, but also about the self of the therapist. Therapists encounter several special challenges in this regard, given the overwhelming amount of darkness, the multiple problems, the vulnerable children, and the frequently high level of conflict in these families. This chapter emphasizes the importance of the therapist understanding and working with personal reactions to these cases, be they actively induced by actions of the clients or be they primarily stemming from the therapist's personal experience.

10

ADAPTATIONS FOR LESS DIFFICULT DIVORCES

This chapter describes adapting this therapeutic approach to less difficult divorces. The methods described earlier in this book presume a family system that is more difficult to work with and in a unique kind of crisis. Yet most of the skill sets are also useful in more typical divorce, adapted to the more typical family. This chapter describes using a similar combination of session formats and intervention strategies, but here in the context of more ambitious goals with a greater focus on client experiencing and healing.

NORMATIVE DIVORCE

Being anchored, as this book is, in difficult divorce, it is easy to lose track of the more normative experience of divorce. Although divorce is an intrinsically painful life event, most families continue to function well enough through this transition to complete developmental tasks. For those in divorcing families, even if they are unhappy, there isn't endless pain and

http://dx.doi.org/10.1037/0000116-011
Treating the Difficult Divorce: A Practical Guide for Psychotherapists, by J. L. Lebow

agony. Conflict, even when present, remains tolerable. It may be challenging to arrive at arrangements for children, but it occurs without long periods of uncertainty and conflict. Children find constructive, if sometimes reluctant, ways to engage with parents in a new way of organizing the family. All family members function without significant psychopathology, even if there are bad days. Families move through this transition into future lives, where the dominant discourse is no longer about divorce. In short, for most, divorce has become a normal, albeit taxing, life transition in Western society, in which approximately half of families engage.

Yet, as noted, normative divorce is still experienced as a major life crisis for most people, in which the core foundation for family life undergoes radical change. The feelings associated with divorce haven't quite caught up with its normative state. Perhaps because for generations it was unthinkable, perhaps because marriage is still framed as forever (at least at the onset, and in stories and films children read and see), or perhaps because of its cataclysmic impact on family organization or core attachment, divorce remains emotionally stirring for most everyone. Feelings are almost invariably powerful, some conflict is typically present, and a state labeled as feeling like I am "not me" (Hetherington, Law, & O'Connor, 1993) is widely prevalent. The transition is considerable and filled with challenges for almost everyone, even for partners who initiate the divorce. Elements of the problems and characteristics in difficult divorce (e.g., high conflict, communication breakdowns, coparenting atrophies) may also flare up for a period in normative divorce. However, one or both partners take leadership in moving to keep the divorce from plunging deeply into and remaining in the territory of "difficult divorce," and eventually life becomes steadier.

As noted in Chapter 2, long-term outcomes are good for most adults and children after this transition. Almost everyone recovers and many even grow through this process (albeit with memories of pain). Yet the waters may be choppy along the way, especially in the first 2 years of the transition (Hetherington & Kelly, 2002). Therefore, there remains much to work on, and many of those going through more typical divorce wisely seek therapy to help mitigate the damage and enhance the possibility of growth with this life transition. Indeed, therapy is often an explicit part of their formula for preventing a decline into difficult divorce.

USING THE MODEL IN NORMATIVE VERSUS DIFFICULT DIVORCE

Although explicitly designed for more difficult, bogged-down, and high-conflict divorce, the integrative approach described in this book is, with modifications, applicable to lower conflict divorce. The major differences between normative divorce and the difficult divorce versions of the model flow primarily from the greater ease in normative divorce in creating and maintaining a working alliance, the greater possibilities for better continuing relationships between the former partners, the availability of the additional option of being able to explore the marriage conjointly with the former partners, and, most of all, the greater possibilities for using this moment in life for self-exploration and to open up a conversation about the future. Further, in more typical divorce, therapy can be more collaborative than in difficult divorce, and the constraints to engaging in "deeper" therapy processes are removed, allowing for affect and meanings to be explored more freely.

In difficult divorce, the therapist's essential task is to keep moving toward the essential, highly practical goals of the therapy. Thus, much of the frame focuses on establishing physical and emotional safety, taking great care for there to be minimal damage when bringing people together, and continually redirecting in-session processes toward therapeutic goals and away from hot buttons for conflict. The therapist's interface, although caring, is often centered on remaining alert to, and anticipating and diminishing, possibilities for damage. To a certain extent, this work requires that the therapist not feel too much; a key to success is maintaining a mindful and steady stance. In working with the more normative divorce process, therapists can experience more fully and remain more open to the experience as it unfolds. When working with more typical divorce, even in times of great sadness and anger, it is far easier to bring a more open feeling state and flexibility to this work than when in the presence of the deeply wounded and attacking clients in difficult divorce.

The Conceptual Model

The conceptual model for intervention and the strategies used in normative divorce are like those for difficult divorce described in Chapters 4, 5, and 6 but with a major difference. The treatment process opens up considerably, with less of a focus on shutting down pathological processes and building very basic skills, and more on working together toward a common end. A combination of family, couple, and individual session formats may be used, with the format(s) selected in relation to who is seeking therapy and the case formulation.

As in the presentation of treatment of difficult divorce, the discussion here is intended to be useful in presenting both a comprehensive approach to therapy in normative divorce that systemically offers therapy to the family system through a variety of treatment formats and a practical set of methods for the therapist who is working with a subsystem or individual in the divorcing family system. This chapter highlights what is special and distinct in working with families in normative divorce from those in difficult divorce and in employing various strategies in this context, rather than comprehensively reviewing the basics of the various strategies involved. The chapter also presents an overview of a typical course of therapy following the model and the treatment strategies used. Actual strategies employed in any specific case will vary with the case formulation, treatment goals, client preferences, context, and therapist skills. Further, given that we are here speaking to more flexible systems than in difficult divorce, there is far more room for the therapy to be effective using a variety of strategies through alternative pathways (see the discussion in Chapter 6).

Given that there is a continuum of difficulty in divorce, an important factor in this therapy lies in how close or far families and individuals are from difficult divorce. To the extent a family has more qualities of difficult divorce within the normative range, more of the highly structured modes described earlier in this book may be needed. A major goal must be to prevent a slide into difficult divorce. To the extent a family is far removed from difficult divorce, a more relaxed and exploratory mode is preferable.

The Therapy Contract

The therapy contract in the normative divorce version of the model is a more typical contract for psychotherapy (Orlinsky & Howard, 1987). In most instances, because the therapy includes more than one individual, the contract is like others in couple and family therapy (Gottlieb, Lasser, & Simpson, 2008). Issues of confidentiality, rights to records, and related issues need to be clearly addressed and fully apparent as in any conjoint therapy, and the written contract for therapy should be well defined, anticipating common problems that may arise (especially if what is a normative divorce veers into more significant litigation). However, the contract does not need to be as specific or detailed as in more difficult divorce, with its ever-present specter of a possibility of legal involvement.

Setting the Format and Framework for Therapy

In this model of working with normative divorce, who best to involve in the therapy is driven largely by client preference, informed by therapist input as to what is likely to be the most useful given the case formulation. The key questions are as follows: What is this client or set of clients seeking, who would be best involved directly in the therapy to address the presenting problem, and how accessible and motivated to be in therapy are those people? This is far less prescriptive than in how the model works in the context of difficult divorce. In normative divorce, there are more available routes toward being helpful; the core assumption is that any of those routes is worth pursuing and that gains can be made even if the ideal client mix is not available.

The therapist enters into collaboration with the client(s) about how therapy might best be pursued. For example, the therapist helps clients understand that conjoint problems are most effectively approached with all of the people involved with those problems (Datchi & Sexton, 2016). If a client calls for therapy concerned about coparenting with a former partner, the therapist presents the potential client with an informed choice as to who might come in, stressing the advantages of involving that partner in sessions. However, sometimes one person is motivated to do something and others are not, or that person's motivation is even dependent on working on the problem alone. The therapist works to collaborate with the client(s) to create the most helpful format for therapy, but not at the cost of sapping motivation to do something. The therapist explains why a format is optimal and discusses concerns about that format, but ultimately clients are full collaborators in structuring the treatment. If the client decides that she or he wants to be seen alone, there is always the possibility of adding a conjoint therapy if that ultimately appears necessary.

The logic is similar in considering treatment for children. If a child or adolescent is looking for someone to talk to about the divorce, responding to this request is usually warranted. Children and adolescents benefit from processing their feelings about divorce. However, it also is important to consider the nature of the issue for which therapy is being sought. Sometimes the request is actually for help with a relational issue, such as the child's relationship with a parent. In this context, the therapist most appropriately lets the parent calling know that it would be best to begin with family sessions and move to working alone with the child if indeed the best solution is to provide an individual space for the child to process feelings.

It also is important to keep in mind that children whose parents are divorcing, are sometimes brought into individual therapy by caring parents in the unusual context of there being no presenting problem other than the family's life transition and no request for help from the child. This is done with the best of intentions—to provide the children a space to understand what is happening and deal with how they are feeling about that, away from loyalty issues to parents. Although typically valuable and involving little risk, the possibilities for such individual work are best considered in the context of also considering the alternative of family therapy. In family therapy, everyone might be able to better process the underlying feelings they are experiencing, and in that context, breakout space for children to meet alone with the therapist could be created if that seems helpful. Nonetheless, in the normative divorce version of this model, the format remains a client–therapist collaboration, and thus, if the clients choose to override the therapist's recommendation, the therapy begins with the format preferred by the clients (bearing in mind that some parent involvement is essential to child and adolescent therapy in this treatment model).

Somewhat ironically, because of the severity of the problems in difficult divorce and because referring sources connected to the court are often involved, assembling the optimal groupings of family members in treatment in relation to the problem is sometimes easier in difficult divorces than more typical ones. Here, with less sense of urgency and fewer external demands, gaining the involvement of the whole family system can be more challenging. This adds to the reasons that this approach, although encouraging the involvement of the entire system, often simply works with whoever is available and motivated to participate in therapy. This may be the whole family, one parent and the children, the former partners, or one former partner. There is both a best-case version of the treatment but also options for working toward the same ends based in the same principles with whoever is available.

Alliance

Therapy begins with alliance-building and assessment. Contrasted with the treacherous territory for alliance of difficult divorce, standard methods for forming alliances in relational contexts work well here (Friedlander, Escudero, & Heatherington, 2006; Horvath, Symonds, & Tapia, 2010; Minuchin & Fishman, 1981). These are easier and generally less fragile people with whom to work, and there are fewer situations in which forces push into therapy those who really don't want to be there.

Still, the major stumbling block to alliance lies in managing the balance of alliances, particularly in families where one or more people feel wronged and hurt. There also are special challenges in maintaining such balance between clients who are more motivated in the therapy process (often adults), and those who less so (typically either leaving partners or children). Recurring experiences in which a client feels sided with or against can also elicit powerful feelings. Conjoint therapy needs to work assiduously to maintain a multipartial alliance (Boszormenyi-Nagy & Spark, 1973) with outreach to those with whom the alliance is weaker.

Alliance problems, when they arise, are often subtler here than in difficult divorce. For example, both former partners may appear cooperative and say that they want to meet conjointly to avoid pitfalls in divorce and coparent in the best possible way, but one former partner may want to engage in the therapy process more than the other. Likewise, tendencies to triangulate the therapist into an unbalanced alliance may occur on a less conscious level.

Therefore, it remains essential here, as in difficult divorce, to track alliances and actively intervene to balance differences in connection before alliance issues become problems in the therapy.

Assessment and Case Formulation

Assessment follows a similar protocol as in difficult divorce. The first question is how close to difficult divorce is this family or individual? As already noted, how families divorce represents a continuum rather than an absolute categorical difference between difficult and normative divorce. Normative divorces often cycle into and out of many of the problems found in difficult divorce. What signs of difficulty are visible, and which are experienced as problems by the client(s)? The answers to these questions suggest not only targets for intervention but also how much the therapist can move away from the protocol for difficult divorce. When there are signs of difficult divorce, a transcendent goal must always be to help prevent a cascade into that painful territory.

This aside, the major focus of assessment lies in using it to develop a case formulation that highlights the problem(s) clients would like to address and processes related to that problem, leading to planning about how to best address it.[1] People in the midst of more normative divorce come to therapy for a variety of reasons. Divorcing partners sometimes seek therapy around conjoint issues, such as exploring the best time-sharing arrangements for children, about perceived blocks in the ability to coparent, or to end the marriage as well as possible. Another frequent reason for seeking help is when one parent looks for assistance with the transition in his or her own household or when one or both parents are concerned about the impact of the divorce on a child or children. Perhaps most common is for one former partner to enter therapy seeking to make this life transition and process the meanings in it, while taking the opportunity to consider the marriage and his or her life going forward.

Several overarching questions often surface around such issues. How can the former couple end the marital relationship in a way that is least damaging? How can they structure life in two homes, and with what degree of coparenting? How can children be helped to have the best possible adaptation to the changes that are occurring? How does one envision postdivorce life and future connections? Is it possible to plan for negotiating differences in parenting that may appear? How will one live life in this new circumstance? How will one deal with the strong feelings that are present? How can one understand what happened and learn from the experience?

---

[1]A difference from difficult divorce here is that in normative divorce, the only stakeholders are the family members.

Goal-Setting and Planning

In this model of therapy, goal-setting in normative divorcing families is a fully collaborative process. Clients are seen as consumers looking to resolve specific problems and work with specific issues. After hearing clients' wishes and concerns, the therapist shares what looks to be the best path toward those goals, and then therapeutic strategies are chosen that most expeditiously and reliably (by virtue of evidence for their impact) will help in working toward those goals.

Whatever the specific goals and whoever is seen, it also is part of the essence of this treatment model that the therapist holds a systemic view of the divorce process. This has a specific important meaning in terms of goal-setting. The therapist considers the collective need to move most successfully through this period, as well as the individual needs and views of the clients(s) she or he is seeing. This prompts conversation with clients about individual needs and those of others, and about proximate goals and long-term benefits. Ultimately, such a systemic view also helps each individual because movements in directions that have an unnecessarily deleterious effect on others are not likely to prove beneficial in the long run; systems always remain systems. An eye is focused not only on the meaning for oneself but that for others as well and whether there are ways to reach the best personal outcomes that are also least damaging for others.

Another place complexities in planning arise is when family members in the therapy have different goals. Here the therapist helps negotiate some approach to the problem that can best serve each client's goals. In those instances where goals are truly incompatible, a proximate goal becomes to at least process these differences in a way that allows more broadly for the best ongoing cooperation.

INTERVENTION STRATEGIES

The intervention strategies employed with normative divorce fall into the same categories as in difficult divorce but are presented in a more collaborative spirit, and with more room for improvisation and typically greater depth of exploration.

Broad Strategies That Set the Stage for More Specific Interventions

Witnessing

Witnessing—empathically listening to client(s) as they share their narrative and move through this time (Weingarten, 2010)—may be the single most important aspect of therapy in normative divorce. The felt presence of the therapist as an empathic listener is often the aspect of therapy clients describe as most important (Elliott, 1986). Rarely experienced events and feelings are present through this time, and having a place to speak about those feelings in the presence of an empathic therapist is itself healing for many.

Psychoeducation

Adults and children going through the process of divorce have a predictable set of experiences and feelings. Psychoeducation draws on the extensive knowledge we have about normative divorce to help clients understand that their feelings and those of the others in the family (both of which may seem strange) are actually normative. There also is much known about how to optimally move through the various challenges of this time and even more about what tends not to work (see Chapter 3). Psychoeducation can help chart pathways to successful transitions about matters such as how to best divide children's time between parents, about decisions such as who will move out and when, about how to tell children about divorce, and about patterns of moving through divorce. Psychoeducation is easier to deliver in normative than difficult divorce, and clients often actively seek it. Furthermore, they typically follow advice they receive.

Maintaining a Solution-Oriented Focus

As in difficult divorce, therapy is more engaging and effective when it is focused on finding solutions. Divorce becomes treacherous when the focus moves to who or why there are problems; it is far better to center on how to avoid or resolve issues. However, there is a necessary difference in how a solution is presented in normative divorces versus difficult divorces. Difficult divorce requires an unmitigated "broken record" directed at offering solutions and pursuing them, with the therapist repeatedly refocusing clients away from complaints and toward possible solutions. Here, with clients who have not already fallen into rigid positions, and absent the constant threat of therapy turning into something harmful, there is more room for the simple acknowledgment of pain, to explore more deeply clients' feelings about problems, and to speak directly to the dilemmas that just can't be solved. The solution focus remains, but it is tempered by room to pursue other conversations.

Orienting to Client State of Change

Orienting to a client's stage of change is, if anything, more salient in the treatment of normative than difficult divorce. In normative divorce, there is much distribution of clients across stages of change. These clients share one common experience—divorce—but may be in enormously diverse positions in relation to it. In normative divorce, some clients mirror those in difficult divorce in being in the precontemplation stage. For former partners, precontemplation typically is manifested in placing responsibility for it fully on one's partner and seeing no need for personal change; for children, it means they see no need for anything to change in their lives despite the divorce. However, in normative divorce, many are in a stage of contemplation or change. Divorce is one of the great precipitants of positive individual transformation.

As in difficult divorce, a focus of therapy becomes to help clients move a stage at a time toward action where they can see themselves as agents of positive change. Clients in normative divorce also present with more fluidity in their stage of change. They frequently oscillate between coping behaviors, thoughts, and emotions and more distressing and provocative ones. This provides greater possibilities for building on the strengths in coping that are already evident at times. Further, the necessity for moving forward in stage of change is less than in difficult divorce, given that an individual and family is functioning in the normal range. Again, absent the hyper-contentious atmosphere of difficult divorce, all these factors add up to more room for flexibility in approach and a greater likelihood of change processes occurring. Paradoxically, even though these clients are more capable of change, the need for change is not nearly as urgent.

Therapy in normative divorce begins with identifying the stage of change of each client, and then collaborating with them in approaching where they each are about change. The most problematic aspect of stage of change in normative divorce comes when there are mismatches in terms of stage of change, a problem more frequently encountered here than in difficult divorce. The wide range of stage of change among clients may mean that clients are in very different places in terms of the work of the therapy. Sometimes a family may even be on the normative side of the continuum of divorce simply because one person is so motivated to be sure the process moves along well enough that it can compensate for the more problematic behavior of other family members. When there are mismatches or when there is a general lack of motivation, motivational interviewing is helpful in clarifying with less motivated clients whether they can see benefits in change. Still, where there are mismatches between clients in stage of change, this leads to conversation and problem-solving in relation to this, not to an imperative for the lower stage of change client to move ahead. There remain many roads people in action can pursue on their own to move their own lives and the collective family life forward. The lower level of urgency of presenting problems allows more space to permit clients to engage from where they are and in the kind of change they seek. Paradoxically, with less need and demand for change, pathways toward change become easier.

Behavior Change Strategies

Behavioral Strategies

Behavioral strategies that invoke operant conditioning, classical conditioning, and social learning also are advantaged in normative over difficult divorce. Much research shows that behavioral strategies work (Datchi & Sexton, 2016; Nathan & Gorman, 2015), but their weakness is that these prescriptions for change may not be filled—that is, the behavioral plan suggested is never tried or followed through (Patterson & Chamberlain, 1994). In the context of normative divorce, the reactivity of difficult divorce is reduced, and more potential solutions are attempted, leaving a better rate of success for behavioral prescriptions.

The specific behavioral tasks are created in relation to the target problems in focus and the case formulation, and thus range widely. Frequently encountered examples include developing structured ways of coparenting, trying out various kinds of arrangements, carrying out tasks having to do with the separation of homes, helping children with their feelings about divorce, and becoming more activated in developing a personal postdivorce life. Such positive experimentation can move families to change in positive ways and move toward their best possible life as divorced family, or at least to develop structured ways of relating that can help life move on as well as possible, avoiding patterns that might lead to further problems.

Systemic Strategies

In a way similar to their response to the behavioral strategies, those in normative divorce are more open in trying out new methods of systemic organization and becoming aware of their individual roles in dysfunctional systemic cycles. Having said this, family reorganization is inevitably difficult and therapies have an important role in helping clients process the changes occurring, placing adaptation to these changes in a normal developmental framework (children almost inevitably have struggles with the pragmatics and emotion of living in two homes), and providing a place for family members to experience, process, and work with the many feelings that arise.

Establishing Reliable, Rule-Driven Methods of Communication
and Good-Enough Coordination, Negotiation, and Problem-Solving

Communication, coordinated problem-solving, and negotiation about shared concerns are crucial vehicles for resolving specific issues and for mitigating future problems. In this approach to normative divorce, the strategies for communication, problem-solving, and negotiation build on the same communication training and problem-solving foundation as the work with difficult divorce, but again there are clear differences. The largest is that a minimal constricted structure for communication and rigid reliable rules to follow are at the center of this module for working with difficult divorce. In those cases, the therapist works to create just enough communication delivered well enough and no more, principally by using a rigid, rule-driven version of the speaker–listener technique (whether in verbal exchanges or through e-mails and texts), which ensures that people hear each other and slows down conflict. Arriving at optimal methods for communication, problem-solving, and negotiation in normative divorce is more a matter of helping family members collaborate about their preferences. A second difference is that in normative divorce, clients typically begin with better abilities to communicate and problem-solve with each other. Thus, this aspect of therapy is more a matter of sorting out blocks to communication than teaching and practicing basic skills, and the work can focus on a more normal mode of communication without the training wheels.

Finally, in normative divorce, part of the negotiation typically focuses on larger questions, such as what type of relationship former partners will have with one another, now and into the future. A wider range of applicable models for postdivorce life is possible in normative divorce than difficult divorce (in difficult divorce, the only relevant model is centered on minimal contact), and therapists can help families negotiate and make intentional decisions among these choices. Some of this decision-making may represent a very different challenge than in difficult divorce. Ahrons (1994) "Perfect Pals" and "Cooperative Colleagues" both represent normative ways of relating between former partners, but disparities in expectations may need to be negotiated between two former partners with differing models of divorce. Communication about emerging expectations about the postdivorce relationship of the partners and negotiation of differences in those expectations can help avoid future problems associated with disparate viewpoints.

Third-Wave Strategies

Mindful Practice

Divorce is a colossal transition for all involved, and there is much that one may not like that needs to be accepted in divorce. Thus, mindful practice, and learning to accept that which is not going to change, have a perfect fit in working with divorcing systems. Given that levels of anxiety and stress are high even in normative divorce, introducing and practicing modes of relaxation and self-care have great preventive value in moving through this time of life. Even in better divorces, there is a continual need to notice when dysregulation in the context of old hot buttons beckons and find better ways to respond in those moments. Mindful practice is one major tool.

Disengagement Skills and Anger Management

Conflict is part of any family life, and all systems need to learn how to deal with it. Even if a family has previously done well in managing conflict, family members in the process of divorce need to develop special skills for working with it in this new context, where the best tools enabling marital repair, such as deep levels of positive sentiment override and intimate connection, are no longer present.

Again, here, as elsewhere, therapy with normative divorce can include a wider range of emotional expression than in difficult divorce. Accessing feelings is encouraged. Even in the best of divorces, there remain negative feelings toward former partners, and children and parents have inevitable struggles. In normative divorce, the therapist has the leeway to create a frame in which some expression of anger is understood as a normal aspect of divorced life (this is not the case in difficult divorce, where it is too risky and almost always sets off negative sequences). Helping clients take a moment to experience their own feelings and those of others or to deal with the various triggers set off by interaction can enable problem resolution.

However, it remains important to keep in context that these families are at a fragile point. Much of the therapist's essential task is to help them continue on the road of normative divorce and find ways to have conflictual moments not spur a downward spiral. Partners are disconnecting, and thus, discharges of angry affect between them are unlikely to be productive. Further, because the threshold for acceptable levels of overt conflict are lower in divorce than in marriage and repair is more difficult, angry behaviors have special salience. Therefore, bringing an awareness of the damage from angry interactions in divorce, and helping further develop tools for positive dialogue about differences, with anger management as needed, becomes an essential part of many divorce therapies.

Radical Acceptance

Accepting that which cannot be changed is a crucial skill in processing divorce. In normative divorce this is less of a project than in difficult divorce (which in part is characterized by immutable thoughts and feelings). Work in the context of this strategy can also be much more collaborative than in difficult divorce. There, the emphasis is often simply on identifying to the clients which aspects of life might be approached as changeable and which as not. In normative divorce, therapists and clients can more readily converse about, and sort through together, which aspects are changeable and which not, and even engage in experiments to see if wished-for changes are possible.

Psychological Strategies

Reattribution and Narrative Change

In normative divorce, there is less tendency to demonize one's former partner than in difficult divorce. The cognitive distortions that occur tend to be less severe, and narratives are more solidly based in reality (albeit nonetheless painful). Nonetheless, in the context of this major transition, cognitive distortions still occur. The changes occurring in attachment, living arrangements, and relationships provoke strong emotion involving the amygdala, which affect individuals' abilities to sift the data available to find a more objective view of reality. Some cognitive distortion is functional in helping enable separation from what has been a primary attachment. The key becomes for the cognitive distortions to remain within a certain range and not to cross over into ones that become so strong as to promote dysfunctional cycles of behavior.

Strategies for testing the accuracy of thoughts and challenging distorted thoughts remain useful with clients in normative divorce. A key question centers on the importance of various distortions. Which ones are benign in enabling coping, and which serve to interfere with learning from the experience or to provoke sequences that move in the direction of difficult divorce? Everyone brings distortions to this time, but intervention most appropriately focuses on those distortions that generate problems. Catastrophic thoughts about the other, the future, or harm to children and thoughts that ignore the feelings of the others in the family are those particularly in need of challenge. Socratic questioning, through which the therapist helps clients learn how to ask themselves questions to establish the objective basis for their conclusions and to consider alternative hypotheses for what may be occurring, is particularly helpful in the context of the greater capacity for more balanced self-exploration in those in normative divorce (J. S. Beck, 2011). The psychoeducational message interspersed is that this is a time of strong feelings and much "not-me" feeling, and thus is a particularly important time to examine one's thoughts and feelings to be sure to avoid the possible waterfalls ahead. When individual cognitions are processed and important concerns about others remain, this most usefully segues into conjoint processing of whatever issue is in focus.

Working with the overarching narratives about divorce among family members is similarly important. The therapist can help cocreate with clients in normative divorce a vision of a trying time of transition that can lead to productive changes, as long as feelings and thoughts are processed and appropriate actions taken.

Exploring Underlying Emotion

Divorce is a time of great underlying emotion. In difficult divorce, the therapeutic task is mostly to contain and soothe strong emotion in conjoint contexts, with additional work, in the circumscribed space of individual sessions, on the depth of experience and what lies behind it, as that work can be tolerated. In contrast, in normative divorce, exploring emotion is a major vehicle for helping clients move beyond the challenging practicalities of life into exploration of the emotional meaning of what is occurring.

There are many useful paths for processing emotion in psychotherapy. I have found Leslie S. Greenberg's (2017) emotion-focused methods to be a particularly good fit for exploring emotion in relation to the issues that arise in normative divorce. Greenberg's methods involve finding the underlying emotion behind what is being expressed and working with the client on that basic emotional state. This process of exploring emotion includes (a) awareness of emotion or naming what one feels, (b) emotional expression, (c) regulation of emotion, (d) reflection on experience, (e) transformation of emotion by emotion, and (f) corrective experience of emotion through new lived experiences in therapy and the world. In divorce, an event accompanied by what inevitably are strong emotional reactions (what Greenberg calls *secondary reactive emotions*) are often powerful. There are complex reactions to primary adaptive emotion, such as becoming caught up in hopelessness or denying one's emotion, rather than experiencing sadness. Emotion-focused exploration of emotion helps clients become more in touch, and thus be able to work, with their primary emotions.

In difficult divorce, experience suggests that such explorations are less productive. These clients tend to be unable to look at themselves in depth and, at worst, become more at risk for becoming dysregulated by experiences designed to help them access their primary emotions. Such experiences in therapy in difficult divorce often segue into clients feeling they have permission to be even more emotionally unrestrained with their partners and children.

Exploring Individual Psychodynamics

The realm of individual psychodynamics and internal processes opens up in normative divorce in a way that lies outside the bounds of what can be expected of clients in difficult divorce. This is a period when examining internal conflicts and the impact of early experience is enormously meaningful, and clients often are motivated to learn more about themselves. The initial questions clients ask themselves (e.g., "What happened?" "How will I manage?" "Why do I feel and act this way?") readily morph into a deeper inquiry into how clients have lived, how they process events, and how early experience shaped their ways of being. Patterns in family of origin about how to function in relationships are particularly productive to examine. So, too, are mutual transferences and object relations that occurred in the marriage, which may have affected how each partner acted and was perceived in the relationship (Wanlass & Scharff, 2016). Sometimes when exploring inner processes in depth, family members can begin to restore their abilities to mentalize one another (Fonagy, 2002) and find some vestige of their positive connection to each other, which may have been put on the shelf as the cascade toward divorce began, even as they continue to have other negative feelings. This is a time of individual change for many people, and a time when understanding what personal qualities or legacies of the relational past were factors in the demise of the marriage can lead to intentional steps to reshape oneself in the future.

Other Strategies

Biological Solutions

Biological solutions are typically not a part of this model for working with normative divorce. During divorce, many people do use antianxiety or antidepressant medications for symptoms secondary to the enormous life change they are undergoing or the off-label use of simply helping them feel calmer and less disturbed through these turbulent times. The present model emphasizes coping and thus looks instead to develop coping strategies (e.g., behavioral, cognitive) for dealing with the normative emotional upheavals of the divorce process. Nonetheless, the value of biological solutions for many clients (especially those with more symptoms) should not be minimized for clients who may find medication useful at this time, especially given that many medications can provide relief quickly.

Spiritual Solutions

For both those in difficult and normative divorce, spiritual solutions and resources can provide a major protective factor during a time of transition. This part of life is most helpful when it involves social support (a clear "difference that makes a difference"), promotes feeling grounded in one's ethical values, and provides acceptance and forgiveness. It is less helpful when religious institutions and communities spur conflict, devalue former partners, or speak of "broken" families. Such messages from religious institutions add additional constraints to resolution.

SELECTING AND USING VARIOUS THERAPY FORMATS

I have spoken thus far to a wide-ranging set of therapy strategies and tools that can help people going through normative divorce. Any of these strategies can be offered in individual, joint former partner, family, or group therapy formats. Nonetheless, some strategies are better suited to different formats, and the work across individual, child, former partner, and family therapy is quite different. In the best case, different tasks are accomplished in different therapy formats in a systemically organized comprehensive way of helping a family through divorce. More often, clients ask for a period of treatment in a specific format, and the therapist works to offer what is possible in that context, negotiating for the addition of other formats as they seem warranted.

Sessions With the Whole Family

There is more opportunity to engage this whole-family approach in normative divorce than in difficult divorce. Because this format represents the old family structure and part of the task of therapy is to morph into a new one, whole-family sessions are typically limited to a few meetings when used at all. Family therapy can provide the best place for parents and children to talk about their feelings with each other and to form plans about how to execute the various decisions parents have made about the next phase of life. It also offers a place for problem-solving about issues in which both parents and children should be involved in decision-making. This context is also helpful in providing a place for parents to explain the divorce to children, provided that the partners have done preparatory work together so that they begin with a narrative about the divorce on which both can agree. Given the value in maintaining boundaries between the issues in the marriage and the life with children, it is important to keep parental issues between the parents so as not to triangulate children.

Sessions Between One Parent and Children

This is the optimal setting for discussing how life is emerging (or will be) in the new parent–children home and for working with the relationship between one parent and the children. Frequently, a parent (and occasionally even a child) will want to use this form of therapy to be more intentional and successful in creating a new life in their home. This format is especially helpful when subclinical problems begin to arise, which can be addressed before they blossom into larger problems.

Former Partner Sessions

Former partner sessions offer the best place for processing the relationship and issues between partners. This is also the best format for discussing difficulties former partners are having with one another, in continuing operations in which both are involved such as parenting, or moving through the challenges of legally obtaining a divorce. It is also an ideal setting for general planning about coparenting and the task of negotiating what future contact between the former partners will be like. For those prepared to go deepest, these meetings also are a place for reviewing what has occurred in the marriage and emotionally connecting around the sadness of the ending of the marriage. In the best of circumstances, couples can review their life together and the decision to part in the context of that history. The select few who can more fully process their experience also use these conversations as a springboard to working through long-standing feelings. This work, which is usually brief, is quite different from couple therapy, which is predicated on the underpinning of enhancing a continuing marital relationship. This is work toward a good ending.

Individual Sessions

Individual sessions allow for the greatest depth of exploration. Divorce is among the most frequent times in life that people seek individual therapy. Even for the least traumatized individual, there is much to process about what has happened, why it happened, how to deal with their former partner and any children, how to deal with the challenges of this new life (which may include being a single parent and/or dating after many years of marriage), and how to process the rush of feelings that is generally inevitable. Perhaps the largest difference in applying this treatment model in normative divorce versus difficult divorce is that here the entire therapist toolkit is relevant. It is not so much for a model to prescribe what is most useful in this work, although there are some interventions such as activation, mindful practice, challenging self-defeating cognitions, and engaging with emotion (as in emotion-focused therapy) that are universally useful. What is most helpful is for individuals to enter a safe space for self-exploration and to use that exploration toward the end of individual growth and greater systemic well-being.

Individual sessions are also the best place to help family members who are the most motivated work to maximize their individual contribution to avoiding and resolving problems. Although conjoint sessions have the possible benefit of multiple people working toward change, multiperson formats inevitably highlight coequal changes. However, the way many family systems avoid difficulties often lies not in coequal change, but in one or more persons finding ways to accept and work with the more problematic behavior of others. Therapists can, in this format, most effectively help motivated family members recognize and accept the limitations of others and find ways to work with those patterns to keep the overall process moving toward therapeutic goals and the divorce from cascading downward. Beyond this, for all family members, individual meetings are the best place to consider what is changeable in self and others and what is not, and to be helped to learn to accept this and work within these limits.

A special aspect of individual work (either in individual sessions as part of a conjoint therapy or in an individual therapy) emphasized in this treatment model lies in maintaining a systemic focus, which considers the others in the family as well as the person in the room. As already noted, during the process of divorce, there is often the temptation on the part of all family members to move toward solutions that are helpful to oneself but harmful for others and thus set off dysfunctional systemic processes. Given the challenges of divorce, the therapist working in this model holds a systemic position that is accepting in relation to the client's exploration of the wide range of their thoughts and feelings, yet challenges those behaviors that will have predictable negative effects for others. Clients make their own decisions about their lives, but therapists in this life circumstance can provide essential feedback about the costs and benefits of various actions for self and others. The specter of difficult divorce hovers, and the therapist can have an important role in helping this ship move to a shore that is safe and secure for everyone.

For example, a father may want to immediately bring a new partner into his children's lives, without considering the inevitable negative reaction that will likely occur. Or a wife who has problems with the ending of the marriage may describe constant efforts to connect with her former partner; this may be personally reassuring in the short term but lead to distress for self and others in the long term. Alternately, a former partner may describe his glee in some destructive cathartic act to his former partner. Such events are not easy to deal with in individual therapy. Clients look for therapist approval and acceptance, but there are ways of challenging the behavior while honoring the client's feelings. Work that probes emotion can be helpful in moving the focus to the underlying emotion, rather than on problematic ways of acting. So too can Socratic questioning, moving to a cost–benefit analysis. In the long run, relating to some of the position of the others in the challenging event that is divorce can also help the individual client, given how valuable systemic calm is to individual progress.

A special word must be added here about individual meetings (or therapy) with children. Even if freed from the extreme conflict and related pathology of difficult divorce, children experiencing normative divorce face a variety of painful feelings. The research of Amato (Amato et al., 1995) and

Emery (Emery & Dinescu, 2016) shows that although children may function well enough, their feelings are strong (and often remain powerful for many years after divorce), especially among those who have come from what they had previously thought of as happy families. Having a safe place to process these feelings with a therapist who can work with them and offer information at their developmental level (perhaps in conjunction with family sessions to discuss issues often not processed) is immeasurably helpful for children trying to make sense out of this experience, some aspects of which they are privy to and some not.

Integrating the Various Formats

As with more difficult divorce, the various formats are best integrated in a systemic approach to therapy. The various session formats can involve one therapist or several, with the pros and cons of one versus many therapists similar to those reviewed in the context of difficult divorce. An overarching message is to encourage drawing on various therapies to the extent the client(s) finds them useful.

There is a bit less urgency for coordination in normative divorce, given that the therapy occurs in a less brittle context. Nonetheless, coordination is always helpful. The integration of the formats allows for intervention strategies to be employed in the format that will likely prove most useful. For example, vulnerable work about self occurs most readily in the individual context. Similarly, dyadic issues such as communication and problem-solving are most efficiently resolved in the former partner or family formats.

What is essential is that there be some bridge between the session formats, such that the work in each moves toward the same ends and with similar language and focus across the session types. Ideally, an issue about which two former partners have different perceptions and narratives might surface in a conjoint session, and then Socratic questioning related to each client's cognitions might move into focus in individual sessions, with any wisdom acquired from that exploration brought back to the joint meetings. Similarly, traumatic feelings might emerge in the family context, with a deeper level of work exploring those feelings in the individual format. Likewise, parents can problem-solve about how to approach children in the former partner context and then bring this set of ideas to the children in the family context.

When one therapist manages all the formats, continuity and tight coordination between types of sessions is relatively simple (although there may be other issues about confidentiality and the perceived psychological safety of the structure of the therapy that may interfere with sharing or about the therapist's comfort level and skill across two very different treatment formats).

When there is more than one therapist, coordination is needed, although not on the level required in difficult divorce. Consistent with the core relative ease of working with normative divorce versus difficult divorce, there is much more leeway for therapists doing different kinds of work with clients in various contexts as long as there is enough effort to bridge those differences and to ensure they do not become isomorphic with family problems. There inevitably is some trade-off in less conversation between the various therapists and specific follow-up of issues across therapies (more such conversation is always better), but given similar underlying goals and some continuing macrolevel coordination, therapies typically work well together in this context.

BRIEF CASE EXAMPLES

Therapy in these families ranges widely. Here are two quite different examples.

A Sad Parting Couple

Herb and William have been a couple for 25 years, although they only married when laws in their state changed to permit same-sex marriage in the past 10 years. They came for therapy after William informed Herb that he had started a new relationship and wanted a divorce. Unlike many couples in similar circumstances, when they began treatment, both were focused on wanting to end the relationship well, rather than focused on tumult secondary to William's new relationship. When that relationship had first become known to Herb, he had considerable anger and felt a keen sense of betrayal, but as they shared and discussed their deeper feelings, the affair had moved into the background. In the foreground was Herb's personal wish to continue the relationship, William's definitive stance that the marriage was ending, Herb's fully digesting that, in fact, the marriage was ending, and a sense on both their parts that they had drifted away from an intimate connection with one another.

The five sessions they had in therapy were moving and productive. The first topic explored involved the pragmatics of dividing their lives. It was already assumed that they would divide time with their 5-year-old daughter. The therapist helped them consider and process details of how they would do this together and remain fully in support of their daughter. They also briefly took up other topics, such as how holidays would be spent (some together). This segued into a frank and complex problem-solving conversation about the boundaries between how they would continue to have a postdivorce connection, how this would interface with William's new relationship, and how the person William was seeing would be involved with their daughter. Here, strong positions surfaced: William wanted a place for his new partner in their daughter's life, whereas Herb wanted to ensure there was a longer term connection before introducing him into their daughter's life. They arrived at what seemed to be a good compromise: They would give their daughter time to digest the divorce and then would gradually introduce William's partner into the mix. Throughout, the therapist mostly followed William and Herb in what they wanted to discuss, providing some structure for negotiation and refocusing when the conversation digressed.

The remaining meetings focused on their mutually sharing their sadness. They recalled the hopes and joys they had together, as well as the key points and markers of their decline in their sense of intimacy and connection in recent years. Both cried at points in these meetings, not in terms of thoughts of continuing the relationship but about parting. They committed to continue to connect with each other in a variety of ways over time.

A Family Dealing With Transition

Brian and Stacy had been married for 15 years. They had not had an easy marriage, but when Stacy informed Brian that she had decided to divorce, it nonetheless came as a surprise. Quickly, things degenerated into arguments about who was going to move out and some close to out-of-control moments of conflict. After one such argument, Brian suggested to Stacy that they meet with a therapist, and she agreed as long as the conversation was restricted to talking about decoupling.

Although Brian expressed his wish that the marriage would continue in the first session, he also accepted that he knew this was not possible. Therefore, the focus quickly moved to collaborating on an agenda of what they needed to do to end the marriage with the least damage possible.

The first specific target for intervention was the spirited, verging on out-of-control, fights they had been having. The therapist approached these arguments in two ways. First, Brian and Stacy collaborated in creating a plan for anger management when arguments began to escalate. This included time-outs when someone was becoming too distressed, individual mindful practice, and work on self-talk. Second, the therapist helped them undertake a behavioral analysis of how such arguments evolved, attending to the topics involved, the timing of the arguments, and the sequences that occurred. The therapist then helped them create a plan for diminishing the risk for these confrontations, by recognizing the cues that acrimony was growing and taking action, but also by bringing back into therapy the issues that needed to be resolved for discussion and negotiation.

This latter list then served to organize a series of sessions focused on problem-solving about the issues over which they clashed. For example, they had both understood from the first that they would share time with the children, but there were major differences between them about how to parent during that time (as often is the case, these were old disputes in a new bottle, such as how to work with the children's eating habits, diet, and discipline). The therapist guided them to arrive at a version of "Mom's house, Dad's house" that allowed each of them to parent as they saw best with good-enough coordination across their major differences. Extremes they might individually pursue about issues such as what the children ate and their bedtimes were negotiated.

A key difference between the parents was that Stacy thought it best to tell the children they were divorcing, but Brian was reluctant to do this until they had a concrete plan for someone to move out. This proved a complex issue to resolve. The therapist directly weighed in on the side of informing the children, explaining that, even beyond the intrinsic value in being honest with children at their developmental level about what is occurring, there were multiple other ways they might find out without the parents telling them, a considerable liability for the strategy of protecting them from the information. A decision was made to tell them together following a standard version of a script for explaining divorce to children, as described by Emery (2004, 2016).

In a touching follow-up session with the children after they had told them about the divorce, the family began to talk together about their feelings. In a particularly poignant moment, when their 7-year-old daughter said she wished they could stay together, Stacy and Brian let her know that wasn't possible. The parents also discussed in session possible time-sharing arrangements, each based on a 50% time in each home division of time, and the children were given an opportunity to voice their preferences. Stacy and Brian, with the help of the therapist, located a Rainbows group in which the children could participate to have another place away from the parents to discuss their feelings.

As the conflict subsided, the therapy wound down. Stacy and Brian did not end up as "perfect pals" but also avoided provocative sequences that might easily result in a cascade into perpetual difficulty.

SUMMARY

This chapter highlighted useful intervention strategies and formats for therapy with normative divorce. Therapy in this context has greater possibility than in difficult divorce. Clients often are more motivated to change at a moment in life when therapy is often found most useful, rather than locked in dysfunctional patterns as occurs in difficult divorce. Further, therapy is not nearly as encumbered by the legal process as in difficult divorce. However, in accentuating this difference, therapists should not underestimate the pain and challenge in dealing with the problems encountered. These include problems located in systemic relationships between family members, those located in the divorcing adults (including for the partner initiating the divorce), and those for children trying to cope with the changes occurring. Those in the process of normative divorce also often slide temporarily into some of the dysfunctional patterns of difficult divorce. The major difference lies in their being less likely to stay stuck in these patterns and remaining able to find ways to remain resilient in the midst of these challenges. Additionally, there are almost inevitably the subclinical internal issues that adults encounter as they face the end of their principal attachment and children face a radical transformation in the structure of their lives.

Therapy with normative divorcing families, partners, or individuals remains an important resource for helping individuals and families cope through these most trying times. At this life transition, therapy with these families, and the individuals in them, can have significant effects, not only on short term coping and avoiding stumbling blocks, but also in eliciting break-throughs in insight and in changing life long patterns. Therapists working with normative divorce optimally build a strong multipartial alliance with clients, engage the other common factors that underlie change in psycho-therapy, and employ a flexible repertoire of interventions that can be adapted to the problems in focus and the case formulation.

11

CASE EXAMPLES: WORKING WITH DIFFICULT DIVORCE

This chapter presents two case examples of families experiencing difficult divorce. Each is court referred, and in each the practitioner served as the therapist to the entire family system. In the first case, the family had serious difficulties from the onset of the divorce onward. In the second case, problems did not emerge until after the addition of a new partner to the family mix.

A HIGH-CONFLICT FAMILY

Stephanie and Troy had a great deal of conflict throughout their 18-year marriage. Stephanie saw Troy as selfish, leaving her with most of the household tasks, in addition to her demanding 8-to-5 job as a paralegal. She also thought he drank too much on the weekends. Troy felt that Stephanie was too angry and critical, and he frequently complained about the low level

http://dx.doi.org/10.1037/0000116-012
Treating the Difficult Divorce: A Practical Guide for Psychotherapists, by J. L. Lebow

of sexuality in their marriage. After many fierce confrontations, Stephanie became convinced that life would be better if she divorced.

When she informed him that she had seen an attorney and launched the legal process, Troy became very upset about Stephanie "giving up on the marriage." Stephanie asked Troy to move out and he refused, saying it was his house as well, that he wanted to remain with the children, and that since she wanted the divorce she should be the one to move out.

Even though they continued to reside in the same home, Troy withdrew from any contact with Stephanie, believing she had by filing for divorce indicated that she didn't want to "have anything to do with him." They also quickly reached an impasse about living arrangements and how they would divide up time with their children, Peter, age 12, and Sasha, age 10. Stephanie believed that because she had done most of the parenting with the children, she should be the one who spent most of time with them and who organized their lives. Tom thought he was entitled to as much parenting time as she was, especially given that she was the one who filed for divorce. In the legal process, they were unable to agree on much at all, leaving them not only with conflicting positions over the long term about custody and children's residence, but also disputes about temporary arrangements while the divorce was proceeding. Stephanie's lawyer filed a motion to have Troy removed from the home, but the judge found no basis to do so.

During the first 2 months after the divorce was filed, family life was mostly characterized by avoidance between the parents. Although they had not agreed on a schedule, they took turns being with the children through a combination of there being many times when only one parent was home at a time and both spending most their time in a different part of the house from the other. Their attorneys made a few calls to try to resolve issues about living arrangements, but doing so wasn't a high priority, and little progress was made. Troy and Stephanie were referred for mediation by the court, as are most parents with disputes over child custody. Stephanie was eager to launch mediation early in the divorce, but Troy would not agree to a mediator or an appointment time. When the court's intervention finally forced them to attend mediation, they had two meetings in which there was a good deal of acrimony that produced no agreements, and Troy refused to schedule any further meetings.

As time passed, overt tensions in the home grew. There were arguments between Troy and Stephanie about who should take the children to school and to doctor visits and about how to parent, with Stephanie favoring setting stricter limits and Troy preferring a more permissive approach with much less monitoring. They also fought about a variety of financial issues. Typically, these arguments had a similar sequence: There would be a dispute about something; someone would take action; the other would confront that person when they were both at home; there would be a loud, belligerent interaction for about 5 minutes; and someone, usually Troy, would storm off. This was followed by another several-day period of radical withdrawal between the parents. Sasha would side with her mother in the arguments, telling father he didn't know what she needed and that he should move out. In contrast, Peter would become highly anxious and withdraw into his room and Xbox.

About 4 months into the divorce, during one of these arguments, Stephanie slapped Troy, and Troy pushed her down. This was followed by emergency motions in court filed by Stephanie for an order of protection to prevent Troy from being near her, and counterfilings by Troy to have Stephanie removed from the home. At that time, the court, although not granting either of the parents' emergency motions, appointed an attorney for the children. Within a few weeks, the children's attorney had met with both parents and both children and recommended to the court that therapy for the family be mandated. The court then issued an order for family therapy to occur that included the parents and children. The court order for therapy was prepared by the attorney for the children with the therapist's input. It named the therapist and mandated the participation of the parents and children to the extent the therapist saw the participation of each as helpful toward therapeutic ends.

First Meetings

Given that participation in therapy was mandated by the court, all parties were fully cooperative with scheduling sessions once the order was entered, even though they had not engaged in previous therapy. Therapy began with individual meetings with Troy and with Stephanie. In these meetings, Stephanie and Troy each shared their narratives about the events that had recently occurred. As is typical in difficult divorce, during most of these first meetings, each focused on the poor behavior of his or her former partner (except when responding to a specific question about personal history). With Troy, it was relatively easy to have him relate his (one-sided) view of what had occurred. With Stephanie, the therapist had a more complex task because telling her story was important to her and she wanted to go through each detail of her marriage and the present conflict. Thus, the therapist scheduled an additional individual meeting with both Troy and Stephanie to be sure each would feel heard at the onset of therapy. In this context, an early alliance was established with both parties. Each seemed relieved to have a place to tell their stories.

At the end of the second meeting with each individual, the therapist presented an initial plan and contract for therapy (typical Health Insurance Portability and Accountability Act–driven service agreements had been presented and signed at the first session). All the family members would be involved in treatment. The next meetings would be one with the two of them together (primarily at this point to see what such a meeting would look like) and a meeting with each of the children separately (with the purpose of learning directly about their reactions to what was occurring). At this point, the therapist also described the ways information would be shared with the attorney for the children (freely, although not about personal information unrelated to the conflict that the parties wanted to keep more private), their attorneys (only about each of them with their own attorney), and the court (there likely would be occasional inquiries about participation and progress).

The therapist also clearly explained the overall purpose of the therapy. These meetings were clearly differentiated from child custody evaluation that would make recommendations to the court about custody and residence and issue a report. Instead, the goals would center on finding ways to solve the problems that they were describing in making the transition through divorce, pinpointing good enough methods of working together, reducing the conflict, and making the present situation more viable for everyone, whether or not the larger issues about child custody could be resolved by them without the judge making that decision. Therapy was not presented as necessarily a solution to the dispute about child custody and residence (achieving that would be an outcome that, although possible, was beyond what might be expected from successful therapy), but instead as a vehicle for accomplishing realistic goals that could help everyone in the family, such as reducing the conflict and the negative impact on children.

The first meeting with the children also went well. This meeting, consisting of 30 minutes alone with each child, aimed to establish some rapport and gain a direct sense of their narratives of this family's life. Peter was relieved to hear that they might get some help. He opened up enough to share how much he hated the fights between his parents. Sasha was also comfortable in the meeting but mostly echoed her mother's thoughts. The therapist thanked each of them for coming in and helping and let them know they would be asked to come back at various times as the meetings went forward.

The primary goals in these initial meetings were to build an alliance with each family member and to begin to assess the problems that were occurring, as well as the sequences and various factors in the family that kept the problems from being resolved. It was surprisingly easy to build therapeutic alliances with Stephanie, Troy, and their children (always a positive sign in cases like this). Stephanie and Troy were frustrated with their present living situation and with each other. Both viewed therapy as a place to vent their feelings and to gain support for their view of the conflict. Both Stephanie and Troy were also clearly in the precontemplative stage of change in terms of understanding their roles in creating and maintaining the problem. Neither saw a specific path they might make toward change, but each was open to participating in therapy sessions. Both Peter and Sasha seemed sad living in the midst of their parents' ongoing conflict and wanted it to be over. They both took some comfort in talking to someone about their feelings.

Assessment

Clearly, this was a couple that was going to divorce. There was no need to consider a diversion into discernment counseling. Neither partner had any desire to consider staying married; each had held to these positions over several months, and they were fully disengaged, save for their conflict. Both Troy and Stephanie were experiencing a profound sense of anger and betrayal about the end of their relationship and the cascade they were caught in with the escalating conflict. The children were suffering collateral damage; each was showing troubling signs.

The broad agenda for the therapy was clearly about helping the couple divorce, reduce the level of conflict, minimize the possibility of further physical confrontations, stabilize family interactions, establish some degree of coparenting, disengage the triangulation that was occurring, and help them pull out of the cascade they were in, so that they can move toward a post-divorce working arrangement. In framing the goals of treatment to the clients, the therapist looked to emphasize resolving those issues that were of principal concern to the family members. The problem list to target included there being too much conflict, anger, and dysregulation; poor communication between the parents; differing and conflicting parenting styles; and children becoming engaged in parental conflict. Given that most of these core difficulties centered on the parents' interactions, sessions with the parents, both together and individually, would be the principal focus of therapy, at least initially.

The therapist's multilevel case formulation, which the therapist did not fully share with the clients, conceived of this family's problems as residing at various levels. In terms of safety, this was a family at high risk. The parents had already had a physical confrontation. However, there wasn't a long or severe history of relational violence that would render safety issues sufficient to rule out conjoint therapy. It was because of this history that the court had decided to allow them to continue to live together despite the physical altercation. Nonetheless, there remained high risk that another "bad moment" could spin out of control, and thus violence prevention had to be a top priority.

In terms of psychoeducational understanding of divorce, this family was an exemplar of one that, in the absence of a conscious understanding of the centrifugal forces in the divorce process, succumbs to them. Neither parent had been divorced previously, all contact with divorce had been with other bad divorces, and they did not fully understand how the legal system worked in relation to divorce. Stephanie thought that because she was the mother, the children would automatically wind up in her care. Troy had read articles that said fathers should have coequal time with mothers, and his friends and family of origin agreed. He certainly hadn't considered the importance of his prior level of parenting or continuity with what the children were most familiar. Each parent thought that when others agreed with them about how horrible their ex-partner was, this was objective feedback. This ignored the powerful pulls toward support triumphing over accurate feedback in such conversations, and that friends and family only had facts as massaged by them, not to mention possibilities of schadenfreude. It also was only beginning to dawn on Stephanie and Troy that their way of approaching the divorce might well result in the legal system not coming to a resolution in their dispute for years. Each initially thought someone would step in quickly and favor them in a judgment. Also, in the realm of psychoeducation, Troy's knowledge of parenting skills, especially structuring, was minimal.

In terms of client stage of change, each parent was locked in precontemplation. Both recognized that they were in a major conflict but blamed the other for this state of affairs. As for communication, throughout their marriage, skills in this area had been marginal at best, but whatever communication there was in the past had now fully broken down into either hot conflict or demand–withdraw. As a result, negotiation and problem-solving were now minimal. Here again, the couple had minimal success in negotiation and problem-solving earlier in their marriage, outside the context of divorce. Previous decision-making was mostly accomplished through division of areas of authority: Stephanie had taken on principal responsibility for decisions about the children, and Troy for financial decisions and large purchases, such as their home.

No mindfulness in relation to the divorce was apparent. Although Stephanie did regularly attend yoga classes in which she did some meditation, she had not thought to apply this skill set to managing her emotions in the conflict with Troy. Similarly, no mutual acceptance between the former partners was apparent. Each of the parent narratives was essentially a story of having been wronged by a disturbed partner. Troy also thought of Stephanie as having a borderline personality disorder because he had, at the suggestion of a friend, read a book about borderline personality disorder and found similarities in Stephanie's expressions of anger toward him (Stephanie did not have a personality disorder). Stephanie spoke of Troy as an alcoholic with major anger management issues.

Each parent was sitting on a powder keg of strong emotion, which easily became dysregulated—something that could readily occur again as they continued to live in the same home. In terms of their individual and collective psychodynamics, early experience had left both with major vulnerabilities.

Their object relations often revolved around projecting anger onto the other by acting in provocative ways, then focusing on the anger of their partner in response. Stephanie described coming from a family in which she was never seen; thus, Tom's patterns of withdrawal poked an old trigger for her. Troy, in contrast, grew up in a family with a high level of conflict and, sometimes, relational violence in which his solution was to withdraw. This had always made for a problematic dance between then, but now, absent of any positive sentiment override, this sequence became relentless. At the level of biology, all family members were healthy, although Troy's alcohol use was of concern. The problematic systemic processes were also clear: circular processes in the generation of conflict, cycles of demand–withdraw, triangulation of children into the conflict, and the major block to systemic reorganization into two family units that would allow for second-order change in the family structure.

In terms of the children's functioning, Sasha's vigorous joining with her mother was of concern, as was Peter's anxiety. The children also each had many strengths: Peter was a fine student, and Sasha did well in most aspects of life. However, there were apparent strains for both in relation to these family conflicts.

In terms of targets for treatment, first, there was the need to ensure safety. Although, as noted, their level of risk was not sufficient for the court to force separation, Stephanie and Troy had already had a physical altercation, and the first priority was to minimize the chances for another. Once there is violence, it receives first attention. Beyond this initial focus, at the systems level, there was a need to calm the frequent crises and alter the circular chains of accusation and counteraccusation that were being unleashed. Toward these ends, it would be important to inculcate a reframed understanding of the dysfunctional patterns to which their family was vulnerable, determine what would work better in this phase of life, and help the family create a vision of how they might work toward the calmer postdivorce life that each expressed a desire for. The family also needed to begin preparation for the next phase of the divorce process, a time during which responsibility for the children would be divided. Both parents would need to learn to find better ways to channel their anger and develop a minimal ability to communicate and problem-solve together. Additionally, to make coparenting more feasible, Troy's parenting skill would need to be further developed.

Given that the preponderance of the issues centered on Troy and Stephanie, the therapy was structured to consist almost exclusively of sessions with them, either together or individually. A few sessions would be scheduled to help the children cope with living in the presence of parental conflicts, but the major thrust of the work would be to reduce such conflict.

The therapist did not fully share this formulation with the clients. To do so would be too technical and time-consuming. Such a comprehensive "case conference" presentation, even if rendered in collaborative language, would too readily digress to some tangent or create blocks in alliance. However, the therapist did share with the parents a more simplified version of the principal goals of therapy: making sure there were no more physical altercations, reducing the number and intensity of verbal altercations, learning about divorce, reducing conflict, improving communication and problem-solving, and exploring and dealing with the other sources of difficulty as they moved into focus. In the first meeting together, Stephanie and Troy agreed that this would be a reasonable agenda. There was a good amount of noise in this conversation, with each former partner complaining about the other, but they agreed to the more neutral version of the goals for these meetings (each perhaps still expecting the other would need to do more). The therapist followed up with a brief communication with the attorney for the children, letting her know that everyone had engaged and that there was an agreed-on plan for making progress centered on the stated goals.

Early Sessions

Although the first meeting between the parents evolved as one might expect, with both partners arguing their positions and not much real communication, there were some hopeful signs. Each partner could see the negative impact, particularly on the children, of the arguments that were occurring. They demonstrated genuine concern for their children, as opposed to cases in which former partners' statements about their children's welfare are governed more by their own needs and desires. Troy, although more limited in his parenting experience, clearly wanted to be a good parent, and Stephanie (the divorce issues aside) was already a good parent. In addition to their complaints, each seemed to be in a "dazed and confused" state. Conflicts in difficult divorce are often battlegrounds of highly armored, battle-tested veterans who aren't simply in the precontemplation stage but are also functioning almost fully in an automatic mode, making any positive movement difficult. In contrast, it was clear that both Troy and Stephanie could still feel, but they were caught up in a vicious, endless cycle that felt mystifying to them and to which their individual behaviors, cognitions, and emotions contributed.

As the treatment evolved early in therapy, conjoint sessions were primarily identified as the place for psychoeducation, joint discussion, problem-solving, negotiation, and practice, while individual sessions were identified as the primary place for inner exploration and work on cognitions, emotions, and psychodynamics to support the work together. The first target was to ensure safety and set a plan for de-escalating conflicts when those arguments began to get too heated. In the first conjoint session, the therapist helped

Stephanie and Troy identify signs that a conflict was developing and might escalate, pointing to both external signs (e.g., raised voices) and internal ones (e.g., feeling states, heart pounding, anger). An experiment was set up to see if they could monitor these states in themselves and let the other know in neutral (rather than attacking) language that they needed to stop the discussion (e.g., "I need to take a break"). The therapist suggested an agreement that gave either permission to invoke a cooling-off period as needed, to be delivered by that person saying what they needed (e.g., "a break"), rather than as a complaint about the other. The therapist also introduced mindful practice and relaxation exercises in this meeting. After a brief introduction to mindfulness and a bit of practice, each agreed to find a way to follow up. Stephanie had some experience with mindfulness from yoga class and identified that she might be able to apply this experience. Troy purchased an app that the therapist suggested and pursued a mindful exercise each day. The mindful practice was further reinforced in individual meetings with both clients that were focused on anger management.

In the following conjoint session, Troy and Stephanie reported not having had any major confrontations between sessions. They each pointed to an occasion they had used the time-out procedure and had been able to stay away from extreme withdrawal. Praising them for their success with this, the therapist emphasized the value of the tool they had developed and the importance of further practice. The remainder of the session focused on psychoeducation. The therapist reviewed how common strong feelings are and that moments of those strong feelings emerged in heated conflict during divorce, that living together through divorce was invariably difficult, that there were expected issues that would come up and feelings that would occur, and that there clearly were better and worse ways for dealing with those feelings when they surfaced. This psychoeducation accentuated that the key differences between families in which children manage the transition through divorce well and those in which children become the casualties of divorce are often precisely about how parents handle the sorts of issues they were facing, pointing to specific situations that have been problematic in their family. Although the therapist left open an opportunity for digression in this part of the conversation to each blaming the other for the problems, an opportunity that Stephanie seized, the therapist was able to refocus back to the key generic point about how the kind of conflict in which they were engaged is toxic for children in divorce. A continuing positive sign was that Troy and Stephanie did seem open to this information. Some parents are so engaged in the fight at this point that they barely attend to this kind of information. Stephanie and Troy were concerned, even if they could not yet see ways out of the problematic cycle in which they were mired.

The monitoring and carrying out of steps to de-escalation continued with beneficial effects in further sessions together. The therapist explored other ways of avoiding conflict and the demand–withdraw pattern. One focus was on beginning simple communication and problem-solving in sessions so that there might be fewer points of problematic contact. That is, could they come up with ways that there would be fewer things about which to argue? They agreed this was a good idea, and they came up with a list of issues to talk about in future sessions. The second focus that emerged was on ways of being less collectively and individually reactive.

In these conjoint meetings, the therapist repeatedly returned to the overarching concept of learning how to better solve problems and move toward solutions. The therapist acknowledged that Stephanie's and Troy's complaints were important and needed to be processed but continually reframed them in systemic terms, emphasizing each partner's role in problem resolution. This made for more than a few early alliance ruptures, when one or the other client felt unheard as each voiced complaints, but fortunately these ruptures remained in balance, so that the therapy overall continued to feel fair and balanced to each of them.

In a few individual meetings with each parent, the therapist followed up with further presenting and practicing of anger management and mindfulness techniques. This segued into a cognitive therapy examination with the powerful thoughts that spurred rage (as well as radical withdrawal) as they emerged as part of the basis for the overwhelming emotional reactions the clients experienced. There was so much to be angry about! The therapist acknowledged this, while continually taking the focus away from the complaints (adding that the therapist would take the specific issue up with the partner when it seemed important to follow up) and on to the importance of how the person in the room processed the complaints. This work did not seek to change how the former partners experienced each other but instead focused on preventing a slide from a (relatively harmless) negative view of the other to powerful thoughts that might invite feeling states that would present difficulties for others (e.g., rage) or themselves (e.g., depression). Both Stephanie and Troy were active participants in this work, and each cooperated in doing thought records with the therapist and at home. In this process, they acquired further tools to help buffer their conflicts even before the conflicts arose.

As conflict deescalated, focus in conjoint meetings moved further into communication and problem-solving, and, as an offshoot of problem-solving, dealing with the largest immediate problem they faced, which was a lack of clarity about which parent would be with which child when. These three foci were interwoven. Communication was needed to problem-solve. Without resolving the core chronic issue that was with them every day, communication was more difficult, and problem-solving was impeded. The therapist suggested directly addressing communication next, and then using it to see if they could resolve the series of problems about which they had differences that they had listed earlier, beginning with the easier problems to resolve and only then moving to the more difficult ones. Stephanie and Troy agreed that this made sense as a plan and began communication training.

The therapist taught them the rule-governed speaker–listener technique (Diamond & Lebow, 2016), which centers on speaking, listening, and repeating what has been heard so that there is certainty the information is conveyed, while minimizing opportunities for escalation. As they practiced this in sessions, they were able to communicate better even about controversial subjects, such as sharing time with the children. The therapist then moved to see if there was a way to move from simply communicating information and what they wanted, without argument, to problem-solving to resolve differences. This exploration began with simpler issues, involving such concerns as what the various expectations would be about sharing food in the kitchen, the kind of food they bought, and cooperating about driving the children places. Stephanie and Troy were able to work out agreements on such small matters, which they then followed. This, in turn, led to some hope for developing a sense of cooperation and perhaps even working through their larger issues, such as the division of time with the children.

In the individual meetings, the therapist looked to explore whether, in this environment of some cooperation and less conflict, there might be possibility for softening of the overly harsh views that they had of each other. The question here wasn't so much whether they could appreciate where their former partner was coming from; that would be an idea that would not fit families who have reached such an impasse. Instead, the emphasis was on what was simply likely to be more functional. Was it necessary to maintain such a rigid negative view of one another? Despite Troy's efforts, Stephanie continued to believe that Troy only wanted to engage in parenting as a way of showing his anger toward her. Through thought records done with Stephanie in session, the therapist examined the present evidence that she had to support this idea. Hesitatingly, Stephanie was able to look at the evidence and consider the possibility that Troy had vastly increased his interest in the children, and it seemed he enjoyed being with them. She did continue to have negative opinions of his competence in several areas of parenting, but, with the therapist's help, she was able to differentiate her concern about his competence from that about his interest in the children. It did seem clear that Troy needed to learn more about certain aspects of parenting, and the therapist assured Stephanie that she would discuss this with him.

Similarly, Troy saw Stephanie as being obstructive to his spending time with the children because of her own anger toward him. When the therapist engaged Troy in a cognitive examination of this thought, although Troy was a bit resistant, he was able to look at the evidence and consider the possibility that she was principally driven by wanting to maintain the kind of relationship she had had with the children and her concern about their welfare. The therapist reframed the changes occurring as a major transition for Stephanie, which Troy might be able to understand.

Troy also reluctantly came to see that his lack of experience, especially in parenting their daughter, might, for good reasons, leave Stephanie with some concerns. The therapist added how common a dilemma this was for families, when one parent who previously had been less involved with children became more involved around the transition to divorce. This piece of psychoeducation readily segued into suggesting to Troy that one path to everyone becoming calmer would be to learn more about the aspects of parenting with which he was less comfortable, especially the structural aspects of parenting and how to be close to an adolescent daughter. When Troy responded positively to this idea, the therapist followed up by speaking to Troy's alcohol use. Troy always defended himself about this topic, maintaining that he never was drunk. The therapist refocused this conversation onto the context of parenting and coparenting. How might he present best to his children? How might he help the therapist convince Stephanie and his daughter that he was competent? A simple cognitive analysis clearly helped him see that there was everything to be said for drinking less. He needed to make this his choice (not Stephanie's) and do it for his reasons (not Stephanie's). Framed this way, he agreed and reduced the number of beers he would drink by half.

The therapist also had two meetings with the children during this phase of therapy. These sessions provided them an opportunity to speak about their concerns and helped them grasp the changes toward which the therapy was aiming. The children showed a significant relief about the changes that were occurring, which made for less conflict and radical withdrawal of their parents from one another. A specific focus in the meeting with Sasha was about whether she now needed to "get in the middle" as she had in the past. With mother and father doing better, the therapist encouraged her to help herself and them by staying out of their conflict. The therapist helped her learn to calm herself with some simple relaxation techniques and engage in self-talk that emphasized focusing more on school and her friends and less on her parents.

Even absent the stressful conflict between mother and father, Peter remained highly anxious. He seemed to have been deeply affected by the conflict, which had triggered something in his already somewhat unrelated anxious personality. Therefore, the therapist discussed with mother and father having another therapist see Peter in individual therapy—not to deal with the divorce but with his more basic anxiety. The parents agreed, and Peter was referred to a colleague, who would be sure to stay closely connected to this therapy (and thus avoid the possibility that the individual therapist's formulation would be that more contact with father was the key ingredient in making Peter highly anxious, a thought that surely that would have been a force returning the family to greater conflict).

Further Sessions

With the situation calmer, the sessions moved toward negotiation about parenting and parenting styles. The therapist was able to develop a set of principles for how each parent would be available and involved with the children during the other's designated parenting time in the home. The children could go see the other parent, as long as it didn't interfere with what they were supposed to be doing, and the parents would remain sensitive to keeping this from turning into a competition for time. Although setting such boundaries in a divorcing couple living together presents challenges (e.g., when one child has math homework and the parent who is not the math expert is the designated parent), establishing such ground rules mostly worked and helped with what had been the constant sense of competing for the children.

Stephanie was also able to communicate to Troy about her desire that he learn more about parenting, especially monitoring, setting rules about aspects such as the children's bedtime and allotted screen time, and being consistent. Both parents agreed that there was a need to enhance the connection between Troy and Sasha. To these ends, Troy had a few more individual meetings with the therapist than Stephanie, for the specifically stated purpose of expanding his parenting repertoire and ways of connecting with his daughter. With less of a sense of being attacked, Troy was not as defensive about his parenting. He agreed to read books about authoritative parenting and discuss those with the therapist; he would also experiment with more structuring for the children and with ways of interacting with Sasha. In the context of the frame that Troy was a well-intentioned parent who needed to learn a bit more about parenting, he was able to consider ways he could improve as a parent, such as learning to set better limits. The changes that evolved led Stephanie to feel more comfortable with his parenting and promoted a positive cycle between them about parenting.

This allowed for discussion in conjoint sessions of Stephanie and Troy's more basic differences in parenting styles. Even with moving toward more competent structuring parental behavior, there were real differences between them in terms of the number of rules set and the strict adherence to those rules. Discussion moved to learning to live with their differences in parenting styles. In these discussions, Stephanie and Troy were able to identify several aspects of parenting about which they agreed (more than one might have thought from their previous behavior), such as the importance of doing homework. They negotiated about other aspects of parenting about which one or the other considered it essential to have a shared vision, such as by what time the children needed to be home at night. However, beyond these areas of agreement, the therapist encouraged the theme of both developing their own (competent) parenting style, adding that it would be easier to establish a "Mom's house, Dad's house" arrangement, different but mutually respectful, for parenting when they no longer lived together.

With both parents on board, they agreed it would be a good idea to have a meeting between Troy and Sasha with the therapist to talk about how to improve their relationship. In the meeting, Sasha told Troy how much she preferred to be with her mother. Now, instead of arguing with her, Troy was able to listen and focus on how they might improve their connection. They identified a couple of activities they might enjoy together and made a plan to begin doing them one on one. Sasha also let father know that it was important to her sometimes to be the one to choose the restaurant or activity in which they engaged. This was followed up with a meeting between Stephanie and Sasha in which Stephanie reassured Sasha that she and Troy were learning to work together better and that it was important to her for Sasha to connect better with her father.

With a new spirit of cooperation, the couple began to talk in sessions about how they might divide parenting time after the divorce. Preliminary discussions seemed positive, and the partners had meetings with their attorneys in which they negotiated a parenting agreement that included joint custody but also the children spending 10 out of 14 days with their mother. Given their respective parenting histories, connections to the children, and time available, this seemed like a wise resolution and was the likely outcome of a child custody evaluation or trial. Clearly, part of why Troy agreed to this plan is that he was now able to be less defensive after receiving feedback about what arrangements were most realistic for a father with his parenting history and to envision Stephanie as supporting him in having a positive role in the children's lives. In sessions, the therapist helped them develop a plan for implementing this arrangement and supporting each other in parenting, as well as communicating about the children when necessary.

Ultimately, Troy moved out of the marital home. Once this occurred, conflict mostly ceased. At the end of therapy, Troy and Stephanie still had negative feelings toward one another. They had not released the reservoir of difficult emotions that developed over years of marriage or the hurt of whose fault it was that the marriage ended. Clearly, this was not a divorced family that was going to have Thanksgiving dinner together. However, they had developed a good-enough way of resolving differences, achieved successful separation of their homes, and found a good-enough method of communicating to coparent when needed. For example, they could both attend the children's sports events without conflict or silently glaring at one another. This allowed Troy and Stephanie and their children to go on with their lives, without the specter of ongoing conflict and drama.

A FAMILY WITH ISSUES INVOLVING A NEW PARTNER

Valerie and Paul had a cordial coparenting relationship during the first 9 months after their separation. With the help of their lawyers, they were working toward a parenting agreement that would give them joint custody of their children, Ethan (age 6) and Max (age 4). The children lived with Valerie during the week, visiting every other weekend and 1 night a week with Paul. They also were in positive talks with their lawyers about a financial settlement. They communicated frequently about the children and made decisions together about their schooling.

Nonetheless, difficulties developed when Valerie and the children began to spend time with Zach 9 months after the separation. Within 1 month of the time they began to date, Zach began to spend most of the time he was not working at Valerie's apartment. Zach was a blue-collar man who had dropped out of high school. His personality was abrasive and outspoken. He was very unlike Paul, who was college-educated and passive. Zach took the children to wrestling matches, showed them injuries he had gotten in fights, and roughhoused with them each evening. Zach also frequently became angry, sometimes yelling at the top of his lungs in the home.

Ethan and Max became afraid of Zach and told their father about their fears. Paul shared his worries about Zach with Valerie, but Valerie told Paul that what Zach did was none of his business. Paul and Valerie began to argue regularly about the situation. The conflict escalated when Ethan sprained his wrist while wrestling with Zach. Ethan told Paul that Zach had become red-faced and twisted his arm to the point where he thought it would fall off. Paul went back to his attorney, initiated an investigation by the local child protective services, and petitioned the court for Zach to be barred from the house and for sole custody of the children. This set off a cycle of accusations and counteraccusations. Valerie filed a petition alleging neglect because Paul would leave the children with his sister during some of his visitations. Paul filed to reduce child support due to Zach's presence in Valerie's home.

After innumerable court appearances and a failed effort at mediation, the children's attorney in the case referred the family for therapy. With the therapist's input, a court order was structured that mandated the participation of the parents, the children, and Zach in the therapy. With the participation in therapy becoming so central a concern of the court, as in many of these cases, all parties were fully cooperative with scheduling sessions once the order was entered.

The therapy began with an individual meeting with each of the parents. During this meeting, the therapist listened to each of their narratives about the events that had been occurring and outlined the therapeutic contract. All the parties would be involved in treatment. A schedule for the first few meetings was agreed on, and the therapist let them know about how the plan was likely to evolve over time. All specific facts about the sessions were to remain confidential, but the therapist would share the extent of their participation, and the therapist's general impressions about what was occurring, with the attorney for the children. The parents also signed releases of information for the therapist to talk with the attorney for the children.

The initial meetings with each parent were followed in short order by two meetings with the children; a meeting with Valerie, Zach, and the children; a meeting with Paul and the children; and a meeting with Valerie and Paul. The primary goals for these initial meetings were to build an alliance with each of the parties and conduct problem assessment. It was strikingly easy to build a therapeutic alliance with Valerie and Paul. Both were frustrated with their present circumstance and saw therapy as a place to vent their feelings and gain support for their view of the conflict. Valerie and Paul were each in the precontemplative stage in assessing their roles in creating and maintaining the problem, but both were open to therapy sessions. The children were also highly cooperative if only to reiterate the viewpoint they shared with their father about Zach. They repeated the history of their interactions with Zach much as Paul had related it and expressed the desire to spend less time with him and have him be less angry. Zach was much more difficult to engage. He feared that the treatment process would be used against him. He obviously was only participating because of the court order and the considerable pressure that Valerie was putting on him to support her in her case.

The therapist's initial assessment was that Zach did not appear to present an ongoing physical threat to the children. The investigations by the child protective agency had judged the allegations of abuse to be unfounded. Moreover, in hearing about the injuries the children had suffered, they seemed to be much more the product of an adult who was trying to be playful and did not fully understand the impact of his size and strength compared with that of the children than physical abuse. Zach was actually in a process of building an attachment with the children, which was easily observed in a session with Valerie, Zach, and the children. Nonetheless, it was equally clear that the relationship between Zach and Valerie posed considerable challenges for the children and the father. Valerie had allowed Zach to move into the children's lives with the privileges of a parent before the children were ready to accept him in this role. Clearly, this also engaged profound feelings of loss and displacement on Paul's part. Furthermore, Zach's temper presented a special problem, and his ways were very different from those of anyone else in the family.

After these first sessions, the therapist felt he had enough information to form an initial assessment. This assessment, which included the working understanding of the family interaction just described, became the basis for the creation of a set of goals and a specific treatment plan for this family. At the systems level, there was a need to calm the frequent crises and break the circular chains of accusation and counteraccusation that had been unleashed. In turn, this depended on being able to create a mutual understanding about the next phase of life, in which there would be relationships with new partners, particularly in terms of how the children would be parented. To achieve this goal, Zach's behavior would need to be tempered, the children would need to build a trusting relationship with him, the parents would need to establish good-enough communication about these issues, Paul would need to process the changes occurring as less threatening, and Paul and the children would need to find ways to deal with the changes occurring rather than engage in the triangulation pattern that was evident.

Because Zach's individual behavior played such a key role in the problem and because the alliance with Zach in the therapy seemed as if it would benefit from more meetings with him, the initial proximate goal focused on building an alliance with Zach and having him begin to work on his aggressive behavior. Engaging Zach in therapy, at first with Valerie and ultimately in individual sessions, and in constructively working at his behavior turned out to be much easier than one might have thought. Zach was a boisterous man, who, although he responded to directives with opposition, was highly cooperative when he felt understood. He saw himself as wanting to have a positive impact on the lives of Valerie and the children. His patterns of behavior with the children mostly represented his way of trying to get closer to them, and he had no trouble identifying a general problem with the expression of anger in his life. Zach also was troubled by the ongoing conflict between Valerie and Paul, which was requiring a good deal of time and money (Zach had also hired an attorney). It helped that the therapist's assessment did not view Zach as the risk that Paul's attorneys had portrayed him to be. The therapist's relationship with Zach's attorney also helped; he assured Zach that he would be fairly treated in therapy.

The therapist was able to refocus Zach on his need to build his relationship with the children. The therapist let him know that he thought Zach was not dangerous but was a bit too rough with these children (the therapist's actual assessment, not a vacuous reframe) and helped him engage in gaining better control over his behavior. He grasped that he was very different from anyone who had spent time with the children, how this presented issues for them, and that he had trouble controlling his anger. Zach agreed to work on anger management in further sessions and on setting rules governing his interactions with the children in sessions with Valerie and the children.

Zach, Valerie, and the children were seen for two family sessions, focused on clarifying expectations about discipline and structuring a system of reward and punishment in relation to the children's behavior. Corporal punishment was clearly placed out of bounds. Almost all of the structuring in parenting was assigned to mother (as it ordinarily might be in a new relationship at this stage).

Intermixed with these sessions, the therapist met with Paul alone, working to help him understand the reattribution of Zach's behavior—that he was rough but not dangerous. The therapist explained to him the kinds of circular causal chains that become unleashed in situations like this, and tried to help him consider the possibility that what he had seen was a worst-case scenario. The therapist also shared how the children had been caught up in the difficulty because of their own complex feelings, and how everyone might move toward a more calming circular path of mutual reassurance. Paul was still not convinced that it was safe for the children to be with Zach. The first time the reframe about Zach's behavior was raised, Paul showed little attitude change. However, he trusted that the therapist had his interests and those of the children in mind and was calmed by the thought that the therapist would be working with Zach on his behavior. The therapist put together a thought record with Paul, contrasting his thoughts with the data available, and challenged him to examine the facts from a different perspective. With time and no further incidents, Paul was able to accept that positive changes were occurring.

During two meetings with the children, interspersed among the other sessions, the therapist focused on giving them an opportunity to talk about their concerns and to help them grasp the changes that the treatment was intended to achieve. The children showed relief about the changes that were occurring. Just after these sessions with the children, in brief meetings between each parent and the children, the therapist also helped them develop guidelines about under what conditions it was appropriate to talk about one parent with the other, and when it was not.

Two meetings were then held between Paul and Valerie, focused on rebuilding constructive communication between them. Convened at a point of their being some constructive possibilities for success, these meetings proved productive, in contrast to the acrimony of the early meeting the therapist had with the two of them. These sessions produced an agreement about when to communicate about various issues with one another and marked a return to better communication about matters such as ill-nesses and joint decision-making when it was needed. Building on their prior positive history of postseparation cooperation, they were able to move beyond disengagement and mutual tolerance, which are more typical goals for those in difficult divorce.

Significantly, after 3 months of treatment, the petitions that had been filed in court for removal of Zach from Valerie's home and full custody to be granted to the father were withdrawn. Paul and Valerie resumed negotiation about their divorce, and soon after, a joint parenting agreement and financial settlement followed. Not only did this mark the success of the intervention, it also had a salutary effect on the process in these families. Zach continued his work with the therapist on his anger management for several months on an intermittent basis, extending his focus to situations beyond the family. Anecdotal 2-year follow-up from reports from the clients and attorneys indicated that the therapy successfully resolved the crisis and helped move the parties on to a life with minimal contact between the parents, but good-enough coparenting to allow for the children's development.

REFERENCES

Achenbach, T. M. (2000). Child Behavior Checklist. In A. E. Kazdin (Ed.), *Encyclopedia of psychology*. Washington, DC: American Psychological Association; New York, NY: Oxford University Press.

Ackerman, M. J. (2001). *Clinician's guide to child custody evaluations* (2nd ed.). New York, NY: Wiley.

Ackerman, M. J. (2008). *Does Wednesday mean mom's house or dad's? Parenting together while living apart* (2nd ed.). Hoboken, NJ: Wiley.

Ackerman, M. J., Kane, A. W., Gould, J. W., & Dale, M. D. (2015). *Psychological experts in divorce actions* (6th ed.). New York, NY: Wolters Kluwer.

Ahrons, C. R. (1994). *The good divorce: Keeping your family together when your marriage comes apart*. New York, NY: HarperCollins.

Ahrons, C. R. (2004). *We're still family: What grown children have to say about their parents' divorce*. New York, NY: HarperCollins.

Ahrons, C. R., & Rodgers, R. H. (1987). *Divorced families: A multidisciplinary developmental view*. New York, NY: Norton.

Ahrons, C. R., & Wallisch, L. S. (1987). The relationship between former spouses. In D. Perlman & S. Duck (Eds.), *Intimate relationships: Development, dynamics, and deterioration* (pp. 269–296). Thousand Oaks, CA: Sage.

Alba-Fisch, M. (2016). Collaborative divorce: An effort to reduce the damage of divorce. *Journal of Clinical Psychology, 72*, 444–457. http://dx.doi.org/10.1002/jclp.22260

Allen, J. G., Fonagy, P., & Bateman, A. (2008). *Mentalizing in clinical practice*. Washington, DC: American Psychiatric Association.

Amato, P. R. (2006). Marital discord, divorce, and children's well-being: Results from a 20-year longitudinal study of two generations. In A. Clarke-Stewart & J. Dunn (Eds.), *Families count: Effects on child and adolescent development* (pp. 179–202). New York, NY: Cambridge University Press. http://dx.doi.org/10.1017/CBO9780511616259.009

Amato, P. R. (2010). Research on divorce: Continuing trends and new developments. *Journal of Marriage and Family, 72*, 650–666. http://dx.doi.org/10.1111/j.1741-3737.2010.00723.x

Amato, P. R., & Booth, A. (2002). A generation at risk: Growing up in an era of family upheaval. *Journal of the American Academy of Child & Adolescent Psychiatry, 41*, 486–487.

Amato, P. R., & Hohmann-Marriott, B. (2007). A comparison of high- and low-distress marriages that end in divorce. *Journal of Marriage and Family, 69*, 621–638. http://dx.doi.org/10.1111/j.1741-3737.2007.00396.x

Amato, P. R., & Irving, S. (2006). Historical trends in divorce in the United States. In M. A. Fine & J. H. Harvey (Eds.), *Handbook of divorce and relationship dissolution* (pp. 41–57). Mahwah, NJ: Erlbaum.

Amato, P. R., Loomis, L. S., & Booth, A. (1995). Parental divorce, marital conflict, and offspring well-being during early adulthood. *Social Forces, 73,* 895–915. http://dx.doi.org/10.1093/sf/73.3.895

Amato, P. R., & Previti, D. (2003). People's reasons for divorcing: Gender, social class, the life course, and adjustment. *Journal of Family Issues, 24,* 602–626. http://dx.doi.org/10.1177/0192513X03024005002

Amato, P. R., & Rogers, S. J. (1997). A longitudinal study of marital problems and subsequent divorce. *Journal of Marriage and the Family, 59,* 612–624. http://dx.doi.org/10.2307/353949

American Psychiatric Association. (2013). *Diagnostic and statistical manual of mental disorders* (5th ed.). Arlington, VA: Author.

American Psychological Association. (2013). *Guidelines for psychological practice in health care delivery systems.* Retrieved from http://www.apa.org/practice/guidelines/delivery-systems.aspx

American Psychological Association. (2017). *Ethical principles of psychologists and code of conduct* (2002, Amended June 1, 2010 and January 1, 2017). Retrieved from http://www.apa.org/ethics/code/index.aspx

Aponte, H. J., & Kissil, K. (2016). *The person of the therapist training model: Mastering the use of self.* New York, NY: Routledge/Taylor & Francis. http://dx.doi.org/10.1007/978-3-319-15877-8_544-1

Arbuthnot, J., Gordon, D. A., & Center for Divorce Education. (2014). *Programs for divorcing parents: A service provider's handbook* (2nd ed.). Athens, OH: Center for Divorce Education.

Association of Family and Conciliation Courts. (2011). Guidelines for court-involved therapy. *Family Court Review, 49,* 564–581. http://dx.doi.org/10.1111/j.1744-1617.2011.01393.x

Baker, A. J. L., Bone, J. M., & Ludmer, B. (2014). *The high-conflict custody battle: Protect yourself and your kids from a toxic divorce, false accusations & parental alienation.* Oakland, CA: New Harbinger.

Ballard, R. H. (2014). A randomized controlled trial of child informed mediation. *Dissertation Abstracts International: Series B. The Sciences and Engineering, 74*(11-B(E)).

Barkham, M., Mellor-Clark, J., & Stiles, W. B. (2015). A CORE approach to progress monitoring and feedback: Enhancing evidence and improving practice. *Psychotherapy, 52,* 402–411. http://dx.doi.org/10.1037/pst0000030

Barlow, D. H. (2014). *Clinical handbook of psychological disorders: A step-by-step treatment manual* (5th ed.). New York, NY: Guilford Press.

Barlow, D. H., Bullis, J. R., Comer, J. S., & Ametaj, A. A. (2013). Evidence-based psychological treatments: An update and a way forward. *Annual Review of Clinical Psychology, 9,* 1–27. http://dx.doi.org/10.1146/annurev-clinpsy-050212-185629

Barlow, D. H., Farchione, T. J., Fairholme, C. P., Ellard, K. K., Boisseau, C. L., Allen, L. B., & Ehrenreich-May, J. (2011). *Unified protocol for transdiagnostic treatment of emotional disorders: Therapist guide.* New York, NY: Oxford University Press. http://dx.doi.org/10.1037/e556572013-126

Barrett, M. J., & Fish, L. S. (2014). *Treating complex trauma: A relational blueprint for collaboration and change.* New York, NY: Routledge/Taylor & Francis.

Becher, E. H., Cronin, S., McCann, E., Olson, K. A., Powell, S., & Marczak, M. S. (2015). Parents forever: Evaluation of an online divorce education program. *Journal of Divorce & Remarriage, 56,* 261–276.

Beck, A. T. (1976). *Cognitive therapy and the emotional disorders.* Oxford, England: International Universities Press.

Beck, C. J. A., Sales, B. D., & Emery, R. E. (2004). Research on the impact of family mediation. In J. Folberg, A. L. Milne, & P. Salem (Eds.), *Divorce and family mediation: Models, techniques, and applications* (pp. 447–482). New York, NY: Guilford Press.

Beck, J. S. (2011). *Cognitive behavior therapy: Basics and beyond* (2nd ed.). New York, NY: Guilford Press.

Benjamin, G. A. H., Beck, C. J., Shaw, M., & Geffner, R. (2018). *Family evaluation in custody litigation: Promoting optimal outcomes and reducing ethical risks* (2nd ed.). Washington, DC: American Psychological Association. http://dx.doi.org/10.1037/0000071-000

Berne, E. (1964). *Games people play: The psychology of human relationships.* New York, NY: Grove Press.

Beutler, L. E., Harwood, T. M., Michelson, A., Song, X., & Holman, J. (2011). Reactance/resistance level. In J. C. Norcross (Ed.), *Psychotherapy relationships that work: Evidence-based responsiveness* (pp. 261–278). New York, NY: Oxford University Press.

Bhatia, G., & Saini, M. (2016). Cultural dynamics of divorce and parenting. In L. Drozd, M. Saini, & N. Olesen (Eds.), *Parenting plan evaluations: Applied research for the family court* (pp. 463–487). New York, NY: Oxford University Press. http://dx.doi.org/10.1093/med:psych/9780199396580.003.0015

Birnbaum, R., Lach, L. M., & Saposnek, D. T. (2016). Children with neurodevelopmental disorders in parental separation and divorce. In L. Drozd, M. Saini, & N. Olesen (Eds.), *Parenting plan evaluations: Applied research for the family court* (pp. 205–242). New York, NY: Oxford University Press. http://dx.doi.org/10.1093/med:psych/9780199396580.003.0008

Black, L. E., Eastwood, M. M., Sprenkle, D. H., & Smith, E. (1991). An exploratory analysis of the construct of leavers versus left as it relates to Levinger's social exchange theory of attractions, barriers, and alternative attractions. *Journal of Divorce & Remarriage, 15,* 127–139. http://dx.doi.org/10.1300/J087v15n01_08

Boring, J. L., Sandler, I. N., Tein, J.-Y., Horan, J. J., & Vélez, C. E. (2015). Children of divorce-coping with divorce: A randomized control trial of an online prevention program for youth experiencing parental divorce. *Journal of Consulting and Clinical Psychology, 83*, 999–1005. http://dx.doi.org/10.1037/a0039567

Boss, P. (2006). *Loss, trauma, and resilience: Therapeutic work with ambiguous loss.* New York, NY: Norton.

Boszormenyi-Nagy, I., & Spark, G. M. (1973). *Invisible loyalties: Reciprocity in intergenerational family therapy.* Oxford, England: Harper & Row.

Bourassa, K. J., Sbarra, D. A., & Whisman, M. A. (2015). Women in very low quality marriages gain life satisfaction following divorce. *Journal of Family Psychology, 29*, 490–499. http://dx.doi.org/10.1037/fam0000075

Bowen, M. (1978). *Family therapy in clinical practice.* New York, NY: Aronson.

Bramlett, M. D., & Mosher, W. D. (2002). *Cohabitation, marriage, divorce, and remarriage in the United States* (Vital and Health Statistics Series 23). Washington, DC: U.S. Government Printing Office.

Braver, S. L., Griffin, W. A., & Cookston, J. T. (2005). Prevention programs for divorced nonresident fathers. *Family Court Review, 43*, 81–96. http://dx.doi.org/10.1111/j.1744-1617.2005.00009.x

Braver, S. L., Griffin, W. A., Cookston, J. T., Sandler, I. N., & Williams, J. (2005). Promoting better fathering among divorced nonresident fathers. In W. M. Pinsof & J. L. Lebow (Eds.), *Family psychology: The art of the science* (pp. 295–325). New York, NY: Oxford University Press.

Braver, S. L., Sandler, I. N., Hita, L. C., & Wheeler, L. A. (2016). A randomized comparative effectiveness trial of two court-connected programs for high-conflict families. *Family Court Review, 54*, 349–363. http://dx.doi.org/10.1111/fcre.12225

Bray, J. H. (2008). Couple therapy with remarried partners. In A. S. Gurman (Ed.), *Clinical handbook of couple therapy* (4th ed., pp. 499–519). New York, NY: Guilford Press.

Bray, J. H., & Kelly, J. (1998). *Stepfamilies: Love, marriage, and parenting in the first decade.* New York, NY: Broadway Books.

Breunlin, D. C., Pinsof, W., Russell, W. P., & Lebow, J. (2011). Integrative problem-centered metaframeworks therapy I: Core concepts and hypothesizing. *Family Process, 50*, 293–313. http://dx.doi.org/10.1111/j.1545-5300.2011.01362.x

Breunlin, D. C., & Schwartz, R. C. (1986). Sequences: Toward a common denominator of family therapy. *Family Process, 25*, 67–87. http://dx.doi.org/10.1111/j.1545-5300.1986.00067.x

Brown, L. K., & Brown, M. T. (1986). *Dinosaurs divorce: A guide for changing families.* Boston, MA: Joy Street Books.

Brown, S. L., & Lin, I. F. (2012). The gray divorce revolution: Rising divorce among middle-aged and older adults, 1990–2010. *The Journals of Gerontology: Series B. Psychological Sciences and Social Sciences, 67*, 731–741. http://dx.doi.org/10.1093/geronb/gbs089

Browning, S., & Artelt, E. (2012a). Stepfamily therapy: The 10 steps. In S. Browning & E. Artelt (Eds.), *Stepfamily therapy: A 10-step clinical approach* (pp. 205–223). Washington, DC: American Psychological Association. http://dx.doi.org/10.1037/13089-003

Browning, S., & Artelt, E. (2012b). Why are some stepfamilies vulnerable? In S. Browning & E. Artelt (Eds.), *Stepfamily therapy: A 10-step clinical approach* (pp. 205–223). Washington, DC: American Psychological Association. http://dx.doi.org/10.1037/13089-002

Buchanan, C. M., Maccoby, E. E., & Dornbusch, S. M. (1996). *Adolescents after divorce*. Cambridge, MA: Harvard University Press.

Campbell, L. F., & Arkles, G. (2017). Ethical and legal concerns for mental health professionals. In A. Singh & l. m. dickey (Eds.), *Perspectives on sexual orientation and diversity* (pp. 95–118). Washington, DC: American Psychological Association. http://dx.doi.org/10.1037/14957-005

Carr, A. (2016). The evolution of systems theory. In T. L. Sexton & J. Lebow (Eds.), *Handbook of family therapy* (pp. 13–29). New York, NY: Routledge/Taylor & Francis.

Carr, A., & Stratton, P. (2017). The Score Family Assessment Questionnaire: A decade of progress. *Family Process, 56,* 285–301. http://dx.doi.org/10.1111/famp.12280

Chatav, Y., & Whisman, M. A. (2007). Marital dissolution and psychiatric disorders: An investigation of risk factors. *Journal of Divorce & Remarriage, 47,* 1–13. http://dx.doi.org/10.1300/J087v47n01_01

Cherlin, A. J. (1992). *Marriage, divorce, remarriage* (Rev. ed.). Cambridge, MA: Harvard University Press.

Cherlin, A. J. (2009). *The marriage-go-round: The state of marriage and the family in America today*. New York, NY: Knopf.

Christensen, A., Dimidjian, S., & Martell, C. R. (2015). Integrative behavioral couple therapy. In A. S. Gurman, J. L. Lebow, & D. K. Snyder (Eds.), *Clinical handbook of couple therapy* (5th ed., pp. 61–94). New York, NY: Guilford Press.

Christensen, A., Doss, B. D., & Jacobson, N. S. (2014). *Reconcilable differences: Rebuild your relationship by rediscovering the partner you love—without losing yourself* (2nd ed.). New York, NY: Guilford Press.

Christensen, A., & Heavey, C. L. (1993). Gender differences in marital conflict: The demand/withdraw interaction pattern. In S. Oskamp & M. Costanzo (Eds.), *Gender issues in contemporary society* (pp. 113–141). Thousand Oaks, CA: Sage.

Coleman, M., Ganong, L., Russell, L., & Frye-Cox, N. (2015). Stepchildren's views about former step-relationships following stepfamily dissolution. *Journal of Marriage and Family, 77,* 775–790. http://dx.doi.org/10.1111/jomf.12182

Conrad, J. (1999). *Heart of Darkness & selections from The Congo Diary*. New York, NY: Modern Library.

Cookston, J. T., Braver, S. L., Griffin, W. A., De Lusé, S. R., & Miles, J. C. (2007). Effects of the Dads for Life intervention on interparental conflict and coparenting in the two years after divorce. *Family Process, 46,* 123–137. http://dx.doi.org/10.1111/j.1545-5300.2006.00196.x

Cooper, G. F. (2014, March 25). Gwyneth Paltrow and Chris Martin "consciously uncouple"—as in, split. *Today.* Retrieved from https://www.today.com/popculture/gwyneth-paltrow-chris-martin-consciously-uncouple-split-2D79437604

Copen, C. E., Daniels, K., Vespa, J., & Mosher, W. D. (2012). First marriages in the United States: Data from the 2006–2010 National Survey of Family Growth. *National Health Statistics Report, 49,* 1–21.

Cowen, E. L., Hightower, A. D., Pedro-Carroll, J. L., Work, W. C., & Wyman, P. A., with Haffey, W. G. (1996). *School-based prevention for children at risk: The Primary Mental Health Project* (pp. 211–235). Washington, DC: American Psychological Association.

Crane, D. R., Newfield, N., & Armstrong, D. (1984). Predicting divorce at marital therapy intake: Wives' distress and the marital status inventory. *Journal of Marital and Family Therapy, 10,* 305–312. http://dx.doi.org/10.1111/j.1752-0606.1984.tb00021.x

Crane, D. R., Soderquist, J. N., & Gardner, M. D. (1995). Gender differences in cognitive and behavioral steps toward divorce. *American Journal of Family Therapy, 23,* 99–105. http://dx.doi.org/10.1080/01926189508251341

Datchi, C., & Sexton, T. L. (2016). Integrating research and practice through intervention science: New developments in family therapy research. In T. L. Sexton & J. Lebow (Eds.), *Handbook of family therapy* (pp. 434–453). New York, NY: Routledge/Taylor & Francis.

Dattilio, F. M., & Epstein, N. B. (2016). Cognitive-behavioral couple and family therapy. In T. L. Sexton & J. Lebow (Eds.), *Handbook of family therapy* (pp. 89–119). New York, NY: Routledge/Taylor & Francis.

DeKeseredy, W. S., Dragiewicz, M., & Schwartz, M. D. (2017). *Abusive endings: Separation and divorce violence against women.* Oakland: University of California Press. http://dx.doi.org/10.1525/california/9780520285743.001.0001

DeLongis, A., & Zwicker, A. (2017). Marital satisfaction and divorce in couples in stepfamilies. *Current Opinion in Psychology, 13,* 158–161. http://dx.doi.org/10.1016/j.copsyc.2016.11.003

Demby, S. L. (2016). Parenting coordination: Applying clinical thinking to the management and resolution of post-divorce conflict. *Journal of Clinical Psychology, 72,* 458–468. http://dx.doi.org/10.1002/jclp.22261

De Shazer, S. (1982). *Patterns of brief family therapy: An ecosystemic approach.* New York, NY: Guilford Press.

De Shazer, S. (1985). *Keys to solution in brief therapy.* New York, NY: Norton.

Diamond, R. M., & Lebow, J. L. (2016). Rule-governed speaker-listener technique. In G. R. Weeks, S. T. Fife, & C. M. Peterson (Eds.), *Techniques for the couple therapist: Essential interventions from the experts* (pp. 51–55). New York, NY: Routledge/Taylor & Francis.

Doherty, W. J. (2001). *Take back your marriage: Sticking together in a world that pulls us apart*. New York, NY: Guilford Press.

Doherty, W. J., & Harris, S. M. (2017). *Helping couples on the brink of divorce: Discernment counseling for troubled relationships*. Washington, DC: American Psychological Association.

Doherty, W. J., Harris, S. M., & Didericksen, K. W. (2016, January 30). A typology of attitudes toward proceeding with divorce among parents in the divorce process. *Journal of Divorce & Remarriage, 57*. Advance online publication.

Drozd, L., Saini, M., & Olesen, N. (Eds.). (2016). *Parenting plan evaluations: Applied research for the family court* (2nd ed.). New York, NY: Oxford University Press. http://dx.doi.org/10.1093/med:psych/9780199396580.001.0001

Eisler, I., Le Grange, D., & Lock, J. (2016). Treating adolescents with eating disorders. In T. L. Sexton & J. Lebow (Eds.), *Handbook of family therapy* (pp. 387–406). New York, NY: Routledge/Taylor & Francis.

Eldridge, K. A., & Christensen, A. (2002). Demand–withdraw communication during couple conflict: A review and analysis. In P. Noller & J. A. Feeney (Eds.), *Understanding marriage: Developments in the study of couple interaction* (pp. 289–322). New York, NY: Cambridge University Press. http://dx.doi.org/10.1017/CBO9780511500077.016

Elliott, R. (1986). Interpersonal Process Recall (IPR) as a psychotherapy process research method. In L. S. Greenberg & W. M. Pinsof (Eds.), *The psychotherapeutic process: A research handbook* (pp. 503–527). Guilford clinical psychology and psychotherapy series. New York, NY: Guilford Press.

Ellis, A. (1962). *Reason and emotion in psychotherapy*. Oxford, England: Lyle Stuart.

Emery, R. E. (1994). *Renegotiating family relationships: Divorce, child custody, and mediation*. New York, NY: Guilford Press.

Emery, R. E. (1999). *Marriage, divorce, and children's adjustment* (2nd ed.). Thousand Oaks, CA: Sage.

Emery, R. E. (2004). *The truth about children and divorce: Dealing with the emotions so you and your children can thrive*. New York, NY: Viking.

Emery, R. E. (2012). *Renegotiating family relationships: Divorce, child custody, and mediation* (2nd ed.). New York, NY: Guilford Press.

Emery, R. E. (2016). *Two homes, one childhood: A parenting plan to last a lifetime*. New York, NY: Avery.

Emery, R. E., & Dinescu, D. (2016). Separating, divorced, and remarried families. In T. L. Sexton & J. Lebow (Eds.), *Handbook of family therapy* (pp. 484–499). New York, NY: Routledge/Taylor & Francis.

Emery, R. E., & Jackson, J. A. (1989). The Charlottesville Mediation Project: Mediated and litigated child custody disputes. *Mediation Quarterly, 1989*, 3–18.

Emery, R. E., Laumann-Billings, L., Waldron, M. C., Sbarra, D. A., & Dillon, P. (2001). Child custody mediation and litigation: Custody, contact, and coparenting 12 years after initial dispute resolution. *Journal of Consulting and Clinical Psychology, 69*, 323–332. http://dx.doi.org/10.1037/0022-006X.69.2.323

Emery, R. E., Matthews, S. G., & Kitzmann, K. M. (1994). Child custody mediation and litigation: Parents' satisfaction and functioning one year after settlement. *Journal of Consulting and Clinical Psychology, 62*, 124–129. http://dx.doi.org/10.1037/0022-006X.62.1.124

Emery, R. E., Matthews, S. G., & Wyer, M. M. (1991). Child custody mediation and litigation: Further evidence on the differing views of mothers and fathers. *Journal of Consulting and Clinical Psychology, 59*, 410–418. http://dx.doi.org/10.1037/0022-006X.59.3.410

Emery, R. E., Rowen, J., & Dinescu, D. (2014). New roles for family therapists in the courts: An overview with a focus on custody dispute resolution. *Family Process, 53*, 500–515. http://dx.doi.org/10.1111/famp.12077

Emery, R. E., Sbarra, D., & Grover, T. (2005). Divorce mediation: Research and reflections. *Family Court Review, 43*, 22–37. http://dx.doi.org/10.1111/j.1744-1617.2005.00005.x

Epstein, N. B., & Baucom, D. H. (2002). *Enhanced cognitive–behavioral therapy for couples: A contextual approach.* Washington, DC: American Psychological Association.

Fackrell, T. A., Hawkins, A. J., & Kay, N. M. (2011). How effective are court-affiliated divorcing parents education programs? A meta-analytic study. *Family Court Review, 49*, 107–119.

Falender, C. A., & Shafranske, E. P. (2012). *Getting the most out of clinical training and supervision: A guide for practicum students and interns.* Washington, DC: American Psychological Association.

Finkel, E. J. (2017). *The all-or-nothing marriage: How the best marriages work.* New York, NY: Dutton.

Folberg, J. (1983, September). A mediation overview: History and dimensions of practice. *Mediation Quarterly*, 3–13.

Folberg, J. (1991). *Joint custody and shared parenting* (2nd ed.). New York, NY: Guilford Press.

Folberg, J., & Milne, A. (1988). *Divorce mediation: Theory and practice.* New York, NY: Guilford Press.

Folberg, J., Milne, A. L., & Salem, P. (2004). *Divorce and family mediation: Models, techniques, and applications.* New York, NY: Guilford Press.

Fonagy, P. (2002). *Affect regulation, mentalization, and the development of the self.* New York, NY: Other Press.

Freedman, J., & Combs, G. (2015). Narrative couple therapy. In A. S. Gurman, J. L. Lebow, & D. K. Snyder (Eds.), *Clinical handbook of couple therapy* (5th ed., pp. 271–299). New York, NY: Guilford Press. http://dx.doi.org/10.1007/978-3-319-15877-8_237-1

Friedlander, M. L., Escudero, V., & Heatherington, L. (2006). *Therapeutic alliances in couple and family therapy: An empirically informed guide to practice.* Washington, DC: American Psychological Association.

Friedlander, M. L., Escudero, V., Heatherington, L., & Diamond, G. M. (2011). Alliance in couple and family therapy. *Psychotherapy, 48,* 25–33. http://dx.doi.org/10.1037/a0022060

Friedlander, M. L., Heatherington, L., & Escudero, V. (2016). Research-based change mechanisms: Advances in process research. In T. L. Sexton & J. Lebow (Eds.), *Handbook of family therapy* (pp. 454–467). New York, NY: Routledge/Taylor & Francis.

Fruzzetti, A. E. (2006). *The high-conflict couple: A dialectical behavior therapy guide to finding peace, intimacy & validation.* Oakland, CA: New Harbinger.

Fruzzetti, A. E., & Payne, L. (2015). Couple therapy and borderline personality disorder. In A. S. Gurman, J. L. Lebow, & D. K. Snyder (Eds.), *Clinical handbook of couple therapy* (5th ed., pp. 606–634). New York, NY: Guilford Press.

Fruzzetti, A. E., Santisteban, D. A., & Hoffman, P. D. (2007). Dialectical behavior therapy with families. In L. A. Dimeff & K. Koerner (Eds.), *Dialectical behavior therapy in clinical practice: Applications across disorders and settings* (pp. 222–244). New York, NY: Guilford Press.

Galatzer-Levy, R. M., Kraus, L., & Galatzer-Levy, J. (2009). *The scientific basis of child custody decisions* (2nd ed.). Hoboken, NJ: Wiley.

Gallagher, M. (1996). *The abolition of marriage: How we destroy lasting love.* Washington, DC: Regnery.

Ganong, L., & Coleman, M. (2018). Studying stepfamilies: Four eras of family scholarship. *Family Process, 57,* 7–24. http://dx.doi.org/10.1111/famp.12307

Ganong, L., Coleman, M., & Chapman, A. (2016). Gatekeeping after separation and divorce. In L. Drozd, M. Saini, & N. Olesen (Eds.), *Parenting plan evaluations: Applied research for the family court* (pp. 308–345). New York, NY: Oxford University Press.

Gardner, R. A., Sauber, S. R., & Lorandos, D. (2006). *The international handbook of parental alienation syndrome: Conceptual, clinical and legal considerations.* Springfield, IL: Thomas.

Glass, J., & Levchak, P. (2014). Red states, blue states, and divorce: Understanding the impact of conservative Protestantism on regional variation in divorce rates. *American Journal of Sociology, 119,* 1002–1046. http://dx.doi.org/10.1086/674703

Goldfried, M. R., & Davison, G. C. (1994). *Clinical behavior therapy.* Wiley series in clinical psychology and personality. New York, NY: Wiley.

Goldstein, M. L. (Ed.). (2016). *Handbook of child custody.* Cham, Switzerland: Springer.

Goodman, M., Bonds, D., Sandler, I., & Braver, S. (2004). Parent psycho-educational programs and reducing the negative effects of interparental conflict following divorce. *Family Court Review, 42*, 263–279. http://dx.doi.org/10.1111/j.174-1617.2004.tb00648.x

Gottlieb, M. C., Lasser, J., & Simpson, G. L. (2008). Legal and ethical issues in couple therapy. In A. S. Gurman (Ed.), *Clinical handbook of couple therapy* (4th ed., pp. 698–717). New York, NY: Guilford Press.

Gottman, J. M. (1999). *The marriage clinic: A scientifically based marital therapy.* New York, NY: Norton.

Gottman, J. M., & Gottman, J. S. (2015). Gottman couple therapy. In A. S. Gurman, J. L. Lebow, & D. K. Snyder (Eds.), *Clinical handbook of couple therapy* (5th ed., pp. 129–157). New York, NY: Guilford Press.

Gottman, J. M., & Levenson, R. W. (1992). Marital processes predictive of later dissolution: Behavior, physiology, and health. *Journal of Personality and Social Psychology, 63*, 221–233. http://dx.doi.org/10.1037/0022-3514.63.2.221

Gottman, J. M., & Notarius, C. I. (2000). Decade review: Observing marital interaction. *Journal of Marriage & the Family, 62*, 927–947.

Gould, J. W., & Martindale, D. A. (2007). *The art and science of child custody evaluations.* New York, NY: Guilford Press.

Gould, J. W., & Stahl, P. M. (2000). The art and science of child custody evaluations: Integrating clinical and forensic mental health models. *Family & Conciliation Courts Review, 38*, 392–414. http://dx.doi.org/10.1111/j.174-1617.2000.tb00581.x

Green, R.-J., & Mitchell, V. (2015). Gay, lesbian, and bisexual issues in couple therapy. In A. S. Gurman, J. L. Lebow, & D. K. Snyder (Eds.), *Clinical handbook of couple therapy* (5th ed., pp. 489–511). New York, NY: Guilford Press.

Greenberg, L. R., Fick, L. D., & Schnider, R. (2012). Keeping the developmental frame: Child-centered conjoint therapy. *Journal of Child Custody: Research, Issues, and Practices, 9*, 39–68. http://dx.doi.org/10.1080/15379418.2012.652568

Greenberg, L. R., & Gould, J. W. (2001). The treating expert: A hybrid role with firm boundaries. *Professional Psychology: Research and Practice, 32*, 469–478. http://dx.doi.org/10.1037/0735-7028.32.5.469

Greenberg, L. R., Gould-Saltman, D. J., & Gottlieb, M. C. (2008). Playing in their sandbox: Professional obligations of mental health professionals in custody cases. *Journal of Child Custody: Research, Issues, and Practices, 5*, 192–216. http://dx.doi.org/10.1080/15379410802583684

Greenberg, L. R., & Lebow, J. L. (2016). Putting it all together: Effective intervention planning for children and families. In L. Drozd, M. Saini, & N. Olesen (Eds.), *Parenting plan evaluations: Applied research for the family court* (2nd ed., pp. 555–584). New York, NY: Oxford University Press. http://dx.doi.org/10.1093/med:psych/9780199396580.003.0019

Greenberg, L. R., & Sullivan, M. J. (2012). Parenting coordinator and therapist collaboration in high-conflict shared custody cases. *Journal of Child Custody: Research, Issues, and Practices, 9*, 85–107. http://dx.doi.org/10.1080/15379418.2012.652571

Greenberg, L. S. (2015). *Emotion-focused therapy: Coaching clients to work through their feelings* (2nd ed.). Washington, DC: American Psychological Association. http://dx.doi.org/10.1037/e602962010-001

Greenberg, L. S. (2017). *Emotion-focused therapy* (Rev. ed.). Washington, DC: American Psychological Association.

Greenberg, L. S., & Goldman, R. N. (2008). *Emotion-focused couples therapy: The dynamics of emotion, love, and power.* Washington, DC: American Psychological Association.

Greene, S. M., Anderson, E. R., Hetherington, E., Forgatch, M. S., & DeGarmo, D. S. (2003). Risk and resilience after divorce. In F. Walsh (Ed.), *Normal family processes: Growing diversity and complexity* (3rd ed., pp. 96–120). New York, NY: Guilford Press.

Grych, J. H., & Fincham, F. D. (1990). Marital conflict and children's adjustment: A cognitive-contextual framework. *Psychological Bulletin, 108*, 267–290. http://dx.doi.org/10.1037/0033-2909.108.2.267

Grych, J. H., & Fincham, F. D. (1992). Interventions for children of divorce: Toward greater integration of research and action. *Psychological Bulletin, 111*, 434–454. http://dx.doi.org/10.1037/0033-2909.111.3.434

Grych, J. H., Fincham, F. D., Jouriles, E. N., & McDonald, R. (2000). Interparental conflict and child adjustment: Testing the mediational role of appraisals in the cognitive-contextual framework. *Child Development, 71*, 1648–1661. http://dx.doi.org/10.1111/1467-8624.00255

Gurman, A. S., & Burton, M. (2014). Individual therapy for couple problems: Perspectives and pitfalls. *Journal of Marital and Family Therapy, 40*, 470–483. http://dx.doi.org/10.1111/jmft.12061

Hahlweg, K., & Baucom, D. H. (2011). Relationships and embitterment. In M. Linden & A. Maercker (Eds.), *Embitterment: Societal, psychological, and clinical perspectives* (pp. 119–128). New York, NY: Springer-Verlag.

Hale, D. (2015). A model of structured separation in couples therapy: Making best use of a separation period. *Journal of Divorce & Remarriage, 56*, 109–116. http://dx.doi.org/10.1080/10502556.2014.996048

Haley, J. (1963). *Strategies of psychotherapy.* Oxford, England: Grune & Stratton. http://dx.doi.org/10.1037/14324-000

Halford, W. K., Hayes, S., Christensen, A., Lambert, M., Baucom, D. H., & Atkins, D. C. (2012). Toward making progress feedback an effective common factor in couple therapy. *Behavior Therapy, 43*, 49–60. http://dx.doi.org/10.1016/j.beth.2011.03.005

Hall, J. H., Fincham, F. D., Fine, M. A., & Harvey, J. H. (2006). Relationship dissolution following infidelity. In M. A. Fine & J. H. Harvey (Eds.), *Handbook of divorce and relationship dissolution* (pp. 153–168). Mahwah, NJ: Erlbaum.

Harrison, K. (2005). *The starter marriage.* New York, NY: New American Library.

Hawkins, A. J., Galovan, A. M., Harris, S. M., Allen, S. E., Allen, S. M., Roberts, K. M., & Schramm, D. G. (2017). What are they thinking? A national study of stability and change in divorce ideation. *Family Process, 56,* 852–868. http://dx.doi.org/10.1111/famp.12299

Hawkins, A. J., Willoughby, B. J., & Doherty, W. J. (2012). Reasons for divorce and openness to marital reconciliation. *Journal of Divorce & Remarriage, 53,* 453–463. http://dx.doi.org/10.1080/10502556.2012.682898

Hawkins, M. W., Carrere, S., & Gottman, J. M. (2002). Marital sentiment override: Does it influence couples' perceptions? *Journal of Marriage and Family, 64,* 193–201. http://dx.doi.org/10.1111/j.1741-3737.2002.00193.x

Hayes, S. C. (2016). Buddhism and acceptance and commitment therapy. In S. C. Hayes (Ed.), *The act in context: The canonical papers of Steven C. Hayes* (pp. 239–248). New York, NY: Routledge/Taylor & Francis.

Hayes, S. C., Strosahl, K., & Wilson, K. G. (2012). *Acceptance and commitment therapy: The process and practice of mindful change* (2nd ed.). New York, NY: Guilford Press. http://dx.doi.org/10.1037/e539472008-001

Hazlett-Stevens, H., & Craske, M. G. (2009). Breathing retraining and diaphragmatic breathing techniques. In W. T. O'Donohue & J. E. Fisher (Eds.), *General principles and empirically supported techniques of cognitive behavior therapy* (pp. 167–172). Hoboken, NJ: Wiley.

Henggeler, S. W., Schoenwald, S. K., Borduin, C. M., Rowland, M. D., & Cunningham, P. B. (2009). *Multisystemic therapy for antisocial behavior in children and adolescents* (2nd ed.). New York, NY: Guilford Press.

Hetherington, E. M. (1979). Divorce: A child's perspective. *American Psychologist, 34,* 851–858. http://dx.doi.org/10.1037/0003-066X.34.10.851

Hetherington, E. M. (1987). Family relations six years after divorce. In K. Pasley & M. Ihinger-Tallman (Eds.), *Remarriage and stepparenting: Current research and theory* (pp. 185–205). New York, NY: Guilford Press.

Hetherington, E. M. (1989). Coping with family transitions: Winners, losers, and survivors. *Child Development, 60,* 1–14. http://dx.doi.org/10.2307/1131066

Hetherington, E. M. (1999). *Coping with divorce, single parenting, and remarriage: A risk and resiliency perspective.* Mahwah, NJ: Erlbaum.

Hetherington, E. M., & Anderson, E. R. (1988). The effects of divorce and remarriage on early adolescents and their families. In M. D. Levine & E. R. McAnarney (Eds.), *Early adolescent transitions* (pp. 49–67). Lexington, MA: Lexington Books.

Hetherington, E. M., Cox, M., & Cox, R. (1985). Long-term effects of divorce and remarriage on the adjustment of children. *Journal of the American Academy of Child Psychiatry, 24,* 518–530. http://dx.doi.org/10.1016/S0002-7138(09)60052-2

Hetherington, E. M., & Elmore, A. M. (2003). Risk and resilience in children coping with their parents' divorce and remarriage. In S. S. Luthar (Ed.), *Resilience and vulnerability: Adaptation in the context of childhood adversities* (pp. 182–212). New York, NY: Cambridge University Press. http://dx.doi.org/10.1017/CBO9780511615788.010

Hetherington, E. M., & Kelly, J. (2002). *For better or for worse: Divorce reconsidered.* New York, NY: Norton.

Hetherington, E. M., Law, T. C., & O'Connor, T. G. (1993). Divorce: Challenges, changes, and new chances. In F. Walsh (Ed.), *Normal family processes* (2nd ed., pp. 208–234). New York, NY: Guilford Press.

Hetherington, E. M., & Stanley-Hagan, M. (2002). Parenting in divorced and remarried families. In M. H. Bornstein (Ed.), *Handbook of parenting: Vol. 3. Being and becoming a parent* (2nd ed., pp. 287–315). Mahwah, NJ: Erlbaum.

Hetherington, E. M., Stanley-Hagan, M., & Anderson, E. R. (1989). Marital transitions. A child's perspective. *American Psychologist, 44,* 303–312. http://dx.doi.org/10.1037/0003-066X.44.2.303

Higuchi, S. A., & Lally, S. J. (Eds.). (2014). *Parenting coordination in postseparation disputes: A comprehensive guide for practitioners.* Washington, DC: American Psychological Association.

Hita, L. C., & Braver, S. L. (2016). Never-married parents in family court. In L. Drozd, M. Saini, & N. Olesen (Eds.), *Parenting plan evaluations: Applied research for the family court* (pp. 488–513). New York, NY: Oxford University Press.

Hiyoshi, A., Fall, K., Netuveli, G., & Montgomery, S. (2015). Remarriage after divorce and depression risk. *Social Science & Medicine, 141,* 109–114. http://dx.doi.org/10.1016/j.socscimed.2015.07.029

Holtzworth-Munroe, A., Meehan, J. C., Herron, K., & Stuart, G. L. (1999). A typology of male batterers: An initial examination. In X. B. Arriaga & S. Oskamp (Eds.), *Violence in intimate relationships* (pp. 45–72). Thousand Oaks, CA: Sage. http://dx.doi.org/10.4135/9781452204659.n3

Hooley, J. M., & Germain, S. S. (2008). Borderline personality disorder. In W. E. Craighead, D. J. Miklowitz, & L. W. Craighead (Eds.), *Psychopathology: History, diagnosis, and empirical foundations* (pp. 598–630). Hoboken, NJ: Wiley.

Horvath, A. O., Symonds, D., & Tapia, L. (2010). Therapeutic alliances in couple therapy: The web of relationships. In J. C. Muran & J. P. Barber (Eds.), *The therapeutic alliance: An evidence-based guide to practice* (pp. 210–239). New York, NY: Guilford Press.

Hynan, D. J. (2014). *Child custody evaluation: New theoretical applications and research.* Springfield, IL: Thomas.

Isaacs, M. B., Montalvo, B., Abelsohn, D., & Isaacs, M. B. (2000). *Therapy of the difficult divorce: Managing crises, reorienting warring couples, working with the children, and expediting court processes.* Northvale, NJ: Aronson.

Jaffe, P. G., Johnston, J. R., Crooks, C. V., & Bala, N. (2008). Custody disputes involving allegations of domestic violence: Toward a differentiated approach to parenting plans. *Family Court Review, 46*, 500–522. http://dx.doi.org/10.1111/j.1744-1617.2008.00216.x

Jewell, J., Schmittel, M., McCobin, A., Hupp, S., & Pomerantz, A. (2017). The children first program: The effectiveness of a parent education program for divorcing parents. *Journal of Divorce & Remarriage, 58*, 16–28. http://dx.doi.org/10.1080/10502556.2016.1257903

Johnson, S. M. (2015). Emotionally focused couple therapy. In A. S. Gurman, J. L. Lebow, & D. K. Snyder (Eds.), *Clinical handbook of couple therapy* (5th ed., pp. 97–128). New York, NY: Guilford Press.

Johnson, S. M., O'Connor, E., & Tornello, S. L. (2016). Gay and lesbian parents and their children: Research relevant to custody cases. In L. Drozd, M. Saini, & N. Olesen (Eds.), *Parenting plan evaluations: Applied research for the family court* (pp. 514–533). New York, NY: Oxford University Press.

Johnston, J., Roseby, V., & Kuehnle, K. (2009). *In the name of the child: A developmental approach to understanding and helping children of conflicted and violent divorce* (2nd ed.). New York, NY: Springer.

Johnston, J. R. (1994). High-conflict divorce. *The Future of Children, 4*, 165–182. http://dx.doi.org/10.2307/1602483

Johnston, J. R. (2005). Clinical work with parents in entrenched custody disputes. In L. Gunsberg & P. Hymowitz (Eds.), *A handbook of divorce and custody: Forensic, developmental, and clinical perspectives* (pp. 343–363). New York, NY: The Analytic Press/Taylor & Francis.

Johnston, J. R., & Campbell, L. E. (1986). Tribal warfare: The involvement of extended kin and significant others in custody and access disputes. *Conciliation Courts Review, 24*, 1–16. http://dx.doi.org/10.1111/j.174-1617.1986.tb00124.x

Johnston, J. R., Lee, S., Olesen, N. W., & Walters, M. G. (2005). Allegations and substantiations of abuse in custody-disputing families. *Family Court Review, 43*, 283–294. http://dx.doi.org/10.1111/j.1744-1617.2005.00029.x

Johnston, J. R., & Roseby, V. (1997). *In the name of the child: A developmental approach to understanding and helping children of conflicted and violent divorce.* New York, NY: Free Press.

Johnston, J. R., Walters, M. G., & Olesen, N. W. (2005). The psychological functioning of alienated children in custody disputing families: An exploratory study. *American Journal of Forensic Psychology, 23*, 39–64.

Kabat-Zinn, J. (2012). *Mindfulness for beginners: Reclaiming the present moment—and your life.* Boulder, CO: Sounds True.

Kabat-Zinn, J. (2013). *Full catastrophe living: Using the wisdom of your body and mind to face stress, pain, and illness* (Rev. and updated ed.). New York, NY: Bantam Books.

Kabat-Zinn, M., & Kabat-Zinn, J. (2014). *Everyday blessings: The inner work of mindful parenting* (Rev. and updated ed.). New York, NY: Hachette Books.

Karam, E., & Lebow, J. (2006). Couples and family treatment of anger difficulties. In E. L. Feindler (Ed.), *Anger-related disorders: A practitioner's guide to comparative treatments* (pp. 165–187). New York, NY: Springer.

Kaufman, R. L., & Pickar, D. B. (2017). Understanding parental gatekeeping in families with a special needs child. *Family Court Review, 55,* 195–212. http://dx.doi.org/10.1111/fcre.12273

Kazdin, A. E. (1979). Unobtrusive measures in behavioral assessment. *Journal of Applied Behavior Analysis, 12,* 713–724. http://dx.doi.org/10.1901/jaba.1979.12-713

Kazdin, A. E., & Rotella, C. (2013). *The everyday parenting toolkit: The Kazdin Method for easy, step-by-step, lasting change for you and your child.* Boston, MA: Houghton Mifflin Harcourt.

Keating, A., Sharry, J., Murphy, M., Rooney, B., & Carr, A. (2016). An evaluation of the Parents Plus-Parenting When Separated programme. *Clinical Child Psychology and Psychiatry, 21,* 240–254. http://dx.doi.org/10.1177/1359104515581717

Kelly, J. B. (2004). Family mediation research: Is there empirical support for the field? *Conflict Resolution Quarterly, 22,* 3–35. http://dx.doi.org/10.1002/crq.90

Kelly, J. B. (2014a). Including children in the parenting coordination process: A specialized role. In S. A. Higuchi & S. J. Lally (Eds.), *Parenting coordination in postseparation disputes: A comprehensive guide for practitioners* (pp. 143–170). Washington, DC: American Psychological Association. http://dx.doi.org/10.1037/14390-010

Kelly, J. B. (2014b). Origins and development of parenting coordination. In S. A. Higuchi & S. J. Lally (Eds.), *Parenting coordination in postseparation disputes: A comprehensive guide for practitioners.* Washington, DC: American Psychological Association. http://dx.doi.org/10.1037/14390-002

Kelly, J. B., Gigy, L., & Hausman, S. (1988). Mediated and adversarial divorce: Initial findings from a longitudinal study. In J. Folberg & A. Milne (Eds.), *Divorce mediation: Theory and practice* (pp. 453–473). New York, NY: Guilford Press.

Kelly, J. B., & Johnston, J. R. (2001). The alienated child: A reformulation of parental alienation syndrome. *Family Court Review, 39,* 249–266. http://dx.doi.org/10.1111/j.174-1617.2001.tb00609.x

Kelly, J. B., & Lamb, M. E. (2000). Using child development research to make appropriate custody and access decisions for young children. *Family & Conciliation Courts Review, 38,* 297–311. http://dx.doi.org/10.1111/j.174-1617.2000.tb00577.x

Kennedy, S., & Ruggles, S. (2014). Breaking up is hard to count: The rise of divorce in the United States, 1980–2010. *Demography, 5,* 587–598. http://dx.doi.org/10.1007/s13524-013-0270-9

Kerns, S. E. U., & Prinz, R. J. (2016). Co-parenting children with attention-deficit/ hyperactivity disorder and disruptive behavior disorders. In L. Drozd, M. Saini, & N. Olesen (Eds.), *Parenting plan evaluations: Applied research for the family court* (pp. 243–277). New York, NY: Oxford University Press.

Killewald, A. (2016). Money, work, and marital stability: Assessing change in the gendered determinants of divorce. *American Sociological Review, 81,* 696–719.

Knapp, S. J., Gottlieb, M. C., Handelsman, M. M., & VandeCreek, L. D. (Eds.). (2012). *APA handbook of ethics in psychology: Vol. 2. Practice, teaching, and research.* Washington, DC: American Psychological Association.

Koel, A., Clark, S. C., Straus, R. B., Whitney, R. R., & Hauser, B. B. (1994). Patterns of relitigation in the postdivorce family. *Journal of Marriage and the Family, 56,* 265–277.

Kramer, L., Laumann, G., & Brunson, L. (2000). Implementation and diffusion of the Rainbows program in rural communities: Implications for school-based prevention programming. *Journal of Educational & Psychological Consultation, 11,* 37–63. http://dx.doi.org/10.1207/s1532768Xjepc1101_04

Krantzler, M., & Krantzler, P. B. (1999). *The new creative divorce: How to create a happier, more rewarding life during—and after—your divorce.* Holbrook, MA: Adams Media.

Lamb, M. E., & Kelly, J. B. (2001). Using the empirical literature to guide the development of parenting plans for young children: A rejoinder to Solomon and Biringen. *Family Court Review, 39,* 365–371. http://dx.doi.org/10.1111/ j.174-1617.2001.tb00618.x

Lambert, M. J. (2013). *Bergin and Garfield's handbook of psychotherapy and behavior change* (6th ed.). Hoboken, NJ: Wiley.

Lambert, M. J. (2015). Progress feedback and the OQ-system: The past and the future. *Psychotherapy, 52,* 381–390. http://dx.doi.org/10.1037/pst0000027

Lambert, M. J., & Ogles, B. M. (2016). Treatment outcome studies. In J. C. Norcross, G. R. VandenBos, & D. K. Freedheim (Eds.), *APA handbook of clinical psychology: Vol. 2. Theory and research* (pp. 465–477). Washington, DC: American Psychological Association.

Laumann-Billings, L., & Emery, R. E. (2000). Distress among young adults from divorced families. *Journal of Family Psychology, 14,* 671–687. http://dx.doi.org/ 10.1037/0893-3200.14.4.671

Lebow, J. (2006). *Research for the psychotherapist: From science to practice.* New York, NY: Routledge/Taylor & Francis.

Lebow, J. (2008). Separation and divorce issues in couple therapy. In A. S. Gurman (Ed.), *Clinical handbook of couple therapy* (4th ed., pp. 459–477). New York, NY: Guilford Press.

Lebow, J., & Rekart, K. N. (2007). Integrative family therapy for high-conflict divorce with disputes over child custody and visitation. *Family Process, 46,* 79–91. http://dx.doi.org/10.1111/j.1545-5300.2006.00193.x

Lebow, J. L. (1995). Open-ended therapy: Termination in marital and family therapy. In R. H. Mikesell, D.-D. Lusterman, & S. H. McDaniel (Eds.), *Integrating family therapy: Handbook of family psychology and systems theory* (pp. 73–86). Washington, DC: American Psychological Association. http://dx.doi.org/10.1037/10172-004

Lebow, J. L. (2002). An integrative approach for treating families with child custody and visitation disputes. In F. W. Kaslow (Ed.), *Comprehensive handbook of psychotherapy: Integrative/eclectic* (Vol. 4, pp. 437–453). New York, NY: Wiley.

Lebow, J. L. (2005). Integrative family therapy for families experiencing high-conflict divorce. In J. L. Lebow (Ed.), *Handbook of clinical family therapy* (pp. 516–542). Hoboken, NJ: Wiley.

Lebow, J. L. (2014). *Couple and family therapy: An integrative map of the territory.* Washington, DC: American Psychological Association.

Lebow, J. L. (2015a). Editorial: Funding couple and family research. *Family Process, 54,* 577–580. http://dx.doi.org/10.1111/famp.12192

Lebow, J. L. (2015b). Separation and divorce issues in couple therapy. In A. S. Gurman, J. L. Lebow, & D. K. Snyder (Eds.), *Clinical handbook of couple therapy* (5th ed., pp. 445–466). New York, NY: Guilford Press.

Lebow, J. L. (2017). Editorial: Mentalization and psychoanalytic couple and family therapy. *Family Process, 56,* 3–5. http://dx.doi.org/10.1111/famp.12277

Lebow, J. L., Chambers, A. L., Christensen, A., & Johnson, S. M. (2012). Research on the treatment of couple distress. *Journal of Marital and Family Therapy, 38,* 145–168. http://dx.doi.org/10.1111/j.1752-0606.2011.00249.x

Lebow, J. L., & Jenkins, P. H. (2018). *Research for the psychotherapist: From science to practice* (2nd ed.). New York, NY: Routledge/Taylor & Francis.

Lerner, H. G. (2005). *The dance of anger: A woman's guide to changing the patterns of intimate relationships.* New York, NY: Perennial Currents.

Lerner, R. M., Easterbrooks, M. A., Mistry, J., & Weiner, I. B. (2013). *Handbook of psychology: Vol. 6. Developmental psychology* (2nd ed.). Hoboken, NJ: Wiley.

Liddle, H. A. (2016). Multidimensional family therapy: Evidence base for trans-diagnostic treatment outcomes, change mechanisms, and implementation in community settings. *Family Process, 55,* 558–576. http://dx.doi.org/10.1111/famp.12243

Linehan, M. M. (2015). *DBT skills training manual* (2nd ed.). New York, NY: Guilford Press.

Linehan, M. M., & Dexter-Mazza, E. T. (2008). Dialectical behavior therapy for borderline personality disorder. In D. H. Barlow (Ed.), *Clinical handbook of psychological disorders: A step-by-step treatment manual* (4th ed., pp. 365–420). New York, NY: Guilford Press.

López, T. J., Iglesias, V. E. N., & Garcia, P. F. (2014). Parental alienation gradient: Strategies for a syndrome. *American Journal of Family Therapy, 42,* 217–231.

Lutz, W., Stulz, N., Martinovich, Z., Leon, S., & Saunders, S. M. (2014). Patient-focused research in psychotherapy: Methodological background, decision rules and feedback tools. In W. Lutz, S. Knox, W. Lutz, & S. Knox (Eds.), *Quantitative and qualitative methods in psychotherapy research* (pp. 204–217). New York, NY: Routledge/Taylor & Francis.

Mahrer, N. E., Sandler, I. N., Wolchik, S. A., Winslow, E. B., Moran, J. A., & Weinstock, D. (2016). How do parenting time and interparental conflict affect the relations of quality of parenting and child well-being following divorce? In L. Drozd, M. Saini, & N. Olesen (Eds.), *Parenting plan evaluations: Applied research for the family court* (pp. 63–73). New York, NY: Oxford University Press. http://dx.doi.org/10.1093/med:psych/9780199396580.003.0003

Mansfield, A. K., Keitner, G. I., & Dealy, J. (2015). The family assessment device: An update. *Family Process, 54,* 82–93. http://dx.doi.org/10.1111/famp.12080

Masurel, C., & Denton, K. M. (2001). *Two homes.* Cambridge, MA: Candlewick Press.

McHale, J., Waller, M. R., & Pearson, J. (2012). Coparenting interventions for fragile families: What do we know and where do we need to go next? *Family Process, 51,* 284–306. http://dx.doi.org/10.1111/j.1545-5300.2012.01402.x

McIntosh, J. E., Pruett, M. K., & Kelly, J. B. (2014). Parental separation and overnight care of young children, part II: Putting theory into practice. *Family Court Review, 52,* 256–262. http://dx.doi.org/10.1111/fcre.12088

McIntosh, J. E., & Smyth, B. (2012). Shared-time parenting: An evidence-based matrix for evaluating risk. In K. Kuehnle & L. Drozd (Eds.), *Parenting plan evaluations: Applied research for the family court* (pp. 155–187). New York, NY: Oxford University Press.

McIntosh, J. E., Wells, Y., & Lee, J. (2016). Development and validation of the Family Law DOORS. *Psychological Assessment, 28,* 1516–1522. http://dx.doi.org/10.1037/pas0000277

McKinney, M. J., Delaney, L. A., & Nessman, A. (2014). Legal standards and issues associated with parenting coordination. In S. A. Higuchi & S. J. Lally (Eds.), *Parenting coordination in postseparation disputes: A comprehensive guide for practitioners* (pp. 35–42). Washington, DC: American Psychological Association. http://dx.doi.org/10.1037/14390-003

McLanahan, S. (2004). Diverging destinies: How children are faring under the second demographic transition. *Demography, 41,* 607–627. http://dx.doi.org/10.1353/dem.2004.0033

Meyer, D. R., Cancian, M., & Cook, F. T. (2017). The growth in shared custody in the United States: Patterns and implications. *Family Court Review, 55,* 500–512. http://dx.doi.org/10.1111/fcre.12300

Miller, H., & Shepherd, V. C. (2016). *The ex-wives' guide to divorce: How to navigate everything from heartache and finances to child custody.* New York, NY: Skyhorse.

Miller, S. D., Duncan, B. L., Sorrell, R., & Brown, G. S. (2005). The partners for change outcome management system. *Journal of Clinical Psychology, 61*, 199–208. http://dx.doi.org/10.1002/jclp.20111

Miller, W. R., & Rollnick, S. (1991). *Motivational interviewing: Preparing people to change addictive behavior.* New York, NY: Guilford Press. http://dx.doi.org/10.4135/9781412950534.n109

Minuchin, S. (1974). *Families & family therapy.* Oxford, England: Harvard University Press.

Minuchin, S., & Fishman, H. C. (1981). *Family therapy techniques.* Cambridge, MA: Harvard University Press.

Mosten, F. S. (2009). *Collaborative divorce handbook: Helping families without going to court.* San Francisco, CA: Jossey-Bass.

Napier, A., & Whitaker, C. A. (1988). *The family crucible.* New York, NY: Harper Perennial.

Nathan, P. E., & Gorman, J. M. (Eds.). (2015). *A guide to treatments that work* (4th ed.). New York, NY: Oxford University Press. http://dx.doi.org/10.1093/med:psych/9780195304145.001.0001

National Center for Health Statistics. (2017). *Marriage and divorce.* Atlanta, GA: Centers for Disease Control and Prevention. Retrieved from https://www.cdc.gov/nchs/fastats/marriage-divorce.htm

Nielsen, L. (2014). Parenting plans for infants, toddlers, and preschoolers: Research and issues. *Journal of Divorce & Remarriage, 55*, 315–333. http://dx.doi.org/10.1080/10502556.2014.901857

Nielsen, L. (2017). Re-examining the research on parental conflict, coparenting, and custody arrangements. *Psychology, Public Policy, and Law, 23*, 211–231. http://dx.doi.org/10.1037/law0000109

Norcross, J. C. (2011). *Psychotherapy relationships that work: Evidence-based responsiveness* (2nd ed.). New York, NY: Oxford University Press.

Norcross, J. C., & Drewes, A. A. (2009). Self-care for child therapists: Leaving it at the office. In A. A. Drewes (Ed.), *Blending play therapy with cognitive behavioral therapy: Evidence-based and other effective treatments and techniques* (pp. 473–493). Hoboken, NJ: Wiley.

Norcross, J. C., Krebs, P. M., & Prochaska, J. O. (2011). Stages of change. In J. C. Norcross (Ed.), *Psychotherapy relationships that work: Evidence-based responsiveness* (2nd ed., pp. 279–300). New York, NY: Oxford University Press.

Norcross, J. C., & Lambert, M. J. (2011). Psychotherapy relationships that work II. *Psychotherapy, 48*, 4–8. http://dx.doi.org/10.1037/a0022180

Norcross, J. C., & Wampold, B. E. (2011). Evidence-based therapy relationships: Research conclusions and clinical practices. *Psychotherapy: Theory, Research, & Practice, 48*, 98–102. http://dx.doi.org/10.1037/a0022161

O'Donohue, W., Benuto, L. T., & Bennett, N. (2016). Examining the validity of parental alienation syndrome. *Journal of Child Custody: Research, Issues, and Practices, 13*, 113–125.

Ogrodniczuk, J. S., Uliaszek, A. A., Lebow, J. L., & Piper, W. E. (2014). Group, family, and couples therapies. In J. M. Oldham, A. E. Skodol, & D. S. Bender (Eds.), *The American Psychiatric Publishing textbook of personality disorders* (2nd ed., pp. 281–302). Arlington, VA: American Psychiatric Publishing.

O'Leary, K. D. (2008). Couple therapy and physical aggression. In A. S. Gurman (Ed.), *Clinical handbook of couple therapy* (4th ed., pp. 478–498). New York, NY: Guilford Press.

Oliphant, R. E., & Ver Steegh, N. (2016). *Family law* (5th ed.). New York, NY: Wolters Kluwer.

Olson, D. H., Russell, C. S., & Sprenkle, D. H. (1983). Circumplex model of marital and family systems: VI. Theoretical update. *Family Process, 22*, 69–83. http://dx.doi.org/10.1111/j.1545-5300.1983.00069.x

Orlinsky, D. E., & Howard, K. I. (1987). A generic model of psychotherapy. *Journal of Integrative and Eclectic Psychotherapy, 6*, 6–27.

Orlinsky, D. E., & Rønnestad, M. H. (2005). *How psychotherapists develop: A study of therapeutic work and professional growth.* Washington, DC: American Psychological Association.

Papernow, P. L. (2013). *Surviving and thriving in stepfamily relationships: What works and what doesn't.* New York, NY: Routledge/Taylor & Francis.

Papernow, P. L. (2015). Therapy with couples in stepfamilies. In A. S. Gurman, J. L. Lebow, & D. K. Snyder (Eds.), *Clinical handbook of couple therapy* (5th ed., pp. 467–488). New York, NY: Guilford Press.

Patterson, G. R., & Chamberlain, P. (1994). A functional analysis of resistance during parent training therapy. *Clinical Psychology: Science and Practice, 1*, 53–70. http://dx.doi.org/10.1111/j.1468-2850.1994.tb00006.x

Paul, P. (2002). *The starter marriage and the future of matrimony.* New York, NY: Villard Books.

Pedro-Carroll, J. (1997). The Children of Divorce Intervention Program: Fostering resilient outcomes for school-aged children. In G. W. Albee & T. P. Gullotta (Eds.), *Issues in children's and families' lives: Vol. 6. Primary prevention works* (pp. 213–238). Thousand Oaks, CA: Sage. http://dx.doi.org/10.4135/9781452243801.n10

Pedro-Carroll, J. (2010). *Putting children first: Proven parenting strategies for helping children thrive through divorce.* New York, NY: Avery/Penguin Group USA.

Pedro-Carroll, J., & Velderman, M. K. (2016). Extending the global reach of a play-based intervention for children dealing with separation and divorce. In L. A. Reddy, T. M. Files-Hall, & C. E. Schaefer (Eds.), *Empirically based play interventions for children* (2nd ed., pp. 35–53). Washington, DC: American Psychological Association. http://dx.doi.org/10.1037/14730-003

Pedro-Carroll, J. L. (2005). Fostering resilience in the aftermath of divorce: The role of evidence-based programs for children. *Family Court Review, 43*, 52–64. http://dx.doi.org/10.1111/j.1744-1617.2005.00007.x

Pedro-Carroll, J. L., & Jones, S. H. (2005). A preventive play intervention to foster children's resilience in the aftermath of divorce. In L. A. Reddy, T. M. Files-Hall, & C. E. Schaefer (Eds.), *Empirically based play interventions for children* (pp. 51–75). Washington, DC: American Psychological Association. http://dx.doi.org/10.1037/11086-004

Pinsof, W., Breunlin, D. C., Russell, W. P., & Lebow, J. (2011). Integrative problem-centered metaframeworks therapy II: Planning, conversing, and reading feedback. *Family Process, 50*, 314–336. http://dx.doi.org/10.1111/j.1545-5300.2011.01361.x

Pinsof, W. M. (1988). The therapist–client relationship: An integrative systems perspective. *Journal of Integrative & Eclectic Psychotherapy, 7*, 303–313.

Pinsof, W. M., (1994). An integrative systems perspective on the therapeutic alliance: Theoretical, clinical, and research implications. In A. O. Horvath & L. S. Greenberg (Eds.), *The working alliance: Theory, research, and practice* (pp. 173–195). Oxford, England: Wiley.

Pinsof, W. M. (2005). Integrative problem-centered therapy. In J. C. Norcross & M. R. Goldfried (Eds.), *Handbook of psychotherapy integration* (2nd ed., pp. 382–402). New York, NY: Oxford University Press.

Pinsof, W. M. (2017). The Systemic Therapy Inventory of Change—STIC: A multi-systemic and multi-dimensional system to integrate science into psychotherapeutic practice. In T. Tilden & B. E. Wampold (Eds.), *Routine outcome monitoring in couple and family therapy: The empirically informed therapist* (pp. 85–101). Cham, Switzerland: Springer. http://dx.doi.org/10.1007/978-3-319-50675-3_5

Pinsof, W. M., Breunlin, D. C., Chambers, A. L., Solomon, A. H., & Russell, W. P. (2015). Integrative problem-centered metaframeworks approach. In A. S. Gurman, J. L. Lebow, & D. K. Snyder (Eds.), *Clinical handbook of couple therapy* (5th ed., pp. 161–191). New York, NY: Guilford Press.

Pinsof, W. M., Breunlin, D. C., Russell, W. P., Lebow, J., Rampage, C., & Chambers, A. L. (2018). *Integrative systemic therapy: Metaframeworks for problem solving with individuals, couples, and families.* Washington, DC: American Psychological Association. http://dx.doi.org/10.1037/0000055-000

Pinsof, W. M., Zinbarg, R., & Knobloch-Fedders, L. M. (2008). Factorial and construct validity of the revised short form integrative psychotherapy alliance scales for family, couple, and individual therapy. *Family Process, 47*, 281–301. http://dx.doi.org/10.1111/j.1545-5300.2008.00254.x

Poladian, A. R., Rossi, F. S., Rudd, B. N., & Holtzworth-Munroe, A. (2017). Family mediation for divorce and parental separation. In J. Fitzgerald (Ed.), *Foundations for couples' therapy: Research for the real world* (pp. 79–87). New York, NY: Routledge/Taylor & Francis Group.

Prochaska, J. M., & Prochaska, J. O. (2014). A stage approach to enhancing adherence to treatment. In D. I. Mostofsky (Ed.), *The handbook of behavioral medicine* (pp. 58–76). Malden, MA: Wiley Blackwell. http://dx.doi.org/10.1002/9781118453940.ch4

Pruett, M. K., Cowan, C. P., Cowan, P. A., Pradhan, L., Robins, S., & Pruett, K. D. (2016). Supporting father involvement in the context of separation and divorce. In L. Drozd, M. Saini, & N. Olesen (Eds.), *Parenting plan evaluations: Applied research for the family court* (pp. 85–117). New York, NY: Oxford University Press.

Pruett, M. K., McIntosh, J. E., & Kelly, J. B. (2014). Parental separation and overnight care of young children, Part I: Consensus through theoretical and empirical integration. *Family Court Review, 52,* 240–245. http://dx.doi.org/10.1111/fcre.12087

Raffel, L. (1999). *Should I stay or go? How controlled separation (CS) can save your marriage.* Lincolnwood, IL: Contemporary Books.

Reilly, P. M., & Shopshire, M. S. (2015). *Anger management for substance abuse and mental health clients: A cognitive behavioral therapy manual.* Rockville, MD: U.S. Department of Health and Human Services, Substance Abuse and Mental Health Services Administration, Center for Substance Abuse Treatment.

Ricci, I. (2012). *The coparenting toolkit: The inspiring new update for mom's house, dad's house.* San Ramon, CA: Custody and CoParenting Solutions.

Riss, S., & Sockwell, J. (2016). *The optimist's guide to divorce: How to get through your breakup and create a new life you love.* New York, NY: Workman.

Rober, P. (2017). Addressing the person of the therapist in supervision: The therapist's inner conversation method. *Family Process, 56,* 487–500. http://dx.doi.org/10.1111/famp.12220

Roddy, M. K., Nowlan, K. M., Doss, B. D., & Christensen, A. (2016). Integrative behavioral couple therapy: Theoretical background, empirical research, and dissemination. *Family Process, 55,* 408–422. http://dx.doi.org/10.1111/famp.12223

Rogers, C. R. (1951). *Client-centered therapy, its current practice, implications, and theory.* Boston, MA: Houghton Mifflin.

Rolland, J. S. (1994). In sickness and in health: The impact of illness on couples' relationships. *Journal of Marital and Family Therapy, 20,* 327–347. http://dx.doi.org/10.1111/j.1752-0606.1994.tb00125.x

Rossi, F. S., Holtzworth-Munroe, A., & Rudd, B. N. (2016). Intimate partner violence and child custody. In L. Drozd, M. Saini, & N. Olesen (Eds.), *Parenting plan evaluations: Applied research for the family court* (pp. 346–373). New York, NY: Oxford University Press. http://dx.doi.org/10.1093/med:psych/9780199396580.003.0012

Rothchild, S. (2010). *How to get divorced by 30: My misguided attempt at a starter marriage.* New York, NY: Plume.

Rowen, J., & Emery, R. (2014). Examining parental denigration behaviors of co-parents as reported by young adults and their association with parent–child closeness. *Couple and Family Psychology: Research and Practice, 3*, 165–177.

Rubin, J. (2002). *My mom and dad don't live together anymore.* Washington, DC: Magination Press.

Rudd, B. N., Ogle, R. K., Holtzworth-Munroe, A., Applegate, A. G., & D'Onofrio, B. M. (2015). Child-informed mediation study follow-up: Comparing the frequency of relitigation following different types of family mediation. *Psychology, Public Policy, and Law, 21*, 452–457. http://dx.doi.org/10.1037/law0000046

Sager, C. J. (1976). *Marriage contracts and couple therapy: Hidden forces in intimate relationships.* New York, NY: Brunner/Mazel.

Saini, M., Johnston, J. R., Fidler, B. J., & Bala, N. (2012). Empirical studies of alienation. In K. Kuehnle & L. Drozd (Eds.), *Parenting plan evaluations: Applied research for the family court* (pp. 399–441). New York, NY: Oxford University Press.

Saini, M., Johnston, J. R., Fidler, B. J., & Bala, N. (2016). Empirical studies of alienation. In L. Drozd, M. Saini, & N. Olesen (Eds.), *Parenting plan evaluations: Applied research for the family court* (2nd ed., pp. 374–430). New York, NY: Oxford University Press.

Saini, M., Drozd, L. M., & Olesen, N. W. (2017). Adaptive and maladaptive gatekeeping behaviors and attitudes: Implications for child outcomes after separation and divorce. *Family Court Review, 55*, 260–272. http://dx.doi.org/10.1111/fcre.12276

Sandler, I., Wolchik, S., Berkel, C., Jones, S., Mauricio, A., Tein, J.-Y., & Winslow, E. (2017). Effectiveness trial of the new beginnings program for divorcing parents: Translation from an experimental prototype to an evidence-based community service. In M. Israelashvili & J. L. Romano (Eds.), *Cambridge handbooks in psychology.* New York, NY: Cambridge University Press. http://dx.doi.org/10.1017/9781316104453.006

Sandler, I. N., Knox, P., & Braver, S. L. (2012). Collaboration of prevention science and the family court. *Administration and Policy in Mental Health and Mental Health Services Research, 39*, 291–300. http://dx.doi.org/10.1007/s10488-011-0367-7

Sanford, K., & Rivers, A. S. (2017). The Parting Parent Concern Inventory: Parents' appraisals correlate with divorced family functioning. *Journal of Family Psychology, 31*, 867–877. http://dx.doi.org/10.1037/fam0000340

Sbarra, D. A., Emery, R. E., Beam, C. R., & Ocker, B. L. (2014). Marital dissolution and major depression in midlife: A propensity score analysis. *Clinical Psychological Science, 2*, 249–257. http://dx.doi.org/10.1177/2167702613498727

Scheinkman, M., & Fishbane, M. D. (2004). The vulnerability cycle: Working with impasses in couple therapy. *Family Process, 43*, 279–299. http://dx.doi.org/10.1111/j.1545-5300.2004.00023.x

Schoen, R., & Canudas-Romo, V. (2006). Timing effects on divorce: 20th century experience in the United States. *Journal of Marriage and Family, 68*, 749–758. http://dx.doi.org/10.1111/j.1741-3737.2006.00287.x

Senko, L. M. (2017). What do the children have to say? Children's perceptions of the Children of Divorce Intervention Program. *Dissertation Abstracts International Section A: Humanities and Social Sciences, 78*(3-A(E)).

Sexton, T., Gordon, K. C., Gurman, A., Lebow, J., Holtzworth-Munroe, A., & Johnson, S. (2011). Guidelines for classifying evidence-based treatments in couple and family therapy. *Family Process, 50*, 377–392. http://dx.doi.org/10.1111/j.1545-5300.2011.01363.x

Sharma, A. (2015). Divorce/separation in later-life: A fixed effects analysis of economic well-being by gender. *Journal of Family and Economic Issues, 36*, 299–306. http://dx.doi.org/10.1007/s10834-014-9432-1

Siegel, J. P. (2010). A good-enough therapy: An object relations approach. In A. S. Gurman (Ed.), *Clinical casebook of couple therapy* (pp. 134–152). New York, NY: Guilford Press.

Sigal, A., Sandler, I., Wolchik, S., & Braver, S. (2011). Do parent education programs promote healthy postdivorce parenting? Critical distinctions and a review of the evidence. *Family Court Review, 49*, 120–139. http://dx.doi.org/10.1111/j.1744-1617.2010.01357.x

Smith, M. L., & Glass, G. V. (1979). Meta-analysis of psychotherapy outcome studies. In C. A. Kiesler, N. A. Cummings, & G. R. VandenBos (Eds.), *Psychology and national health insurance: A sourcebook* (pp. 530–539). Washington, DC: American Psychological Association.

Smyth, B. M., McIntosh, J. E., Emery, R. E., & Howarth, S. L. H. (2016). Shared-time parenting: Evaluating the evidence of risks and benefits to children. In L. Drozd, M. Saini, & N. Olesen (Eds.), *Parenting plan evaluations: Applied research for the family court* (pp. 118–169). New York, NY: Oxford University Press.

Speck, R. V., & Attneave, C. L. (1974). *Family networks.* New York, NY: Vintage Books.

Sprenkle, D. H., Davis, S. D., & Lebow, J. L. (2009). *Common factors in couple and family therapy: The overlooked foundation for effective practice.* New York, NY: Guilford Press.

Stallman, H. M., & Sanders, M. R. (2014). A randomized controlled trial of Family Transitions Triple P: A group-administered parenting program to minimize the adverse effects of parental divorce on children. *Journal of Divorce & Remarriage, 55*, 33–48. http://dx.doi.org/10.1080/10502556.2013.862091

Stanley, S. M., Markman, H. J., & Blumberg, S. L. (1997). The speaker/listener technique. *The Family Journal, 5*, 82–83.

Stanton, M., & Welsh, R. (2011). *Specialty competencies in couple and family psychology.* New York, NY: Oxford University Press. http://dx.doi.org/10.1093/med:psych/9780195387872.001.0001

Steinbach, A. (2018). Children's and parents' well-being in joint physical custody: A literature review. *Family Process*. Advance online publication. http://dx.doi.org/10.1111/famp.12372

Stith, S. M., & McCollum, E. E. (2009). Couples treatment for psychological and physical aggression. In K. D. O'Leary & E. M. Woodin (Eds.), *Psychological and physical aggression in couples: Causes and interventions* (pp. 233–250). Washington, DC: American Psychological Association. http://dx.doi.org/10.1037/11880-011

Straus, M. A. (1979). Measuring intrafamily conflict and violence: The Conflict Tactics (CT) Scales. *Journal of Marriage and the Family, 41*, 75–88. http://dx.doi.org/10.2307/351733

Straus, M. A. (2004). Cross-cultural reliability and validity of the Revised Conflict Tactics Scales: A study of University Student Dating Couples in 17 Nations. *Cross-Cultural Research: The Journal of Comparative Social Science, 38*, 407–432. http://dx.doi.org/10.1177/1069397104269543

Szigethy, E., Weisz, J. R., & Findling, R. L. (2012). *Cognitive-behavior therapy for children and adolescents*. Arlington, VA: American Psychiatric Publishing. http://dx.doi.org/10.1176/appi.books.9781615370955

Templer, K., Matthewson, M., Haines, J., & Cox, G. (2017). Recommendations for best practice in response to parental alienation: Findings from a systematic review. *Journal of Family Therapy, 39*, 103–122. http://dx.doi.org/10.1111/1467-6427.12137

Tesler, P. H., & Thompson, P. (2006). *Collaborative divorce: The revolutionary new way to restructure your family, resolve legal issues, and move on with your life*. New York, NY: Regan Books.

Tilden, T., & Wampold, B. E. (Eds.). (2017). *Routine outcome monitoring in couple and family therapy: The empirically informed therapist*. Cham, Switzerland: Springer. http://dx.doi.org/10.1007/978-3-319-50675-3

Tumin, D., Han, S., & Qian, Z. (2015). Estimates and meanings of marital separation. *Journal of Marriage and Family, 77*, 312–322.

Waller, M. R. (2012). Cooperation, conflict, or disengagement? Coparenting styles and father involvement in fragile families. *Family Process, 51*, 325–342. http://dx.doi.org/10.1111/j.1545-5300.2012.01403.x

Wallerstein, J. S. (1991). The long-term effects of divorce on children: A review. *Journal of the American Academy of Child & Adolescent Psychiatry, 30*, 349–360. http://dx.doi.org/10.1097/00004583-199105000-00001

Wallerstein, J. S. (1998). Children of divorce: A society in search of policy. In M. A. Mason, A. Skolnick, & S. D. Sugarman (Eds.), *All our families: New policies for a new century* (pp. 66 94). New York, NY: Oxford University Press. http://dx.doi.org/10.1007/978-1-4684-7021-5_2

Wallerstein, J. S. (2005). Growing up in the divorced family. *Clinical Social Work Journal, 33*, 401–418. http://dx.doi.org/10.1007/s10615-005-7034-y

Wallerstein, J. S., Corbin, S. B., & Lewis, J. M. (1988). Children of divorce: A 10-year study. In E. M. Hetherington & J. D. Arasteh (Eds.), *Impact of divorce, single parenting, and stepparenting on children* (pp. 197–214). Hillsdale, NJ: Erlbaum.

Wallerstein, J. S., & Kelly, J. B. (1974). The effects of parental divorce: The adolescent experience. In E. J. Anthony & C. Koupernik (Eds.), *The child in his family: Children at psychiatric risk*. Oxford, England: Wiley.

Wallerstein, J. S., & Kelly, J. B. (1975). The effects of parental divorce. Experiences of the preschool child. *Journal of the American Academy of Child Psychiatry, 14,* 600–616. http://dx.doi.org/10.1016/S0002-7138(09)61460-6

Wallerstein, J. S., & Kelly, J. B. (1976). The effects of parental divorce: Experiences of the child in later latency. *American Journal of Orthopsychiatry, 46,* 256–269. http://dx.doi.org/10.1111/j.1939-0025.1976.tb00926.x

Wallerstein, J. S., & Kelly, J. B. (1980). *Surviving the breakup: How children and parents cope with divorce.* New York, NY: Basic Books.

Wallerstein, J. S., & Lewis, J. M. (2004). The unexpected legacy of divorce: Report of a 25-year study. *Psychoanalytic Psychology, 21,* 353–370. http://dx.doi.org/10.1037/0736-9735.21.3.353

Wallerstein, J. S., Lewis, J., & Blakeslee, S. (2000). *The unexpected legacy of divorce: A 25-year landmark study.* New York, NY: Hyperion.

Walsh, F. (2006). *Strengthening family resilience* (2nd ed.). New York, NY: Guilford Press.

Walsh, F. (Ed.). (2009). *Spiritual resources in family therapy* (2nd ed.). New York, NY: Guilford Press.

Walsh, F. (2012). *Normal family processes: Growing diversity and complexity* (4th ed.). New York, NY: Guilford Press. http://dx.doi.org/10.4324/9780203428436

Wampold, B. E. (2015). Routine outcome monitoring: Coming of age—With the usual developmental challenges. *Psychotherapy, 52,* 458–462. http://dx.doi.org/10.1037/pst0000037

Wampold, B. E., & Imel, Z. E. (2015). *The great psychotherapy debate: The evidence for what makes psychotherapy work* (2nd ed.). New York, NY: Routledge/Taylor & Francis.

Wang, H., & Amato, P. R. (2000). Predictors of divorce adjustment: Stressors, resources, and definitions. *Journal of Marriage and the Family, 62,* 655–668. http://dx.doi.org/10.1111/j.1741-3737.2000.00655.x

Wanlass, J., & Scharff, D. E. (2016). Psychodynamic approaches to couple and family therapy. In T. L. Sexton & J. Lebow (Eds.), *Handbook of family therapy* (pp. 134–148). New York, NY: Routledge/Taylor & Francis.

Warshak, R. A. (2010). Family bridges: Using insights from social science to reconnect parents and alienated children. *Family Court Review, 48,* 48–80. http://dx.doi.org/10.1111/j.1744-1617.2009.01288.x

Warshak, R. A. (2015). Ten parental alienation fallacies that compromise decisions in court and in therapy. *Professional Psychology: Research and Practice, 46,* 235–249. http://dx.doi.org/10.1037/pro0000031

Watzlawick, P., Bavelas, J. B., & Jackson, D. D. (2011). *Pragmatics of human communication: A study of interactional patterns, pathologies, and paradoxes.* New York, NY: Norton.

Webb, E. J., Campbell, D. T., Schwartz, R. D., & Sechrest, L. (1966). *Unobtrusive measures: Nonreactive research in the social sciences.* Oxford, England: Rand-McNally.

Weiner-Davis, M. (1992). *Divorce busting: A revolutionary and rapid program for staying together.* New York, NY: Summit Books.

Weingarten, K. (2010). Reasonable hope: Construct, clinical applications, and supports. *Family Process, 49,* 5–25. http://dx.doi.org/10.1111/j.1545-5300.2010.01305.x

Weingarten, K. (2012). Sorrow: A therapist's reflection on the inevitable and the unknowable. *Family Process, 51,* 440–455. http://dx.doi.org/10.1111/j.1545-5300.2012.01412.x

Weingarten, K. (2015). The art of reflection: Turning the strange into the familiar. *Family Process, 55,* 195–210. http://dx.doi.org/10.1111/famp.12158

Weiss, R. L., & Cerreto, M. C. (1980). The Marital Status Inventory: Development of a measure of dissolution potential. *American Journal of Family Therapy, 8,* 80–85. http://dx.doi.org/10.1080/01926188008250358

Weitzman, L. J., Dixon, R. B., Arendell, T., Krantz, S. E., Riessman, C. K., Ahrons, C. R., & Rodgers, R. H. (1992). Divorce and remarriage. In A. S. Skolnick & J. H. Skolnick (Eds.), *Family in transition: Rethinking marriage, sexuality, child rearing, and family organization* (7th ed., pp. 217–289). New York, NY: HarperCollins.

Wilde, J. L., & Doherty, W. J. (2013). Outcomes of an intensive couple relationship education program with fragile families. *Family Process, 52,* 455–464. http://dx.doi.org/10.1111/famp.12012

Winslow, E. B., Braver, S., Cialdini, R., Sandler, I., Betkowski, J., Tein, J.-Y., . . . Lopez, M. (2017, April 25). Video-based approach to engaging parents into a preventive parenting intervention for divorcing families: Results of a randomized controlled trial. *Prevention Science.* Advance online publication. http://dx.doi.org/10.1007/s11121-017-0791-3

Wolchik, S. A., Sandler, I. N., Jones, S., Gonzales, N., Doyle, K., Winslow, E., . . . Braver, S. L. (2009). The new beginnings program for divorcing and separating families: Moving from efficacy to effectiveness. *Family Court Review, 47,* 416–435. http://dx.doi.org/10.1111/j.1744-1617.2009.01265.x

Wolchik, S. A., Tein, J.-Y., Sandler, I. N., & Kim, H.-J. (2016). Developmental cascade models of a parenting-focused program for divorced families on mental health problems and substance use in emerging adulthood. *Development and Psychopathology, 28,* 869–888. http://dx.doi.org/10.1017/S0954579416000365

Young, J. E. (1990). *Cognitive therapy for personality disorders: A schema-focused approach.* Sarasota, FL: Professional Resource Exchange.

Young, J. E., Klosko, J. S., & Weishaar, M. E. (2003). *Schema therapy: A practitioner's guide.* New York, NY: Guilford Press.

INDEX

Abandonment, 73, 209
Abusive parents, 115, 119. *See also*
    Relational violence
Acceptance
    failure to accept divorce, 214–215
    as goal of therapy, 122–123
    in high-conflict case study, 266
    radical, 148, 155, 223, 249–250
    in therapy in difficult divorce, 34
    treatment strategies to improve,
        145, 146
Acceptance and commitment therapy,
    148
Acceptance strategies, 192. *See also*
    Radical acceptance strategies
Access to information, 90–91
Acrimony, 22–23, 173, 191
Action stage of change, 118
Adolescents, 43, 98, 174
Adversarial processes, judicial, 166,
    173, 180
Affairs, extramarital, 212–214
Affordability, of therapy, 99
Age, divorce rate and, 37
Ahrons, C. R., 42, 43, 53–54, 63,
    142, 248
Alienating behaviors, parental,
    202n3, 205
Alienation, 6, 28, 201–209
Alliance ruptures, 104–106
Alliances. *See also* Therapeutic alliance
    between court and therapist,
        176–177
    between disengaged children, 206
    multipartial, 105, 213, 242
    other–therapist, 107–108
    parent–child, 30
    self–therapist, 107
    within-client, 104
    within-system, 108
Alternative dispute resolution, 174, 175
Amato, P. R., 40, 41, 43, 46, 49 50, 255
Ambivalence, about divorce, 121–122
American Psychiatric Association
    (APA), 202

American Psychological Association
    (APA), 187
Anger issues, 146–147, 194, 249
Anger management skills training,
    146–148, 194, 197, 249
Angry Associates, 53, 54
Anxiety, 199, 272–273
ApA (American Psychiatric
    Association), 202
APA (American Psychological
    Association), 187
Arbitration, 176, 185
Assessments
    and child custody evaluations,
        110–112
    of danger, 114–115
    in high-conflict case study, 265–268
    in integrative treatment model in
        difficult divorce, 109–118
    multilevel, 115–118, 265
    in new partner case example,
        276–277
    in normative divorce cases, 243
    of problem in focus, 112–113
    of relational-problem severity, 115
    of therapeutic progress, 160–161
Association of Family and Conciliation
    Courts, 187
Attachment, 108, 118, 127, 159
Attorneys
    ability to pay for, 48–49, 174
    in "better" divorce, 31
    for children, 172, 179, 181
    collaboration of therapists with,
        179–183
    communication between therapists
        and, 85
    conflict encouraged by, 167, 172
    in difficult divorce, 23, 33
    and divorce therapy, 167
    for divorcing partners, 180, 181
    interactions of therapists and,
        176–183
    leverage from, in therapy, 178–179
    in mediation, 175

Attorneys, *continued*
    negative attributions by, 166
    relationships of therapists with,
        177–178
    roles of, in judicial system, 172–173
    sharing information with, 101
Avoidance, 124, 201

Balance, in systemic perspective, 90–91
Beck, A. T., 82, 117
Behavior(s)
    alienating, 202n3, 205
    in biopsychosocial model of
        assessment, 116–117
    challenging of clients', 255
    conflict-provoking, 70
    denigrating, 202n2
    divorce-related issues with, 32, 44–46
    and inclination to divorce, 70
    negative, 139
    negative attributions of, 149–150, 166
    of new partners, 25
    nonverbal, 117. *See also*
        "Four Horsemen" of divorce
    parent rejecting, 202n2
    psychoeducation about, 132
    troubling, 192–193
Behavioral experiments, 201, 247
Behavioral plans, 247
Behavioral strategies, 138–140, 247
Behavior change
    alliance and promotion of, 107
    as goal of therapy, 122–123
    in new partner case example, 277–278
    treatment strategies encouraging,
        138–145, 155, 247–248
Best expert, client as, 93
Best interests of child
    in child custody conflicts, 193
    goal-setting related to, 125
    in judicial system, 166, 173
    psychoeducation about, 133, 135
    in typology of divorcing partnerships,
        54
Better divorce, 30–31
Bias, 111, 233–234
Biological treatment strategies,
    153–154, 252
Biopsychosocial model of assessment,
    115–118

Black and white thinking, 82
Blame, 30, 134, 202, 203
Boszormenyi-Nagy, I., 105
Boundary violations, 19–20
Bowen, M., 18, 151
Brief therapies, for treating parental
    alienation, 203
Broad treatment strategies
    for difficult divorce cases, 130–138
    guaranteeing safety, 130–131
    motivational interviewing, 137–138
    for normative divorce cases, 244–246
    psychoeducation, 132–135
    solution-oriented focus in, 136–137
    and state of change, 137–138
    witnessing, 131
Brown, L. K., 135
Brown, M. T., 135
Buchanan, Christine, 43
Burnout, preventing, 231–232

Calming of conflict, 125, 128
Case formulation
    and assessment, 111
    for divorce due to marital infidelity,
        213–214
    for families in chaos, 218
    for families in normative divorce, 243
    in high-conflict case study, 267–268
    in integrative treatment model,
        121–127
    for treating parental alienation,
        203–204
    and treatment strategy selection,
        154–155
Catastrophizing, 117, 250
Change
    paths to, 9–10, 34
    resistance to, 161–162
    stage of. *See* Stage of change
Chaotic families, 218
Child custody and visitation
    in difficult divorce, 33
    in divorce, 54
    and financial negotiations, 49
    in high-conflict case study, 270–271
    in joint parenting agreement, 168
    judicial decisions on, 170
    mediation of conflicts over, 78
    setting goals related to, 123

as source of conflict, 46–47
treatment strategies for conflicts
    over, 190–194
trends in, 37
Child custody evaluations
assessments in therapy vs., 110–112
confidentiality in, 100–101
coordination on, 184–185
therapist as treating expert in, 182
Childless couples
communication for, 142
divorce for, 63, 124
treatment strategies for, 217–218
Child problems, 113, 158, 215, 217
Children
acceptance of parents' divorce by, 215
best interests of, 54, 125, 133, 135,
    166, 173, 193
in better divorce, 30
boundaries between parental conflict
    and, 19–20
in difficult divorce, 6–7, 33, 86–87
disengagement between parent and,
    201–209
effects of divorce on, 42–47
in high-conflict families, 195–196
initial meetings with, 264
judicial system contact for, 166
in mediations, 78
parent–child difficulties, 27–28
with psychopathology, 45, 215, 217
reactions of, to divorce, 132–133
as reluctant clients, 222
with special difficulties, 28–29, 143
talking to, about divorce, 133–134
therapy with. See Child therapy
time with, conflicts over, 190–194,
    274
triangulation of, 18–19
Children of Divorce program, 76
Child therapy
in cases involving marital infidelity,
    214
in high-conflict case study, 272
in individual sessions, 81, 158–159,
    255–256
in normative divorce cases,
    241–242, 253
prevention programs, 76
psychoeducation, 134–135

resolving child custody conflicts in,
    193
risks of, in difficult divorce, 88
sessions involving one parent and
    children, 253
in treatment of parental alienation,
    204, 206
Classical conditioning, 138, 139
Client privilege, 103
Clients, adaptations of therapists to,
    233–236
Clinical Outcomes in Routine
    Evaluation, 161
Coaches, in collaborative divorce, 80
Cognitions, relational functioning and,
    148–149
Cognitive behavior therapy, 194–195
Cognitive distortions, 117, 250
Cognitive strategies, 148–150, 155
Cohabitating units, partings in, 38
Collaboration
in goal-setting, 125–126
in normative divorce cases, 239,
    241, 244
of therapists, court, and attorneys,
    179–183
during treatment, 127–128
Collaborative divorce, 80
Commitment level, 50–51, 71
Common factors, 81, 84, 109
Communication
assessing level of, 112, 117
with attorneys, 85, 179–181
in better divorce, 30
with court, 177, 179–181
in difficult divorce cases, 21–22,
    29–30, 155
establishing methods of, 141–144
for families residing in the same
    house, 197
goal-setting related to, 123
in high-conflict families, 195,
    270–271
in new partner case example, 278–279
in normative divorce cases, 82,
    247–248
with parenting coordinators, 176
rule-governed, 141–144, 247–248
treatment strategies for improving,
    155, 247–248

Compassion fatigue, 231
Competence
    of parents, 113, 210
    of therapists, 89, 119
Confidentiality, 78, 100–102, 104
Conflict de-escalation, 268–269
Conflict-provoking behavior, 70
Conflict resolution, 190, 191
Conflicts. *See also* High-conflict
        families
    adapting treatment strategies to
        deal with, 190–200
    attorney's encouragement of,
        167, 172
    in better divorce, 31
    calming of, 125, 128
    in difficult divorce, 6
    emotional dysregulation and, 17
    goal, 122
    internal, examining, 251–252
    less-conflictual difficult divorce,
        29–30
    between parents, 18–20, 46–47
Conflict Tactics Scale–Revised, 114
Conjoint therapy sessions
    considerations with, 157, 158
    for families with history of relational
        violence, 131, 199
    in high-conflict case study, 268–271,
        273–274
    marital, 65
    in normative divorce cases, 254–255
    for parents with no history of
        coparenting, 210
    sharing of emotion in, 151
    therapeutic alliance in, 106–107
    in treatment of parental alienation,
        206
Consciousness raising, 205
Conscious uncoupling, 42
Consent, in therapeutic contract, 96
Contemplation stage of change, 69,
        118, 246
Contempt, 23
Contract, therapeutic, 11, 96–104, 240
Control, scheduling as means to exert,
        235
Control groups, 43
Cooperation, with new partners, 25
Cooperative Colleagues, 53–54, 248

Coordination
    establishing methods of, 141–144
    in normative divorce cases,
        247–248, 256
    between therapists, 257
    of therapist with other helping
        professionals, 183–187
Coparenting
    assessments for, 111
    for children with psychopathology,
        217
    conjoint sessions with
        ex-partners on, 157
    in difficult divorce, 21
    families without a history of,
        209–211
    goal-setting related to, 124
    in partings other than divorce, 38
Coping skills, 82, 147, 252
Cotherapy, 89
Countertransference, 64, 74, 86, 230–231
Couple therapy, 58–68
    acceptance and behavioral change
        in, 123
    approaching topic of divorce in,
        60–62
    assessment of inclination for
        divorce in, 69
    decision to divorce as aspect of, 58
    defining, 58–59
    evaluating outcome of divorce in,
        59–60
    personal values of therapist in,
        62–65
    process for considering divorce in,
        65–68
    risks of, in difficult divorce, 87
    therapeutic alliance in, 104
    transition to individual treatment
        from, 73–74
Court. *See also* Judges
    alliances between therapist and,
        176–177
    collaboration of therapist with,
        179–183
    familiarity with procedures of,
        177–178
    interactions of therapists and,
        176–183
    leverage from, in therapy, 178–179

Court-involved cases
    assessments in, 112–114
    child custody disputes in, 168
    confidentiality in, 100
    ending of therapy in, 163
    expectations about therapist
        participation in, 183
    learning procedures for, 177
    leverage from court and
        attorneys in, 178
    postdivorce divorce issues in, 220
    process for, 170–172
    stressors in, 166
    therapeutic alliance in, 108
    therapeutic contract for, 96, 99
Court-mandated treatment, 178
Covert triangulation, 19
Creative Divorce (Krantzler &
    Krantzler), 62–63
Crisis management, 235–236
Cross-cultural intermarriages, 53
Culture(s)
    adapting to clients of other, 233–234
    and experience of divorce, 50, 52–53
    of judicial system, 177
Custody, defined, 168
Cutoffs of positive contact
    assessing, 112–113
    and communication, 21–22
    in difficult divorce, 3, 6, 21–22
    goal-setting related to, 123
    and parent–child difficulties, 28
    treatment strategies for alleviating,
        201
    withdrawal of parent as cause of,
        211–212

Danger, 114–115, 119
Decision making
    about divorce, 57, 58
    about taking difficult divorce case,
        119–120
Decisiveness, 228
Delivery, of psychoeducation, 135
Demand–withdraw patterns
    in difficult divorce, 22
    in families with child custody
        conflicts, 190
    in high-conflict families, 194
    treatment strategies for dealing with,
        196–197

Demonization of others, 83
Denigrating behaviors, 202n2
Denton, K. M., 135
Depositions, 170
Depression, 44
Detection of Overall Risk Screen, 114
Developmental approach, 92, 159
Developmental process, divorce as,
    47–54
Developmental tasks, 20, 30
Diagnostic and Statistical Manual of
    Mental Disorders, Fifth Edition
    (ApA), 202
Dialectical behavior therapy, 195
Difficult divorce, 13–34. See also
    Integrative treatment model in
    difficult divorce
    better divorce as alternative to,
        30–31
    characteristics of, 16–30
    and characteristics of marriage, 6
    competent practice in, 89
    defining, 5–7
    framework for therapy in, 31–34
    helping clients get unstuck in, 32
    implications of, for therapists,
        14–18
    importance of systemic perspective
        in, 90–91
    individual therapy with clients in,
        67–68
    interventions with families in, 76–80
    mediation and, 79
    normative vs., 5–6, 17, 238
    prevalence of, 4
    preventing slide from normative
        divorce to, 240, 255
    and risks of therapy, 84–86
    risks of therapy in, 84–89
    treatment strategies in. See
        Treatment strategies in
        difficult divorce
Dinosaurs Divorce (Brown & Brown),
    135
Discernment counseling
    considering, in couple therapy,
        61–62, 66
    defining, 59
    goals of, 121–122
    in individual therapy, 66

Discovery, in judicial process, 169, 170
Disengagement
    adapting treatment strategies for
        level of, 200–212
    extreme, 200–201
    improving disengagement skills,
        146–148, 249
    and parental alienation, 201–209
    for parents with no history of
        coparenting, 209–211
    and withdrawal of a parent after
        divorce, 211–212
Disequilibrium, feelings of, 132
Dissolved Duos, 53, 54
Divorce, 35–55. *See also* Difficult
        divorce; "Four Horsemen" of
        divorce; Normative divorce
    across life cycle, 51–52
    approaching, as couple therapy topic,
        60–62
    assessing inclination for, 61, 68–71
    better, 30–31
    change in societal views of, 41–42
    child arrangements in, 54
    collaborative, 80
    complexity of therapy with
        couples in, 13–14
    conflict between parents in, 46–47
    considering, in couple therapy,
        65–68
    cultural variation in, 52–53
    demography of, 35–39
    as developmental process, 47–54
    developmental transitions in, 24
    "easy," 5
    emotional/behavioral issues
        related to, 44–46
    evaluating outcome of, 59–60
    expectations about, 31n1
    failure to accept, 214–215
    financial ramifications of, 48–49
    gender differences in, 52
    impact of, on family members, 42–47
    individual differences in, 49–51
    in LGBTQ relationships, 39
    meaning of, 10, 69
    partings other than, 38
    prevalence of, 35–37
    as process, 7, 57
    in psychotherapy, 57–74

reasons for, 39–41
and remarriage, 38–39
in second marriages, 221–222
separation vs., 71–72
social science research on, 43–44, 62
and therapist's personal values, 62–65
withdrawal of parent after, 211–212
"Divorce busters," 62
Divorce decrees, 168, 171, 175
Divorce rates, 35–37
Divorce therapy
    considering, in couple therapy, 65
    defining, 59
    empirical studies on, 163–164
    exploring individual psycho-
        dynamics in, 152
    and judicial system, 166–167
    moving to, 73
    research on, 12
    seeking of, 75
    therapist for, 99–100
Divorcing families
    interventions with. *See* Interventions
        with divorcing families
    negative emotions in, 225–226
Divorcing partner(s)
    attorneys for, 180, 181
    failure to accept divorce by, 214–215
    as participants in therapy, 97–98
    partnership typology for, 42, 53–54
    transition from couple to individual
        treatment for, 73–74
Doherty, W. J., 59, 61, 62, 66, 69
Domestic terrorism, 83, 200
Dornbusch, Sanford, 43

Early experience, 118, 251–252
Early marriage, divorce in, 52, 63, 217
"Easy" divorces, 5, 16
Educational level, divorce rate and, 37
Emergency motions, 169
Emery, R. E., 43–44, 46, 78–79, 134,
        256, 259
Emotion(s)
    about former partners, 134
    in assessment of inclination for
        divorce, 68–69
    of children in normative divorce,
        255–256
    exploring underlying, 150–152, 251

negative, in divorcing families, 225–226
in normative divorce experience, 238, 255–256
psychoeducation about, 132, 134–135
secondary reactive, 251
Emotional issues, 44–46, 123
Emotional pain, 46, 212, 225–226
Emotional regulation
in better divorce, 30
biopsychosocial model of assessing, 118
in difficult divorce, 17
in families in normative divorce, 82
for high-conflict families, 194, 266–267
Emotion-focused therapy, 151, 155, 251
Empathy, 105, 227–228, 230
Empirical support, for treatment strategies, 163–164
Ending of therapy, 162–163, 193, 228
Engagement, in therapy, 65, 109, 222–223
Ethical issues, 103–104, 187, 213
Ethical Principles of Psychologists and Code of Conduct (APA), 187
Ethnicity, divorce rate and, 37
Ex-partners. *See* Former partners
Expertise, in difficult divorce work, 89, 119
Exposure strategies, 138, 139, 201, 204
Extended family members
adapting strategies to include, 218–219
in better divorce, 31
in difficult divorce, 23–24
as participants in therapy, 97, 159–160
Externalization, 40
External locus of control, 83
Extramarital affairs, 212–214
Extreme disengagement, 200–201
Extremity of problem, assessing, 115

Fairness, 90–91
Family Assessment Device, 161
Family law cases, 168–169, 172
Family members
in biopsychosocial model of assessment, 117

contribution of, to problem in focus, 115
impact of divorce on, 42–47
information sharing by, 101–102
negotiating treatment goals between, 124–125
therapy in difficult divorce for, 32
Family-of-origin issues, 118, 252
Family sessions, 156, 253
Family structures
in better divorce, 30
lack of agreement on, 190–192
systemic strategies for improving, 140–141
uncertainty in, 17–18
Family subsystems
in biopsychosocial model of assessment, 116
integrative model for, 8, 92
referrals of, 120
therapy with, 156
Family system
adapting treatment strategy to, 217–219
meaning of divorce in, 69
therapy with, 97, 156, 253
Family systems-based therapy, 7–8
Family therapy
for families in normative divorce, 241–242
for families with history of relational violence, 199–200
in new partner case example, 278
risks of, in difficult divorce, 87–89
therapeutic alliance in, 104, 107
Fathers, prevention programs for, 77
Feedback, on therapy, 160–161
Feelings. *See* Emotion(s)
Fiery Foes, 53, 54
Financial issues, 33, 48–49
Financial means, difficulty of divorce and, 48–49
Finkel, E. J., 212
Follow-up plans, 163
Former partners
conjoint sessions with. *See* Conjoint therapy sessions
connections between, 47–48
feelings about, 134

"Four Horsemen" of divorce
   in assessment of inclination to
      divorce, 70
   in consideration of divorce, 65
   defining, 40
   discussing, in couple therapy, 60–61
   and exploring underlying emotion
      in therapy, 151
   in multilevel assessment, 117
Fragile families, 38

Gatekeeping parent, 33, 97–98
Gender-based bias, of therapists, 234
Gender differences, in divorce, 52
Goals
   of couple therapy, 58, 59
   for difficult divorce cases, 16
   divorce as treatment goal, 58
   mutually stated, 125–126
Goal-setting
   for collaboration with other mental
      health professionals, 186–187
   for families with child custody
      conflicts, 191
   for high-conflict families, 268
   in integrative treatment model,
      121–127
   in normative divorce cases, 244
   for treatment of parental alienation,
      204
   for treatment of postdivorce divorce
      issues, 219
Gottlieb, M. C., 187n12
Gottman, John, 23, 29, 32, 40, 65, 70,
   117, 151, 197
Gottman, Julie, 197
Gould, J. W., 101, 182, 184
Gould-Saltman, D. J., 187n12
Grandparents, effect of divorce on, 219
Greenberg, L. R., 101, 182, 184,
   187n12
Greenberg, Leslie S., 251
Guardians, attorneys as, 173

Haley, Jay, 19
Happiness
   postdivorce, 49–50
   unhappy marriages, 40, 45, 46, 50
Harris, S. M., 59, 61, 66
Hawkins, A. J., 41

Health Insurance Portability and
   Accountability Act (HIPAA),
   96, 104, 183
Helping professionals, coordination
   with other, 183–187
Heterosexual marriages, gender
   differences in experience of
   divorce after, 52
Hetherington, E. M., 134
Hetherington, Mavis, 4, 15, 43, 44, 132
High-conflict divorce
   anger management skills training in,
      146–147
   goal-setting for partners in, 124
   implications of, for therapists, 15
   individual therapy for children in,
      158–159
   risks of therapy in, 84
   toxic effects of, 75
High-conflict families
   adapting treatment strategies for,
      194–197
   difficult divorce for, 3, 6
   effects of divorce in, 45
High-conflict family case example,
   261–275
   assessment, 265–268
   background, 261–263
   early sessions, 268–273
   first meetings, 263–265
   further sessions, 273–275
Highly contested divorce cases, 169–172
HIPAA. *See* Health Insurance
   Portability and Accountability Act
Hohmann-Marriott, B., 41, 49–50
Homicide, in divorcing families, 26
Honesty, 20
Hopelessness, 230

Immigration status, divorce rate and, 37
Indirect patient system, 64, 83
Individual differences, in divorce, 49–51
Individual problems, difficult divorce
   and, 4
Individual psychodynamics, 152–153,
   251–252
Individual therapy
   with children, 81, 158–159, 255–256
   consideration of divorce as reason for
      seeking, 66–68

divorcing partners' transition to, 73–74

in families with history of relational violence, 199

in high-conflict families, 195, 270, 271

integrative model for, 92

in new partner case example, 277, 278

in normative divorce cases, 241–242, 254–256

other therapy formats vs., 157–158

risks of, in difficult divorce, 87

therapeutic alliance in, 107–108

in treatment of parental alienation, 204–205

Information sharing

about marital infidelity, 213

with child custody evaluators, 184

with court/attorneys, 180–181

in difficult divorce work, 90–91

with other mental health professionals, 186

Initiator. *See* Leaving partner

In-laws, 219

Integrative behavior couple therapy, 123, 148

Integrative Psychotherapy Alliance Scales, 105

Integrative systemic therapy (IST), 9, 91–92, 129, 152

Integrative therapy, 8–9

Integrative treatment model in difficult divorce. *See also* Treatment strategies in difficult divorce

adapting, for normative divorce, 238–244

assessments in, 109–118

case formulation and goal setting in, 121–127

common factors in, 109

deciding to take referred cases, 119–120

described, 91–94

empirical support for, 163–164

ending of therapy in, 162–163

extended family as participants in, 159–160

impasses and resistance in, 161–162

integrative systemic therapy vs., 91–92

progress assessments and feedback in, 160–161

structure of, 95–128

theoretical underpinnings of, 7–10

therapeutic alliance in, 104–109

therapeutic contract in, 96–104

therapy formats for, 156–159

treatment plan formulation, 127–128

and treatment strategies for psychopathology, 216

Interminable issues, 29

Internal conflicts, 251–252

Interventions with divorcing families, 75–94

collaborative divorce, 80

families in difficult divorces, 76–80

families in normative divorces, 80–84

integrative model of, 91–94

mediation, 77–79

parenting coordination, 79–80

prevention programs, 76–77

risks of therapy in difficult divorce, 84–89

systemic perspective in, 90–91

Intimate partner violence, 26

Intrafamilial violence, 25–26

Irreconcilable differences, 28–29

IST. *See* Integrative systemic therapy

Johnston, J. R., 23, 202, 203

Joint custody, 54, 168

Joint parenting agreements, 168, 171

Judges. *See also* Court

communication with, 179, 181

relationships of therapists and, 177

roles of, 168–169

Judicial process, 167–172

limitations of, 173–174

and role of judges, 168–169

steps in, 170–172

Judicial system, 165–183. *See also* Legal system

attorneys' roles in, 172–173

comfort with, 229

culture of psychotherapy vs., 177

divorce therapy and, 166–167

ethical and legal issues for therapists, 187

Judicial system, *continued*
   judges' roles in, 168–169
   limitations of process, 29, 173–174
   mediator's role in, 174–175
   parenting coordinator's role in,
      175–176
   processes in, 167–172
   therapists' interactions with court
      and attorneys, 176–183

Kelly, J. B., 42, 134, 202, 203
Kin-wars, 23–24
Krantzler, M., 62–63
Krantzler, P. B., 62–63

Late-emerging issues, 219–222
Late-life divorces, 52
Law, knowledge of, 187
Leaning-in partner, 61, 63, 121
Leaning-out partner, 61, 63–64
Leaving partner (initiator)
   experience of divorce for, 49, 50
   marital infidelity by, 212–213
Left partner, experience of divorce for,
   49
Legal action, 22–23, 31
Legal divorce, 53, 171
Legal system. *See also* Judicial system
   and conflict between parents, 46–47
   difficult divorce in, 4
   factors encouraging divorce in,
      36–37
   therapist's interactions with, 15, 16
Lesbian, gay, bisexual, transgender, or
   queer (LGBTQ) couples, 39, 235
Less-conflictual difficult divorce, 29–30
Levenson, R. W., 40
Leverage, from attorneys/court,
   178–179
LGBTQ couples, 39, 235
Life cycle of participants, divorce across,
   51–52
Life transitions, postdivorce, 47
Long-standing problems, 115
Loyalty, 24

Maccoby, Eleanor, 43
Maintenance stage of change, 69
Marital infidelity, 212–214
Marital Status Inventory, 70

Marital therapy, 99–100. *See also*
   Couple therapy
Marriage(s)
   difficult divorce and characteristics
      of, 6
   effect of individual therapy on,
      66–67
   expectations about, 41–42
   partners who will not accept end of,
      214–215
   perpetual issues of, 29
   prevalence of, 36
   separation in, 71–72
   "starter," 41
   unhappy, 40, 45, 46, 50
   Western views of, 212
Marriage counseling. *See* Couple therapy
Martin, Chris, 42
Masurel, C., 135
Maudsley therapy, 8
Maximization, 117
Mediation
   in difficult divorce, 77–79
   empirical studies of, 164
   negotiation in therapy vs., 144
   by parenting coordinators, 176
   as requirement of judicial system,
      169
Mediators, 77–78, 174–175
Men, experience of divorce for, 52
Mental health issues. *See also*
   Psychopathology
   assessing parental, 112
   difficult divorce and, 4, 5
   in divorcing families, 44
   for people in separation and divorce,
      16–17
Mental health professionals, 101,
   185–187
Mentalization, 152–153, 252
Midlife divorce, 51
Mindful practice
   in difficult divorce cases, 145–146
   in high-conflict case study, 266, 269
   implementation of, 155
   in normative divorce cases, 248–249
   in treatment of parental alienation,
      204
Minimization, 117
Minor child, legal definition of, 174

Minuchin, Salvatore, 18
Motivational interviewing
    in difficult divorce cases, 137–138
    for families with child custody
        conflicts, 193
    in normative divorce cases, 246
    for parents with severe
        psychopathology, 216
    in treatment of parental alienation,
        204
Multidimensional family therapy for
    adolescent delinquency, 8
Multilevel assessments, 115–118, 265
Multipartial alliances, 105, 213, 242
Multiple-therapist model, 99–100
Multisystemic therapy for adolescent
    conduct disorder, 8
Mutually stated goals, 125–126
My Mom and Dad Don't Live Together
    Anymore (Rubin), 135

Narratives about divorce
    after withdrawal of a parent, 212
    black and white thinking and, 83
    changing, in normative divorce
        cases, 250–251
    couple therapy as part of, 59
    in difficult divorce, 7
    financial motivations for
        behavior in, 49
    and goal-setting in therapy, 122
    reasons for divorce in, 40
    and therapists' personal values,
        63, 64
    witnessing of, 131
Narrative therapy, 149
Nature of activity, in therapeutic
    contract, 102–103
Negative attributions of behavior,
    149–150, 166
Negative behavior, reinforcement of,
    139
Negative emotions, 225–226
Negotiation
    in high-conflict case study, 274
    in normative divorce cases,
        247–248
    of session content, 126
    strategies for improving, 144–145
    targeting blocks to, 192–193

New partners
    in better divorce, 31
    case example, 275–279
    and issues related to remarriage,
        220–222
    negative experience of, 25
    premature introduction of, 24
Nielsen, L., 54
No-fault systems, 36–37
Nonmarital relationships of short
    duration, 38, 209–211
Nonverbal behavior, 117. See also
    "Four Horsemen" of divorce
Normative divorce, 237–260
    adapting integrative model for, 11,
        84, 238–244
    case examples involving, 257–259
    child therapies in, 88
    communication in, 142
    difficult vs., 5–6, 17, 238
    experience of, 237–238
    gender differences in experience of, 52
    integration of therapy formats for
        clients in, 256–257
    interventions with families in, 80–84
    reasons for, 40
    relocation of parents in, 29
    sharing of emotion in, 151
    therapy formats for clients in,
        253–256
    treatment strategies used with,
        244–252
"Not me" state, 4, 15, 44, 132, 238, 250

Object relations, 230, 267
Older couples, childless, 217–218
One-therapist model, 99
Operant conditioning, 138, 139
Optimism, of therapist, 227
Orders of protection, 114, 130
Other–therapist alliance, 107–108
Our Family Wizard, 142
Outcome Questionnaire, 161
Overgeneralization, 117
Overnight visits, effects of, 54
Overt triangulation, 19

Pain, emotional, 46, 212, 225–226
Painful experiences, families with,
    212–217

Paltrow, Gwyneth, 42
Parallel parenting, 21
Parent(s)
    abusive, 119
    competence of, 113, 210
    disengagement between child and,
        201–209
    extreme disengagement between,
        200–201
    initial meetings with, 263–264
    with personality disorders, 26–27
    with psychopathology, 27, 123,
        215–217
    relocation of, 29
    withdrawal of, 211–212
Parental alienation, 201–209
    case example, 207–209
    strategies for treating, 201–206
Parental alienation syndrome, 202
Parental Denigration Scale, 202n2
Parent–child alliances, 30
Parent–child difficulties
    assessing, 112–113
    in difficult divorce, 27–28
Parent–child relationship,
        reestablishing, 206
Parent education programs, 77
Parenting. See also Coparenting
    assessing problems with, 112
    behavioral strategies for improving,
        139–140
    and difficult divorce, 3–4
    extending, in divorcing families, 28
    in high-conflict case study, 273–274
    irreconcilable differences in, 28–29
    in normative divorce cases, 17
Parenting coordinators
    coordination with, 185
    interventions in difficult divorce by,
        79–80
    role of, in judicial system, 175–176
Parenting skills development, 210
Parent rejecting behaviors, 202n2
Participants in therapy
    for families in normative divorce,
        240–242
    specifying, in therapeutic contract,
        96–98
    variation in engagement by, 222–223
Parting Parent Concern Inventory, 161

Passive-aggression, 190
Payment arrangement, 98–99
Pedro-Carroll, J., 134
Perfect Pals, 42, 54, 142, 248
Perpetual issues, of marriage, 29
Personal experiences, of therapists, 231
Personality disorders, 26–27
Personality issues, as factor in difficult
        divorce, 33
Personality traits, of therapists, 226–227
Personal reactions, of therapists, 229–233
Personal values, of therapists, 62–65
Pervasiveness of problem, 115
Perverse triangle, 18–19, 116
Pinsof, W. M., 60, 83, 97, 107
Positive outcomes, 60, 66, 81
Positive sentiment override, 197
Postdivorce divorce issues, 219–220
Postdivorce families, successful, 47–48
Postdivorce litigation, 172
Poverty, 49
Precontemplation stage of change
    and assessment of inclination to
        divorce, 69
    and interventions for divorcing
        families, 75–76
    orienting therapy strategies to,
        137–138, 246
    psychoeducation on, 135
    therapeutic alliance with clients in,
        104
    treatment planning, 118
Pregnancy
    as factor in difficult divorce, 24
    in nonmarital relationships of short
        duration, 38, 209–211
Pretrial judicial processes, 170
Prevention programs, 76–77
Primary prevention programs, 76
Problem in focus, assessment of, 112–113
Problem-oriented focus, 136–137, 245
Problem solving
    assessing problems with, 112
    in better divorce, 30
    biopsychosocial model of assessing,
        117
    in high-conflict case study, 270–271
    in normative divorce cases, 247–248
    strategies for improving, 144–145, 155
Prochaska, J. M., 137

Progress, in difficult divorce cases,
228–229, 231
Psychodynamics, individual, 152–153,
251–252
Psychoeducation
in cases involving marital infidelity,
213
with children, 159, 217
empirical studies of, 164
for families with child custody
conflicts, 191
in high-conflict case study, 265–266,
269, 272
in normative divorce cases, 82, 245,
250
for parents with no history of
coparenting, 209–210
for partners who will not accept
divorce, 215
in prevention programs, 76–77
on remarriage, 221
in treatment of extreme
disengagement, 201
in treatment of parental alienation,
204
treatment strategies providing,
132–135, 155
Psychological abuse, 115
Psychological availability, of divorce, 41
Psychological testing, 110
Psychological treatment strategies
cognitive strategies, 148–150
for difficult divorce cases, 148–153
exploring individual
psychodynamics, 152–153
exploring underlying emotion,
150–152
for normative divorce cases, 250–252
Psychopathology. *See also* Mental health
issues
adapting treatment strategies for
participants with, 215–217
children with, 45, 215, 217
parents with, 27, 123, 215–217
Psychopharmacology, 154, 252
Psychotherapy
assessing inclination to divorce,
68–71
with couples in divorce, 13–14
couple therapy, 58–68

divorce as focus of, 57–74
divorce therapy, 73
risks of, in difficult divorce, 84–89
and separation in marriage, 71–72
transition from couple to individual
treatment for divorcing
clients, 73–74
Public health function, of therapists,
176–177

Race, divorce rate by, 37
Radical acceptance strategies, 148, 155,
223, 249–250
Rainbows program, 76
Rational-emotive therapy, 149
Reactivity, reducing, 178–179, 222
Reattribution, 149–150, 250–251
Reconciliation, 71, 120, 122
Record-keeping, 104, 183
Referrals, deciding whether to take,
119–120
Reframing
of extended family's role, 160
of narrative involving marital
infidelity, 214
of problems, 113, 136
Reinforcements, 138
Relational problems, 12, 158
Relational strategies, 199
Relational violence, 114–115, 130–131,
198–200
Relationship building, 277–278
Relationship satisfaction, 70–71
Releases, for custody evaluators, 184
Religious communities, 153, 252
Religious divorces, 53
Relitigation rates, 172
Relocation, of parent, 29
Remarriage, 24, 38–39, 220–222
Resilience, therapists', 226
Resistant clients, 109, 161–162, 222
Responsiveness to treatment, family
members', 222–223
Retraumatizing experiences, 139, 199
Rogers, Carl, 84, 105
Role differentiation, for parents, 209
Rolland, J. S., 50
Rubin, J., 135
Rule-governed communication,
141–144, 247–248

Sadness, dealing with, 257–258
Safety
    as block to custody negotiation,
        192–193
    in difficult divorce, 239
    goal-setting related to, 123
    guaranteeing, 130–131
    in high-conflict case study, 267
Same-sex marriages, 234–235
Sanger, Clifford, 71
Satisfaction, relationship, 70–71
Scheduling issues, 162, 235
Schemas, challenging, 150
Secondary prevention programs, 76
Secondary reactive emotions, 251
Second marriages, 221–222
Self-reflection, 152
Self-report measures of inclination for
    divorce, 70
Self-selection for difficult divorce work,
    15, 226–227
Self–therapist alliance, 107
Separation in marriage, 71–72
Seriously distressed marriages, 49–51
Session Rating Scale, 105
Severity assessments, for relational
    problems, 115
Sexual orientation, client's, 234–235
Shared single households, 197–198
Side-taking, by therapist, 105, 230–231
Skill-building therapies, 86
Sleeper effect, of divorce, 43
Social learning theory, 138–140
Social network therapy, 97
Social roles, in divorcing families, 44
Social support, 233
Socioeconomic status, 234
Socratic questioning, 150, 250
Sole custody, 54, 168
Solution-oriented therapy, 136–137, 245
Speaker-listener technique, 142, 248, 271
Special difficulties, children with,
    28–29, 143
Spiritual treatment strategies, 153, 252
Stage of change
    biopsychosocial model of assessing,
        118
    in high-conflict case study, 266
    mismatches between clients', 246
    orienting to client's, 245–246

treatment plan and, 128
    treatment strategies based on,
        137–138
"Starter" marriages, 41
Status calls, 169
Stay-at-home parents, 52
Stepfamilies, 38–39, 214, 221–222
Storytelling, psychoeducation via, 135
Strength, in therapeutic stance, 227–228
Superordinate goals, 123, 125
Supervision of families, by therapists,
    120n5, 199–200
Supportive therapy, 16, 84
Symmetrical escalation, 132, 180
Systemic approach
    to assessment, 116
    coordination of mental health
        professionals in, 185–186
    for families with variable
        engagement, 223
    for high-conflict families, 194
    in individual sessions, 255
    in integrative treatment model, 92
    in interventions with divorcing
        families, 83, 90–91
    in normative divorce cases, 244
Systemic runaway, 116, 132
Systemic strategies, 140–141, 247
Systemic Therapy Inventory of Change,
    60, 161
Systems theory, 8–9, 92

Team approach to difficult divorce work,
    232–233
Therapeutic alliance
    and communication with court/
        attorneys, 180
    in difficult divorce cases, 85
    in high-conflict case study, 264–265
    in integrative treatment model,
        104–109
    leverage from court and attorneys in
        building, 178
    in new partner case example, 276
    in normative divorce cases, 242–243
    and personal values of therapist, 63
    and progress in therapy, 160–161
    and witnessing, 131
Therapeutic contract, 11, 96–104, 240
Therapeutic stance, 227–229

Therapist(s), 225–236
    adaptations of, to clients, 233–236
    communication between attorneys
        and, 85
    competence of, 89, 119
    coordination between, 257
    court and attorney interactions for,
        176–183
    difficulties in divorce intensified by, 4
    effective therapeutic stance for,
        227–229
    as factor in treatment strategy
        selection, 156
    implications of difficult divorce for,
        14–18
    and interventions in normative
        divorce, 81
    multiple-therapist model, 99–100
    and negative emotions in divorcing
        families, 225–226
    other helping professionals and,
        183–187
    personal reactions of, to difficult
        divorce work, 229–233
    personal values of, 62–65
    relationships of, with judges and
        attorneys, 177–178
    resources of, in decisions about
        referrals, 120
    role of, 14, 99–100
    self-selection of, for difficult divorce
        work, 15, 226–227
    threats to, 131
    as treating experts, 182–184, 223, 228
    triangulation of, 73, 84–85
Therapist passivity, 93
Therapy coaching, 151
Therapy formats
    integrating, 256–257
    for integrative treatment model,
        156–159
    in normative divorce cases, 240–242,
        256–257
Therapy structure, importance of, 95
Third-wave strategies
    for difficult divorce cases, 145–148
    for families residing in the same
        house, 197
    for normative divorce cases, 248–250
Thought records, 150

Thoughts, about divorce, 41
Time with children, conflicts over,
    190–194, 274
Timing, of therapeutic contract, 103
Transference, 74
Transition, dealing with, 258–259
Trauma, in divorcing families, 235–236
Treating experts, 182–184, 223, 228
Treatment dose, 93
Treatment plans, 127–128, 244
Treatment strategies in difficult divorce,
    129–164
    behavior change strategies, 138–145
    biological strategies, 153–154
    broad treatment strategies, 130–138
    combining and order of, 154–156
    empirical support for, 163–164
    implementation of, 154–163
    for individual therapy with
        divorcing partner, 68
    and integrative treatment model,
        92, 93
    psychological strategies, 148–153
    spiritual strategies, 153
    third-wave strategies, 145–148
Treatment strategy adaptations, 189–223
    of behavior change strategies,
        247–248
    of biological and spiritual treatment
        strategies, 252
    of broad strategies, 244–246
    for conflict-related issues, 190–200
    for disengagement-related issues,
        200–212
    for families with painful experiences,
        212–217
    family context as basis for, 217–219
    for issues that emerge over time,
        219–222
    for normative divorce, 244–252
    of psychological strategies, 250–252
    for therapy-participation variability,
        222–223
    of third-wave strategies, 248–250
Trial, contested divorce cases at, 170
Triangulation
    of children, 18–19, 170
    in high-conflict families, 195–196
    in new partner case example, 277
    setting goals related to, 123, 124
    of therapist, 73, 84–85

Troubling behavior, by parent, 192–193
Two Happy Homes, 142
Two Homes (Masurel & Denton), 135

Uncertainty, in family structures, 17–18
Uncontested divorce, 169
Unhappy marriages, 40, 45, 46, 50
Unmarried couples
    "difficult divorce" for, 6, 113n3
    legal conflicts between, 172
    partings in, 38
    pregnancy in nonmarital
        relationships of short
        duration, 38, 209–211

Very young children, overnight
    visits for, 54
Violence
    false accusations of, 130n2
    intimate partner violence, 26
    intrafamilial, 25–26
    relational, 114–115, 130–131,
        198–200
Visitation. *See* Child custody and
    visitation

Waivers to confidentiality, 102
Wallerstein, Judith, 42
Wang, H., 49
Western society
    divorce rate in, 36
    gender and divorce in, 234
    normative divorce in, 238
    views of divorce in, 10, 31n1,
        41–42
    views of marriage in, 212
Wisconsin, custody arrangements in,
    168n2
Withdrawal of parent, 211–212
Within-client alliance, 104
Within-system alliance, 108
Witnesses in legal proceedings,
    therapists as, 183
Witnessing, 131, 213, 244–245
Women, experience of divorce for, 52
Written communication, 142–143

Young adults, 52, 174
Young children, psychoeducation for,
    135
Young couples, 52, 217, 219

ABOUT THE AUTHOR

Jay Lebow, PhD, ABPP, is senior scholar and senior therapist at the Family Institute at Northwestern and a clinical professor of psychology at Northwestern University in Evanston, Illinois. He is editor-in-chief of the journal *Family Process*. Dr. Lebow has authored or coauthored six books, including *Couple and Family Therapy: An Integrative Map of the Territory*; *Research for the Psychotherapist: From Science to Practice*; *Integrative Systemic Therapy: Metaframeworks for Problem Solving With Individuals, Couples, and Families*; and *Common Factors in Couple and Family Therapy: The Overlooked Foundation for Effective Practice*. He is the editor of seven other volumes, including *Clinical Handbook of Couple Therapy*, *Handbook of Family Therapy*, and *Encyclopedia of Couple and Family Therapy*. He has written over 200 articles and book chapters, most of which focus on couple and family therapy, research about psychotherapy, therapy for high-conflict divorce, and the relationship between research and practice. For more than 30 years, he has engaged in clinical practice, supervision, and research; is board certified in couple and family psychology; and is an American Association for Marriage and Family Therapy–approved supervisor. Dr. Lebow served as president of the Society of Couple and Family Psychology and has received the Society's Family Psychologist of the Year award as well as the American Family Therapy Academy's Lifetime Achievement Award.